Cretan Cult ~~and Fe~~

sel~~f~~ ~~~tain~~

a

C~~r~~

th

THE AUTHOR

R. F. WILLETTS was born in 1915. In 1937 he obtained a B.A. Honours degree (1st Class) in Classics at Birmingham University, his M.A. in Classics the following year, and a Diploma in Education in 1939. He is Senior Lecturer in Greek at Birmingham University.

He has published articles on Classical subjects in the learned journals, and his versions of *Lysistrata* and the *Plutus* of Aristophanes have been performed on the stage. His verse translation of the *Ion* of Euripides was published by Chicago University Press in 1958 and h~~e was a~~ contributor to *Landmarks in the ~~History of~~ Physical Education*, Routledge & ~~Kegan~~ Paul 1957.

CRETAN CULTS AND FESTIVALS

CRETAN CULTS
AND
FESTIVALS

by

R. F. WILLETTS, M.A.

Senior Lecturer in Greek in the
University of Birmingham

ROUTLEDGE AND KEGAN PAUL

LONDON

First published 1962
by Routledge & Kegan Paul Ltd
Broadway House, 68-74 Carter Lane
London, E.C.4

Made and printed in Great Britain by
William Clowes and Sons, Limited
London and Beccles

TO
MY MOTHER

Κρήτη τις γαῖ᾽ ἔστι, μέσῳ ἐνὶ οἴνοπι πόντῳ,
καλὴ καὶ πίειρα, περίρρυτος· ἐν δ᾽ ἄνθρωποι
πολλοί, ἀπειρέσιοι, καὶ ἐννήκοντα πόληες·
ἄλλη δ᾽ ἄλλων γλῶσσα μεμιγμένη· ἐν μὲν Ἀχαιοι,
ἐν δ᾽ Ἐτεόκρητες μεγαλήτορες, ἐν δὲ Κύδωνες,
Δωριέες τε τριχάϊκες δῖοί τε Πελασγοί·
τῇσι δ᾽ ἐνὶ Κνωσός, μεγάλη πόλις, ἔνθα τε Μίνως
ἐννέωρος βασίλευε Διὸς μεγάλου ὀαριστής.

HOMER

Contents

Preface   *page* ix
Acknowledgements   xiii

PART ONE: PAST LEGACIES

1. Introduction: Principal Economic and Social
   Developments   3
2. Initiation Practices and Other Mainland
   Links with Crete   43
3. Minoan-Mycenaean Cults   54
4. Homer on Crete   120

PART TWO: TRANSITION AND CONTINUITY

5. The Caves   141
6. The Cretan Goddesses   148
7. The Birth and Death of a God   199
8. Asklepios   224

PART THREE: CRETAN OLYMPOS

 9. Zeus   231
10. Hera   252
11. Apollo   256
12. Artemis   272
13. Athene   278
14. (a) Aphrodite; (b) Ares; (c) Hermes; (d) Posei-
    don; (e) The Twelve Gods   284
15. Strangers to Olympos   292

vii

PART FOUR: CRETAN KOSMOS

16. Religion and Law   297
17. The Role of the *Polis*   301
18. Poetry and Music   308

    Appendix: The Song of Hybrias the Cretan   317
    Bibliography   325
    Subject Index   338
    Index of Deities, Persons, Places   350

Preface

THIS account of the cults and festivals of ancient Crete is designed as a companion volume to my earlier *Aristocratic Society in Ancient Crete*. In that work the religious ideas and practices of the Cretans received only incidental treatment, since my purpose was to investigate the social and political institutions of the Cretan aristocracies. Also, as I observed in my preface, the subject of religion, 'from its nature, cannot be restricted to datable confines and isolated within a period, and an adequate treatment would demand far more space than could be envisaged within the scope and purpose of this volume'.

Since then, my investigations have expanded to the scope of a second volume. This lengthy treatment is justified by the amount of material which was at my disposal and by the inherent importance of the subject. For no student of Greek religion can afford to ignore Crete. It is therefore my hope that this work will not only adequately serve as a supplement to my account of the institutions, an enlargement of the attempt there made to account for the peculiar characteristics of Cretan aristocracy, but may also provide a self-contained exposition of the Cretan cults and festivals.

As I was completing the earlier work, the proposed decipherment of the Linear B script was announced; and the student of Crete could expect novel and early written sources to supplement the other means at his disposal. Hence the lack of any discussion of the Linear B materials in the text needs explanation. The omission is partly due to my belief that the criticisms, on linguistic grounds, of Beattie, Grumach and others have not been properly answered.

But, even if all doubts had been dispelled on this score, the poverty of the present material and the difficulty of its interpretation would remain as obstacles preventing its use for immediate historical purposes—as some at least of the Continental scholars who support the decipherment would agree. This objection seems to me to have been confirmed rather than diminished by the careful

ix

article of W. K. C. Guthrie on *Early Greek Religion in the Light of the Decipherment of Linear B*.[1]

Professor Guthrie makes clear at the outset that the amount of light shed by the Linear B tablets on the basis of the proposed decipherment is meagre. 'In spite of the exciting and welcome array of divine names,[2] one's first impression of the Linear B tablets is that the amount of indubitable religious information which they convey is tantalizingly small. Against almost every facet of religious life at which they seem to hint—vegetation-cult, initiation, divine kingship, Dionysiac *orgia*—one must simply put, in the end, a large question-mark. That is, if one confines oneself strictly to the texts of these highly specialized and partially unintelligible documents themselves.' (*Ib.* 35.)

To meet the difficulty Guthrie argues that some resort to comparative methods in the interpretation of the texts is not only permissible but inevitable if they are to yield any coherent message. 'Often these methods provide the only possible criterion for choosing between one interpretation and another, although obviously comparisons themselves will provide probability rather than certainty.' (*Ibid.*)

Three chief types of religious material are noted as available for comparison, and suitable as guides for the elucidation of the Linear B texts. These are, in order of priority: (1) the evidence about Minoan-Mycenaean religion from the uninscribed monuments, studied by scholars like Nilsson, Persson and Picard; (2) the evidence from the religion of historical Greece; (3) the pattern of religion found in earlier or contemporary Near Eastern countries. Since I have myself drawn upon these same sources, Guthrie's assessment of their value for our understanding of early Greek religion may be usefully compared with mine. For it is his judgment of the subject in the light of these classes of evidence that naturally for me constitutes the chief value of his article.

There are a number of conclusions stated by Guthrie on the basis of his three non-textual classes of evidence which substantially agree with my thesis at various points:

1. The warnings of Finley (*Econ. Hist. Rev.* (1957), 140) that 'discontinuity between the Mycenaean world and the Greek was so great

[1] BICS 6.35–46.
[2] The large number of proper names is, of course, for critics of the proposed decipherment, a suspicious feature.

that it is fruitless to look to the latter for guidance in the former' are considered to have less weight in the religious than in the social or economic sphere. Classical Greek religion was full of survivals from the earlier period, particularly in the nature-religion associated with the fertility of the soil. (Guthrie *ib*. 36.)

2. There are parallels, too close for coincidence, between the mythology of Greece and that of Hattusas and Ugarit; there is the historical fact of direct Mycenaean contact with the Eastward and Southward regions; and it has never been denied that Greek religion was an amalgam of Indo-European and indigenous Aegean elements, these Aegean elements being fertility-cults like, in general, those of the kingdoms further East. Though we must be wary of basing speculation on the assumption that a single universal cult pattern was transferred from the Near East to Greece, the possibility is by no means excluded 'that there was, at least in outline, some sort of Near Eastern and Aegean religious pattern to which the Mycenaeans were not immune'. (*Ib*. 36–7.)

3. A feature of Cretan religion from the earliest times was the use of cave-sanctuaries. (*Ib*. 38.)

4. The evidence from seals, rings and other art-forms suggests a rustic vegetation-worship, a great-goddess, a young male figure, ecstatic dancing and probably mourning, animal-daemons, the cult of trees and plants seemingly connected with the axe, stones and pillars. (*Ibid*.)

5. In Minoan-Mycenaean religious art it is difficult to see a clear-cut polytheism. (*Ib*. 39; cf. my remarks p. 76 below.)

6. As for gods, the dominant figure of Minoan-Mycenaean religion is the so-called Master of Animals, consort-son of the Mother-goddess, hitherto convincingly identified with the Cretan Zeus Kouros or Koures. (*Ib*. 40.)

7. There is overwhelming evidence from all periods that the religion of Crete was ecstatic and mystic, devoted to a god who was born, lived as babe and youth and died; and who also appeared in taurine form. This religion is all that we mean by Dionysiac, but to the Greeks the primeval Kouros of Crete was Zeus. (*Ibid*.)

Guthrie accepts Nilsson's judgment that the Minoan and Mycenaean religions were identical in their outward forms and that, for practical purposes, we must treat them as one. For Guthrie the paramount lesson of the Linear B decipherment is that the Mycenaeans are finally proved to be Greeks; the gods were Greek gods, not confined to palace circles, but worshipped by the people at large.

But I have sought to establish differences between the Minoan and Mycenaean phases. In my view the former is dominated by the worship of a goddess, the latter by the worship of male deities; although the male deity begins to emerge in the Minoan phase, the process must have been accelerated when Crete became subject to Mycenaean influence; and a part may well have been played in this process by Greek-speaking Achaeans from the mainland.

The conjecture and the speculation I have indulged in, in my introductory chapter, were necessary if certain questions were to be posed and some tentative answers supplied; and the chapter had to be written to provide a social framework and some social terms of reference for the changing pattern of religious conceptions, if these were not to be treated in isolation. Nothing is more prone to become a speculative abstraction than a cult divorced from its social context.

It has been my purpose to attempt to discover, wherever possible, the social needs which the cults and the festivals were designed to satisfy or to represent. Where they were survivals, I have tried to track them down to their more rudimentary social contexts. Where they were new, I have tried to explain their novelty. Finally, when they became ossified, I have tried to find the reason why they were perpetuated at home and admired elsewhere. Since my purpose was historical I could not but begin with a sketch of the changing social matrix to give some shape to what follows.

What follows is treated under four main headings, which the nature of the material itself seemed to warrant. Any attempt at more rigid demarcation would have been arbitrary. The discussion of Past Legacies led to the treatment of the theme of Transition and Continuity, and the nature of the Cretan Olympos needed to be seen against the reality of the motives behind the Cretan Kosmos.

R. F. W.

Birmingham,
October, 1961

Acknowledgements

I AM GRATEFUL to colleagues of the University of Birmingham and elsewhere for advice of various kinds; more particularly, to Professor George Thomson for stimulating discussion on many aspects; to Mr. R. T. Rundle Clark for guidance in matters of Egyptian history and religion; to Mr. E. W. Whittle for his comments on portions of my theme; to Mr. P. Lekatsas for some valued discussions in Athens; to Dr. N. Platon, Ephor of Antiquities and Director of the Herakleion Museum, and to his Assistant, Mr. K. Davaras, for their kindly assistance.

Acknowledgements are due to the editors of journals in which some of the material presented here made its first appearance, namely, *The Classical Quarterly, Eirene, Hermes, International Review of Social History* and *Klio.*

Finally, I wish to thank the University of Birmingham Research Committee for its continued encouragement.

Part One

PAST LEGACIES

And like a subterranean wind that stirs
Some forest among caves, the hopes and fears
From every human soul, a murmur strange
Made as I passed: and many wept, with tears
Of joy and awe, and winged thoughts did range,
And half-extinguished words, which prophesied of change.

SHELLEY

CHAPTER 1

Introduction: Principal Economic and Social Developments

I. NEOLITHIC PHASE

THE earliest known inhabitants of Crete were neolithic folk, no traces having been found of palaeolithic food-gatherers. The island is readily accessible from the mainland of Greece, from the Delta, from Syria and from Anatolia; and wind and currents favour the sea traveller. Neolithic immigrants had arrived in mainland Thessaly and the Peloponnese during the course of the fourth millennium. We may suppose that immigrant neolithic farmers arrived in Crete, partly from Anatolia, partly from the Delta, bringing their technical knowledge and equipment with them, certainly not more than a few centuries before the beginning of this period. Excavation of neolithic habitations, though still as yet partial, is sufficient to indicate, firstly, that in extent if not in density, the neolithic area of occupation was roughly equal to that of the Bronze Age; secondly, that with certain exceptions, neolithic settlements lay away from the coasts; thirdly, that a preference for cave habitations, at not a few sites, is a further indication of the general uncertainty of living conditions; finally, that 'Neolithic Crete may be regarded as an insular offshoot of an extensive Anatolian province'.[1]

Beneath the oldest Minoan levels at Knossos, ruins of neolithic villages formed a tell 6·5 m. high, and it seems therefore that the principal centre of Minoan civilization was also the earlier site of one of the largest neolithic settlements in Europe and the Near East.[2] 'Thus, when men first settled on this spot, they settled on a low knoll, overlooked by the surrounding hills, a knoll on which, so far as we know, there existed no spring, though the Kairatos

---

[1] Evans PM 1.14; cited by Childe DEC 17.
[2] 'The selection of Knossos . . . is a problem very difficult of solution.' Pendlebury AC 37.

stream runs close below. Although the coast nearest to them faces directly towards the Mainland of Greece and the Islands of the Aegean, their connexions were with Egypt to the far South and with Asia to the East.'[3]

The deposit at Knossos has been divided into Lower, Middle and Upper Neolithic periods,[4] but the fact remains that our knowledge of Cretan neolithic culture can hardly be described as extensive. It is at least clear, however, that this culture was relatively advanced before the settlement was made at Knossos, judging by the nature of the pottery and the implements from the lowest strata. Lower Neolithic pottery was hand-made from coarse brownish clay burnished inside and outside, but undecorated. The Middle Neolithic style of pottery reveals improved modifications, decoration being done by burnishing, rippling and incising. Pebbles were ground and polished to make plump celts. But the obsidian cores found in this stratum, though worked on the spot, were probably imported from Melos and Yali, thus indicating some lack of self-sufficiency.[5]

We have valuable and interesting evidence of the style of Upper Neolithic architecture from Knossos and from Magasa, near Palaikastro. At Magasa there is a rock shelter, consisting of an overhanging ledge with the front roughly walled in, and a house with one entrance room and one inner living room: a single layer of large undressed blocks of limestone remains.[6] Later developments from this simple type are the houses below the central court at Knossos, with their cluster of small rooms around the main room; their fixed hearths of clay and small stones either in the middle of a room or against a wall, and of a type familiar in Asia Minor and in Greece of the early Bronze Age; their clay floors often running under dividing walls of undressed limestone blocks laid in clay and pebbles.[7] The flat axe of copper[8] found on the floor of a house with stone celts confirms other indications[9] that the period was short and transitional. Pottery declines in technique, but not so the celts and flaked obsidian.

Even if it were possible to suppose that the neolithic peoples were indigenous, we should be justified in examining better attested conditions elsewhere, so as to supplement by analogy the

[3] Pendlebury *ibid*.
[5] Pendlebury *ib.* 38–9; Childe *ib.* 16–17.
[7] Evans PM 2.i, 7 ff.
[9] Pendlebury *ib.* 41.

[4] Pendlebury *ibid*.
[6] ABSA 11. 261 ff.
[8] *Ib.* 2.i, fig. 3 f.

scanty direct evidence of the structure of Cretan neolithic economy and social life. But the advanced stage of the earliest strata of excavation seems to rule out the possibility of a purely indigenous neolithic culture.[10] On the other hand, the probability of neolithic immigration from Asia Minor and the Delta is a valuable pointer in the search for comparative data, even when we have made allowances for the fact that neolithic cultures are not uniform but rather characterized by their variety. For the climatic changes which followed upon the close of the last Ice Age produced the conditions which facilitated the economic and social transition from palaeolithic food-gathering to neolithic food production, which had its origins in the Middle East. The older techniques of hunting and food-gathering, appropriate to bands of nomads wandering over the wide expanse of prairie lands, which had stretched almost uninterruptedly over North Africa into Asia as far as Iran, were no longer adequate when the former grassland had been replaced by stretches of desert enclosing the oases and river-beds. Concentrated in such fertile areas, the descendants of the hunters and food-gatherers were compelled to devise fresh means for the exploitation of nature. Animals and plants could no longer simply be used: continuity of crop and offspring had to be ensured by human co-operation and by human understanding and control of nature. Animals were domesticated, plants were now cultivated.

The first step in these radical changes, it would appear, was taken when, while the men still hunted, the women began consciously to sow the seeds of the wild grasses which were the earliest strains of wheat and barley. There are many barbarian societies known to modern ethnography which have not advanced beyond the cultivation of cereals or plants. The neolithic peoples of the Middle East and Mediterranean also domesticated such animals as sheep, goats, cattle and pigs; and the oldest neolithic societies known to us consist of mixed farmers who were stockbreeders as well as tillers of the soil, and ensured themselves continuous supplies of milk, meat and grain. The new economy did not only develop new food resources but was also responsible for the techniques of pottery, spinning and weaving. To assist them in the construction of dwellings—made of mud, reeds, logs, stone or withies, plastered with clay—these societies required and developed new tools, conspicuous among these being the axe-head.

[10] Pendlebury *ib*. 37.

Within the neolithic village there was division of labour between the sexes. The ethnographic evidence reveals the remarkable part played by women in the invention of the major technical resources of neolithic economy. It continued to be their task to cultivate the village plots, to grind and cook the grain, to spin and weave cloth, to make clothes, and also pottery. Such tasks as the manufacture of tools and weapons, hunting, building, the care of livestock and the clearing of land for cultivation—all these probably fell within the province of the men.

This type of village economy became more and more widespread as more and more land was brought under cultivation. The ready accessibility of Crete to the seafarer resulted in its becoming what has been described as 'the most important extension of the Anatolian province as a whole'.[11] The archaeological evidence supports the likelihood of a very early immigration from southwest Anatolia and also intercourse with Egypt and other centres. The favourable position and the natural resources of the island were to have the most important and enduring consequences. 'Its fertile lowlands guarantee a living to farmers and orchardists; its resources in timber, copper and other raw materials can supply the needs of secondary industry; its natural harbours are not only bases for fishermen but havens for merchants who can transport Cretan produce to urban centres and bring back in return the manufactures and also the science of older cities.'[12]

The characteristic unit of the palaeolithic period was the clan, based on the principles of kinship and common ownership. Membership of the clan was determined by descent from an assumed common ancestor, a totem. Totems are either edible species of animals and plants or natural objects. Organic totems must be presumed to have come first because of their connexion with the food supply; while inorganic totems, such as stones, man-made implements, rain, wind, are later types developed by analogy. The clan formed a firm circle of blood relations, intermarriage between them being prohibited. The clan was exogamous, and a number of intermarrying clans formed a tribal grouping. The close ties thus formed between clans led to the development of classificatory systems of relationship, much more complex and comprehensive systems than those based on the

[11] Hawkes PFE 77; cf. Childe *ib*. 16–18; Pendlebury AC 41–2.
[12] Childe *ib*. 16–17.

family as the social unit.[13] Membership of the clan, though based on kinship, also involved systematic forms of initiatory training, according to ritual custom, in childhood, which reached their culmination in the initiation ceremonies at puberty. Participation in the same rites could ensure the adoption into the clan of non-clansmen.

The clan form of social organization developed in the palaeolithic period and continued into the neolithic period.[14] It may be assumed that the first neolithic settlers transplanted their social institutions to Crete, including that of communal land tenure, a normal feature among modern barbarians. It can be further assumed that the foundations of Cretan economy at this stage included both the cultivation of unidentified cereals together with olives and other fruits and also the breeding of cattle, goats and pigs.[15] None but the most speculative attempt to assess the balance between cultivation and stock-raising is possible. But it may be significant that sheep are not osteologically attested until the Late Minoan period.[16] Perhaps more significant for the assumption of a possible early and continuing bias in favour of cultivation, at least in the fertile lowlands, is the marked survival of matrilineal traditions well into the historical period, especially at Gortyna.[17] Modern ethnography reveals many examples of transition from matrilineal to patrilineal descent, but none of the reverse process—[18] which creates a presumption that the former is the earlier. Each successive mode of production in primitive society is marked by a different division of labour between the sexes. Among pure cultivators, owing to the predominant role of women in the economy, descent is matrilineal. Among stock-breeders, since economic and social influence rests with the males, descent is patrilineal. Granted the temporary priority of matrilineal systems, it is possible to recognize a gradual transition from matrilineal to patrilineal systems. This process, markedly accelerated with the introduction of stock-raising, receives a setback with the early phases of agricultural work, before garden tillage has been replaced by field tillage and when the hoe has not yet given place to the cattle-drawn plough. It may be that Cretan matrilineal in-

---

[13] For linguistic data relating to the kinship terminology of the classificatory systems see Thomson AA 6, 25–30, 132, 387–417; SAGS 1.58–78; 145–6; Benveniste in BSLP 46 (1950) 20–2; Isachenko in *Slavia* 22.1 (1953) 43–80.

[14] Cf. Childe WHH 59.   [15] Childe DEC 22.
[16] Hazzidakis TEM 77.   [17] Willetts ASAC 24, 36, 71, 73, 76, 80, 93, 95.
[18] Hartland PP 1.256.

stitutions survived, especially among the descendants of the older inhabitants who continued to do the work of agriculture, because cultivation was initially more important than stock-breeding; while the accompanying social institutions, once firmly established, were enabled to persist because garden tillage continued to play an important economic role.

2. MINOAN PHASE

(a) The Early Minoan Period
c. 2800?–1800 B.C.

In the course of this period the original settlers were joined by more immigrants from Asia and also perhaps by a small wave of settlers from Libya. Metal-working was introduced, foreign relations were maintained with Asia, Egypt and Libya, and overseas trade was chiefly directed towards Egypt and the Cyclades. The population rapidly increased. The eastern part of the island was the most prosperous and important coastal towns were founded at Palaikastro, Pseira, Mokhlos and Gournia. It is suggested that the eastern area played the major part in Early Minoan culture in all probability because of its veins of native copper, for flat copper axes now appear with the old plump stone type.[19]

The basic features of neolithic economy may be assumed to have survived, but there were also some important new developments. 'But now,' Gordon Childe has written, 'specialized craftsmen—jewellers, coppersmiths, lapidaries—must have been supported by the surplus produce of the peasantry. And so, in addition to rural hamlets, larger agglomerations of population must be assumed though no Early Minoan township has been fully excavated. Soundings at Vasiliki in East Crete and beneath the palace at Knossos give hints of the existence of complexes of rectangular houses of brick and timber on stone foundations, like the contemporary towns of Anatolia and Mainland Greece. But even as late as MM I, we find the rural population living in isolated house-complexes more reminiscent of a big farm than even a village.'[20]

Since there are different burial practices and different ceramic

[19] Hawkes *ib*. 88.
[20] DEC 22. Childe adds that similar conclusions might be drawn from the graves: *ibid*.

traditions, it can be inferred that Crete did not possess a single unified culture, but was divided into heterogeneous groups. These, however, must be assumed to have lived together without strife, in view of the absence of signs of fortification. But since there is no similar disparity in kinds of metal tools, stone vases, jewellery and seals it seems that the economic system was much more uniform. 'This system secured and distributed foreign materials, gold, silver, lead, obsidian, marble, and perhaps amber (from the tholos of Porti), Egyptian and Asiatic manufactures such as faience beads and stone vases that were copied locally and perhaps Cycladic figurines. Individual artisans needed seals (buttons, beads and prisms) that might bear scenes symbolic of their craft; merchants stamped therewith bales of goods exported to Asine and other mainland ports. But no regular system of writing and ciphering was yet needed nor publicly sanctioned for correspondence or accounts.'[21]

(b) The Middle Minoan Period

c. 1800–1500 B.C.

The development of bronze-working within this period was the most conspicuous basic feature determining the character of what now clearly emerges as the so-called Minoan 'civilization'. The term has been as freely applied to the Cretan society of the Bronze Age as to other Bronze Age states of the Near East, because the archaeological evidence, from its nature, has drawn most attention to the analysis of the characteristics of the urban centres of these states. But the term cannot be justified as wholly valid in the context until it is seen to be applicable as a description of such states in their totality, alike of the cities which formed their centres as of the agricultural and artisan communities within their bounds which nourished their economy. The evidence for these centres, though still deficient in many respects, is relatively abundant as compared with that which is available for a proper assessment of the conditions of social life and social production which prevailed within their tributary or dependent communities. Crete is not exceptional in this respect. We are not yet in a position to explain at all precisely when, why and how the basic features of

[21] Childe *ib.* 25. On the affinities between early Cretan seals and Africa and Asia, Matz FS; Frankfort CS 300-1; cf. Kenna 12 and n. 1.

neolithic economy, assumed to have survived into the Early Minoan period, became transformed to typical Bronze Age features, except in the case of a few urban centres. So far as the major part of the population is concerned—the tillers of the soil and the artisans—we can only speculate upon the degree to which primitive communal relations of production became converted into tributary relations at this time.[22]

The earlier Bronze Age states of the Near East had depended upon the technical processes of pottery, spinning and weaving, the smelting and casting of copper, the manufacture of bronze from copper and tin, the plough, the wheeled cart, the harness and the sailing ship, followed, early in the third millennium B.C., by the bellows, the tongs and the *cire-perdue* process of bronze-casting.[23]

In the case of Egypt and Mesopotamia, aside from the development of bronze-working, the other major development of productive forces which determined the growth of the typical Bronze Age state was irrigation. Irrigation was dependent upon the tools supplied by Bronze Age economy, and the large-scale agriculture which produced the vast surplus appropriated by the ruling classes was equally dependent upon irrigation.

The rich alluvial soil contributed to the production of an abundant agricultural surplus in Babylonia, which was, however, wholly deficient in raw materials. The agricultural surplus was therefore exchanged for raw materials, including metal and timber, from abroad. Nevertheless, commodity production was, on the whole, apart from foodstuffs, restricted to luxury goods. Even though international commerce which facilitated the exchange of material goods was a characteristic feature of Babylonian society from the earliest times, the internal economy as a whole remained, in the main, a natural economy.

The cities of the Mesopotamian region were obliged to secure their sources of raw materials by a process of expansion which led to the development of trading routes with Anatolia and Egypt and with the coasts of Syria and Palestine. Thus the old Bronze Age culture and economy of the Afro-Asiatic hinterland was given access to the Mediterranean region, with the rise of another group of city-states on the Syrian coastline having the natural advantages of good harbours, access to fertile valleys and to mountains rich in such resources as timber, stone and tin. Their geographical

[22] Cf. my remarks in ASAC 252.   [23] Lilley 1–8; 12–13.

environment made these cities less dependent on centralized irrigation and also, consequently, less able to produce an agricultural surplus. This deficiency was compensated by a more intense industrial production. Luxury goods such as jewellery and cosmetics were manufactured; there were dyeworks; copper foundries; workshops producing bronze tools; and shipyards, where a variety of vessels were built, including transports large enough for ninety men.[24]

A tablet from Ras Shamra (Ugarit) refers to the local dyeing of wool, about 1500 B.C.[25] The wool, dyed black-purple and red-violet, was sold by weight, in lots of about 300 shekels. Most of the names of dealers are of west Semitic (north Syrian) origin. The very high degree of proficiency achieved by the artisans of this region is exemplified by the ornate battle-axe of Mitannian origin from Ras Shamra, of about 1300 B.C. It is wrought from three metals. The blade is of iron, the socket of copper with gold inlays. The iron of the blade contains a high percentage of nickel, a treatment involving much technical skill combined with a considerable metallurgical knowledge. The copper socket, which was produced by the *cire-perdue* method, was cast round the blade, the contraction of the copper on cooling being adequate to secure the blade without rivets.[26]

The specialist craftsmen of these states were early organized in fraternities and guilds. In the administrative documents of Ugarit[27] men are often segregated according to their occupations or guilds, which tended to be hereditary. They included different kinds of warriors and priests, as well as craftsmen such as smiths, builders, wainwrights, potters, launderers, sculptors, fowlers, shepherds, grooms and gatekeepers. Members of other professions, such as scribes, are listed individually, so far without evidence of their guild, but there is some indication that they were organized in the same way. The administration of obligations to the state, as also the benefits provided by the state, was done partly through town-districts, partly through the guilds.

The kingdom was divided into administrative districts, each consisting of a township with dependent suburbs. Taxes and dues to the state were exacted in silver, by labour service or in kind.

[24] Schaeffer CTRS 38–9.
[25] Thureau-Dangin, F., in S. 15.137; Thompson, R. C., JRAS (1934) 781.
[26] H. H. Coghlan in Singer pp. 618–19 and fig. 418.
[27] Gordon UL 122–6.

Benefits from the state, such as payment for public service, were paid in silver or in kind. Military and naval manpower was supplied by draft quotas imposed on the various communities and guilds.

These tendencies developed at the expense of the old tribal system. But the population still preserved its tribal traditions. Though it is more common to find names qualified by the name of their local township, the older form of qualification by the tribal name still occurs. The king as head of state was believed to have divine sanction. Therefore members of the king's clan and other politically important clans were placed in important offices, such as the priesthood.

The ancient Ugarit was a busy port, where the goods of Syria and of the Hittite kingdom were exchanged with those of Egypt, Cyprus, Knossos and later Mycenae. The ancient city of Alalakh, on the north Syrian coast near Alexandretta, as we know from excavations, played a similar, if less important, role. In general, such cities must have played a vital part in the carrying trade between Mesopotamia and the Mediterranean regions; and their prosperity was, to a very considerable extent, based on the accumulation of merchant capital. The merchants themselves, it seems, counted among their necessary professional attainments a knowledge of several languages and of several scripts. Commercial requirements thus influenced the spread of literacy from older centres of culture, the development of written records and the invention of an alphabet.

Ugarit had a continuous history from the earliest times of settlement in Syria. Its most influential and most flourishing period, however, lies between 1800 and 1200 B.C. The people spoke a dialect closely akin to Phoenician and Hebrew, with certain phonetic peculiarities. From the library of a temple a great number of tablets have been recovered, many in ordinary cuneiform which can be readily deciphered. But about 600 of them are written in a script different from any known system of cuneiform, with a limited number of signs, indicating that the script was alphabetic. It has transpired that they were written in an alphabet which consisted of cuneiform signs invented to express the phonemes peculiar to the Semitic dialect of Ugarit. In 1949 Schaeffer found a tablet which enumerated the Ugaritic alphabet in the order of its letters, corresponding with the order of the Hebrew and Phoenician alphabets, except for the insertion of eight additional letters of the Ugaritic alphabet, representing sound-values either absent or unexpressed in Phoenician and Hebrew. This alphabet seems also to have approximated to the Arabic, in differentiating between shades of guttural, dental and sibilant sounds. Its origin is still unknown, but it is clear that quite remarkable progress was made, from the middle of the second millennium B.C., towards the invention of a proper alphabetic system. The eventual failure of the Ugaritic system has been explained as being due to the fact that the Phoenician was already competing with it, because clay was not a natural writing material in Palestine and because the destruction of Ugaritic civilization in the thirteenth century B.C. contributed to the disappearance of its script.[28] We also know that seven different languages were spoken at Ugarit in the period of its greatest prosperity, including Babylonian, Hittite and Egyptian.[29]

The rise of the Cretan Bronze Age city-states to their eminence in the Middle Minoan period was contemporaneous with the Syrian, which they resembled in their economic and political organization. The close ties existing between the Syrian and Cretan cities at this period and their consequent bearing upon the character of Minoan society and the ultimate origins of Hellenic civilization have been increasingly emphasized by archaeologists and scholars.[30]

The common features in the economic sphere can be readily appreciated through a review of the technical resources available to the Bronze Age Cretans which fully illustrate the debt which they owed to Asiatic traditions. Although metal ousted stone but slowly in the Near and Middle Eastern regions, it is assumed that metallurgy was widely practised there soon after 4000 B.C. In Assyria polished stone celts had largely given way to implements of bronze by 3000 B.C., in Egypt by 2000 B.C. and in the Aegean by 1500 B.C. Thus Cretan metallurgy was in general based upon these Asiatic traditions which had previously matured over a very considerable period.

The oldest surviving portion of a potter's wheel, found at Ur, has been dated 3250±250 B.C. A complete clay disk, 90 cm. in

---

[28] S. H. Hooke in Singer 762–3. [29] Schaeffer CTRS 31.
[30] Pendlebury AC 94–179; Childe DEC 26–7, WHH 146–8; Schaeffer CTRS 3; Woolley FK 77, cf. JHS 56.125; Demargne CD *passim*; Thomson SAGS 1.28, 376, 2.107; Levi GC *passim*; Page 180. Cf. Gordon UL 122: 'Even islands of the Mediterranean, notably Crete and Cyprus, were integrated into the One World of the Amarna Age.'

diameter and 8 cm. thick, was buried with its owner at Erech, in Sumer, about 2000 B.C. The disks of varying sizes from Minoan Crete all belong to genuine wheels, though the classification of these wheels is still uncertain. It may be that the pivoted disk and the foot-wheel were in use in Crete from 1800 B.C. The potter's wheel was used in Sumer or Iran, or both, earlier than in China or Egypt or Syria or Crete; and the farther we move westward from the Persian Gulf and the Tigris the later is the appearance of wheel-made vases.[31] A social surplus sufficient to support the potter and his family by providing an effective market for his wares is a prerequisite for the use of the wheel. The market had to be local, since primitive conditions of transport normally precluded the export of such fragile and bulky wares as pots over any great distance. But the low productivity of primitive farming would not, on the other hand, have made it worth while to set up a wheel in a village of less than 200 households. This density of population was first reached in the Near East and the great river valleys. North of the Alps in Europe no settlement approached it before 500 B.C. Population remained scattered from neolithic times in hamlets of from ten to fifty houses.[32] Not that we need to rely on inferences from evidence of such a general kind to indicate a social surplus in Crete sufficient to maintain an increased population by the early second millennium B.C. The social surplus required for the support of a potter, compared, for instance, with that required for a smith, is not large. But already by the end of the third millennium B.C. a surplus beyond the capacity of a wholly neolithic economy, in part for export, in part sufficing to support smiths, carpenters, goldsmiths, jewellers and seal-cutters, had become available from the skill of Cretan orchardists in cultivating the vine and the olive, and also from the utilization of local resources of timber, copper and the murex-shell.

The main technical effect of the introduction of the wheel in Crete, as elsewhere, must have been to speed production of existing shapes and to favour tendencies to elaboration.[33] It may be that, like the modern Cretans and the Nagas, ancient Cretan

---

[31] Childe in Singer 199–200, 202–3. 'Some likely approximate dates are: Sumer 3250±250; Mediterranean coast of Syria and Palestine 3000; Egypt 2750; Crete 2000; mainland Greece 1800; south Italy 750; upper Danube-upper Rhine basins 400; southern England 50 B.C.; Scotland 400 A.D.; the Americas 1550 A.D.' Ib. 203.

[32] Childe ib. 203.

[33] Scott in Singer 404; cf. ib. 397–8; 399 (cf. Evans PM 1.177); 403 (cf. PM 1.180 and 223–5).

potters now became part-craftsmen, part-farmers.[34] Socially, there were other consequences. 'After the introduction of the wheel, pottery seems to have become an exclusively masculine industry, as in India, China, Crete and Brittany.'[35]

Not only the ceramic industry but transport also was revolutionized by the application of the wheel. The oldest vehicles known in the archaeological record, and those most common in non-industrialized countries in our own times, share the distinctive characteristics of solid wheels and paired draught. Solid-wheeled vehicles were used in Sumer soon after 3500 B.C.; in Elam and probably Assyria about 3000 B.C.; on the upper Euphrates round about 2250 B.C.; in south Russia and also in Crete about 2000 B.C. The available data perhaps indicate lower Mesopotamia as the centre of diffusion of wheeled vehicles.[36]

Solid-wheeled vehicles are perfectly adequate for the slow transport of goods. The invention of the lighter and more efficient spoked wheel added speed and manœuvrability to the initial advantages of wheeled transport. Hence its rapid transference to warfare in the form of the spoked-wheel war-chariot. Spoked wheels are first represented about 2000 B.C., in northern Mesopotamia and in Cappadocia. They were used in Egypt soon after 1600 B.C., and they feature on clay tablets from Knossos about 1500 B.C. Four-spoked wheels were common to the Cappadocian vehicles depicted on seals, to Egyptian chariots before 1400 B.C., and to all Minoan and Mycenaean chariots in the Aegean area.[37] It will be necessary to refer again to the appearance of the spoked wheel in Crete when the consequences of the arrival of the Achaeans are discussed.[38]

Among other impressive crafts which contributed to the splendid appurtenances of Minoan society may be mentioned dyeing, fresco painting and ivory-work. Saffron, the orange-yellow dye from *Crocus sativus*, made from the dried stigmas of the flowers, was common in Crete, and was also produced in Syria, Egypt and Cilicia. And within this period Crete shared with Ugarit an early knowledge and appreciation of the Tyrian purple so generally admired in classical times.[39]

Originality has been claimed[40] for the Cretan technique in

[34] Scott *ib.* 407.
[35] Scott *ibid.*
[36] Childe *ib.* 211.
[37] Childe *ib.* 211–13.
[38] Pp. 34–5.
[39] Forbes in Singer 247; cf. Pendlebury AC 281.
[40] Forbes *ib.* 242.

frescoes which it now seems necessary to deny. Colouring was applied when the stucco (of lime-plaster) was still moist, a technique unknown to the Egyptians. It appears that this technique was, however, transferred to Crete from the Asiatic mainland.[41]

The outstanding excellence displayed by Cretan ivory-workers is in contrast with their apparent neglect of sculpture on a large scale.[42] The craft of ivory-working is assumed to have originated in the Near East where a ready supply of elephant ivory was available,[43] but Syria formed another source of supply.[44] Hence the art of carving in the round was early developed by Syrian, Phoenician and Palestinian craftsmen. In advising that the most useful approach to ancient ivory-working is to consider it as the product of a long-lived craft, Barnett makes some remarks concerning the organization of artisans which may be quoted here in full, since they have a bearing on a most important feature of the Minoan economy which has not been fully appreciated. Barnett writes:[45] 'As the ancient economies developed surplus wealth, they found the means to support specialist artisans. Craftsmen were early organized into fraternities and guilds, and came to form a recognized part of ancient city and temple life. Sometimes the organized guild faded into a social group of kindred, or a caste with special rites and privileges.

'Guilds of ivory-workers, however, are not mentioned in ancient Oriental sources, except in India. Their existence is doubtless masked under a more general heading, such as carpenters, but we can trace them by their works. Often itinerant, they spread their products and cultural traditions far and wide. Transmitting technical traditions from father to son, they imparted to their craft features which were incredibly long-lived. Some of their traditions are still alive in the Near East. Thus ivory combs are now made in Aleppo by Armenian workmen of exactly the shape of those of north Syrian craftsmen 3000 years ago. Furniture

[41] Woolley FK 77.
[42] Cf. Barnett in Singer 672, Pendlebury AC 217–18.
[43] Barnett *ib.* 663, who, however, points out that 'this statement may require limitation when more is known about early Indian and Chinese civilizations, but for the present it holds good'.
[44] Barnett *ibid.*: 'Another source of supply of elephants was Syria, where lived a separate sub-species now long extinct and seldom mentioned by naturalists.' The ivory used by the Mycenaeans was presumably imported from Syria. See Wace ABSA 50.250 n. 2. Cf. Barnett JHS 68; Dunbabin 38–9.
[45] *Ib.* 664–6 (and cf. fig. 456).

and trinket-boxes are to this day inlaid at Damascus with ivory, mother-of-pearl and coloured woods in a tradition that may have descended from Phoenician times.'

What Woolley describes as Level VII at Atchana (ancient Alalakh) is dated 1780–50 B.C. and here was found the evidence for the transference of the technique of fresco painting to Crete. 'It is here, in our Level VII, that for the first time we can trace connexions with Crete, but now they are unmistakable. The methods of construction employed in Yarim-Lim's palace are the same as those of Knossos—the polished stone slabs lining the base of the walls, the half-timber construction (though in the stony island of Crete rubble naturally takes the place of mud brick), the free use of cement, the wooden columns on plain circular stone bases, even details of planning such as the lay-out of the audience-chamber; and the frescoes are identical in colouring, technique and style. In Crete all this appears suddenly in the palace of Minos and contemporary buildings, there being no sign of local development, and after the Minoan age it all disappears; but Yarim-Lim's palace is in the old tradition, and its features are reproduced in later buildings right down to the seventh century B.C.; moreover Yarim-Lim's palace antedates by more than a century the Cretan examples in the same style. There can be no doubt but that Crete owes the best of its architecture, and its frescoes, to the Asiatic mainland. And we can say more than this. The exchange of goods by international trade is one thing, and a most important thing, but it has its limits; one cannot export a palace on board ship, nor is the "art and mystery" of fresco-working a form of merchandise. These professional techniques require direct contacts, and we are bound to believe that trained experts, members of the Architects' and Painters' Guilds, were invited to travel overseas from Asia (possibly from Alalakh itself, seeing that it had its Mediterranean harbour) to build and decorate the palaces of the Cretan rulers.'[46]

It seems therefore possible that such well-organized 'guilds' of craftsmen, with their inherited skills passed from generation to generation, but with powers of mobility and initiative denied to their fellows in the already severely stratified older Bronze Age centres, took advantage of the opportunities offered to them in a rapidly expanding Cretan economy which was vigorously adapting Asiatic techniques. The relative prosperity which skilled workers

[46] Woolley FK 76–7; cf. *ib.* 15, 109, 156–7, 158–9.

enjoyed even in provincial centres not dominated by palaces, the respect which would be shown to their technical mastery, and the enjoyment of a general atmosphere of social freedom, must all be considered to have contributed in no small measure to the quality of Minoan social life, and to the vitality of its maturing culture, still so readily and delightfully to be apprehended from its surviving monuments.

Although Cretan urbanization had an early history, the typical Minoan town is a planless structure, indicative of flexible social relations. Nor could Cretan agrarian economy be directed from a single centre with control of irrigation. Cretan agricultural resources had already long before begun to be exploited by skilful specialists who presumably maintained an independent social tradition. The consequent dependence of the Minoan towns on commercial wealth may have ensured that immigrant craftsmen and others who acquired their skills were encouraged to preserve and foster their 'guild' traditions in a society where the ties of kinship were still of paramount importance.[47]

For why was it that 'the organized guild faded into a social group of kindred, or a caste with special rites and privileges' in the older Bronze Age societies? The medieval guild was a modified form of the craft or occupational clans which developed within the higher grades of tribal society as a natural means of transmitting hereditary occupations.[48] But this pedigree only partly justifies the application of the term 'guild' to the Bronze Age groupings which, at least in the Greek tradition, continued to have close associations with the ties of kinship fostered by the persistent institutions of the clan. The strong influence of such associations is testified in the Greek myths of Daidalos ('the Cunning Worker', 'the Artist'), which were a folk-memorial of the lasting achievements of the bronze-workers and other craftsmen of Minoan Crete. The Daidalidai of Attica claimed their descent from him, and Athens tried to claim him as an original Athenian. But his origin, like his work, was Cretan.

The terminology used elsewhere in Greek tradition about the origin of 'castes' in Crete has a special relevance in this connexion. The tradition is reported by Aristotle,[49] who informs us

---

[47] Two interesting examples of cult are quoted by Barnett (in Singer 665 n. 1, citing A. Boissier, OL 2.236): 'in Egypt, Horus was patron of the smiths of Edfu; at Lagash in Sumer, Nintukalamma was god of metal-workers'.

[48] Grönbech 1.35.   [49] *Pol.* 1329a 40–1329 b5.

that the 'caste'-system still in existence in Egypt and Crete in his own day was first established in Egypt by the legislation of Sesostris and in Crete by that of Minos. The word which is often rendered as 'caste' in this context (i.e. *genos*) means, basically, 'kin' and is the regular word for 'clan'. The usage is not unique. Other Greek writers who described the social system in Egypt used the same or similar terminology. Their statements will have to be considered in more detail when we try to decide what Aristotle meant by the 'legislation' of Sesostris and Minos.[50]

The centre from which this developing economy was fostered, directly or indirectly, was the palace, the focal point from which radiated the impulses of its growth and whose ruins were destined to serve as the dramatic symbol of its decay. The palaces that arose in central Crete, at such places as Knossos, Phaistos, Mallia, Tylisos and Haghia Triada, testify to an increase in wealth such as is usually accompanied by an increase in population; and increase in the native population would have been augmented by immigration.[51] This fact has been more readily appreciated, however, than the no less important prerequisite of a corresponding increase in the food supply. We must indeed suppose that there was such an increase on an appreciable scale. We must again suppose that increased urbanization provided further stimulus to the already established methods of specialist farming we have noticed. It is also reasonable to suppose that there were important changes in methods of cultivating arable land, designed to increase corn-production, and also of stock-raising. But such supposition has little basis in fact, because our knowledge of agricultural techniques at that time is regrettably deficient. For example, we may know that the plough was very like the Egyptian plough, but we do not even know what were the draught-animals.[52]

Pending the discovery of factual information (for various reasons hard to come by, but not wholly to be despaired of), we have no alternative but to fall back upon conjecture, inferred from data of other kinds.

Cattle-raising is normally men's work and, as garden tillage gives way to field tillage and the hoe to the cattle-drawn plough, there is a tendency for the work of agriculture to be transferred

---

[50] Pp. 31-2. [51] Cf. Childe DEC 26.
[52] Pendlebury AC 270.

from women to men, accompanied by a gradual transition from matrilineal to patrilineal descent.[53] It may well be that the larger populations, the higher levels of economic and social achievement of the Middle Minoan period, were accompanied by a more efficient exploitation of agricultural resources with the introduction of better methods of tillage and of stock-raising on a relatively larger scale. Just as other techniques had arrived from Asia, so these advances in agricultural techniques may well have been due, at least in part, to Asiatic influences borne along the trade routes and to the arrival of Asiatic immigrants. Such possibilities will have to be more closely examined when we consider the cults of historical Gortyna.[54]

In the meantime we have to proceed with further general conjecture, beginning with a modification of the tendency noted above as it may have applied in Cretan conditions. In view of the marked surviving traces of matrilineal descent in historical Crete,[55] it may be that any tendency for the work of agriculture to be transferred to the men, with consequent transition from matrilineal to patrilineal descent, was complicated by factors operating in reverse. The geographical conditions of the island, part mountain, part forest, part plain, would tend to operate in favour of uneven development. We expect more advanced techniques in the plains. But even there it is legitimate to ask if a further complicating factor was not supplied by the continuing marked importance of techniques of specialist farming which were modified forms of garden tillage.

Such inferences are supported by myth and by archaeology. For Demeter is said to have reached Greece from Crete,[56] where, as we shall see, she was an emanation of the Minoan Mother-goddess.[57] She it was who supplied Triptolemos with seed-corn and a plough and sent him over the world to teach mankind the art of agriculture.[58]

The appearance of Triptolemos in myth seems to coincide with a more active part played by men, as opposed to women, in agricultural work. Again, the standard Minoan burial custom at all periods was collective interment in natural caves, stone

[53] Westermarck ODMI 1.634, 2.273; Landtman OISC 15; Hobhouse MCSISP 22; Heichelheim WA 1.14; Lowie PS 71, 174, 184; Childe MMH 138.
[54] Pp. 152–68 in particular.
[55] Willetts ASAC 24, 36, 71, 73, 76, 80, 93, 95.   [56] h.Cer. 123.
[57] Pp. 148–52.   [58] Harrison PSGR 273; cf. Paus. 8.4.1.

chambers or tholos tombs.[59] At Mokhlos and in the Messara the grouping of the graves implies the association of several kindreds in a single village settlement.[60] But individual interment in stone cists, jars and clay coffins began before the end of Early Minoan times and this custom steadily increased later.[61] Such a practice points to disintegration of the clan. But the intensity of any such process should not be over-estimated. For, in the first place, the jar burials may be exceptional cases, many being designed for infants. (The custom of burying infants in jars, in or near the house, is widespread; its purpose is to reimpregnate the mother with the dead child's spirit.)[62] Secondly, individual interment did not become standard. Thirdly, the *oikos*, perpetuating, on a restricted basis, the collective customs of the clan, tenaciously survived in Crete well into the historical period.[63]

The influence of the *oikos* (the 'household')[64] as a unit of social organization can be seen both in the architecture and in the functioning of the palace. It has been observed that the Minoan palace is a symbol of a great household like the divine households of Sumer, where the various kinds of work done collectively by the members of a neolithic household became differentiated and consequently divided among specialists, maintained by the surplus food supply concentrated within the temple granaries and dependent upon the household store for raw materials. Such dependency resulted in a loss of social prestige and freedom which the craftsmen had earned under barbarism.[65] We have seen reason to

[59] Childe DEC 22–3; Evans PM 1.70–2; Hall CGBA 44. Minoan chamber-tombs persist into sub-Minoan and Protogeometric; so do tholoi in remoter districts. Cremation was, it seems, gradually introduced before the influence of Attic Protogeometric was felt, during the sub-Minoan period. The practice of cremation in pithos burials at Olous may even belong to the latest Minoan; but the cremations at Tylisos and Mouliana are probably contemporary with, or later than, the introduction of Attic Protogeometric influence; so Desborough 307; cf. 324–7 for detailed references to sites. (Local Protogeometric may have emerged in north central Crete *c*. 950–*c*. 900 B.C.: *ib*. 294.) Cf. Brock *passim*.

[60] Childe DEC 24; Pendlebury AC 63–5.

[61] Childe *ibid*.; Evans PM 1.149–50.

[62] Cf. Frödin 437; Earthy 66, 153; Karsten 34–5, 246–7, cf. 251–2.

[63] Willetts ASAC 29, 59–63, 65, 252–3, 255.

[64] The Indo-European correlatives of the Greek word *oikos* (originally *woikos*) show its original connexion with (*a*) the clan and (*b*) the village. The Indo-European form is *woiko-s* yielding Latin *vicus* ('village', 'group of houses', town-quarter'). The Anglo-Saxon loan-word from Latin was *wīc*, appearing in such modern English words as Warwick and Greenwich. Later lexicography proves that the word never lost its collective associations in Greek. See further Boisacq s.v.; LSJ s.v. ο῎ικος, cf. οἰκία; Willetts ASAC s.v.

[65] Childe WHH 146; cf. 85 and 53.

suggest that the development of specialist production under the patronage of the Minoan palaces resulted, not in a loss, but rather in a fresh acquisition of such prestige and freedom.

The long traditions of settled habitation had an early influence on the forms of architecture which were to make Crete readily receptive to the development of the palace styles. For, apart from a few Early Minoan tholos tombs in the Messara and elsewhere which could possibly indicate recollection of circular nomadic huts, Cretan houses develop in plan from a 'but-and-ben' two-compartment structure, with a single entrance, into rectangular houses—shallow, wide and with terraced flat roofs. By the early second millennium B.C. there is more complex planning, the rooms being grouped around central courts and light-wells.[66]

According to Seton Lloyd, palaces developed logically from an elaboration of the contemporary house-plan, but there are fundamental differences of arrangement and construction between those of Crete and those of Mycenae. In Crete there is the vast labyrinthine complex at Knossos, and another at Phaistos on the south side of the island. These buildings had no fortifications, since military security depended upon sea-power, but their own walls were sturdy enough. Up to a certain height they were built of ashlar masonry with a layer of clay between courses and a backing of rubble, held rigid by a framework of timber beams. These upper wall-faces were plastered over, and painted with elaborate decorative frescoes or sometimes in imitation of their internal construction. From the third Middle Minoan period onwards, ashlar masonry was used within the timber framework and the faces were left exposed. At Knossos the Cretan preference for flat roofs and terraces proved easily adaptable to the steep slope of the site chosen for the Palace of Minos. Its plan also to some extent reflects the extremes of temperature to be expected from the Cretan climate. The main living-rooms have a minimum of outside exposure, being grouped for the most part around rectangular light-wells, from which the sun was reflected through columned peristyles. The main halls were approached through ranges of doorways with deep reveals, into which the doors could be folded back in the summer. Whether by chance or otherwise, a similar arrangement was adopted by the Hittites.[67] Terracing, and

[66] ABSA 11.270; 14.365; Pendlebury AC 63–5; Mallowan in *Iraq* 2 (1935) 28; Seton Lloyd in Singer 484–5; cf. *ibid*.: 'On the Greek mainland, the circular nomadic hut formed the basic element from which the house-plan evolved.'

[67] Bittel DRBHH fig. 38.

the choice of an upper storey as a *piano nobile*, laid some emphasis on staircases, which now for the first time in history received attention as domestic architectural features. That in the 'King's Suite' is 1.8 m. wide with a central newel-post 90 cm. square. Its 45 cm. treads are each cut from a single slab of gypsum, built 18 cm. into the wall on either side and dressed on the underside, to form a stone ceiling to the flight below. The development of Cretan architecture introduced a completely new element into column-design. For the first time the pillars, which are of cypress wood, taper sharply from the top downwards. Their stone bases were at first tall in proportion, and were made of variegated stone. In the Late Minoan period flat disks of limestone were preferred.

But we have seen that the sudden onset of the architectural style of the palaces is dependent on Asiatic influences, which may, incidentally, perhaps also account for such a common arrangement noted above as being adopted both by Cretans and Hittites. The progress of archaeology will no doubt bring other common features to light[68] and enable us to assess more accurately the blending of native tendencies with foreign influence.

Nor can the absence of fortification be attributed to a military security dependent on sea-power. Such a hypothesis presupposes a centralization for which there is no evidence at this period. No doubt the geographical position of Crete gave it a large measure

[68] Thus Woolley, FK 108–9, describing the excavation of the palace of Level IV Alalakh (*c.* 1450–*c.* 1370 B.C.), writes: 'The building-methods used are indeed those which were traditional in the country, and even the details of the plan have much in common with the Yarim-Lim palace of three centuries before; the architecture is native, developed in Asia, and when we find parallels in other lands they are due to those lands borrowing ideas from Asia and not *vice versa*. And such parallels do exist. When in 1937 we unearthed just this part of the palace—the steps with their flanking platforms and the entrance-chamber, we found a solid mass of mud brick-work running across from one door-jamb to the other; it was not easy to get a true wall-face, but since the bricks were not loose but firmly compacted with their mud mortar we could only conclude that this was a wall, and a wall *in situ*, although its surface had suffered badly and although it seemed anomalous in that it blocked the head of the steps. Suddenly it struck me that the whole thing had a remarkably Cretan appearance, but in Crete there would have been at the top of the steps two columns with a door opening between them; accordingly I marked out two circles and told the workmen to dig away the brickwork there, and when they looked scandalized at the idea of destroying a standing wall said that they would find in each marked spot a stone column-base. They dug, and the stone column-bases duly appeared, set on the limestone threshold which had been hidden hitherto; our "wall" was indeed a wall, but it was that of the upper storey which with the burning of the wooden architrave above the columns had fallen down into a coherent mass on the threshold. I think that the story illustrates better than anything else the close analogy between Alalakh and Knossos.'

of initial security. But this security appears to have been further guaranteed by the commercial character of Cretan economy in the urban centres. From an early period the Cretan townships had arisen where there were good harbour facilities, sometimes without access to arable land.[69] We have seen that the heterogeneous groupings of the third millennium B.C. had managed to live together apparently without strife. In the Middle Minoan period the emphasis on commerce seems to have allowed of a similar peaceful development. Cretan economy had not so far fostered internal strife between its main centres nor did it invite suppression from abroad. Its close commercial relations overseas were not so designed. Internal economic and social development must have contributed much in this direction. The unplanned and unfortified Cretan towns grew out of village communities centred around a market-place where the settlement began, at once the hub of its social and religious life and also the centre for the exchange of commodities. It is significant that, in contrast with the decorative and pictorial art of Asia and Egypt, Cretan art is lacking in scenes of war and battle.

There are other significant differences. The Cretan palaces, like the Oriental temples, were also factories and warehouses. The palaces have shrines, but the towns have no temples. The temple as centre is replaced by the market-place. Theocratic domination is replaced by commercial enterprise. Thus at Knossos and Phaistos magazines and workshops are, in proportion, more conspicuous and occupy a relatively larger area than those in the temples of Erech or Lagash.[70] Hence the inference that a smaller proportion of their contents and products was absorbed in supplying the needs of the household, the balance being used for trade. This means that the economic power centred in the palaces must, to a very great extent, have been dependent upon secondary industry and commerce as compared with agricultural production.[71] Agricultural production could be controlled only indirectly in the main, not centrally controlled. And so the village communities could have retained, at this time, their ancient autonomy and their ancient social traditions relatively unimpaired, except for the disruptive economic influences which may have occurred in certain places, as a result of a fairly free play of economic forces.

[69] Cf. Childe WHH 129. [70] Childe *ib.* 146.
[71] Childe *ib.* 147.

Hence the 'priest-king' of the Cretan town-palaces is also different from his Oriental counterparts. He is in no position to reflect all the forces of his society so as to appear before that society overwhelmingly as god manifest. He is intermediary as priest, as he is intermediary as merchant. And he is one among many. His fellow-merchants are his social peers, his counterparts in the other palaces are his religious peers. The peculiarities of Cretan urban and agrarian economy account for the peculiarities of the Cretan 'priest-king'.[72]

The development of this kind of economy resulted not only in the building of such commercial requirements as harbours, bridges and roads, but in Crete, as in other Bronze Age countries, led also to three other considerable consequences. A rudimentary form of money was required, to be weighed out against other commodities, of the kind exemplified by the copper ingots occurring at Haghia Triada, Tylisos, Mokhlos and Knossos;[73] exchange transactions further required measurement by weights;[74] and a written script became necessary as a means of recording such transactions, of preserving the inventory of exchange.

The various types of script which appeared in the course of archaeological investigation were divided by Evans into pictographic and linear scripts. The linear scripts were further divided into Linear A and Linear B. The earliest pictographic signs, of the third millennium B.C., are engraved on seals and it is still doubtful whether they represent actual writing. Pictographs of a more developed kind date from about 2000 B.C., on seals and also on tablets and bars, their signs resembling the Hittite signary and Egyptian hieroglyphs.

The linear script A appears about the middle of the seventeenth century B.C., and Linear B in the course of the fifteenth century B.C. Both are pre-alphabetic cursive scripts; but pictorial signs continued to be used until the end of Minoan times.

It is then clear that commodity production, if mainly of luxury goods, developed to a considerable extent in the Middle Minoan period. Production of commodities for the market, for exchange and for export stimulated the absorption and development of techniques and the expansion of a class of specialist craftsmen, dependent on the economy fostered by the palace but enjoying a

---

[72] See further pp. 82–92 . [73] Pendlebury AC 212.
[74] All weights until *c.* 1450 are of stone; Skinner in Singer 779, cf., for Crete, Pendlebury AC 213.

large measure of social freedom and power of initiative. There was a parallel expansion and an increasing social influence of a class of merchants, occupying themselves with the exchange of commodities, concerned to increase wealth by their control of such exchange. A steady growth of trade, a no less steady accumulation of merchant capital, combined with the peculiar features of a Bronze Age economy owing much to geographical environment, would all appear to have checked any tendency for the traditional system of land tenure, associated with primitive communal relations of production, to be drastically modified. We are not yet in a position to assess to what extent, if any, primitive communal relations among food-producers had been modified by tributary relations, as had been the usual case elsewhere; but the possibility of the onset of such a process, at least in the central areas, should not be excluded. There was also, no doubt, a tendency for patriarchal slavery to increase, especially in the palace households. But social freedom and prestige of artisans could mean that slavery played only a minor part in the economy and was, at best, only indirectly linked with the production of commodities. These inferences concerning tributary relations and slavery have to be retrospectively derived from conditions existing in the Late Minoan period. They are, in the present state of our evidence, quite speculative.

The essence of the problem can be expressed by raising specific questions. Was the peasantry called upon to contribute, in the form of labour services, to the building of the palaces, roads, aqueducts, bridges and harbours? To what extent was such work carried out by household slaves from the palaces? Did the exportable surplus of wine and olive-oil find its way into the hands of merchants as a form of tribute assessed from the palace, or did the specialist cultivators exchange their products in the market-place against wares supplied by the merchants?

(c) The Late Minoan Period
c. 1550–1100 B.C.

This period is marked by three main features, all of which must be borne in mind if we are to present a plausible account of the climax and disintegration of Bronze Age civilization in Crete. These are: (a) on the one hand, the continuity and development of indigenous Minoan culture; (b) on the other hand, the interpenetration of this indigenous culture with the culture of mainland Mycenae; and (*c*) the violent destruction of the main centres of Minoan civilization about 1400 B.C. Let us review these features in reverse order, arriving at the most difficult last of all.

The destruction was thoroughgoing. Indications of its violent character, accompanied by burning, are apparent at Knossos, Phaistos, Haghia Triada, Gournia, Mokhlos, Mallia and Zakros.[75] Though no similar evidence of burning was found, there was certainly a break in habitation at Palaikastro, Pseira, Nirou Khani, Tylisos and Plate.[76]

The theory that this destruction was due to a severe earth-quake[77] was questioned by Pendlebury: 'It has been seen . . . that woodwork was more sparingly used at this time than before, and that previous earthquakes,[78] which were strong enough to fling great blocks of the Palace at Knossos into the houses below, had neither caused fires, though the woodwork was more extensive, nor had they caused such a complete break and set-back in the culture. Rather they had acted as a spur to fresh endeavours. Furthermore, at Knossos the first damage an earthquake of such magnitude would have done would be to shake down the Domestic Quarters and particularly the Grand Staircase, where four floors at least were supported on wooden columns. A very mild earthquake in 1931 snapped and shifted the upper part of a reinforced concrete column no less than 6 cm. But the Grand Staircase remained complete and practically undamaged long enough for it to be silted up with debris and earth which preserved the landing on a level with the Central Court to within $1\frac{1}{2}$ metres of its original position. The marks of fire are most obvious on the Western or official wing.'[79]

Pendlebury therefore concluded: 'Everything, indeed, points to a deliberate sacking on the part of enemies of the most powerful cities in Crete.'[80] The hypothesis that these enemies should be identified with the Homeric Achaeans is based on archaeological and linguistic evidence. The Mycenaean culture of the mainland, to which the Achaeans belonged, had become, in the course of its development, increasingly interfused with the Minoan. The view

[75] PM 4.942 ff., 786, 885; *Gournia* 21; AJA 13.301; *Mallia* 1.45; ABSA 7.142; Pendlebury AC 228.
[76] ABSA 10.259, 20.6; *Pseira* 10; 'Αρχ. 'Εφ. (1922) 24; PM 4.786; Pendlebury *ibid.*
[77] PM 4.942 ff.
[78] On their effects see PM *passim*; Pendlebury AC *passim*; cf. Childe DEC 27.
[79] Pendlebury AC 228-9.   [80] *Ib.* 229. Cf. Kantor 54 and n. 117.

that Minoan culture was carried to the mainland by forcibly incorporating it within the Minoan dominions, advanced by Evans and supported by Pendlebury, now receives less favour than the view which would allow Mycenaean culture to have become Minoanized in regard to its external and material aspects, but would emphasize its possession of certain marked characteristics, independent of Minoan elements, which continued to be fostered while the Mycenaeans, at a lower level of development, became familiar with Crete and its higher culture, and persuaded or compelled Minoan craftsmen, scribes and so on to settle among them.[81] When Pendlebury conceded that 'though superficially Minoanized, the Mainland still kept a good deal of its native culture and taste', he seemed also to be abandoning much of the substance of the first view. But the second view appears to have the weakness of conceding to the Mycenaeans an economic initiative overseas, at an early stage of their development, such as they may not have possessed until later in their career. What cannot be disputed, however, is that 'by 1400 B.C. the Mainland had thoroughly mastered Minoan techniques and assimilated the Cretan industrial system.'[82] Though we can still merely speculate upon a number of alternative means by which artisans and equipment were transferred, we are better equipped to explain the resulting adjustment in Helladic economy than we were even a few years ago.

The kings and queens buried in the Shaft Graves at Mycenae belonged to the dynasty which came into prominence shortly before 1600 B.C., fortified Mycenae and Tiryns, assumed control of a territory which reached to the Corinthian Isthmus and maintained relations with Orchomenos and Thebes. Although there are scant traces of Minoan influences in the earliest of the graves, they later become markedly conspicuous. The dynasty of this period gave place to the Tholos Tomb Dynasty about 1500 B.C., which developed closer relations with Orchomenos and Thebes, and made Mycenae a commanding power in the Peloponnese, with its control of communications between south-east and north-west. After 1400 B.C. the hegemony of the Aegean world passed to Mycenae. Over the previous two centuries the mainland had been receiving the products of Minoan economy—weapons of war,

---

[81] See Nilsson HM 71–82 for a convenient summary of earlier views; cf. Childe DEC 78–9.
[82] Childe DEC 81.

pottery, jewellery and luxury commodities. Minoan techniques had been absorbed by native specialists. Already, by the eighteenth century B.C., Cretan commercial products, judging by the distribution of Minoan pottery, had reached mainland Greece, the islands of the Aegean, Cyprus, Syria and Egypt. At first probably restricted to luxury articles, this commerce later included cheaper goods for a wider market, exported in pottery, such as olive-oil. This latter tendency was developed by the Mycenaeans, whose pottery was directly exported in large quantities eastwards to Troy, to south-west Asia Minor, Syria, Palestine, Egypt, and westward to Sicily and south Italy. Indirectly the sphere of commercial influence was extended even farther westward.[83]

The city of Mycenae was reconstructed during and after the fourteenth century B.C. A wall at least ten feet thick now surrounded the city, built of massive stone blocks; the Lion Gate was the chief entrance. A palace occupied the centre of the citadel; and the people probably lived in hamlets around the citadel.[84]

The martial character of the Mycenaeans is conspicuously exemplified in the fortification of their urban centres, affording a marked contrast with the unfortified cities of Crete. There are other differences which have been recognized as elements of northern origin preserved despite the borrowing and adaptation of Minoan culture.[85] The 'megaron' of the Mycenaean palace is a house-type distinct from Minoan architecture;[86] the abundant finds of amber on the mainland compared with their scarcity in Crete point to northern connexions; there are differences in dress, and also in religion.[87]

Although the various ethnic groupings of which Mycenaean society was composed have still to be strictly defined, the 'Heroic Age' of mainland Greece, symbolized by the Achaeans of the Homeric poems, shares certain general characteristics with other 'heroic ages' elsewhere.[88] Barbarian newcomers, with a militarized tribal organization, assimilate the superior culture and techniques of the social system which they disrupt. In the process their tribal system undergoes further drastic changes; and the appropriation of new resources of wealth, in land and in movable goods, brings about marked social inequalities. In the case of the Achaeans, as

---

[83] Wace M. 22–3, 107–8; Mylonas 12–14.
[84] Mylonas *passim*; Wace M 22.   [85] Nilsson HM 72–82.
[86] *Ib.* 72–5; cf. *ib.* MMR 12 n. 1; Boëthius in ABSA 24 (1919–21) 161.
[87] See further Ch. 3.   [88] Analysed by Chadwick HA, GL.

the citadel dominates the hamlets, so the kings and chieftains dominate the battlefield with their expensive war-gear, their chariots and their weapons of bronze. Their heroic stature is a reflection of their control of Bronze Age techniques adapted to war.

Yet, even in war, an Agamemnon enjoys only a loose hegemony, his control often disputed by his chieftains. This in turn reflects the sterner reality of the inability of the Achaeans to organize a centralized Bronze Age economy of the older type. Geographical conditions on the mainland were even more opposed to the possibility than in Crete; there could be no centralized irrigation and no centralized agrarian system over a sufficiently wide area to necessitate the development of a comprehensive bureaucratic state. Moreover, the very process of disruption of tribal traditions, based on the growth of social inequalities, promoted faction and favoured decentralization. Appropriation of wealth might tear asunder the egalitarian system of the clan, but inequalities developed within the clan in direct proportion to the increased power of the clan chieftains.

It is clear from the Homeric evidence that older forms of communal property existed side by side with newer forms of private property.[89] Light is thrown upon the early process of development of private ownership, especially in land tenure, from a study of comparative institutions.[90]

Such comparisons should serve to remind us of the connexion, in Bronze Age economies, between the growing diversity of forms of land tenure and the parallel growth of social divisions of labour, including special categories of persons who were dependent on the surplus provided by the labour of others and so freed to devote themselves to administrative and military pursuits. The growth of social inequalities sprang from the control of technical resources by persons or groups removed from direct participation in productive labour. For concentration of wealth, tributary exactions and militarization of the economy are developing features equally characteristic not only of Hittite and Mycenaean society in the latter half of the second millennium B.C., but also of China in the same period.[91]

The latter comparison is instructive also in demonstrating that

[89] Nilsson HM 212–47.
[90] Cf. the remarks on Hittite land tenure by Gurney 102–3.
[91] Wu Ta-k'un 1–3.

common features in economic systems are motivated by economic causes. Conquest, borrowing, adaptation, dynastic fusion—all these may become important modifying factors in the operation of such causes. Since no such factors, however, can possibly help to explain such common features as existed between Mycenaean and Chinese societies in the late second millennium B.C., the dominance of inherent economic motivation is, in these cases, quite plain. Hence we are obliged to examine the possibility of an independent development of Late Minoan Cretan society which could have manifested 'caste' features by returning to Aristotle's proposition that the caste-system was established, according to tradition, in Egypt by the legislation of Sesostris and in Crete by that of Minos. The proposition occurs in a context where Aristotle is at pains to demonstrate that it is no original or recent discovery of political philosophy that the state should be divided into 'castes' (or 'classes') and that the fighting men should be distinct from the farmers; and that a system which had continued up to his time in Egypt and in Crete had a considerable antiquity.[92]

As was mentioned earlier,[93] the word which is rendered as 'caste' (*genos*), or something similar, is used not only by Aristotle among Greek writers with reference to Egypt. Thus Herodotos[94] enumerates the seven distinct 'castes' (*genea*) into which he says the Egyptians were divided—priests, warriors, cowherds, swineherds, tradesmen, interpreters, boatmen. The warriors, who came from certain specified districts, were forbidden to practise a trade and enjoyed special privileges denied to all other Egyptians except the priests. Each warrior had twelve *arourai* of land (altogether about 9 acres) allotted to him free of tax. In addition to these privileges, he also received, during his year of special service in the king's bodyguard, a daily ration of meat and drink. Herodotos, it is true, makes no mention of cultivators as forming a special caste, but the omission is perhaps due to the fact that he is at pains to stress the prohibition of trades to the Egyptian warriors.[95] But Diodoros,[96] who is as careful as Aristotle to stress the antiquity of the Egyptian system, is more specific than Herodotos about land tenure. He states that the entire country was divided into three parts, the first allotment going to the priestly hierarchy, who, with the income derived from their holdings, performed all the sacrifices through-

[92] *Pol.* 1329 a 38–1329 b 5.   [93] P. 19.
[94] 2.164–8.   [95] Cf. Isoc. *Busir.* 18; Plu. *Lyc.* 4.
[96] 1.73–4.

out Egypt, maintained their staffs and supported their own needs. The second allotment goes to the kings to bring in the revenues to pay for their wars, the splendour of their entourage and the rewards bestowed for distinguished service. The third allotment goes to the warriors, whose profession, like that of the priests, is hereditary. There are three other 'orders' (*syntagmata*) in the state, continues Diodoros, namely herdsmen, cultivators and artisans. The cultivators rent on moderate terms the arable land held by the king, priests and warriors, and they devote all their time to the work of tilling the soil. Craftsmen too are forbidden to follow any but their own craft.

Now Isokrates attributes the separation of the warriors from those who pursue other professions not to Sesostris but to Busiris.[97] But Diodoros says that it was Sesoösis (Sesostris) who not only performed the most outstanding military exploits of the Egyptian kings but also systematized the legislation respecting the warrior caste (*ethnos*).[98]

There is no agreement as to the precise identity of Sesostris, but there is no doubt that to the Greeks he was a conqueror, a Pharaoh of the kind most likely to be associated with the militarized New Kingdom (1580–c. 1100 B.C.), roughly contemporaneous with the Cretan Late Minoan period.[99]

Bronze Age economy in the second millennium B.C., therefore, at a certain stage of its development among the Chinese, the Hittites, the Egyptians and the Achaeans exhibits the common characteristics of (*a*) militarization; (*b*) social inequalities now firmly based on rigid divisions of labour; (*c*) forms of service to a central authority; (*d*) the maintenance of royal, military, administrative and priestly hierarchies through the systematic appropriation of surplus from the major internal economic resource of land and the consequent development of a major class of tribute-paying cultivators; (*e*) the extension of this general system to other territories through conquest, coercion or dynastic alliances. In general, these characteristics owed their origin to the monopoly control by the ruling groups of bronze, as expensive as it was essential for the manufacture of products by craftsmen which

[97] *Busir.* 15.
[98] 1.94.4 For *ethnos* in the sense of 'class', 'caste', 'tribe', cf. Pl. *Lg.* 776d, *Plt.* 290b; X. *Smp.* 3.6; Pl. *Grg.* 455 b, cf. Arist. *Ath. Fr.* 3; D. S. 17.102; of 'orders' of priests, *OGI* 90.17; of 'trade-associations' or 'guilds', *PPetr.* 3 p. 67; of 'rank' or 'station', Pl. *R.* 420 b, cf. 421 c, D. 21.131.
[99] Cf. Pendlebury AC XXV.

chiefly benefited the wealthy. An intensified search for further wealth by these ruling groups was an outcome of a one-sided economic relationship whereby an agrarian surplus had provided for craftsmen, and craftsmen had then produced mainly luxuries and weapons for merchants, soldiers, priests and administrators. The communal relations still maintained among the peasantry in varying degrees contrasted with the unequal distribution of wealth. The degree of their survival was an index of the degree to which the cultivators failed to benefit from the products of the craftsmen, of the degree to which communal labour was still necessary to compensate deficiencies in technique.

From the agrarian surplus the specialist handicraft workers have been maintained and have multiplied; their products have been exchanged and the process of exchange has led to the appearance of specialist merchants; social production and commerce must now be organized centrally; the organizers of production, who, like the craftsmen, owe their social origin to the granting of a surplus from the collective labour of the cultivators of the soil, further expand this surplus in all its developing forms and their social status becomes expanded in corresponding degree. What was bestowed now becomes what is due. Tribute and services are obligatory. The area from which they are exacted is forcibly expanded. Force and wealth go hand in hand.

There are indications that Cretan society was independently developing analogous characteristics in the Late Minoan period before there was any fusion with Mycenaean culture.[100] The process of unification, under the hegemony of Knossos, was completed. A network of good roads, protected by forts at intervals, linked the Minoan towns together.

'Though it is clear,' commented Pendlebury,[101] 'that the period must have been peaceful in the extreme, the main roads were carefully guarded, as can be seen from the number of small sites which must have been forts or police stations along their course. This is particularly noticeable along the great road from Komo to the harbour town of Knossos, and I would attribute to the same period the forts along the road from Zakros to Ampelos. . . .' Against whom did these main roads have to be guarded in a

---

[100] Cf. the view of Banti, for whom the similarities existing between Knossos and the mainland in LM II 'seem to be due to a Greek conquest of Knossos': MPA 310.

[101] Ib. 184.

period of extreme peace and why did the maintenance of peace require forts or police stations?

The well-known fresco from Knossos called the 'Captain of the Blacks' probably belongs to L.M. II.[102] It shows 'a smart Minoan officer in a yellow kilt and a horned cap of skin, carrying two spears and leading a file of black troops at the double.'[103] This revealing fragment is to some extent paralleled by the scene on the handleless cup (The Chieftain Vase) from Haghia Triada early in the period. A young prince gives orders to a subordinate officer and a file of men. 'The contrast between the proud bearing of the Prince and the deferential attitude of the officer is admirably brought out.'[104]

Such knowledge as we have of the development of Cretan arms and armour indicates an increased attention to the practices of warfare. In discussing the figure-of-eight shield, Evans emphasized both its antiquity and its religious character.[105] But the importance which this shield seems suddenly to have acquired in LM Ia was explained by Evans as due to the rise of a new militaristic dynasty which destroyed Gournia and other towns of east Crete.[106] Scenes of fighting which involve this shield have not yet been found in Crete, but two seals from Knossos show lines of marching warriors with figure-of-eight shields covering their right sides.[107] They date from the early part of the period (LM Ia). Both the sword and the spear underwent a marked development in Crete at this time and influenced the types discovered on the mainland.[108] But the most revolutionary change in the field of armament was undoubtedly effected by the introduction of the chariot. 'Considering the relatively small total resources available to early urban societies, the war chariot is fairly comparable to the tank of today; it was an engine which only a

[102] PM 2.755.

[103] Pendlebury, AC 200–1, who comments: 'The evidence for the Sudanis is the knee of one figure on a blue background and the back of the head of another on a white background': ib. 200 n. 5. Cf. Banti MPA 309: 'The Minoans were interested in nature more than in man; their paintings show a peaceful and fascinating, but rather frivolous, life in an enchanted Fairyland, where warriors, like the so-called "Captain of the Blacks", look as if they belonged to musical comedy, or had been drawn by a cartoonist.' This is special pleading. The point is that the warriors, unlike musical comedy and cartoonists, are *there*.

[104] Ib. 214 and Plate XXXVII, 2; cf. RL 12.324. See further pp. 84–9.

[105] PM 3.314 ff.; cf. ib. 2.50 ff.; Lorimer HM 137.

[106] Ib. 308; Lorimer ib. 137.

[107] Evans PM 3.313, figs. 204–5; cf. Lorimer ib. 138.

[108] Lorimer ib. 254 ff.; ib. 261 ff.

rich civilized state could produce and maintain, and against which no barbarian tribe or rebellious peasantry could compete.'[109] Just as the chariot probably helped Mycenae to acquire supremacy in the Peloponnese, both as a means of communication with the centre and as an instrument of war,[110] so it may have helped Knossos in its acquisition of similar supremacy in Crete. Such is the inference that may plausibly be drawn from the inventories of the Knossian accounts, among which muster-rolls of chariots and lists of weapons conspicuously feature.[111] And the Knossian inventories of men and women, flocks and herds, vases and their contents, olive trees and saffron, indicate a meticulous care in the recording of property and the management of commerce such as would be natural to the centre of a tributary system.

The development of a highly organized bureaucratic system, with its centre at Knossos, was matched by a corresponding expansion of external influence so marked that it has all the signs of a considerable imperial hegemony in the Aegean, which included the Cyclades, Argolis and Attica, and perhaps extended as far as Sicily. This expansion, which was perhaps facilitated by actual Minoan colonization,[112] was dependent upon the maintenance of close commercial relations with Egypt and with Syria.[113] The scanty mainland evidence of direct contact with Egypt has been taken to indicate a deliberate policy of exclusion by the Minoans.[114] Such a monopoly of trade, which would have denied the developing mainland economy a natural outlet to the most flourishing markets and perhaps guaranteed that some portion of its benefits accrued to the Minoans in the form of tribute, would not only have caused increasing tension between Crete and the mainland but could only have been sustained by force. Hence the Minos of Greek tradition became a tyrant and imperial overlord; and this tradition of Minoan thalassocracy is not only too firm to be rejected but derives, in all probability, not from a 'Mycenaean Minos', but from the period of the 'priest-kings' of Knossos, before its destruction.[115]

---

[109] Childe in Singer 209–10.   [110] Lorimer *ib.* 322.
[111] Evans PM 4.785 ff.; Pendlebury AC 219; Childe WHH 147.
[112] Evans *ib.* 2.626.   [113] Pendlebury AC 230. Cf. Schaeffer 12.
[114] *Ibid.*
[115] Hall CGBA 265–6; Pendlebury *ib.* 229–31; Thomson SAGS 1.371 and n. 5; cf. Th. 1.4. Changes in the architecture of the period indicate a shortage of timber. Was this shortage partly due to intensive naval construction? Cf. Evans PM 2.518, 565; Pendlebury *ib.* 188. See further pp. 88–9.

But sudden as was the final destruction of the main centres of Minoan supremacy, there must have been a prior period of fusion between Minoan and Mycenaean cultures in Crete itself. For the Linear B script appears to have been the palace style of recording at Knossos from *c.* 1450 to *c.* 1400 B.C. The details of such a process of fusion, as also the reasons for the final destruction, are the subject of much controversy which can only be settled as further concrete evidence accumulates. But the results which followed upon the destruction of the centres are not in doubt. The focus of imperial power shifted to Mycenae, as the seat of an indubitably militarist dynasty, which, adapting its monopoly control of inherited Minoan Bronze Age techniques to warfare, enjoyed that brief supremacy which is immortalized by Homer, and was used to hasten its own destruction. Wealth was amassed at one pole of society, but no means was found of using it to promote any fresh advances in technique to offset the continuing characteristic one-sidedness of Late Bronze Age economy. Hence Mycenaean society as a whole became increasingly poorer during the course of the late fourteenth and thirteenth centuries B.C.

The collapse of the Minoan imperial bureaucracy is a special case of the decay of the Bronze Age cultures of the Mediterranean, which was to become general by about 1200 B.C. We have seen some reason to suggest that the economic basis of the one-sided expansion which prompted the rise of the Minoan thalassocracy was being firmly laid at the beginning of the Late Minoan period, if not earlier. It seems, however, that the ruling groups who promoted the expansion and controlled those special features of the economy which made expansion possible were those who suffered most from its collapse, as also the urban centres from which they exercised their control. Thanks to the one-sided nature of the economy, the Cretans as a whole were able to continue their traditional way of life without much interruption. They were thus in the end able to benefit from the inability of the rulers to use the wealth derived from their control of tribute and of the products of the craftsmen in such a way as to change radically the economic system outside the main urban centres. All the indications are that Minoan culture continued without interruption, but, of course, at a lower level. Now that they could no longer be employed on elaborate work in the palaces, it is likely that a large number of specialist craftsmen found employment either on the mainland or in Egypt. The chief stimulus to the concentration of wealth within Crete had been removed with the loss of dynastic autonomy. With overseas trade out of Cretan control, there developed a tendency for the population to disperse, especially over the hitherto sparsely inhabited western districts.[116] This decentralization was to have significant consequences in the religious sphere. The further exploitation of natural resources which the dispersal implies, coupled, no doubt, with Mycenaean commercial influences, helped to maintain society in traditional, though subdued, Bronze Age forms until the end of the Bronze Age and the collapse of the Mycenaean Empire, with which Crete was now linked, under the impact of fresh invaders to the mainland, the Dorians.

3. FROM BRONZE TO IRON

Of the details of the social and economic changes which occurred in Crete from *c.* 1100 to *c.* 800 B.C., that is to say from the end of the Bronze Age until the island was becoming thoroughly 'Dorian', concrete evidence remains regrettably deficient.[117] The existing evidence, such as it is, appears to support the following general conclusions: With the collapse of the Achaean Empire, there was a drastic fall in Cretan population. Most of the coastal sites and inland towns were abandoned; and the palace site at Knossos was also finally deserted. Elaborate styles of architecture were no longer feasible. But building techniques did survive, though the now-common built tombs are our chief source of knowledge in this field. So too did the craft of the potter, and there were Cretan innovations in styles of pottery even in the so-called sub-Minoan, Protogeometric and Geometric periods. By the beginning of the eighth century more settled conditions prevailed and a few of the old Minoan sites such as Haghia Triada, Phaistos and Mallia were again inhabited. In the next two centuries

[116] Pendlebury *ib.* 237–9. Cf., on the artistic consequences of the dispersal of Cretan emigrants, Frankfort CS 267–8.

[117] Cf. the fascinating report of 'Karphi. A City of Refuge of the Early Iron Age in Crete': ABSA 38.57–145. On sites of sub-Minoan and Protogeometric remains see Pendlebury AC 313 ff.; Desborough 233–71. In the period of the Greek colonization movement, which was well under way by the close of the eighth century B.C., there are archaeological indications that Crete was again influenced, as before in the Bronze Age, by Phoenicians and other Semitic peoples. The extent of this influence is considered to be extensive enough to justify the label 'orientalizing', applied to seventh-century Greek culture. See, for Crete, Demargne CD 307–56; Dunbabin *passim*; on Crete and Cyprus as intermediaries, Frankfort CS 314.

there was a considerable increase both in wealth and in population. New cities were founded and existing ones expanded.

There are three general factors which can be isolated as having played the most important part in establishing the social and economic system as it appears in outline by the eighth century B.C. These three factors must have interacted, but precisely how cannot be estimated because of our lack of information about social conditions over the preceding three centuries. They are: (1) the replacement of bronze by iron; (2) the development of Dorian supremacy; (3) the remarkably tenacious survival of Minoan traditions throughout the troubled and confused period from the Bronze Age into the times when a Hellenic social system could become firmly based on Iron Age techniques.

There had been rapid growth of native iron-working in Iran, Transcaucasia, Syria and Palestine between 1200 and 1000 B.C. Cyprus, Caucasia and Crete were not slow to follow. 'The new processes which made steel a material equal, and even superior, to bronze found their way prepared in all these countries by earlier attempts at iron-smelting. This explains why the smelting of iron spread so much more quickly than that of bronze.'[118] Iron gradually replaced bronze as the chief metal, though fine work continued to be done in bronze, including a number of important works of art.[119] Iron was cheaper and much more abundant than bronze and its widespread availability must have helped considerably in the establishment of the separatist communities which so markedly differentiate the Crete of the historical period from the centralized Late Minoan system. In contrast with the characteristic trends of Bronze Age economy, the spread of iron-working would lead to the attachment of domestic industry to agriculture; and their combination would have helped to bring about a self-sufficiency of village producers independent of markets.[120]

---

[118] Forbes in Singer 595.

[119] Pendlebury AC 336; cf. Kunze KB. It is agreed that Cretan metallurgy in the archaic period, by continuing a very ancient tradition, was one of the most developed in the whole of Greece.

[120] Cf. Th. 1.2.2: τῆς γὰρ ἐμπορίας οὐκ οὔσης; ib.1.7.1:—ἐμπορίας τε ἔνεκα. While iron is absent from the Protogeometric level at Amyklai, the Protogeometric period in Athens coincided with its more and more common use. Though still a precious metal in the sub-Mycenaean period, iron became the normal weapon from Early Protogeometric onwards. But iron weapons found in Crete belong to an earlier date than Cretan Protogeometric, and they may antedate Attic Protogeometric. Hence the Cretans used iron weapons, as they also practised cremation, without influence from Attica: Desborough 288, 301–2; cf. 252, 255.

The Dorians moved into southern Greece at the end of the second millennium B.C., and then extended overseas to the southern Cyclades, Crete, Rhodes and the Carian coast. They arrived as a league of three tribes: the Hylleis, descended from Hyllos, son of Herakles; the Dymanes, who worshipped Apollo; the Pamphyloi, 'those of all tribes', who worshipped Demeter. The Dorians held firmly to their traditional form of tribal organization, and their tribal customs, institutions and nomenclature endured in Crete, though in continuously modified ways, throughout the period of the supremacy of the aristocratic systems which have become closely associated with their name.[121]

The details of the Dorian dispersal over Crete remain obscure. But the epigraphic record confirms that Cretan Doric became in general the language of the rulers of the city-states of the Iron Age. It may be assumed that the danger and the conflicts which are likely to have accompanied this settlement further encouraged the conscious fostering of tribal traditions, including a confederate organization, with the bonds of kinship as its basis, expressed through the medium of a common language. But since this tribal organization was superimposed upon an already existing social and economic order, it became steadily transformed from an association of kinsmen into a rudimentary apparatus of state in the different areas, at first perhaps under royal leadership.[122] The earliest inscriptions show that the political forms of aristocratic government had taken firm shape. Such powers as had formerly been exercised by kings or chieftains had been taken over by boards of chief magistrates known as *kosmoi*, selected from privileged hereditary groups, with Councils of elders made up of former magistrates, and Assemblies of citizens functioning beside them.

The process of dispersal over Crete cannot have been uniform, for there are indications that the Dorians were ready to adapt themselves to existing conditions so as to bring about, in some areas, an amalgamation with indigenous ruling groups.[123] But whether independently by Dorians, or in conjunction with other rulers, in general the land and the tillers of the land were appropriated as instruments of production by aristocratic minorities.

This original land settlement was the product of the amalgamation of two systems, of the indigenous Minoan-Mycenaean and of

---

[121] See further Willetts ASAC 230 *et passim*.   [122] *Ib*. 103.
[123] *Ib*. 254 and n. 1.

Doric tribalism. To what extent the tributary system (which had, in all probability, already modified the communal village system in the later Bronze Age) had then been further modified in the period before the Dorian supremacy is a matter of speculation. It seems likely that the Dorians became, through a process of conquest and oppression, the masters in an already existing 'caste-system', continued from the Bronze Age. Certainly their supremacy was founded upon a system of vassalage. The tillers of the soil were serfs, subject to systematic tribute, at first in the form of rent in kind and then developing into money-rent.[124] The Dorian rulers of Sparta imposed a tribute of fifty per cent upon their serfs. But, in Crete, it appears that the tribute was not so highly assessed. The serfs belonged inalienably to the *klaroi*, the estates from which the ruling class drew tribute. But so did the houses in which they lived, which could be furnished by the serfs from their own means. And the serfs could also possess cattle in their own right; could marry and divorce; and they could even, at least at Gortyna as late as the fifth century B.C., inherit the *klaros* which they worked, in the event of there being no citizen heirs available. These conditions, which allowed the numerous class of cultivators, on which the whole economy so long depended, to preserve their own ancient traditions, even though subordinated, largely contributed to the stability of the aristocratic system.

Nevertheless, the primary features of this system were economic, social and political inequality, with four main classes of the population distinguished. The minority of free citizens, out of which was formed the ruling classes of landlords and officials, had their dwellings, their *syssitia* and gymnasia in the city, the centre of the political, social and religious life of each separate state. The phratry (originally a group of clans), in its Cretan form of the *hetaireia*, became an exclusive association of male citizens, preventing women and all non-citizens from exercising political rights. The chief motive for the distribution of the land and the cultivators themselves among the ruling minorities, in accordance with their tribal custom, was to ensure a continuous food supply for themselves and their dependants, so that they were free to concentrate upon administrative and military pursuits. It appears that contributions derived from tribute were made individually, and in kind, in the first instance, by members of the *hetaireiai* to a common fund. This system later became centrally organized

[124] *Ib.* 16, 20–1, 49, 139–40, 152, 193.

through the state apparatus and it was no doubt in this stage that rent in kind began to be supplemented by money-rent. The organization and education of the citizen youth, centred upon the *agelai*, retained many characteristic tribal features.

The *apetairoi* were a class of free men, free, that is to say, in the sense that they were neither bonded nor enslaved. But, as their name implies, they were excluded from the *hetaireiai* and they lacked the political rights enjoyed by the citizens. It is possible that this class included the members of various communities subject to one or another city-state. In addition to the large class of subject serfs, there was also a distinct class of chattel slaves.[125]

The process of adaptation of Dorian tribal institutions to new conditions would have been facilitated by the fusion with those native tribal institutions which are likely to have persisted from Bronze Age times among the cultivators. Another consequence of the impetus derived from contact with the traditions of the older civilization was the rapidity with which the new Cretan society became centred upon cities. Yet another was the active and relatively early practice of alphabetic writing.

The distribution of land and cultivators brought about successive modifications in the system of inheritance among the ruling clans. We have seen how the Minoan 'household' exercised its influence in the one-sided development of Bronze Age economy. Now, in new conditions, the tendency developed for smaller units of relationship to grow within the wider circle of the clan system of the rulers, especially marked by the growth of the institution of the *oikos* ('household') which was closely related to the possession of the *klaros*, the 'lot' or family estate.[126] Changes in the system of inheritance were accompanied by corresponding changes in the system of marriage, as tribal kinship and inheritance gave place to a family system based on individual ownership. In the cities where commerce once more began to develop to a significant degree, and with the introduction of a system of coinage in the early fifth century B.C., the break-up of the older tribal systems, represented at this period by the transitional form of the *oikos*, was accelerated. Coined money made possible the alienation of estates which became general by the Hellenistic period. Even so, forms of common ownership (especially perhaps where rights of pasturage, as opposed to cultivation, were concerned) appear to have survived.

[125] See further *ib*. Chs. IV and VI.   [126] See further *ib*. Ch. VII.

Alienation and the consequent freedom to acquire unlimited amounts of land would imply an increasing proportion of free landless persons. There were, in fact, demands for a redivision of the land in Hellenistic times, but this never came about owing to the operation of a variety of opposing factors. The successful maintenance of the tribute system which kept the *syssitia* in being, the incessant warfare which ravaged the cities from the middle of the fourth century B.C. until the Roman occupation, the subjection of weaker by stronger states, the absorption of surplus manpower in large-scale piracy and in mercenary service within the same period, all helped to stave off the application of drastic reform. But the most important single obstacle standing in the way of change was the continued dependence of the whole agrarian economy on serf labour. No major internal economic advance, of the kind which occurred in democratic city-states, was possible without the liberation of the serf-class as small-scale, independent producers.

With the development of the *oikos* as an economic and social unit within the clan, restricted kinship groups acquired political dominance. Ruling clans were succeeded by the system of close oligarchy of the fifth and fourth centuries B.C. The Hellenistic period was one of economic and political instability, as Crete was drawn into contact with conflicting overseas powers in Europe, Asia and Africa. Close oligarchy was modified to some extent, but the aristocracies maintained their political power and successfully resisted fundamental change.

The economic and social history of Crete, over a period of more than 2000 years before the Roman occupation, was such that it could never emancipate itself from the abiding influence of tradition. The importance of this generalization in relation to the history of Cretan religion must not be underestimated.

CHAPTER 2

Initiation Practices and Other Mainland Links with Crete

THE evidence for the dominance of old traditions in the Cretan cults will be presented in detail in the following pages. Before this detailed exposition begins, however, it will be helpful to sketch in general terms and with a few illustrative examples some of the more important principles which will emerge from our survey.

Firstly, the hypothesis that early settlers in Crete had transplanted and developed tribal institutions comparable with those familiar in the ethnographic record elsewhere leads us to the acceptance of a totemic basis for Cretan religion. The controversial nature of this viewpoint will be mentioned later, when it will be tested in the case of an important myth with a Minoan background, which will help us to understand the prevalence of the motif of the cycle of birth and death in Cretan religion. It will be argued that this cycle was originally totemistic.

If the ancestors of the early clans were, in Crete as elsewhere, animals, birds and natural forces, we can explain many characteristic features of later Cretan religion as totemic survivals. These include the traditions, in cult, myth and in coinage, relating to the bull, the goat, the sow, the snake, the dove and the sacred tree. The pillar, which functions in a similar way to the sacred tree, the horns of the bull and the double-axe, sanctified both as a tool for felling trees and as a sacrificial weapon in contact with the blood of the bull, derived their emblematic power from the same conception.

Secondly, since constant reference will be made to initiation, it must be emphasized that initiation is an inherent part of the totemic cycle; and it follows that indications we shall find of initiatory practices, both in cult and in social institutions, supplement the evidence for the survival of a totemic basis in various forms.

Primitive communities are divided into age-grades on a physiological basis, transition from one grade to another being brought about through rites of initiation. The newborn child is looked upon as an ancestor come to life again, the clan totem reincarnated. At puberty, the child undergoes its most important transition. For the adolescent dies as a child and is born again as a man or a woman. Similarly, the adult man or woman is transformed into an elder. At death, the elder enters the highest grade of all, being now counted among the totemic ancestors. Eventually he will re-emerge from this category and the whole cycle will begin again. In this cycle, birth is death and death is birth, complementary aspects of an everlasting process of change, of decay and renewal. The death and rebirth of the initiate is dramatically represented, often with a contest and an ordeal of some kind. This practice has left a deep imprint on the whole character of Cretan religion.

Thirdly, we must anticipate a later argument by pointing out that, with the decline of the Mother-goddess, the bull became associated with the Minoan kingship, which had important functions in relation to the calendar. Hence the bull becomes a symbol of the sun. Both are fertility symbols and, through their agency and their link with the kingship, the totemic cycle undergoes a change. In its changed form it has left its traces not only in Crete but wherever early Cretan influences penetrated. Bull-worship and, to a lesser extent, snake-worship, remain involved with traditions of the prehistoric kingship.

There is a legend, common in folklore, of an exposed baby which is suckled by animals. We shall find that this legend is common in Crete, particularly with reference to the infant Zeus. Since Cretan Zeus is a god who dies and is born again, we must regard the sow, the goat, the bees and other creatures who nursed him, according to the myths, as totemic survivals in a vegetation cycle of decay and renewal which replaced the simple totemic cycle.

It is not only the god, or his animal symbol, who continually dies and is born again. The same kind of cycle persists in the training of those for whom certain kinds of deity have a particular regard, the youth of the city-states of the historical period. For, even in the more sophisticated Greek communities, there remained indications of more primitive forms of social organization dependent on tribal initiation. This helps to explain why physical education continued to be an always important and often decisive factor in Greek education, even where it was most advanced. In such places the relationship between intellectual education and physical education was typified by that common feature of the city-state, the gymnasium. The bonds between gymnastic, music and philosophy were reflected in the activities, arrangement and the architectural form of the gymnasium.

In the more backward Greek states, where education remained, for the most part, physical education, primitive forms of training were naturally more conspicuous. Here we find embedded in the educational system a form of nomenclature apparently more suited to cattle than to human beings. But this nomenclature was not intended to be undignified—assuming that it derived ultimately from cattle-worship, from the close bonds between human and animal life reflected in totemistic beliefs. It will later be argued that these forms of organization, together with their nomenclature, may well go back to the Minoan Age. But here we are concerned with their historical nature; and we may look to Sparta first of all because it presented the most primitive traces.[1]

As soon as a Spartan child was born it was taken before the elders of its tribe and, if considered to be a weakling, it was exposed. The male Spartan was subjected to state-regulated discipline from the end of his sixth year until his sixtieth. After the sixth year the boy began his progress through a number of different age-grades. Though many details of the organization of their training are still obscure, it seems probable that boys of different ages lived under the supervision of a young man called an *eiren*, eating and sleeping together as members of a community called a 'herd' (*agela*), corresponding to the communities of the adult males. These communities crossed those of the age-classes, each age-class being divided into 'herds of oxen' (*bouai*), headed by 'ox-herd leaders' (*bouagoi*) of the same age. Instruction in gymnastics was given by the *eirenes*. Two or more 'herds', each commanded by its 'leader', took part in contests under the supervision of an *eiren*.

During the six-year period which lasted until the completion of his twelfth year, the boy entered upon the first stage of his training, but did not become involved in competitive exercises in music, dancing or athletics until he was ten. At the end of the twelfth year, the boys shaved their heads, wore only one cloak in

[1] Cf. Michell S *passim*; Nilsson DGSL.

a year, summer and winter, and were not allowed to bathe or anoint themselves except on special occasions. In the summer they slept on rushes plucked by hand from the Eurotas. In winter they were allowed to add leaves of wolf's-bane to their bedding.

The period of adolescence, from thirteen to eighteen, marked the third six-year period. At the age of eighteen the young Spartan acquired the status of *melleiren*, being now a candidate for the rank of *eiren*, reached in the nineteenth year. A severe test of physical endurance is a familiar feature of rites of initiation among primitive peoples, and the public scourging of the *melleirenes* at the altar of Artemis Orthia was an institution of this general type. Plutarch tells us that he had frequently seen youths die under this ordeal. However, there is some reason to believe that this ceremony, which lasted until the fourth century A.D., acquired its more brutal features in Roman times.

When he had completed his twenty-fourth year the Spartan ceased to be an *eiren* and became a first-line soldier. When he was thirty he became a full citizen and a member of the Assembly of citizens. He could now live with his wife and family.

Their early forms of military training prepared the young men for service with the *krypteia*, perhaps between the ages of eighteen and twenty. The word *krypteia* is sometimes translated as 'secret police' or 'secret service'. The atmosphere of secrecy implicit in the word more probably derived, however, from the fact that the *krypteia* formed a special part of the series of initiations from boyhood to manhood. For a period of withdrawal from the tribal settlement, spent in hiding in the bush and living on whatever nature and human resourcefulness can provide, is a common feature of tribal life.

Spartan girls were also organized in 'herds'. They took their meals at home but were encouraged to live an outdoor life, training their bodies so as to be able to bear strong children. They took part in gymnastic and musical training, in wrestling, running, swimming and throwing the discus and the javelin. At some festivals they danced and sang before the young men, praising the brave and deriding misbehaviour. Until they were married the women wore no veils and mixed with the men.

The Dorian institutions of Crete were in some respects similar to those of Dorian Sparta, but there were differences.[2] Thus, although the names of a fair number of Spartan age-grades have

[2] For more detailed comparisons cf. Willetts ASAC *passim*.

been preserved, this is not the case in Crete, except where puberty and the transition from youth to manhood are concerned. A number of age-distinctions appear in the Code of Gortyna as applicable to the free citizens; of these, *anoros* or *anebos* signify the boy or girl below the age of puberty[3] and *ebion, ebionsa* and *orima* the boy or girl after puberty.[4]

The importance attached to foot-racing is indicated by the terms *dromeus* and *apodromos*.[5] *Dromeus* means 'a runner' and was the term applied to an adult, a citizen in his own right. Although the exact age at which a youth became a 'runner' is uncertain, it must have been at about twenty. The term implies the right to exercise in the public gymnasium. The term *apodromos* was applied to a minor, one who was not yet allowed to take part in the public athletic exercises.

The Cretan youths were also organized in 'herds'. One of the most interesting points in Strabo's account of the educational system is his statement that those who were promoted from the 'herd' were obliged to marry at the same time.[6] This is undoubtedly a tribal feature of great antiquty and it implies that Cretan marriage was a state-controlled and public ceremony, involving all who belonged to the same age-grade.

It seems likely that the special term *apageloi* concerned the adolescent in the period immediately preceding entry into the 'herd'. For we know from Hesychios that *apageloi* were the same as *skotioi* ('secret ones').[7] A scholiast on Euripides (*Alcestis* 988) says that in Crete the boys were called *skotioi* because they lived in the women's apartment. But it is more likely that *skotioi* was a suitable term to apply to boys who were about to undergo the transition from boyhood to manhood, which involved a period of seclusion outside the city for two months. Hence we may compare Cretan *skotios* with Spartan *kryptos* (*krypteia*).[8] This explains why, as we shall see, Aphrodite was known in Phaistos as Skotia, the patron goddess of those about to undergo initiation into manhood and marriage.

Since Athenian women lived in seclusion, education in Athens, as was usual in most Greek states, with the exception of Sparta and Crete, was mainly for boys. There were three stages of formal

---

[3] IC 4.72. VII. 30, 45, VIII. 46, XI. 19, cf. IC 2. V. 25, A. 7 (Axos).
[4] *Ib.* VII. 37, VIII 39.
[5] Cf. Willetts ASAC 7–8, 10–14, 80–1, 123.   [6] 10.482.
[7] Hsch. s.v.; Jeanmaire CC 426.   [8] Willetts ASAC 14 and n. 6.

education: a primary stage from the age of six to fourteen, a secondary stage from fourteen to eighteen and a third stage from eighteen to twenty. This third stage was made compulsory by the state and is, in this respect as in others, comparable with the Spartan and Cretan systems. In the two years from eighteen to twenty the youths of Athens formed a special category of the population and were called *epheboi* ('youths'). The system of ephebic training was reorganized in the latter part of the fourth century. Although the relevant evidence is chiefly late, it is probable that some of its essential features derived from older times. This is indicated in some of the archaic traces of the oath which was taken by the novices. Moreover, as in Sparta and Crete, the ephebic training was organized by the state and not primarily for intellectual pursuits, at least in the Classical period. It was developed by the state as an organized system of military training and only became inseparable from the general educational system at a later date.

When he was eighteen, the Athenian youth entered upon the first stage of his enrolment and training as a citizen. The various tribes each selected three men over the age of forty, one of whom was finally chosen by the assembled people to supervise the *epheboi* of each tribe. After their supervisors had been appointed, the *epheboi* were taken round the temples, put into garrisons and started their training. They were taught the use of arms and spent much time in gymnastic training. The *epheboi* of each tribe took their meals together. They participated in festivals and a special place in the theatre was reserved for them. After completing the first year of their training, they had to demonstrate their skill at a public review in the theatre. Afterwards they received a spear and a shield from the state, and these arms were looked upon as sacred. The second year was spent in patrolling the frontiers and manning the forts.

While they were *epheboi* the youths wore a special cloak, originally dark or black, later white. Since emphasis is laid by ancient writers on the rough cloaks of the Spartan and Cretan boys, and since black or dun was the traditional mourning colour in Greece—except in Argos, where it was white—it is likely that, in all three cases, the wearing of this special garment was originally connected with the primitive belief in the death of the child at initiation.

In the third century the numbers of Athenian *epheboi* diminished to small proportions, and, since brothers are found serving together, the age qualification cannot have been so strictly observed.

But the system of grouping by age-classes continued in the Hellenistic period. Most Greek cities, small or large, had a system of ephebic training. The ages of the *epheboi* differed from place to place, but their form of organization very much continued to influence the educational system of the Greek world. In the main, where cities had lost their independence and were now ruled by monarchs who could command standing armies, military training as a dominant feature of the training of the youth was no longer required.

But Crete remained an exception to this general tendency. Though the island became more subject to outside influences of all kinds, the Cretan cities were never joined into any complete federal union and maintained their separatism until the Roman conquest in the first century B.C. Many traditional institutions remained unimpaired, including the 'herd', training in which was still a necessary preliminary for entry into the citizen body. The enrolment of the youth in 'herds' is well attested by inscriptions throughout the Hellenistic period.

The Athenian *epheboi* began their training in Boedromion (September–October) and had to perform important duties in Elaphebolion (March–April). It was then that they sacrificed a bull to Dionysos, under the direction of the archon.[9] At Magnesia on the Maeander a bull was presented to Zeus Sosipolis at the new moon of Kronion (October–November), with prayers for the safety of the city, peace, plenty and a good harvest. It was fattened during the winter and was sacrificed on the 12th of Artemision (April–May).[10] This sacrifice was performed by the *stephanephoros*, a priest found in several Ionian cities. He had the right to wear a crown and probably also purple as a sign of royalty; and he also gave his name to the year.[11] He is comparable with the Athenian *archon basileus*, who exercised sacred duties derived from the ancient kingship. A similar festival took place at Miletos.[12]

At Olympia the priests known as *Basilai* sacrificed to Sosipolis on the Hill of Kronos at the vernal equinox.[13] The name of the priests reveals their origin ('kings'); and, although we do not know

---

[9] Mommsen FSA 176; CIA 2.471 (IG 2.471); cf. CIA 4.318b (IG 2.478).
[10] SIG 589.   [11] Str. 14.648, cf. 633; SIG 589. 1.
[12] Hsch. Διὸς βοῦς.   [13] Paus. 6.20.1.

what the victim at the sacrifice was, a parallel with the Magnesian festival is indicated by the association of the snake with the god Sosipolis in both cults.[14] The god Dionysos, generally closely connected with Zeus and very comparable with the Cretan Zeus, was worshipped as a bull and a snake.[15] At Kos a specially selected bull was sacrificed to Zeus Polieus by the *geraphoros basileon* ('bearer of the king's privileges') on the 20th of Batromios (probably February–March).[16]

If festivals of this kind, revealing traces of a bipartite year, divided, as in Babylonia, at the equinox, and with their links with the kingship, the bull and the snake, derived ultimately from Mesopotamia, the inference is that they were brought to Greece in Minoan times by way of Crete; and the presentation of the bull must have been a very old feature.[17]

In the course of our survey, the relationship between the Minoan kingship and an octennial system of time reckoning, indications of which survive in the later mythology and cult of the Greek world, will be examined. One of the most familiar Athenian myths which recalled a bygone connexion with Minoan Crete concerns the journey of Theseus to Crete to kill the Minotaur. By this means he freed his compatriots from their obligation to send to Minos a sacrificial tribute of seven boys and seven girls every eight years. This myth was dramatized in the Crane Dance, with its representation of the windings of the labyrinth, before the horned altar of Apollo at Delos. The dance probably took place on the 7th of Thargelion, in the course of a festival to celebrate the birth of Apollo and Artemis. On the day before, the Athenians celebrated their deliverance from the old tribute by a pilgrimage to Delos, when the festival of the Thargelia began. In this festival two human victims were put to death, one on behalf of the men, the other on behalf of the women. Tradition said that this rite originated as an expiation of the death of Androgeos, the son of Minos.[18]

The sphere of Minoan influence penetrated farther into mainland Greece; and we find traces of the survival of that preeminence of the Mother-goddess which precedes the influence of a male deity in Minoan religion. In Crete, as we shall see, Hera

[14] Harrison T 241, fig. 61.   [15] *Id.* T 449, PSGR 398–400.
[16] SIG 1025.   [17] Cf. Thomson SAGS 2.113.
[18] Plu. *Thes.* 15, 21; Call. *Del.* 307–13; *Il.* 18.590–606; Hsch. Θαργήλια; D.L. 2.44; Anon. *VPlat.* 6 Cobet; Plu. *M* 717 d; X. *Mem.* 4.8.2; Pl. *Phd.* 58 a–b; Phot. *Lex.* φαρμακός; Suid. φαρμακούς; Phot. *Bibl.* 534.

appears to be a form of this Mother-goddess. For she was worshipped at Knossos along with Zeus in a sacred marriage, which derived from the Minoan palace-cult; and not far from Knossos Hera gave birth to Eileithyia, in the cave of Amnisos. On the mainland the chief centre of her worship was the Argive Heraion. Hence it can be inferred that she came to the Argive plain from overseas. The oldest image of Hera in the Heraion was made of pear-wood and had been brought from Tiryns. Tiryns was only a short distance away from Nauplia, which had probably been a chief port of call for Minoan traders. At Nauplia itself there was a cult of Hera Parthenos ('The Maiden'). At Hermione, to the south-east, there was another good harbour. Here there was a tradition that Zeus and Hera first landed when they arrived in Greece from Crete.[19]

The sacred marriage continued to be one of the most characteristic features of the worship of Hera. At Plataiai an effigy draped as a bride was escorted to the top of Mount Kithairon. At Athens there was an annual feast celebrating her marriage with Zeus. In Euboia the marriage reputedly took place on Mount Okhe. At Samos Hera was again represented by the effigy in bridal costume. Annual mysteries were enacted at the spring in Nauplia where she bathed after her marriage to renew her virginity—and the local Hera Parthenos was thus reconciled with the wife of Zeus.[20]

But one of the most interesting of these sacred marriages was remembered at Hermione in the form of a totemic myth. Zeus often appears as a lover disguised as a bird and it has been suggested that such myths, appearing in old Mycenaean centres, recall the Minoan belief in the bird epiphanies characteristic of their goddess.[21] In this case Zeus transformed himself into a cuckoo, on a mountain henceforth known as Cuckoo Mountain (Kokkygion).[22]

It was not only Hera who was remembered as coming from Crete, but the hero who was 'called after Hera' (Herakles), whose exploits were located in main areas of Mycenaean culture.[23] This suggests that the saga of Herakles was of Minoan origin and that he himself was the male partner of Hera, the Mother-goddess.[24]

[19] Paus. 2.17.5, 38.2; St. B. Ἑρμίων cf. Theoc. 15.64 sch.
[20] Paus. 9.3.3–9; Phot. ἱερὸς γάμος; St. B. Κάρυστος; Aug. CD 6.7; Lact. Inst. 1.17; Paus. 2.38.1.
[21] Nilsson MMR 552.   [22] Paus. 2.36.2.
[23] Nilsson MOGM 207.
[24] Pi. fr. 291; EM Νεῖλος, cf. Kretschmer MN 122.

It also explains why joint cults of Herakles and the Mother were common in country districts.[25] According to the local tradition, the Olympic Games were founded by the Idaian Herakles, who came from Crete.[26] On the Hill of Kronos which overlooked the sacred grove at Olympia there was a shrine of the goddess of childbirth, Eileithyia, whose cult was prominent in Crete. The shrine housed a snake called Sosipolis ('the saviour of the state'), and it was fed on honey-cakes by a priestess, who alone was allowed to enter, with her head veiled.[27] The shrine has been identified as the Idaian Cave mentioned by Pindar.[28] The statue of Sosipolis at Elis held the horn of Amaltheia, a Minoan symbol, recalling the legend that Zeus was reared on Mount Ida by the nymph Amaltheia on goats' milk out of a cornucopia. Herakles brought with him from Crete, to found the Olympic Games, his companions Paionios, Epimedes, Idas and Iasios.[29] Of these, Idas is clearly named after Cretan Mount Ida and Iasios recalls the Iasion whom we shall find featuring in the earliest attested form of the sacred marriage.

Hence the very name of the Hill of Kronos, with its 'priest-kings', the Basilai, the Idaian Cave and the Idaian Herakles, the cult of Eileithyia and the snake, and other points of detail, indicate the Minoan Age of Crete as their point of origin. They have parallels in parts of Arcadia, where a variety of local cults refer to Rhea and the birth of Zeus.[30]

The sun-god of Crete was later known as Talos and under this name became identified with Zeus. A similar identification took place among the Laconians. For it appears that they had had a fertilizing sun-god, like Talos, whose position was eventually taken by Zeus. The high peak of Mount Taygeton was known as Mount Taleton. It was sacred to the sun and horses were among the sacrifices offered to him there.[31] The mountain-god Zeus Taletitas derived his title from the mountain. He was here associated with the fertility-goddesses Auxesia and Damoia, Peloponnesian counterparts of Demeter and Kore, a familiar Cretan pair. At the site of their worship traces of an Eleusinion have been found.[32] We shall see good reason to credit the ancient tradition

[25] Farnell GHC 129.   [26] Pi. O. 10.23–59; Paus. 5.7.6–7.
[27] Paus. 6.20.2.   [28] Pi. O. 5.8; C. Robert SO 41.
[29] Paus. 5.7.6.
[30] Paus. 8.28.2, 8.38.2, 8.41.2; Str. 8.387, cf. Paus. 4.31.9, 4.33.1.
[31] Paus. 3.20.4.   [32] Cf. Cook Z 2.890.

that Crete was the home of the mysteries, including the Eleusinian Mysteries.

Thus some of the general principles underlying Cretan religion have their parallels in myth and cult in areas outside Crete where the Minoan traditions had been planted. We must now turn to the examination of these traditions in more precise terms.

CHAPTER 3

Minoan-Mycenaean Cults

THE heritage of cult practice (with its associated ritual and developing mythology) taken over by the Cretan communities of the historical period and adapted by them to their own new conditions of life can be roughly divided into three interrelated streams. There is, firstly, the enduring stream of influences from the neolithic period—enduring, both in the sense that the surviving images of that period cannot, in the words of Evans, be dissociated 'from those that appear in the shrines of the Great Minoan Goddess';[1] and also in the sense that their later imitations have continued to be discovered in the archaeological deposits of the advanced historical period, for many centuries after they have contributed to the development of Cretan sculpture. Secondly, there is the equally pervasive, but more complex, stream of influences derived from the dominance, at the height of the Bronze Age, of the Great Goddess, in her various manifestations. And, thirdly, there is the later stream, which is the product of the amalgamation of these two anterior traditions with a variegated polytheism, which, developing from the later Bronze Age, becomes firmly established in the city-states of the historical period and eventually unites the Cretan with the main established tradition of Hellenic polytheistic religion. The older phases of this combined heritage were dominated by the making of a goddess: the later phases by the intrusion of gods.

It is the purpose of the present chapter to summarize the more outstanding features from each of these streams of tradition; and also to indicate their relationship to the evolution of Cretan society from the neolithic period until the onset of the Iron Age, as sketched in the first chapter.

[1] PM 1.52.

1. FIGURINES

The interpretation of those monuments of the mural art of the Upper Palaeolithic hunting culture, which survive in caves and rock shelters, in the light of the traditions of recently surviving hunting peoples, as complex as it is still conjectural, nevertheless establishes a firm connexion between the hunting and the sex rites of the palaeolithic hunters.[2] The hunting imagery of the cave of Montespan includes the remains of clay figures torn to pieces in the rites.[3] When the game was painted on the rock face, the action of killing could be realistically illustrated or confined to a mimic dance.[4]

'The sex rites, on the other hand,' wrote Klingender, 'are illustrated by the masked human couples shown, at Les Combarelles and elsewhere, in exactly the same position as the men and women in the Bushman dances, and by animal couples, such as the bisons of Tuc d'Audubert. But sexual imagery is all pervading from the first. The migration of the Gravettians from Lake Baikal to the Atlantic seaboard is marked by the "Venus" figurines which tend to be replaced at later stations (notably la Ferrassie in the Vézère valley, where the whole development is documented) by more or less conventionalized symbols of the vagina or by pregnant animals. Most telling among these allusions is, however, the siting of the sanctuaries in caves. What a "kloof enclosed with hills and precipices" was to the Bushmen, the cave was to the northern hunters: the magic womb in which the fertility of the totem was maintained. To these sacred sites only the initiated could penetrate. To enter the Montespan cave, for example, one must dive beneath an overhanging rock through an ice-cold stream. . . . Nor are we left in any doubt, in the light of the evidence quoted, concerning the rituals of creation which took place in these sacred enclosures. They are also, moreover, vividly illustrated in postglacial settings by paintings or engravings in which a man and a woman are linked by a line which is then carried around them, like a cave or stone-circle.'[5]

This close connexion between hunting and sex rites reflects the simple but profound unity of contradiction so conspicuously inherent in the conditions of a primitive hunting economy.

---

[2] Klingender PRPSE; cf. Hawkes 38–9.
[3] Tombe CPMG; Klingender *ib.* 144–5.   [4] Klingender *ib.* 145.
[5] *Ib.* 145–6. On Bushman rites cf. the absorbing account in Van der Post LWK.

Human existence is assured by the killing of animals to provide the food supply. But the further renewal of this food supply is dependent upon the reproduction of animal life. In the same way, the appropriation of a food supply provides for the continuing existence of the hunter only for a limited period. The hunter too must reproduce his kind. The life and death of animals and human beings are indissolubly linked, and the relationship becomes objectified in the form of totemic representations, symbolic alike of ancestry and of rebirth. Similarly, the widespread practice of staining objects and persons with red ochre is symbolic of the renewal of life. The bones of the dead are stained with red ochre in Upper Palaeolithic burials.[6] And when the girls of the South African Valenge perform a dance during the initiation ceremonies of puberty, they too are covered in red ochre.[7]

The Upper Palaeolithic Gravettian culture has yielded the earliest statuettes, most usually female and, as it seems, often pregnant. While the breasts, hips and buttocks are emphasized, the facial features are normally ignored.[8] The distribution of such statuettes in Europe has been considered to reinforce the notion of an Eastern origin for the Gravettian.[9]

The figurines so commonly discovered in neolithic and chalco-lithic sites in central Europe, the Mediterranean region and the Near East are generically similar to the palaeolithic types. Usually made of clay, less often carved in stone, the statuettes are normally female; but male figures and models of animals also occur.[10] Since the communities which produced these figurines had now become settled food-producers, it is naturally assumed that the magic rituals of the hunters had become the fertility cults of cultivators, involving a complex extension of the association between the cycle of human existence and reproduction and the same cycle in nature. The common bond of life between nature and society is now the earth, as opposed to the creatures who rove upon it. This common bond is for long envisaged as a female principle. Since the work of agriculture does not become transferred to men until field tillage and the cattle-drawn plough replace garden tillage and the hoe, the tendency is for matrilineal descent to continue until that stage has been reached. The dominance of the female figurine

---

[6] Hawkes 38; Burkitt 191.   [7] Earthy 111–24.

[8] Are the Cyrenaic female funerary busts, without facial features (going back to the end of the sixth, and beginning of the fifth, century B.C.) remote descendants of the palaeolithic 'Venus'? See Chamoux 293–300.

[9] Hawkes 39.   [10] Hawkes 84.

in cult thus corresponds with the dominance of the female in the cycle of human reproduction and the vital importance of female labour in the work of agriculture. But to seek a more precise understanding of the role of these figurines in a particular 'cult-ritual' is difficult.

'It is agreed that these objects were intended somehow to promote fertility. So much indeed is in some specimens obvious. But there the problem has been left. In attempting to solve it, several considerations must be kept in mind. In the first place, cults involving the use of human effigies are not confined to this region of the world nor to the past. Secondly, since the remains present a continuous series from Late Palaeolithic to the Iron Age, we must be prepared to find that they served different purposes at different times. Between the first and last of them lies almost the whole history of magic. Thirdly, the circumstances of discovery demand attention. Most were found in tombs; many of the later examples must have been votive offerings, some being perforated for suspension. In some cases too the postures and gestures are obviously intended to be significant. And lastly, the sequence revealed in the stratified cultures of the Danube, Gumelnita, and Thessaly suggests that they should be studied against the background of the primitive agricultural matriarchate. . . . They go back to the time when the connexion between copulation and conception was unknown, as it still is among the lowest savages. The magic for which they were made was directed in the first place to menstruation and parturition, and extended later to initiation, marriage, disease, and death—to every crisis that demanded the infusion of reproductive energy, the renewal of life.'[11]

The Cretan types of figurine, found together with clay birds and animals in the neolithic strata of Knossos, were discussed by Evans.[12] Though fragments of male figures were identified, the majority of images in human shape were female. They are of two

[11] Thomson SAGS 1.240-3. Cf. Nilsson MMR 290-2: 'It is a commonly accepted view that these figures are idols in the sense of images of a goddess who, owing to the maternal forms of the figures, is termed a Mother Goddess. But this opinion is not founded on any proofs of a special order. . . . Images are also used for magical purposes by primitive man and this magic use precedes on the whole the religious representation of gods. . . . There are consequently other points of view also which ought to be taken into consideration in trying to understand the female figures. It might be said that these theories may all be justified to a certain extent; the images may have been used and conceived in more than one sense. It can certainly not be claimed that such a plurality of meaning is *a priori* impossible.'

[12] Evans PM 1.43-55; cf. Nilsson MMR 290.

main types. The rarer type is flat and broad; the more frequent type is short, stumpy, steatopygous, either squatting with the legs bent under the body or sitting with knees drawn up and feet drawn together. Both types were assumed to have a common origin, with close parallels on the Anatolian side.[13] Generic relationships with the Upper Palaeolithic types cannot, of course, be directly established, but, together with the changing pattern of magical associations suggested above, could be assumed as part of the inherited traditions of neolithic immigrants.[14] The continuing importance of Cretan caves and rock shelters as centres of cult from the earliest times tends to reinforce this inference.[15]

The Early Minoan images are considered to be due to foreign influence, partly Egyptian, partly Cycladic.[16] The Parian marble of which the Cycladic idols imported into Crete were made makes their origin clear. Yet, despite (perhaps also because of) these influences, we may assume that the ideas attaching to the images underwent modification and extension rather than fundamental change. Thus the many examples from the later Middle and Late Minoan periods, of terracotta and of bronze, are divided into three classes: votive images from sanctuaries, cult idols from shrines and those discovered in graves and tombs.[17] The variety of attitudes assumed by these figurines, including the 'gesture of benediction', may, in certain cases, recall the actual postures of a sacred dance. Since the familiar sitting or squatting posture of the earliest specimens may have represented that actually assumed in childbirth, the varied gestures of the later types may have been supposed to exercise a beneficial influence in childbirth and also over the growth of the crops; as puppets the images could be efficacious in connexion with death, as well as with birth, and this would account for their presence in graves and tombs; as votive offerings they could represent either the worshipper appealing for the protection of a goddess—in sickness or childbirth, at initiation, marriage or bereavement—or the goddess herself, in the form of a

[13] Evans *ib.* 45, 47; cf. 51: 'We have to do with parallel phenomena, the operation of which is traceable throughout a geographically continuous region extending from the Aegean, and the Adriatic, to the Persian Gulf and even beyond the Caspian.'

[14] Cf. Evans *ib.* 45. 'It may be that some distant connexion will ultimately be established between this Neolithic family and the still earlier images of the Aurignacian Age with the organs of maternity so prominently shown—of which the "Venus of Brassempouy", and that of Willendorf in Lower Austria, stand as classical examples.' Also *ib.* 51–2; Nilsson MMR 290; Hawkes 84 and 89.

[15] See further Ch. 5. [16] Nilsson MMR 293.

[17] Nilsson *ib.* 295.

gift-offering for her patronage.[18] Minoan cave sanctuaries have become familiar as votive sites of figurines;[19] and it is likely that the other principal varied usages of the figurines had become well established before the end of Minoan times. Protogeometric and Geometric figurines continue obviously to exhibit the Minoan tradition; and figurines of animals also continue to be found together with male and female human types.[20] The ancestral idols of magic did not easily yield to the succeeding deities of religion.[21]

2. THE CYCLE OF BIRTH AND DEATH

In the preceding section it was assumed that the Cretan figurines and the traditions associated with them must somehow be connected with palaeolithic predecessors, implying an extension of these traditions from the cycle of human and animal birth and death to the similar cycle of growth and decay in conditions of settled cultivation of crops. This assumption followed upon a more general earlier hypothesis that the first neolithic settlers transplanted their social institutions to Crete.[22] These institutions would be based on the clan. Since membership of the clan is normally determined by descent from an assumed common totemic ancestor, acceptance of the general hypothesis must involve the likelihood of a totemic basis for Cretan religion. Such a possibility has been as firmly rejected by some students of early Greek religion as it has been firmly considered by others to be fundamental to a proper understanding of the subject.

Thus, among contemporary authorities, Nilsson adds to his judgments 'that there is nothing in the Greek religion which necessarily demands a totemistic explanation', and that 'it is unproved and doubtful whether totemism ever existed among the forefathers of the Greeks',[23] the remark that 'the images of animals found in the palaeolithic age and later, e.g. in the neolithic remains of Knossos, are—quite rightly I think—not accepted as images of

---

[18] Cf. Nilsson *ib.* 298-9. [19] Nilsson MMR 63-4, 69-70.
[20] Pendlebury 312, 322.
[21] A small temple of the Late Geometric period on the site of a sub-Mycenaean settlement at Gortyna has recently been excavated. A votive deposit on the slopes below the altar yielded hundreds of fragments of clay plaques with figure reliefs showing traces of painted decoration, terracotta figurines, vases, etc. The figurines, it is claimed, represent all stages from Late Mycenaean to Roman times. In archaic times the goddess is naked and wears a polos crown; but in Classical and Hellenistic times she is replaced by an image of Athene: JHS 75 (Sup.). 17; Levi GSAG.
[22] P. 7. [23] HGR 77-8; cf. also H. J. Rose. in SK 375.

gods in animal shape, or totems'.[24] On the other hand, Thomson, in his discussion of snake-worship as a totemic survival, writes: 'Those who deny the presence of totemic elements in Greek religion have only been able to maintain their position by isolating the subject from its proper context in the general history of religion. And the result is that one of the most conspicuous features of Greek culture—the part played in myth and ritual by plants and animals—is left unexplained.'[25] We must return later to the subject of the Minoan snake-cult. At present we are concerned with the task of trying to find some actual trace of a totemic cycle of birth and death, partly to test the assumption, partly because such a line of inquiry may throw some incidental light on the initiation of the Dorian youth in the Cretan city-states of the historical period. For initiation is closely bound up with the totemic cycle. 'Death does not imply the extinction of life. It only implies a transition from one form of life to another. . . . Thus, the human life, including a part of the animal and the plant life, presents an eternal circular course where there is apparently no beginning and no end, where the only things changing are the successive incarnations and transformations through which the soul has to pass.'[26]

The starting point of Persson's valuable study of the nature of prehistoric Greek religion was his analysis of the myth of Glaukos.[27] Accounts of the myth are preserved by Apollodoros and Hyginus and there are also references in later writers.[28]

According to the version preserved by Apollodoros, Glaukos, the son of Minos and Pasiphae, while still a child, was drowned by falling into a jar of honey as he was chasing a mouse (or a fly). When he disappeared, Minos made an energetic search and asked the advice of diviners as to the best means of conducting it. The Kouretes told him that he had, among his herds, a cow of three different colours, and that the man who could give the best description of the cow's colouring would restore his son to him alive. When the diviners had been assembled, Polyidos, son of Koiranos, compared the cow's colouring to the fruit of the bramble and,

[24] MMR 291 n. 10.   [25] SAGS 1.114.

[26] Karsten CSAI 416. The common habit (prevalent in many parts of the world, including Greece) of naming a child after a grandparent stems from the primitive view that the newborn child is an ancestor come to life again: Frazer TE 2.302, 3.298; Daremberg-Saglio 7.88; Dieterich ME 23; Seebohm SGTS 54; Karsten ib. 417.

[27] Persson 5–24.

[28] Apollod. *Bibliotheca* 3.3 f.; Hyg. *Fab.* 136; Tz. Sch. *ad* Lyc. 798; Eust. 369. 20; 894. 42; cf. Kirchner in *RE* s.v. Glaukos.

compelled to search for the boy, found him by some means of divination. But Minos declared that he must recover the boy alive, and Polyidos was therefore shut up with the dead body. Polyidos was in a state of great perplexity; and then he saw a snake going towards the corpse. He threw a stone at the snake and killed it, afraid that he would be killed himself if any harm befell the boy's body. Then a second snake appeared and, when it saw the first one dead, went away, but returned with a herb which it placed all over the body of the dead snake, which was thereupon restored to life. Surprised at the sight, Polyidos applied the same herb to the body of Glaukos and raised him from the dead. Although Minos had now his son restored to life again, he did not allow Polyidos to return to Argos until he had taught Glaukos the art of divination. Polyidos did so under this compulsion and, when he was sailing away, he told Glaukos to spit into his mouth. Glaukos obeyed and forgot the art of divination.

According to Hyginus, Glaukos, son of Minos and Pasiphae, fell into a jar filled with honey when he was playing ball. His parents searched for him and also questioned Apollo, who answered: 'A portent has been born to you, and he who can interpret it can also restore your son.' Upon hearing this oracle, Minos began to question his people about the portent. They told him that a calf had been born which changed its colour twice a day, every four hours, first being white, then red and then black. Minos called his diviners together and, when they could not interpret the portent, Polyidos, son of Koiranos, showed that it was like the fruit of the mulberry tree, which is first white, then red and finally, when it is ripe, black. Then Minos said to him: 'You are to restore my son to me in accordance with Apollo's answer.' As Polyidos continued to pursue his divination, he saw a night owl perched on a wine-cellar, driving away bees. Understanding this omen, he drew the lifeless boy from the jar. Minos then said to him: 'Now that you have found the body, you must also restore its soul.' When Polyidos said that he could not do this, Minos instructed that he should be shut up in a tomb together with the boy, and that a sword should be placed with them. When they had been shut up, a snake suddenly approached the boy's body and Polyidos, thinking it would eat up the boy, promptly struck it with the sword and killed it. A second snake came in search of its mate, saw that it was dead and brought a herb with whose touch it restored the first snake to life. Polyidos did the same to the boy.

Their cries were heard by a passer-by, who reported to Minos; and he ordered the tomb to be opened, received his son unharmed and sent Polyidos back to his country with many gifts.

As Persson pointed out, although the myth is given in detail only in these two late sources, and in fragmentary form in other later writers, the antiquity of the myth itself and the authenticity of the sources available to later writers are best demonstrated by the fact that Aeschylus (in *Kressai*), Sophocles (in *Manteis*) and Euripides (in *Polyidos*) all dealt with the subject. So did Aristophanes. According to Lucian,[29] the myth also formed the basis of a panto-mime. In another version, referred to elsewhere,[30] it was Asklepios, and not Polyidos, who restored Glaukos to life.

In his analysis of the myth, Persson drew the following conclu-sions: (1) The tradition that Glaukos fell into a jar of honey in-volves a direct reference to the practice of burying the dead in honey;[31] and, moreover, 'since the custom of pithos burial after the end of the Middle Bronze Age is to be met with only sporad-ically in the Greek culture area, occasionally in eastern Crete, in the Dipylon necropolis, and at the periphery of the world of Greek culture, there seems to me some reason for suspecting that this detail of the Glaukos story is of Minoan or pre-Mycenaean origin'.[32] (2) The dead boy, mourned and restored to life, the tree, the life-giving plant, the serpent, and so on, are different elements derived from an ancient vegetational religion. (3) Since Glaukos was the son of Minos, since a cow or a calf takes part in the story, and since Glaukos himself was closely related to Ariadne, the legend must be treated together with other material concerning Minoan religion, available in the form of Minoan-Mycenaean signet rings (described by Persson as the 'textbook' of the Minoan-Mycenaean religion). And, to quote the words of Persson's own summary: 'Successive analyses of a number of related representa-tions on Minoan-Mycenaean gold rings gave us an illustrative-narrative series which proved to be demonstrably associated with a vegetation cycle. Pictured for us were the changing seasons as they were celebrated in private cult practice and official festival.'[33]

This vegetation cycle, whose importance in Minoan religion Persson certainly demonstrates, must have had, as he himself sug-gests, an earlier origin. 'For primitive man the task of sustaining

[29] *Salt.* 49.
[31] Preller 2. 475.
[33] *Ib.* 164.

[30] Sch. *ad* E. *Alc.* 1; Hyg. *Fab.* 49.
[32] Persson 14. Cf. *ib.* p. 15.

life is the Alpha and Omega of all his actions and decisions. This applies to a savage who lives on roots and fruit as well as to a more agricultural people.'[34] But the savage is hunter as well as root- and fruit-gatherer. And there are indications in the myth of Glaukos which recall the totemic cycle of birth and death, whose traditions, we must suppose, were handed down from the ancestors of the first immigrants into Crete. These indications point to a very early origin of those rites of initiation which, in changed forms, persisted in Crete down to the Hellenistic period.

The significance of the part played by the Kouretes in that version of the myth handed down to us by Apollodoros was noticed by Jane Harrison.[35] More recently, Jeanmaire has interpreted the story as a ritual simulation of death and resurrection in an initiation rite.[36] The story, Jeanmaire reminds us, recalls that of another Glaukos, of Anthedon, 'city of the flower (or herb)'.[37] This other Glaukos saw the fishes on the beach restored to life through the touch of a plant. Tasting the plant himself, he (according to various versions) became mad; or was changed into a sea-god and leaped into the sea; or became immortal but grew old and leaped into the sea (thus becoming identified with the 'old man of the sea'). The leap was a ritual leap and the metamorphosis followed upon the tasting of a magical herb. Immersion in a jar of honey to the point of suffocation is an ordeal similar to a leap into the sea: hence the proverbial expression, 'Glaukos rose from the dead after he had drunk honey'.[38] The details of the later part of the Cretan Glaukos story lend support to the view that the particular type of initiation may have been preliminary to admission into a specialist guild of diviners, whose technique was passed from master to pupil.[39] The significance of the spitting episode is quite clear in this connexion. The magic power which Glaukos had received from Polyidos returns to the master when the pupil spits into his mouth.[40] Similarly, the initial problem which Polyidos is

---

[34] *Ib.* 165.

[35] 'The Kouretes are also, as all primitive magicians are, seers.' T 26.

[36] Jeanmaire 444–50.

[37] Ath. 7.48; Tz. *ad* Lyc. 754; Sch. *ad* A.R. 1. 1310; Ovid *Met.* 13.924 ff.; Paus. 9.22.6; Ausonius *Mosella* 276 ff.; Serv. *ad* Verg. *Georg.* 1.437; Jeanmaire 445; Persson 21–2.

[38] Γλαῦκος πιὼν μέλι ἀνέστη: Apostol. *Cent.* 5.48; Jeanmaire *ibid.*; Persson 11.

[39] Jeanmaire 446; cf. Persson 21.

[40] When Apollo spat into Cassandra's mouth, she was unable to convince anyone of the truth of her prophecies: Serv. *ad* Verg. *A.*2.247. On saliva in magic see Pliny *NH* 28.35 ff.; de Mensignac 41 ff.; Gruppe 887.

asked to solve, namely, how best to describe the changing colours of the cow, is a riddle of a type commonly associated with initiation practices. Riddles, as ancient as they are widespread, are originally designed for catechism in the secrets of initiation.[41] The three different colours of the cow, analogous to the three different colours of the ripening mulberry, probably allude to three different stages of the initiatory rite.[42]

A number of other details strengthen this interpretation of the myth. As proof of the popularity of the story of Glaukos in the time of the great dramatists, Persson refers us to its portrayal on the Sotades bowl, now in the British Museum,[43] showing a grave mound in section, with Polyidos and Glaukos inside the mound. Polyidos is aiming his staff at one of the snakes. There is, comments Persson, 'a certain naïveté in the representation of the boy, who does not appear to be as one dead; rather, the crouched position in which he is pictured gives the impression of a cowering living being who watches the preparations being made for his own revival'. If, however, the artist was aware that Glaukos was both the chief participant and also a witness of a mimetic rite, we must not apologize for his naïveté, but rather pay to his skill in conveying the correct impression of the scene a tribute at least equal to that which has been paid to the elegance and delicacy of his drawing.[44]

That Glaukos and Polyidos are, in a sense, different aspects of one and the same person, is also appreciated by Persson. Having stated that Glaukos is the 'grey-blue one', while Polyidos is 'he who knows many things',[45] he then draws upon the parallel theme of Glaukos of Anthedon to conclude that 'Glaukos, the "grey-blue one", is identified with the smooth and grey-blue sea before a storm—he becomes a diviner; wisdom and age follow—he becomes "the old man of the sea"'.[46] But there is no need to go to Anthedon to find the clue to this interrelation of youth and age, the uninitiated and the initiated, the pupil and the teacher. There is much evidence to show that *glaukos* signified originally that

[41] Schulz in *RE* s.v. Rätsel; Chadwick GL 3.152–3, 834–6, cf. 1.474; Jeanmaire 448; Thomson SAGS 1.499. Kalchas, the soothsayer, died of vexation when he failed to solve a riddle put to him by a rival; and, in Boiotia, at the Agriania, the women went in search of the lost Dionysos and spent the evening, after supper, in asking riddles: Str. 14.642–3; Plu. *M.* 717a; Thomson *ibid.*, cf. AA 143, 189–91. On riddles especially associated with initiations cf. Krige RRQ 138.

[42] Jeanmaire 449.   [43] Persson 12 and frontispiece, after Pfuhl no. 526.

[44] Cf. Persson 12.   [45] *Ibid.*

[46] *Ib.* 22.

which gleams but is not coloured, in the sense that water or the moon is colourless, 'white'.[47] Now when Hyginus is describing the changing colours of the calf and the mulberry, he uses the word *albus* of the first colour; and *albus* means 'white' or 'colourless' in the sense that it is opposite to *ater* ('black'). Glaukos then is like the calf and the mulberry before they change colour. He must, as it were, also change complexion—pass from his initial age-grade—before he can become black, ripe, 'one who knows many things'.

It is clear, moreover, that these three colours were not fortuitously chosen. They are the successive colours of Io, as a cow;[48] and of the sacred bulls of Augeias.[49] We have seen that when the Athenian boys became *epheboi* they wore a distinctive cloak, originally black or dun in colour, later white; black or dun was the traditional colour of mourning in all parts of Greece, except Argos, where it was white; Spartan and Cretan boys of the historical period also wore distinctive rough cloaks: hence the possibility that the Spartan, Cretan and Athenian cloaks all had a ritual origin, surviving as a vestige of the primitive belief in the death of the child at initiation.[50] At Sparta too it was the custom to place no offering in the tomb of the dead; but the body was wrapped in the red cloak of the Spartan soldier and laid on olive leaves. The Spartan soldier was one who had passed out of the *agela* of the youths and had been initiated into adult life. The colour of his cloak recalls the intermediate red of the calf and the mulberry in the myth of Glaukos; and, like the plant in the myth, the olive leaves on which the body was laid signified renewal of life.[51]

Since the three colours continued to have a ritual significance, we should look with a sharper eye at another detail of the story, which could otherwise be too readily dismissed as fortuitous. According to Apollodoros, the Kouretes told Minos that 'in his herds he had a cow of three different colours and that the man who could best describe that cow's colouring would also restore his son to him alive'. For the 'herds' of Minos, Apollodoros uses the word *agelai*, which is also the word regularly used of the bands into which the Spartan and Cretan youths were organized before

[47] Cf. L.S.J. s.v.
[48] Str. 10.1.3; St. Byz. s.v. Argura; Suid s.v. Isis.
[49] Apollod. 2.5.5 and 7.2; D.S. 4.13; Paus. 5.1.7; Tz. *ad* Lyc. 41; Hyg. *Fab.* 14.
[50] P. 48.
[51] Plu. *Lyc.* 27; cf. Frazer GB 1.1.101; Dieterich ME 49.

they were initiated into adult status.[52] The possibility that the Spartan and Cretan *agelai* had a Minoan origin cannot be ruled out.

The new phenomenon which is required to be explained in the story is the appearance of a cow with three different colours; and the Kouretes (or Apollo) require this to be explained in terms of something already known. As soon as the seer, the one 'who knows many things', compares the cow with the mulberry, the riddle is solved, the new is understood in terms of the old—and the old is the familiar sacred tree. This aspect of the myth can therefore be interpreted as representing the fusion of a cow-cult with the cult of the tree. This is a topic to which we must return,[53] noting, for the time being, that if such a cow-cult were a later addition this does not weaken the argument for the priority of the totemic, as compared with the vegetation, cycle.

The cults of the sacred tree and of the snake are so important in Minoan religion that they must be separately considered. But the snakes in the myth seem to be a totemic feature, symbolic of the power of resurrection.[54] The dead snake is restored through the magical agency of the living. It is also a ghost, a dead man's ancestor. In vase paintings a snake is not uncommonly shown on the grave mound, to indicate that a hero dwells in his tomb in snake form.[55] When the boy Glaukos died he became a snake-ghost. The resurrection of the dead snake is the means and symbol of his own restoration to life. If we regard Glaukos as a snake we can also understand why he should die in a honey-jar while pursuing a mouse. The snake represented in a relief discussed by Jane Harrison[56] was identified as one of a species practically harmless to man, but poisonous to its proper prey, which includes mice and rats. A traditional diet of snakes was honey, perhaps because of their taste for bee-grubs.[57] The ghost ancestors must have their food supply; and Glaukos too was embalmed in honey, because it was a source of immortality.

For honey is a very primitive intoxicant and plays an important part in ancient Greek, and also in Minoan, ritual.[58] This is why Polyidos saw bees being driven away from the entrance of a wine-cellar by an owl—a spirit in the form of a bird.[59] Apollo (in the version of Hyginus) makes the prophecy which leads to the

---

[52] Cf. Jeanmaire 449.   [53] Pp. 165-8, cf. 117.
[54] Cf. Thomson SAGS 1.114-20; Frazer *Apollod.* App. 7.
[55] Harrison PSGR 329.   [56] *Ib.* 328; cf. *ib.* 18.
[57] Evans PM 4.156-8.   [58] Harrison PSGR 443-4, Nilsson MMR 542.
[59] Cf. Harrison PSGR 332.

solution of the whole problem by Polyidos, perhaps because his specifically Cretan epithet connects him with mice—Smintheus.[60] Smintheus, it is true, was a prophet, but the origin of his cult may have been due to his interest in protecting the crops from field-mice. Glaukos would have laid Apollo-Smintheus under a special obligation by dying while pursuing a mouse.

The details may remain conjectural, but the myth of Glaukos clearly is built upon a simple and familiar pattern of ritual. The boy at puberty is lost, dies as a boy, is mourned and is restored to life. There are later accretions, but the basis remains totemic.

3. THE TREE AND THE STONE

The Achaeans, who thought of themselves as *dioi*, born of gods, would naturally scorn less flattering accounts of human origins. When Penelope, for example, is pressing the disguised Odysseus to give an account of his country and his birth and kin, she jokingly reminds him that he could not have sprung from legendary rock or tree.[61] The phrase had already become proverbial.[62] To Hesiod, however, writing in the epic tradition but less sophisticated than Homer because of his close links with the peasantry, the legendary tree is more real, and he records a race of men sprung from ash-trees.[63] This account represents a compromise. For, since Zeus, according to Hesiod, made the race from ash-trees, the conception of man spontaneously created out of trees was fused with the conception of man created by gods; and the men sprung from trees, moreover, were not the first, but the third, race of men on earth.[64]

At the conclusion of the basic work[65] in which he established the connexion between the cult of sacred tree and sacred stone, Evans described an arresting personal experience, as proof of its tenacious survival into recent times. In the course of archaeological investigations in upper Macedonia, he heard of a sacred stone at the Turkish village of Telekiöi, venerated by Moslem and Christian alike. He visited the shrine and, in order to understand the ritual, went through the appropriate ceremony. After explain-

---

[60] Str. 13.613; Swindler 29-33. Cf. n. 82 and pp. 269-70, where Apollo-Smintheus is more fully discussed.
[61] *Od*. 19.162-3.   [62] Cf. Pl. *Ap*. 34d, R. 544d, *AP* 10.55 (Pall.).
[63] *Op*. 143-5.   [64] Sinclair *ad loc*.
[65] MTPC; cf. further *id*. PM *passim*.

ing how the suppliant must pray for what he most wishes, and then embrace the stone so that the fingertips meet at its farther side, his description continues: 'The worshipper who would conform to the full ritual, now fills a keg of water from a spring that rises near the shrine—another primitive touch—and makes his way through a thorny grove up a neighbouring knoll, on which is a wooden enclosure surrounding a Mohammedan Saint's Grave or Tekke. Over the headstone of this grows a thorn-tree hung with rags of divers colours, attached to it—according to a widespread primitive rite—by sick persons who had made a pilgrimage to the tomb. The turbaned column itself represents in aniconic shape the visible presence of the departed Saint, and, conjointly with the thorn-bush, a material abode for the departed Spirit, so that we have here a curious illustration of the ancient connexion between Tree and Pillar Worship.'[66]

Despite the criticisms levelled against the view of Evans that constructional Minoan pillars were aniconic images of deity,[67] his more general explanation of the associated cult of stone and tree can be accepted as a characteristic feature common to many other primitive religions. Light is thereby thrown upon the survival of tree and stone in the worship of the anthropomorphic divinities of Classical times, of which the laurel and omphalos of Apollo are the most obvious examples.[68]

Not the least valuable feature of Evans's study was his insistence upon the evidence for transition from aniconic cult to anthropomorphic worship. 'The co-existence of this more realistic imagery side by side with the material objects of primitive cult certainly betrays elements of transition. We discern already foreshadowings of the time, not far distant, when the mental conception of individual divinities would leave its impress on the rude stock or stone or more artistically shaped pillar which from time to time was supposed to become possessed with its spiritual essence.'[69] The dual cult was, in the opinion of Evans, so widespread that it might be said to mark a definite early stage of religious evolution, and he preferred to treat the cult of trees and pillars, or rude stones, as an identical form of worship.[70] This wise preference indicates that the evidence was such that the author regarded the question of the initial priority of stone or tree

[66] *Ib.* 105. [67] See Nilsson MMR Ch. VII.
[68] Evans MTPC 22; Harrison T 165–6, 340, 396–424; Harris OCH.
[69] *Ib.* 26; cf. Persson RGPT 167. [70] *Ib.* 7.

as being irrelevant. They were an inseparable and constant combination.[71]

Nevertheless, the sanctity of stone and pillar could be considered as due to a variety of causes. It might be connected with some particular manifestation supposed to be of a spiritual nature —to the interpretation of a sign, or of a dream, as in the case of Jacob's pillar. Artificial pillars might owe their indwelling spiritual being to the holiness of the spot where they were set up, to religious symbols like the double-axe carved on their surface, or to some special rite of consecration. Wooden columns often took over their sanctity from the sacred tree out of which they were hewn. Natural blocks derived their baetylic qualities from the fact that they were of meteoric origin; while the stage in aniconic worship in which the pillar was of a purely artificial kind and the stone was, as it were, offered to a spiritual being as a place of habitation, marked an advance on the primitive idea of a holy stone as one that had in some way manifested itself as being in spiritual possession; and, further, the two conceptions of the pillar-image of divinity and of the tombstone as the dwelling place of a departed spirit met in the idea of a mortal god, a conception most familiar in the traditions of the Cretan Zeus.[72] To these observations others of a more speculative and abstract kind have since been added.[73]

In searching for the origin of the cult of tree and stone, however, insufficient attention has perhaps been paid to the fact that, before the onset of the more complex Bronze Age society, man's principal tools had been made of stone. Before the age of settled cultivation he had also gathered fruits from the tree; with settled cultivation, timber had to be felled, and the sanctity which con-

---

[71] 'In India, where worship of this primitive character is perhaps best illustrated at the present day, the collocation of tree and stone is equally frequent.' Evans, *ib.* 8.

[72] *Ib.* 20–3.

[73] '(Primitive man) came to observe that water and light are essential for vegetation; yet they remained manifestations too difficult to apprehend as objects of worship. But the sun is the giver of light, and the spring or well the giver of water . . . the spring needs a symbol or figure to represent it. An approach is made to this through associated objects, which draw attention to it from a great distance or impress it on the mind, for example the cliff from which the spring gushes forth, or the tree which grows near it. Thus, just as the wheel becomes a symbol for the sun, the tree or the stone become symbols for the well or spring: they represent the indwelling power of the flowing water or of the vegetation nurtured by it. The tree and the stone become, so to speak, the basic elements in the sacred place.' Persson RGPT 166.

tinues to be attached to the Minoan double-axe derives, it has been suggested, from its use for hewing timber; and hewing timber (like garden tillage) is in primitive society women's work.[74] We have seen that specialist orchardist cultivation is early attested in Crete.[75] If we suppose that sacred tree and sacred stone derived their sacral combination from the labour process of neolithic economy, it is possible to conceive the more readily of their continued association through the Bronze Age, when the vegetation cycle had become paramount and when that cycle was in turn beginning to be superseded by anthropomorphic conceptions. The lasting importance of orchardist cultivation would also help to explain why the sacred tree especially is of such widespread importance in Minoan religion. The work of Mannhardt and Frazer, in the opinion of Nilsson, established the tree-cult as one of the best-known features of primitive religion and modern folklore; while the discovery of its specific prominence in Minoan religion was the result of the pioneer work of Evans.[76]

Lest the derivation suggested above of the sacral combination of tree and stone from the labour process be considered too crudely simple, it is necessary to recall the evidence that has been offered for the association between the later vegetation cycle and the earlier totemic cycle on which it may ultimately have depended. One of the primary characteristics of this cycle, as we saw, is the close association between man and nature established in the very early phases of human society. Even when human society and the life processes of nature, of animals and crops, had become more distinct in the mind of man, no exact separation between secular and religious conceptions as yet occurred. Economy and cult continued to be infested with magic.

The point may be illustrated from another part of the world, where, after four centuries of Christian influence, corn is still regarded as sacred, as a living being. Explaining why this conception is fundamental to the Maya way of thinking, J. E. S. Thompson repeats the following Maya legend:[77]

'Maize was once stored beneath a great mountain of rock. It was first discovered there by the marching-army ants, which made a tunnel to its hiding-place beneath the rock and began carrying the

[74] Mason 133. The Minoan double-axe is never in the hands of a male god, but, on rings and seals, is carried by ministers of the cult or by women. Pendlebury AC 274; Nilsson MMR 226.

[75] P. 6.   [76] MMR 262.

[77] RFMC 240.

grains away on their backs. The fox, who is always curious about his neighbours' doings, saw the ants carrying this strange grain and tried some. Soon the other animals and then man learned of this new food, but only the ants could penetrate to the place where it was hidden.

'Men asked the rain gods to help them get at the store. In turn, three of the rain gods tried, but failed, to blast the rock apart with their thunderbolts. Then the chief rain god, the oldest of them all, after many refusals, was prevailed upon to try his skill. He sent the woodpecker to tap the surface of the rock to find the weakest spot. When it had been discovered, he told the woodpecker to take cover under an overhanging ledge while he tried to split the rock. With all his strength he hurled his mightiest thunderbolt against the weak point, and the rock was riven asunder. Just as the thunderbolt struck, the woodpecker, disobeying orders, stuck out his head. A flying fragment of rock hit him on the poll, causing it to bleed freely, and ever since the woodpecker has had a red head. The fiery heat was so intense that part of the maize, which had been entirely white, was charred. Some ears were slightly burned, many were discoloured with smoke, but some escaped all damage. There resulted four kinds of maize—black, red, yellow, and white.'

Long ago, as he observed the customs of the native people conquered and ruled by the Incas, Pedro de Cieza de León recorded that: 'All held the sun to be the chief god; all believed that there is a Maker of all created things who, in the language of Cuzco, they call Tici-Viracocha. But in spite of this belief, in olden times they worshipped trees and stones and the moon and other things imposed upon them by the devil, our enemy, with whom those designated for that purpose spoke, and they obeyed him in many things. . . .'[78]

4. ANIMALS AND BIRDS

The coinage of the Classical and Hellenistic periods provides a ready demonstration of the lasting importance of animals and birds in the Cretan mythological tradition. In Minoan times the bull, dove and snake had already achieved a special prominence in religious associations. Other creatures had not been entirely superseded, especially outside the framework of official cult. But even

[78] Von Hagen 67.

within that framework there was preserved a link with savage custom which deserves initial comment.

In his interpretation of the pictures of the Haghia Triada Sarcophagus, Paribeni was the first to recognize the true nature of a garment worn by the chief officiants at the sacrifice, both female and male.[79] Beginning at the waist, and fastened with a girdle, it falls without folds, its lower outline being rounded and almost semicircular and having at the back what appears to be a short tail. Nilsson accepts as beyond doubt Paribeni's conclusion that this garment is an animal's hide, and comments: 'The animal's hide was man's first garment, and no doubt was once worn by the first inhabitants of Crete as well as by other savage peoples, and was preserved in the cult because of religious conservatism.'[80] It seems proper to observe that, if the neolithic inhabitants of Crete were anxious to retain the costume of palaeolithic hunters in their cults, the possibility that their religious conservatism extended also to the content of their rites ought not to be excluded. Since totemism is as common a phenomenon among hunters as the wearing of animal hides, there seems to be no reason why the religious conservatives of early Crete should radically have repudiated all association with it.

The large numbers of votive terracottas found in the Middle Minoan sanctuary on the peak of Petsofa near Palaikastro in eastern Crete included figurines of oxen, goats, rams, swine, dogs, tortoises, hedgehogs, vermin such as stoats and weasels, and also birds, apparently doves.[81] The models of human heads, arms, legs, and of the whole body cloven from crown to fork, were presumably prophylactic offerings. Their association with models of vermin has led to a comparison with the golden emerods and mice which were made as 'trespass offerings' by the Philistines.[82] Finds

---

[79] MA 19.1.

[80] MMR 157. See further Persson *ib.* 42–3.

[81] Myres in ABSA 9.356; Evans PM 1.151; Nilsson MMR 68.

[82] Whether this interest should also be extended to the protection of human beings from plague carried by mice and rats (cf. Swindler, *ib.* 33 and n. 28) is a question of some importance. Since the Philistines were, partly at least, of Cretan origin, the description of their prophylactic offerings of golden emerods and mice is of particular interest in this connexion: 'Then said they, What shall be the trespass-offering which we shall return to him? They answered, Five golden emerods, and five golden mice, according to the number of the lords of the Philistines: for one plague was on you all, and on your lords. Wherefore ye shall make images of your emerods, and images of your mice that mar the land; and ye shall give glory unto the God of Israel: peradventure he will lighten his hand from off you, and from off

of the same kind have been made at other such similar sanctuaries at Mount Juktas and the cave of Psychro.[83]

There is little doubt that the birds so frequently depicted in religious contexts of the Minoan Age, perched on double-axes, columns, trees, idols and so on, represent divine manifestations.[84] Bird figures also occur from the Neolithic Age, together with animal and human figures, and it is natural to conclude that they had religious significance.[85] Terracotta birds are often found in domestic shrines, at Gournia, Haghia Triada, Palaikastro and elsewhere; but, as compared with animal figures, they are rarely found in the votive deposits of caves and open-air sanctuaries. Hence it appears that the birds of the domestic shrines are not votive offerings, but actual representations of deity. The idea that birds were manifest forms of the spirits of the dead continued to be persistent in later Greek religion.[86] We can assume that birds derived their religious sanctity from totemic associations.[87]

By far the most prominent Minoan domestic cult, however, is that of the snake, especially in association with the so-called snake-goddess. Such snake-cults are of world-wide provenance,

---

your gods, and from off your land.' I. Sam. 6.4, 5: cf. Myres in ABSA 9.382, n. 2; Evans *ib.* 1.153.

Some commentators have argued that we are presented here with an account of bubonic plague. But J. F. D. Shrewsbury (*The Plague of the Philistines* in *Journal of Hygiene* 47.244–52) finds this conclusion to be unsupported by the epidemiology of plague. He argues that the concurrent plague of field-mice must be eliminated from the pestilence that devastated the Philistines. But if there were two plagues, it is clear from the context that they were of equal importance. And if the field-mouse (*Arvicola arvalis*), which attacks seed, growing corn and stored grain, was most probably the animal concerned, it is equally clear that this species could exist in sufficient numbers to constitute a formidable menace to food supply. Thus, in an agricultural community, a deity who protected the crops from the devastation of such pests could have played an important role, aside from any conjectural association with plague.

[83] Evans PM 1.153, cf. Cook Z 2.939; Evans JHS 17.350; Orsi and Halbherr *Mus. It.* 2.905; ABSA 6.94; Nilsson MMR Ch. I *passim*, HGR 12.

[84] Cf. Nilsson HGR 18, MMR Ch. X.

[85] As suggested by Evans PM 1.44; but denied by Nilsson MMR 336.

[86] Cf. Harrison PSGR 200–1, 305, 332, T 110–17; Nilsson MMR 340.

[87] Cf. Nilsson MMR 340: 'Except for the idea that certain birds belong to certain gods, there is no reason why various birds should not also be the epiphanies of the gods. So much can confidently be stated; to go further involves us in uncertain and very questionable hypotheses, which cannot be warranted by the testimony of the monuments, our only source of indisputable knowledge.' But the testimony of monuments is rarely elicited without interpretation, comparison, hypothesis— especially where they exist without written records.

dependent on the belief that snakes are incarnations of the dead.[88] But the snake also signifies immortality. Because it casts its slough and renews itself it becomes a symbol of the ability to be born again.[89] Hence it is not only an object of reverence and dread, but also a beneficent spirit, a guardian of the house.[90] Snake-worship is a constant phenomenon in later Greek religion and plays a part in modern Greek folklore.[91] We have seen how the snake in the myth of Glaukos readily operates as a symbol of resurrection. This symbolic role of the snake in mythology, folklore and cult was already being consolidated, it would appear, in the Minoan Age. The totemic cycle of birth and death no longer operated in its primitive form. It had been modified by the vegetation cycle, as the hunters became settled cultivators. With the increasing complexity of social organization, the link between man and nature, birth and death, was realized in a more subtle, abstract fashion. The Minoan snake-cult is so prominent partly because the snake served to symbolize these past associations, partly because its abstract force was also now serving as the basis for the development of a further refinement of conception in the form of anthropomorphic deity—first in association with a goddess, later in association with the male deities who succeeded her.[92] Among these latter Asklepios played a part of especial importance in the Cretan cults of the historical period.[93]

5. THE MINOAN GODDESS

As we have seen, Evans concluded that it was impossible to dissociate the neolithic female figurines from those that occur later in the shrines and sanctuaries of what he termed the 'Great Minoan Goddess'. This goddess became dominant by Middle Minoan times, as the result of what must have been a long process of development. We are no more in a position to grasp the details of this process than we are able to recover the successive stages

[88] Briffault 2.641–51, 660–73; cf. Picard 113; Nilsson MMR 328; Harrison PSGR 232–7, 327–32, T *passim*.

[89] Cf., for Melanesia, Briffault 2.643; for Egypt, Budge GE 2.377, cf. Rundle Clark s.v. Serpent; for Phoenicians, Eus. *PE* 1.10.

[90] Nilsson HGR 13, MMR 325; Harrison T 267. Cf. Junod LSAT 2.384; Hollis MLF 307–8; Krige SSZ 53, 62, 65, 174, 285.

[91] Nilsson HGR 13, 103–4, MMR 325; Harrison PSGR 332; Plu. *Cleom.* 39; *Sol.* 9, *Thes.* 10; Paus. 1.36.1; Apollod. 3.12.7; D.S.4. 72; Hes. *fr.* 107; Str. 10.393; Polites P 2.58; Demetrakos s.v. δράκος.

[92] Cf. Nilsson MMR 329.

[93] Cf. Ch. 8.

whereby the original settlers transformed their neolithic conditions and developed the flourishing Bronze Age society which we
associate with the Middle Minoan period. However, as we saw,
just as Cretan metallurgy was based upon Asiatic traditions, so the
Cretan cities, the centres of the social system, resembled the Syrian
in their economic and political organization. Indications of flexible
social relations imply tolerance of earlier forms of social organization, especially among farmers and orchardists. Geographical
conditions in Crete, with its areas of mountain, forest and plain,
did not favour an even economic development. Even on the
plains special factors presumably operated in favour of the
continuing importance of the role of women. Of special significance in this connexion was the 'household' character of the
palaces. There was an increasing tendency for production and
commerce to be organized centrally. Yet development was
necessarily one-sided and the traditional way of life of the
agrarian producers was relatively undisturbed.

The appearance of the goddess has prompted as much attention,
and even more speculation, than the rise of the palaces. Both are
equally remarkable and the dominance of the one in the religious,
of the other in the social sphere, are complementary. The
palace is the central feature of Minoan civilization. That an
anthropomorphic female divinity is the central feature of Minoan
religion is a fact whose general recognition has been obscured by
the attempt to answer a question to which different answers have
been given and which is, from the nature of the case, unanswerable
—namely, was Minoan religion monotheistic?[94]

The goddess is represented in a rich variety of associations: with
animals, birds and snakes; with the baetylic pillar and the sacred
tree; with the poppy and the lily; with the sword and the double-
axe. She is a huntress and a goddess of sports; she is armed and she
presides over ritual dances; she has female and male attendants.
She has dominion over mountain, earth, sky and sea; over life and
death; she is household-goddess, vegetation-goddess, Mother and
Maid.

She is, like the figurines shaped by human hands out of which
she grew, an eclectic figure. But her dominance in all spheres also

[94] On the goddess and her attributes, and initial discussion of the problem see
Evans PM Index s.v. Minoan Goddess 59–61; full discussion in Nilsson MMR Ch.
XII and later authorities there cited; Persson RGPT *passim*. On the similarity with
Cyprian prehistoric cult; Dikaios, S 13.345–54; Dussaud *ib*. 27.57–81.

demonstrates that she operated, in all her particular associations, as an abstract and unifying principle. She is both one and many. This inherent contradiction of her character, reinforced by analogy and by study of the nature of later Greek religion, has given rise to contradictory interpretations. Despite a variety of modifications, these interpretations follow two main lines. Either the goddess is always virtually the same goddess under a variety of aspects, which is open to the objection that peoples at a similar stage of development to the Minoans often have a plurality of gods and goddesses. Or we must suppose that the various manifestations of the goddess indicate a whole number of separate female divinities with different names, which is open to the simple objection that we do not know these names; and, further, that we divide one goddess into several goddesses by concentrating attention upon the variety of her associations at the expense of that essential unity which she appears intended clearly to represent. In fact, this strong impression of unity would not be radically affected even if the goddess had been, quite early, called by different names.[95] We should feel, as in analogous cases in later Greek religion, that, when two deities are fulfilling the same function, function is more important than name. It therefore seems desirable, in the present state of our knowledge, to accept the goddess as a contradictory figure, both as one and many, and to concentrate attention on the functional aspect.

In this connexion, the fashion of her dress is of interest as an indication of her close association with social life and its changing aspects. Aside from her never wholly discarded habit (inherited from the neolithic period) of appearing naked, the goddess, from the beginning of the Middle Minoan period, whether plastically or pictorially represented, wears the latest style of dress. The figurines of ivory and faience from palace shrines carefully preserve the details of the fashionable clothes of the Court ladies of the latest Middle and early Late Minoan periods. This is the case not only when she is worshipped in formal surroundings, but when she hunts, descends from on high, or emerges from the earth.[96] We can conclude that in her most sophisticated form the goddess belongs to the palaces. But, just as the social and economic role of the palaces, though highly important, was partial in the

[95] On their possible origin as invocatory epithets see Persson *ib.* 124–7, 135–6, 141; cf. Nilsson *ib.* 395.
[96] Evans PM 4.27; cf. *ib.* 401–2.

sense that other spheres of human activity were relatively unchanged by their presence, so the goddess retained those earlier, and sometimes quite primitive, associations which, we must suppose, had more meaning to many (perhaps most) of her worshippers than her latest styles of dress. In short, the goddess may be regarded as the symbolic reflection of the one-sided development of the society which paid her such respect. In the urban palaces were concentrated the principal characteristics of Minoan Crete and the controlling influences which developed them in distinction from the past forms of social life which, nevertheless, still flourished outside the centres and, in remoter areas, at quite primitive levels. In the goddess likewise is first concentrated the unique religious characteristic of the age, an anthropomorphic conception of divinity which is, however, realized through association with still-vigorous cult survivals from the past. The society centred on the palaces objectifies nature only partially. Its goddess still mirrors the close association of man, plant and animal. As an abstract force she still has many concrete supports.

Why should this anthropomorphic realization have taken female shape? Foreign influences can be set aside as a basic explanation. The goddess, as we shall see, has many Eastern connexions, apart from her more local origins. But, if she had been wholly foreign, we should still have to explain why her worshippers were ready to receive her. To explain her merely as the representation of a supreme female principle is to make her more abstract than she ever pretended to be. The reality behind this 'principle' was connected with the high position of women in Minoan society, which is apparent from the portrayal of women in the frescoes and to which Evans drew attention in arriving at a similar conclusion[97]— a conclusion confirmed by so many of the attributes and associations of the goddess.

We have seen reason for supposing that the collective forms of social organization survived from the neolithic period into the Bronze Age of Crete. Though the part played by tribe, clan and household has to be largely conjectured from analogy and inference, there are certain factors, including the evidence of late survivals into the historical period, which strengthen the possibility that these social units continued to be matrilineal. Within such a matrilineal social framework, the women would have played a predominant part in the maintenance of the clan- and

[97] *Ib.* 3.58–9; cf. 227.

household-cults. Households with special prestige arising from seniority or other causes would have been likely to acquire special responsibilities regarding the cult of the clan ancestress. Since the palaces were also households, as well as being the centres of social development in general, changes in cult practice must have been there most intensified. It is in the palaces that we can most readily imagine the development of the neolithic figurine into a goddess attended by the priestesses who conceived of her as the reflection of their own increasing social stature. This line of evolution would account for the presence beside the goddess of the magical fetishes and totemistic symbols through which the ancestral spirits of the clan had first been envisaged, now perpetuated by association with the vegetation cycle.

Of the primitive roots of these fetishes and symbols, in the form of tree and stone, animal and bird, something has been already said. A few further matters of importance remain to be considered here. It is clear, from certain of the monuments, from the nomenclature of later deities, and from mythology, that the goddess was a moon-goddess as well as (or rather by virtue of being) a fertility-goddess. The worship of the moon in its various phases is closely associated with the time-keeping which is indispensable to any moderately advanced agricultural community. This aspect of the subject must be discussed when the problem of the calendar is considered.[98] But moon-worship must also have contributed to the cult of the goddess from the point of view of human fertility and from the special associations of the moon with the physiological functions of women.[99] Sacrificial animals offered by women to the moon universally belong to small species, chiefly the hare, goat and pig; the dove, especially in Semitic women's cults; and the cat.[100] The close relationship of the Cretan goddess with the goat and the dove needs no emphasis, and the pig and the cat are represented in a variety of contexts.[101] The general choice of these small species was probably associated with the domestication of animals, the huntsmen bringing home the young which the women kept as pets.[102] The snake, as a fertility symbol accompanying the goddess as protectress of the household, is likely to have

[98] Pp. 92–103.
[99] Cf. Briffault 2.432, 583–4; Nilsson PTR 149; Roscher LGRM 2.2687, 4.1470; Robertson Smith RS 133; Plu. M 376e; Arist. HA 7.2 (582b), GA 2.4.9; Sor. Gyn. 21 (Rose 185), cf. Gal. 9.903.
[100] Briffault 2.610–23.   [101] Evans PM Index s.v.v.
[102] Thurnwald 77; Frazer TE 1.14–15; Briffault 2.619.

been under the special provenance of women in a similar way, except that it was not sacrificed.[103]

The moon is commonly regarded, in primitive societies, as the stimulus of fertility in plants and vegetation. The tending of plants was included among the early social tasks of women, and herbal magic is everywhere their province, since plants, flowers and seeds were commonly used by women at menstruation, childbirth and pregnancy. The lily was, above all, the Minoan sacred flower.[104] Ritual dances take place before the goddess in a field of lilies; a lily appears at her feet when she is enthroned; she is offered a bunch of lilies by her female attendants. Sometimes she is offered poppy capsules.[105] As late as the time of Pliny, the lily was considered to be a check to menstruation; and the poppy for long continued to be regarded as a symbol of fecundity.[106]

6. THE MINOAN GOD

The late appearance and subordinate status of a male deity underline the overwhelming importance of the goddess. There was no conception of a male anthropomorphic divinity in the neolithic period. Although his appearances are by no means frequent in the Middle and Late Minoan periods, two conclusions emerge from the evidence. The god is a secondary deity; but by the end of the Minoan Age the tendency to raise him to a superior status is clear. The social implications are important. Just as the dominance of the goddess reflects the social importance of women, based on the survival of communal relations and of matrilineal rights of inheritance and descent, the rise of the god similarly reflects the pressure exerted on this system by the changing social status of men.[107]

---

[103] Many birth stories current in antiquity are associated with the snake. Philip deserted Olympias, mother of Alexander, when a snake was seen stretched beside her, either from fear of her enchantments or because he dared not violate the sanctity of one wedded to a greater than himself. We are told that the women of Macedonia had from early times been addicted to Orphic and Dionysiac orgies; and that Olympias made the rites still more barbarous and abandoned by carrying in the dances huge tame snakes which kept creeping out of the ivy in the mystic cradles and coiling round the women's wands and crowns, striking terror into the men: Plu. *Alex.* 2, cf. Suet. *Oct.* 94. Similarly, Nikoteleia, mother of Aristomenes the Messenian, was said to have been visited by a *daimon* or a god in the likeness of a serpent: Paus. 4.14.7; Frazer *ad loc.* Cf. Harrison T 270.

[104] Evans PM 2.776-7.   [105] *Ib.* 3.458; Persson RGPT 74-5.

[106] Plin. *NH.* 23.159-60, 24.50, 21.126; Eus. *PE* 3.11.6. Cf. Call. *Cer.* 45, Theoc. 7.155-7.

[107] Cf. Persson RGPT 123.

But the counterbalancing factors earlier noticed[108] as continuing to operate in the economic and social field in favour of matrilineal rights have their correspondence in the religious sphere. The emergence of the god to any sort of eminence is so slow that there is only one certain example of his full-size portrayal, in the form of a nude figure standing between horns of consecration on the gem found near Kydonia.[109]

This youthful god pushed his way to the fore in a variety of forms and under a variety of names after the Minoan Age, and he will have to be considered in further detail from this point of view.[110] It will be sufficient, at this stage, to summarize a few matters of general importance concerning his Minoan role.

The researches of Frazer demonstrated the connexion between the youthful god and agrarian magic. This god must die so that the crops may live. Crops have to be sown, brought to their seasonal maturity in the fields by the operation of nature, and then harvested. The operation begins again with the seed, gathered and preserved after the harvest, then returned to the earth at the proper time. The element of continuity in this vegetation cycle is represented by the goddess, who also maintains the continuity of human life. The element of discontinuity, of growth, decay and renewal, is a god. He is male because he personifies the seed and, because he shares in its mortality, he is a dying god. And he dies as the son or the lover of the goddess. Hence Evans, in commenting upon the mortal character of the Cretan god, wrote: 'That his death and return to life were of annual celebration in relation to the seasonal re-birth of Nature is an almost irresistible conclusion.'[111] The Cretan goddess and the youthful Cretan god are involved in the same essential pattern of Oriental ritual which gave rise to the myths of Ishtar and Tammuz, Isis and Osiris, Venus and Adonis.[112]

The youthful god is often armed, with bow, spear or shield. Since these weapons would be used in hunting as in war, it is, no doubt, incorrect to suppose that the god was armed because he was a warrior-god. The peaceful disposition of the Minoans has been considered to be an argument against such a possibility.[113] A further argument is that the conception of the young armed

[108] Pp. 7–8.
[109] Evans PM 1.708, cf. 3.465; Nilsson MMR 354, cf. 358.
[110] See Ch. 7.   [111] PM 3.467.
[112] Evans PM 3.468; Persson RGPT Ch. 4. But cf. Nilsson MMR 404 and 412.
[113] Nilsson MMR 411.

hunter must have been familiar in social life from early times. The ritual associations of such a conception, deriving from the totemic cycle, would precede (as they would also foster) the appearance of a youthful armed god in a vegetation cycle dominated by a goddess. An interesting demonstration of this line of evolution is supplied by the chryselephantine image of a boy-god of adolescent age.[114] Its shorn head indicates ritual cutting of the hair at puberty, a widespread custom which features in ancient Greece. Although the custom is not recorded in historical times in Crete, this may be due to accident. The likelihood is that the Cretan boy reached formal puberty at the age of twelve and, like his Spartan counterpart, cut his hair. Since the practice of initiation of Cretan boys survived so persistently in historical times, and since the neolithic Cretans must have been exceptional if they did not bring a similar practice into the island with them, a ritual dedication of the hair could have been associated with initiation at puberty in the Minoan Age.[115]

The initial purpose of such a practice was to initiate the youth into the techniques of adult hunters. But this purpose was bound to be changed as social life changed. In the historical period, as we have seen, initiation was closely bound up with the life of the city-state.

Similarly, in the Minoan period, we can conjecture that the young were initiated into appropriate social responsibilities. With the onset of militarization in the later Bronze Age,[116] we can imagine that the Minoan youth adapted their arms from hunting to warfare. We cannot therefore dismiss the possibility of a similar change in the religious conception of the armed god, in his aspect of guardian of the youth, as distinct from his role of guardian of the crops. Such a change would help to account for the fact that, later in his career, the Minoan god begins to discard the ordinary male loincloth. Instead he now favours the cylindrical helmet, the fighting pose and the Syro-Egyptian kilt of the Syrian lightning-god, Resheph.[117]

[114] Evans PM 4.468, considered this to be undoubtedly genuine. Cf., however, Nilsson MMR 314 n. 20. Whether the figure is that of a god or of a human boy hardly affects my argument here.

[115] Cf. my argument in ASAC 11; also Evans PM 4.477: 'At Delphi, where the early cult was so closely connected with that of Minoan Knossos, it was customary for boys about to enter on the estate of manhood to have the forepart of their hair cut off at the spot where Theseus was said to have practised the same rite.'

[116] Cf. pp. 26–37.

[117] Evans PM 4.401; and (with Syrian and Hittite comparisons) 3.477–80.

7. THE 'PRIEST-KING'

Evans applied the term 'Minoan' to the early Cretan civilization, with the general approval of his contemporaries.[118] For Greek memories of this preceding civilization were concentrated in the differing traditions of Minos. 'On the one side we gain a vision of a beneficent ruler, patron of the arts, founder of palaces, stablisher of civilized dominion. On the other is depicted a tyrant and destroyer.' Evans blamed Athenian chauvinism for exaggerating the tyrannical aspect of the early sea-dominion. Archaeology had demonstrated that the palace envisaged as an ogre's den had been in reality the peaceful abode of 'priest-kings', even though Minos 'the destroyer' may have existed from the standpoint of subject peoples. The application of the term by the Greeks to traditional settlements from prehistoric Crete showed that they were accustomed to conceive of the word 'Minoan' in an ethnic or dynastic as well as a personal sense. This dynastic use of the term could be compared with the Egyptian use of Pharaoh. As the bearer of a divine title, the Cretan Minos could be compared with the divine 'priest-kings' of the religious centres of Anatolia, who represented a god, wore his dress, wielded his authority and often bore his name. The almost universal divine nature of primitive kingship[119] was well exemplified in the case of Egypt. But in Egypt the temple overshadowed the palace; whereas, in the Anatolian centres, royal and sacerdotal dwellings were combined. The conditions of Minoan Crete were more like those of Anatolia than of Egypt. For the Knossian palace was permeated with religious elements. The sign of the sacred double-axe or *labrys* appears constantly on its stone blocks, on stucco and painted pottery, on seals, on the altar of a shrine. Wall-paintings have direct or indirect religious associations. Large parts of the palace consisted of small shrines for ritual use. The so-called 'Room of the Throne' was clearly designed for religious functions. The arrangement of the throne, of the surrounding stone benches, and of the tank opposite the throne, suggested close comparison with the 'Hall of Initiation' in the sanctuary of Mên Askaënos and a Mother-goddess, near the Pisidian Antioch,[120] leading to the presumption that the much

---

[118] PM I.1–7.

[119] Evans cited Frazer LEHK 128 ff. Cf., on the relation between king and vegetation deity, Hooke L 226; Engnell 25–38; Widengren 42–58.

[120] JHS (1912) 111 ff.; ABSA 18.37 ff.

earlier 'Room of the Throne' at Knossos was intended for similar rites of initiation and purification, presided over by a Minoan 'priest-king', adopted son on earth of a Cretan Great Mother.

A whole number of place-names and personal names appear to derive from a very early linguistic substratum, common to Crete and to those regions in Asia where 'priest-kings' were a normal institution.[121] They include the words Knossos, Minos and the word for 'king' or 'prince', *basileus*.[122]

Nilsson has agreed[123] that, in the light of our knowledge of the Minoan religion, Evans correctly described the king of Knossos as a 'priest-king'. For the palace was a sacred house in which cults were practised. Moreover, at Mycenae itself and in two other important Mycenaean towns, Athens and perhaps Tiryns, the temple of the divine protectress of the Greek city-state, Athene or Hera, is built upon the ruins of the palace of the Mycenaean king. Even after the abolition of the kingship in Greece, republican sacral officials continued to hold the title of *basileus*.[124] At Athens the Council used to meet in the King's Porch under the presidency of the *archon basileus* (the 'king archon'), who was responsible for the care of the Eleusinian Mysteries, for law-suits concerning sacrilege and impiety, priesthoods and murder.[125] The inference is that this important republican magistrate took over the sacral functions of the old king. The name of 'king', attaching to the highest sacral officials, was especially common in Ionian towns; and the Ionians, of all the Greek peoples, came first and most permanently into contact with Minoan culture.[126]

Although the Cretan 'priest-kings' shared some of the typical characteristics of Oriental despotism, they differed markedly in other respects. These similarities and differences emphasize those specific features of Minoan economic and social development sketched in the previous chapter.

The direct evidence of the institution from the monuments is, admittedly, slight. Evans himself exhausted the possibilities of

---

[121] Fick VOQVG 26–7; Kretschmer EGGS 401; Haley in AJA 32.141; Nilsson HM 64–5.

[122] Meillet AHLG 40; Wackernagel 212; Nilsson *ibid.*

[123] MMR 486. Cf. A. Furumark in SK 370: 'There is . . . much evidence in favour of the view that in Minoan Crete there existed a sacral kingship of much the same nature as those of Oriental cultures.'

[124] Arist. *Pol.* 1322 b 20.   [125] Arist. *Ath.* 57.

[126] Nilsson *ib.* 485 and n. 1. The Ionians may have been Mycenaeans: Chadwick GDGP; cf. Thomson SAGS 1.392; 518–26.

inference from the materials available to him, both of a direct and indirect nature, in establishing his conception of a 'priest-king' analogous to Oriental prototypes. That conception has already been summarized and some detailed points of hypothetical interpretation can now be added before we consider the two representations on which all speculation must eventually depend.

The series of LM II signet impressions from the Central Palace Shrine shows the Minoan Mother-goddess, Lady of the Double-Axe, standing on a rocky peak between guardian lions, receiving the adoration of a votary who was perhaps a 'priest-king'.[127] The scene on the Sarcophagus of Haghia Triada could indicate that the cult of deceased and heroized members of the line of Minoan 'priest-kings' was associated with that of their divine mistress in the Palace Sanctuary of Knossos.[128] There is some evidence to suggest that a divinity or the 'priest-king' himself was carried in a palanquin.[129] At Mallia a platform where ritual functions might have been performed before the assembled people in the Court below was approached by a flight of four steps. In an alcove near by were found three bronze weapons: a dagger, sword and single-bladed axe. Oriental comparisons suggested that they formed the personal insignia of a 'priest-king', the ceremonial attributes of spiritual and temporal power.[130] Similar attributes were elsewhere associated with the goddess, and it is possible therefore that they were transferred on occasion to her vicegerent, the 'priest-king'.[131] The long-robed votaries of the Camp-Stool Frescoes, on the borders of the 'Sanctuary Hall' at Knossos, argued Evans, stood in a close relation to the hierarchical system in vogue at the palace in the last epoch of its history. The Hall itself, he suggested, might have had a special connexion with a Sacral College, consisting of young persons, male and female, belonging to the inner circle of the Court of the Priest-kings, including perhaps actual 'Children of Minos'.[132] In other supposed representations, sometimes the religious, sometimes the military and secular, aspect of the 'priest-kings' is brought to the fore. In one such case the 'priest-king' has beside him the dolphin badge of sea-power.[133]

The two representations which can be more definitely accepted as those of a ruler or 'priest-king' are the 'Chieftain Vase' from the

[127] PM 1.159.
[129] Ib. 1.224.
[130] Ib. 1.270–7. Found with a jar of LM I a provenance.
[132] Ib. 4.397–9.
[128] Ib. 1.447.
[131] Ib. 2.792–5.
[133] Ib. 4.412–13.

earlier prehistoric palace at Haghia Triada,[134] and the fresco described by Evans as 'The Priest-King Relief'.[135]

The scene represented on the Vase was originally explained by Paribeni as a young military commander giving orders to a subordinate officer who is himself attended by three soldiers. This conception of a military ceremonial has been generally agreed, with differences of opinion as to details. The officer, standing to attention and with his head slightly bowed, wears a neck ring and a single bracelet. His hair, though closely cropped, has a top-knot. He carries a long sword sloped over his right shoulder, and in the left hand, stretching from his waist above his left shoulder and head, is another object with a stiff handle and flexible tail. This was recognized by Evans to be a lustral sprinkler of the kind used by the Roman *pontifices*, such as that too which survived into the service of the Christian Church. The sword and the lustral sprinkler he considered to be portrayed, this time in the hands of the goddess, in a gem from the palace at Knossos. He therefore concluded that they were emblems of spiritual and temporal power, which were, on some ceremonial occasions, carried by the 'priest-king', as earthly representative of the goddess, or held out before him by another personage as in the case of the scene on the Vase.

The objects carried by the three men attending the subordinate officer have always been considered to be hides, perhaps simplified versions of the Minoan figure-of-eight shield.[136] (This consisted of an entire ox-hide cut to a circular, or oval, shape and stretched over two staves placed at right angles. In detailed representations its surface is dappled after the manner of bulls in Minoan and Mycenaean wall paintings and reliefs, which indicates that the hair of the hide was retained.)[137] K. Müller preferred to regard the hides as cloaks of leather worn by ambassadors or prisoners-of-war, and Evans suggested they might be elephants' skins, spoils of hunters returned from Libya.[138] Although Evans did not himself place the hides in a religious context, his identification of the lustral sprinkler has provided Forsdyke with the clue to a fresh interpretation of the Vase scene.[139] The development of this

[134] Paribeni in RL 12; Evans PM 2.790 ff.
[135] Evans PM 2.253, 427, 644, 685, 774-95, frontispiece, Pl. xiv; 4.6, 323, 400.
[136] Paribeni *ibid.*; Lorimer 137.   [137] Lorimer 134-5.
[138] FR 246; Evans PM 2.742.
[139] Forsdyke MC; cf. Groenewegen-Frankfort AM 207.

interpretation has a general bearing on the argument of the preceding chapter.

Skins of animals, Forsdyke pointed out, are worn like skirts by some of the ministrants in the sacrifice on the Haghia Triada Sarcophagus. Also, the dead man standing outside his tomb is wrapped in a cloak of hide. Frequent representations of water-demons clothed in fantastic skins imply that hides were worn in ritual masquerades; and Paribeni identified as hides the baggy breeches worn by men and women in seal-designs of a religious context, the wearer in some sense impersonating the animal.[140] Forsdyke rejects the idea that the hides in the Vase scene are shields, or ritual garments.[141]

Against the normally accepted view that the sword is a military weapon or sword of state, Forsdyke opposes objections[142] leading to the alternative view that it was, like the sprinkler, a sacrificial instrument. The Vase scene is then a ceremonial presentation of bulls' hides, after a sacrifice, to the king; who, if himself a god, also shared the honours of sacrifice. This would explain the sub-missive attitude of the priest leading the procession. If we ask why the king should want hides, the answer is that, since ceremonial religious rites were centred in the palace and hides were used in them, the skins of sacrificial animals would be a necessary property of the king. Another royal use for ox-hides, perhaps religious as well as secular, was in the manufacture of soldiers' shields. If, as seems certain at the period, Minoan military forces were sent overseas, there must have been a heavy demand for ox-hides. Some magic or religious purpose must lie behind the frequent

---

[140] MA 19, pl. I; Forsdyke 14.

[141] On the grounds that the garment of the seal-designs 'seems to be the stiff hide or skirt tucked up for freedom of movement so that it approaches the form of the loincloth. In all these instances the spring of the tail, which marks the material as an animal's skin, is on the lower edge of the garment; that is to say, the direction of the skin is naturally adjusted to the head and feet of the wearer, who in some sense personates the animal. On the cup the tails are at the side; the hides are there-fore not being worn, but are being carried horizontally. Stiff ritual garments are represented elsewhere as either shaped to the body or symmetrical. The projection of these hides in front (seen only in the leading figure) is much greater than behind. They are certainly not shields.'

[142] Namely, that the regal cult of the sword, if not nordic, was at least an insti-tution of the Iron Age, when swords first became reliable in battle, the effective weapon of the Bronze Age being the spear. (This argument is of doubtful validity, in the light of our knowledge of the Cretan rapier: see Lorimer 261–7. Forsdyke finds it difficult to explain why a sword, rather than a dagger, should be used for sacrificial purposes.)

representation of shields, and, since the bull was a sacred creature, its occurrence with the shield or gems indicates a close and practical connexion between the bull and the protective symbol. We need not necessarily accept the interpretation of a ceremonial presentation of bulls' hides after a sacrifice to agree (*a*) about the need for a constant supply of hides and (*b*) about the religious association of bull and shield. Whether the subordinate is military or priestly, the three men soldiers or attendants, the hides are either shields or are destined to become shields, and the 'priest-king' has become a military functionary.

Nor need we accept the suggestion that the figure of the king or prince is a representation of Minos (rather than, say, a local 'priest-king') to agree with the force of the arguments adduced in favour —some of which have been made familiar in earlier discussions of the data. The first important consideration is that the figure of the Vase has been called a prince or a young commander because of his apparent youth. And was not Minos by a regal fiction always young? For Homer calls him a nine-year king, familiar friend of Zeus.[143] Though different explanations have been given by ancient and modern commentators, the meaning is made clear by comparison with ancient and modern examples of periodic kingship. A precise parallel is to be found in the Greek text of the Rosetta Stone, where Ptolemy V is described as the lord of thirty years (the nominal period from the accession of a king of Egypt to his *Sed* festival).[144] According to Plutarch, the Spartan ephors watched the night sky every ninth year, and, if they saw a shooting star, the king might be deposed.[145] The Greek tradition, recorded by Plato and others, that Minos retired every ninth year to the cave of Zeus and renewed his familiar intercourse with the god, is interpreted as meaning that Minos renewed his kingship in the cave, his familiar on these occasions being, however, not Zeus, but one of the Minoan deities. For the king of Egypt was a living god, the human embodiment of Horus. If Minos was also a god, he has to be identified with the young god of Crete who renewed his youth every year. Therefore we need not hesitate, it is argued, to accept a youthful representation of the king. 'Facial portraiture was beyond the competence of Minoan artists, if not beyond their

---

[143] *Od.* 19.179.
[144] In view of the following argument (in Section 8a) it should be mentioned that the ceremony of the *Sed* is understandable on a lunar basis. See Parker 80 n. 23.
[145] *Agis.* 11.

comprehension. But this regal figure is none the less a vivid portrait.'[146]

That we should accept a youthful representation of the king seems indisputable. What has to be more thoroughly explored is the supposed identification of a 'priest-king', whose kingship was renewed every eight years, with a god whose youth was renewed every year.[147]

The Minos referred to by Homer was not the great king of Knossos, but the grandfather of Idomeneus. This king would have been an Achaean conqueror who, if he called himself Minos, would have assumed the name and the honours of his Cretan predecessors.[148] For Greek folk-memory, argues Forsdyke, is too heavily contaminated by literary interference to be acceptable in its details. Though containing a record of prehistoric events, times and persons associated with these events tend to be confused or invented. The self-contradictory Greek traditions consequently have to be assessed against the facts of archaeology or contemporary statements in the history of other countries. The contradictory accounts of Minos in Herodotos and Thucydides are cited as an example. According to a Cretan tradition reported by Herodotos,[149] the Carians were, in ancient times, subjects of Minos. They were called Leleges, they occupied the islands, and they paid no tribute. But they manned the ships of Minos whenever he required them to do so. Since Minos subdued an extensive territory and prospered in war, the Carians were by far the most considerable of the peoples of that time. According to Thucydides,[150] Minos was the first person known by tradition to have established a navy. He made himself the master of what was known in the time of Thucydides as the Hellenic sea, ruled over the Cyclades, into most of which he sent the first colonies, expelled the Carians, appointed his own sons governors and thus did his best to suppress piracy as a means of securing the revenues for his own use.

Herodotos and Thucydides agree that Minos was a powerful

---

[146] Forsdyke 17.
[147] See pp. 92–103.
[148] Forsdyke *ibid.*; cf. Thomson SAGS 1.370–1, Hall CGBA 265–6.
[149] 1.171. Herodotos expressly says that he had checked, to the best of his ability, the tradition that they paid no tribute. The implication is that other peoples were subjected to tribute and that the Carians were exempt because of their service as sailors. The testimony of this Cretan tradition therefore substantiates my argument concerning the development of tributary relations in Chapter 1. It is interesting that, in historical times (third century B.C.), the Stalitai were obliged to serve Praisos by undertaking sea voyages: see my ASAC 130.
[150] 1.4.

ruler, possessing a navy and overseas dominions. But whereas, according to Herodotos, the Carians manned his ships, according to Thucydides he drove them out of the islands. It appears that they are attributing the activities of different times and tendencies to a single person. A different solution was adopted by the Parian chronicler, who reconciled the conflicting traditions by assuming that there were two kings of the name Minos.[151] However, the Cretan command of the sea must have lasted from c. 1600 B.C. until the fall of Knossos, c. 1400 B.C. It cannot be restricted to the life-span of a single king. This power may have reached its culminating point at the time (c. 1500 B.C.) of the first Minoan embassies to Egypt in the reigns of Hatshepsut and Thothmes III.[152] The grandfather of Idomeneus, on the dating of Eratosthenes, must have lived c. 1250 B.C.; he it was who may have driven the Carians out of the islands.[153] Though conceding the possibility that there may have been a king of Crete, about the middle of the eighteenth Egyptian Dynasty, who bore the name of Minos and impressed it upon posterity to the exclusion of other names, Forsdyke follows Evans in supposing that the title was dynastic, and not individual.

Though the Chieftain Vase cannot be precisely dated, it cannot be later than 1400 B.C., when the palace at Haghia Triada was destroyed. Its shape and style indicate that it belongs to c. 1500 B.C. Some conclusions can be drawn from the fashion of the dress. In the tomb paintings of Senmut and Useramon at Thebes (c. 1490–1480 B.C.), which are the first Egyptian pictures of Minoans, the envoys wear the traditional loincloth with frontal sheath. But in later tombs, beginning with the tomb of Rekhmara, the nephew of Useramon (c. 1460 B.C.), they wear the kilt without the sheath. The kilt may then be a new fashion introduced as a result of closer contact with Egypt and Syria. Since the figures on the Vase wear very short kilts, they can be taken to represent a transitional stage from the loincloth to the kilt, to be dated, on the Egyptian evidence, to c. 1470 B.C. This date would fall within the generation ascribed by the Parian Marble to the earlier Minos.[154]

---

[151] *Marmor Parium* 11, 19. Cf. Plu. *Thes.* 20, D.S.4.60.

[152] Forsdyke 18.

[153] Forsdyke *ibid.*; cf. Thomson SAGS 1.170, 370. Forsdyke adds (citing Homer *Od.* 14.256–72) ' . . . if he got as far as Egypt it was only to be driven off by the seamen of Rameses or Merneptah. It was in the fifth year of Merneptah, about 1230, that the great attack on Egypt of the Libyans and the Peoples of the Sea, among whom the Achaeans are specified, was defeated at Piari in the Western Delta.'

[154] *Ibid.*

As for the figure on the 'Priest-King Relief' (the only one hitherto recognized as Minos), though fragmentary, it shares one mark of distinction with the figure of the Vase—an elaborate necklace. Since the crown is worn by one of the women, and also by the persons in the chariots, on the Haghia Triada Sarcophagus, it was not apparently royal. Whether the action portrayed on the Sarcophagus be an apotheosis, or a sacrifice to a dead king who was in life divine, it is concerned with after-life, and the crown may be an Elysian attribute. Therefore Evans' 'conjecture that the king enjoys, like Rhadamanthys and Menelaos,[155] the amenities of an other-worldly garden, would be correct'.[156]

The conclusion of Forsdyke's argument is as follows: 'In his first restoration of the fresco, Evans gave the king a sceptre, which he doubtless borrowed from the figure on the cup. The sceptre was an emblem of divinity as well as royalty in Achaean and later Greek times. Minoan deities hold plain staffs which are usually described as spears, but I believe that if the Minoan artist had wanted to represent a spearhead he would have done so, as he did when he showed the young god as a hunter. In the design on an electrum ring from Mycenae, the young male figure manifestly bears a sceptre. Evans called this scene a *sacra conversazione* of the young god with the Mother-goddess.[157] It would be the only piece of evidence for the association of the god with a goddess, and for that reason Nilsson does not accept it as a religious document.[158] But no mortal woman could sit enthroned among rocks to welcome a diminutive young man in any domestic or social relation. She must be a goddess, and if no Minoan god was associated with her, the youth must be a sceptre-bearing king. Is not this the scene in the cave described by Plato, where Minos renewed every ninth year his familiar converse with the deity? It is an entirely satisfactory picture of that visit, and the only objection to this interpretation is that the coincidence of the literary and archaeological records seems too good to be true, like the encounter of Oidipous with the sphinx on the "Thisbe" seal. But the style and pedigree of the Mycenae ring are above suspicion.'

[155] *Od.* 4.563 f.
[156] Forsdyke 19; for the Sarcophagus cf. Nilsson MMR ch. 13.
[157] PM 3.464.
[158] MMR 352; cf. Persson RGPT 69–70: 'the very rendering of such a scene on a gold ring attests sufficiently its sacred character. . . . It is as if the goddess had accepted a promise from the lesser god.'

It seems then that the Minoan 'priest-king' was a young man whose tenure of office was dependent upon the sanction, periodically granted, of the Minoan goddess, for whom the male deity, Zeus, was substituted in Homeric and later Greek tradition. The nature of this periodic tenure will be examined later. Meantime, however, something remains to be said, in general terms, of the nature of Oriental kingship in relation to Cretan conditions.

Evans cautiously advanced the opinion that the 'priest-kings' might be thought to have been identified with the male deity to a certain extent.[159] When such evidence as that of the Haghia Triada Sarcophagus, the Chieftain Vase, the Priest-King Relief and the gem from Mycenae is introduced in support of this identification, the dating acquires a more than usual significance. The Sarcophagus cannot be dated by the external evidence of objects found in the tomb, but is ascribed, for stylistic reasons, to the transitional period between Late Minoan II and III.[160] The date of the Vase, as we have seen, is likely to have been *c.* 1500 B.C.; that of the Relief seems to be approximately the beginning of the Late Minoan period;[161] and that of the gem must presumably have been approximately the same as the rest. So far as the evidence goes, it therefore appears that any impulse towards deification occurs rather late in the Minoan Age, when the centralized power of Knossos has been established. It is significant that Nilsson should conjecture (in his discussion of the Sarcophagus) that 'the impulse towards deification may have come from Egypt, where the king was worshipped as a god after his death and every man was believed to become an Osiris. For the Egyptian elements in the accessories of the cult figured on the Sarcophagus are undeniable.'[162] When the peculiar conditions of Cretan economy of the Middle Minoan period were discussed in the first chapter, it was suggested that the Cretan 'priest-kings' were different from their Oriental counterparts because, unlike them, they were unable to appear as the divine abstraction of all social forces; and that they were intermediary as priests, as they were intermediary as merchants. It follows that any later tendency to deify the king would be closely associated with the despotic centralization of the later Bronze Age (and was perhaps restricted to Knossos?). Even

---

[159] PM 4.401.
[160] Paribeni MA 19.71; Rodenwaldt in *Tiryns* 2.198; Nilsson MMR 426.
[161] Evans PM 2.777.   [162] MMR 438.

so, it appears that he was never able to free himself of his status as intermediary *vis à vis* the goddess.[163]

Bronze Age Egypt and Mesopotamia were alike in that their agriculture was wholly dependent on irrigation. In Egypt the kingship was exceptionally stable, owing to the need for unified control of the Nile flood and also to the isolation of the country. The worship of the dead, though not confined to Egypt, developed there in a peculiar form. Mummification was made possible because of the absence of rain. The Egyptian kings could lie in state in their pyramids as though they had never died.[164] In Mesopotamia the relations between neighbouring cities were unsettled. Various kings of various cities, having established a temporary hegemony over others, endeavoured to establish claims to divinity. But the doctrine never became firmly established.[165] Nor did it in Crete, but for different reasons. The economic basis of 'kingship' in the Cretan Bronze Age rested, not on irrigation, but on commerce. The later centralization, in turn, depended on commercial expansion accompanied by internal and external tributary exaction. The Cretan male god developed independently in association with the vegetation cycle. It is only when centralization has been achieved that a blurring of distinction between the 'priest-king' and the male god becomes at all possible. The 'priest-king's' claims to divinity are late; and this may explain, as we shall see, why his tenure of office has to be renewed every eight years, while the male god (if we accept the implications of the vegetation cycle) dies every year.

8(*a*). THE MINOAN CALENDAR

Reference has been made already to the role of the Cretan goddess as moon-deity and of her consequent special association with (*a*) fertility and (*b*) primitive time-reckoning in this connexion.[166] It is to this second aspect that we must now devote some further consideration.

The observation of the moon is the oldest systematic form of reckoning time.[167] The basic unit of this reckoning is the month, which is practically everywhere denoted by the same word as the

---

[163] Cf. Persson's remark cited in n. 158 above.
[164] Cf. Thomson SAGS 2.73.
[165] *Ib*. 79–82; Frankfort KG 223, 228, 230.   [166] P. 78.
[167] Nilsson PTR 148.

moon.[168] The two phases first observed are the new moon and the full moon. Then the crescent of the waning moon is added, giving the tripartite division of waxing, full and waning moon.[169] The Babylonians were the first to effect a quadripartite division, based on the halving of the originally observed halves of the month— the origin of our four weeks.[170] The lunar month has 29·53 days; a lunar year of twelve months has 354·36 days. So long as economy remains at a primitive level, the waxing and waning moon can remain a symbol of fertility and of the growth, decay, death and renewal of life. Moreover, the regularly occurring phases of the moon are adequate units of measurement of the necessarily monotonous pattern of events of social life.[171] But with the development of agriculture, attention becomes directed to the seasons, and to the consequent importance of observing their recurrent cycle. This cycle of seasons corresponds with the solar astronomical year of 365·24 days. The discrepancy of almost eleven days between the lunar year and the solar year has to be reconciled. When the months are retained, but extended or adapted to a period which roughly corresponds with the seasonal cycle of 365·24 days, the solar calendar replaces the lunar reckoning. But when the lunar calendar is periodically reconciled with the solar reckoning by adding a thirteenth month, a lunisolar calendar is adopted. The cycle of intercalation differs. When, as in Egypt, an extra month is added in nine years out of every twenty-five, we have a twenty-five-year cycle.[172] When, as in Mesopotamia, the extra month is added in seven years out of every nineteen, we have a nineteen-year cycle.[173] There was also a lunisolar calendar in Greece, where, although the city-states had independent calendars, there was uniformity in their structure.[174] The year was divided into twelve months which alternated between twenty-nine and thirty days. To make good the deficit of eleven days, a thirteenth month was intercalated in three years out of every eight. This gave the octennial cycle, known as the *oktaeteris*, or, since a new octennium was regarded as beginning in every ninth year, the *ennaeteris*.[175]

[168] Nilsson *ibid.* A common base underlies our words for 'moon', 'month', 'measure': Thomson SAGS 1.211.
[169] Nilsson *ib.* 155.
[170] *Ib.* 171; Langdon BMSC 86–7.
[171] Cf. Nilsson *ib.* 217.
[172] Parker CAE.
[173] Neugebauer 97, 101, 123.
[174] L. Bischoff in *RE* s.v. Kalender; Nilsson ERBGK, SS.
[175] Cens. *ND* 18.4–6; Nilsson PTR 264.

The many correspondences between Greek and Babylonian festivals have led to the hypothesis that the two calendars had a common basis;[176] and, further, that if certain Greek festivals, connected with an ancient co-ordination of equinoctial rites, were ultimately of Mesopotamian origin, they must have been brought to Greece in Minoan times by way of Crete.[177] Nilsson, maintaining that the Greek calendar was of foreign origin, argued that it was introduced into Greece not earlier than the seventh century B.C., or at most the eighth, under the supervision of the Delphic priesthood.[178] Thomson accepted the first part of this argument as correct in the sense that the Greek calendar did not belong to the indigenous tradition of the Greek-speaking immigrants into the Aegean. They must have adopted it from the cultures with which they came into contact; and if, as Nilsson maintained, it was a religious product, the presumption is that, 'like so much else in Greek religion, it was a heritage from the Minoan Age, and there are positive reasons for believing that it was older and less dependent on Delphi than (Nilsson) allows'.[179] The Attic-Ionic and Doric calendars appear to derive from a prehistoric original located in central Greece, with an Oriental connexion (through Europa) with Minos.[180] 'In regard to Homer,' Thomson pointed out, 'it is a mistake to suppose, as Nilsson has done, that the Homeric Greeks had no names for the months just because they are not mentioned in the poems. Since their aim was to present an idealized picture of the heroic past, the epic poets avoided all mention of institutions that had only a local or contemporary interest; and on this principle allusions to the calendar were excluded, because its nomenclature varied from city to city.'[181]

There is clear evidence from literary, mythological and archaeological sources of a close connexion between the octennium and the kingship.[182] The most important and the most familiar of these allusions occurs in that passage of the *Odyssey*, previously mentioned, where Minos is described by Homer as a nine-year king, familiar of Zeus.[183] Literally interpreted, the word *enneoros* in this passage means 'for nine years', not 'for eight years'. But since, in

---

[176] Thomson SAGS 2.111; cf. Langdon BMSC 86–7.
[177] Thomson *ib*. 113.
[178] PTR 362–9; ERBGK 29.
[179] SAGS 2.114.
[180] *Ib*. 116; see further pp. 152–68.
[181] *Ib*. 117. Cf. Nilsson PTR 345–6.
[182] Cf. Frazer GB 3.58–92.
[183] *Od*. 19.178–9: τῆσι δ'ἐνὶ Κνωσός, μεγάλη πόλις, ἔνθα τε Μίνως/ἐννέωρος βασίλευε Διὸς μεγάλου ὀαριστής. Cf. p. 87; also sch. *ad loc*., Pl. *Min*. 319c., *id*. *Lg*. 624d., Str. 10.476, D.S. 5.78.3, Max. Tyr. 38.2, Val. Max. 1.2.ext.1, *EM* s.v. ἐννέωροι.

94

reckoning intervals of time numerically, the Greeks included both the terms separated by the interval (whereas we include only one), *enneoros* must mean at 'intervals of eight years'. Similarly, the *ennaeteris*, though meaning literally 'a period of nine years', was a term defining the octennium or eight-year cycle.[184] The passage was, however, variously interpreted, even in antiquity. But Plato, followed by Strabo and by most moderns, understood that Minos consulted with Zeus 'every ninth year'; that is to say, at each octennium.[185]

[184] Cens. *DN* 18; Frazer GB 3.59 n. 1. (Cf. Greek *trieteris*, a cycle of two years (literally 'a period of three years').) The existence of the accompanying term *ok-taeteris* is an example of the inconsistency of the Greeks in this matter, which caused ambiguity in antiquity, as it does for us.

[185] Depending on the view taken of the meaning and syntax of *enneoros*, five interpretations have been offered, within the strict context. (Cf. H. L. Jones *ad* Str. 10.476.) (1) Minos reigned as king 'for nine years', i.e. 'at intervals of eight years' —the view supported here and adopted by Frazer: cf. Hoeck 1.244, Müller D 2.96 and other authorities cited by Frazer GB 3.70-1 n. 3; or (2) Minos was nine years old when he became king (so Butcher and Lang, and A. T. Murray); or (3) held converse with Zeus for nine years (possibly? the view of Heraclid. Pont: FHG 2 p. 211); or (4) held this converse every ninth year; or (5) reigned as king when he had come to mature years.

That the Homeric *enneoros* could mean 'nine years old' seems to be settled by the description of the Aloidai (*Od.* 11.311) as being, in their ninth year, nine cubits wide and nine fathoms tall—the parallelism being so obviously intended. But there has always been difficulty in adopting this straightforward meaning when the word is used of an ox (*Od.* 10.19), of swine (*ib.* 390), of unguent (*Il.* 18.351). The usage in the latter context indicates that *ennea* could be taken as a round number and that *enneoros* could therefore mean 'of full age', 'mature' (cf. sch. *Il. l.c.*). Aristotle. (*HA* 575b 6) says that an ox is in its prime when it is five years old and goes on to couple the Homeric *pentaeteros* (used of a hog, *Od.* 14.419) with *enneoros* used of the ox (cf. *pentaeteros* of the ox in *Il.* 2.403), adding that the terms signify the same thing (δύνασθαι γὰρ ταὐτόν). *Pentaeteros* and *enneoros* can only mean the same thing, in the literal sense, if we suppose that *-oros* signifies, not a year, but a season, i.e. 'a half-year' and *enneoros* = 4½ years. The objection is that 4½ years is not, in the literal sense, the equal of 5 years. The alternative is to suppose that Aristotle, also, supposed that *pentaeteros* and *enneoros* amounted to the same thing in a metaphorical sense, i.e. 'full grown', 'mature'.

How did this notion of perfection and maturity arise? A clue to the solution of all this confused commentary is perhaps given in what appears to be the most confused single comment on *enneoros*. Eustathius explains *enneoros* in *Od.* 10.390 as meaning 'nine seasons, that is, two years and one month'. Rightly observing that the 'one month', instead of 'one season', seems incongruous, H. L. Jones (*ad.* Str. 10.476) remarked: 'This suggests that the present passage (i.e. *Od.* 19.178-9) might mean that Minos held converse with Zeus during a period of one season every other year.' But the original meaning of *oros* seems to have been 'year' (cf. Boisacq s.v.), and not 'season', as Eustathius subjectively supposed. But, assuming the octennial cycle, the odd month incongruously mentioned by Eustathius may be the intercalary month. For, in early Greece, according to Geminos (8.26, cf. 8.33) the practice had been to intercalate a month in every other year. But this system brings about too many intercalations; the calendar, after eight years, is

The octennial festivals of Thebes (as of Delphi) were associated with the calendar and the kingship. At the Daphnaphoria, an olive trunk hung with balls symbolizing sun, moon and stars, and 365 chaplets representing the days of the solar year, was carried by girls in procession.[186] A rite which enacted Apollo's slaying of the Delphic dragon took place at the Stepterion, in a hut which was supposed to represent a royal palace.[187]

The octennial confirmation of the Spartan kingship after an inspection of the stars by the ephors has every appearance of being an ancient custom brought in from central Greece, since the Spartans claimed descent from Hyllos, son of Herakles, who was born at Thebes, and also from Kadmos.[188]

The tribute of seven boys and seven girls, sent every eight years by the Athenians to Minos, appears to be associated with that octennial renewal of kingly authority attested by the passage from the *Odyssey* discussed above.[189]

The Athenians were absolved from this tribute when Theseus had killed the Minotaur. The myth of Theseus and the Minotaur was celebrated in the Crane Dance at Delos.[190] The probable date of this dance was the 7th of Thargelion (in the course of a festival which commemorated the birth of Apollo and Artemis),[191] which would account for the number of victims: seven for Apollo, seven for Artemis. It is further significant that the Athenians commemorated their deliverance from the tribute by an annual pilgrimage to Delos on the 6th of Thargelion.[192] The festival of the Thargelia began at Athens on the same date. According to tradition, a custom of putting to death two human victims, one on behalf of the men, one on behalf of the women, had been established in expiation of the death of Androgeos, a son of Minos.[193]

ahead of the solar year by a whole month. One of the four intercalations in an octennium had to be omitted. Intercalations thus fell at intervals of three, two and three years, in the third, fifth and eighth years. (Cf. Hdt. 2.4.1 and Thomson SAGS 2.118–20.) Thus, both *pentaeteros* and *enneoros* would have had common sacral associations, derived from the octennium; and the common metaphorical meaning of 'prime', 'mature', may in turn have derived from these associations.

[186] Procl. *Chr.* 26; cf. Paus. 9.10.4.   [187] P. 268.

[188] Plu. *Agis* 11 says that the custom was observed at 'intervals of nine years', i.e. at 'intervals of eight years' according to our reckoning: cf. n. 185.

[189] Plu. *Thes.* 15, D.S. 4.61, Paus. 1.27, Ovid *Met.* 8.170; cf. Serv. *ad* Verg. *A.* 6.14, Hyg. *Fab.* 41.

[190] Plu. *Thes.* 21, Call. *Del.* 307–13, *Il.* 18.590–606.

[191] Hsch. Θαργήλια, D.L. 2.44, Anon. *VPlat.* 6 Cobet, Plu. *M.* 717d.

[192] X *Mem.* 4.8.2, Pl. *Phd.* 58a–b.

[193] D.L. 2.44, Phot. *Lex.* φαρμακός, Suid. φαρμακούς, Phot. *Bibl.* 534.

The Homeric evidence indicates that Nestor's kingdom at Pylos was probably organized on a tribal basis, and that divisions of nine played a special part, as did the sacrificial bull, which had a specific relation to the Minoan kingship. When Telemachos visited Pylos the people were mustered on the beach, indicating that they were gathered for a special occasion.[194] This occasion was a sacrifice of bulls to Poseidon, ancestor of the House of Nestor. There were nine '*hedrai*' on the beach, each of which had nine bulls to offer. These '*hedrai*' (each of 500 men) were separate 'seats' or areas marked out for the nine divisions of the people on the beach. The divisions are analogous to the nine territories of Nestor's kingdom. The total number of people on the beach ($9 \times 500 = 4500$) tallies with the number of men on board the ninety ships which Nestor led to Troy ($90 \times 50 = 4500$).[195] The Pylos divisions have been compared with the 'ninths' (*enatai*) into which each of the Dorian tribes at Kos and Sparta were divided, and of which we may have traces in historical Crete. The bull sacrificed to Zeus Polieus at Kos was selected from twenty-seven bulls presented by the tribes, three from each 'ninth'. Nine huts were erected at the Spartan Karneia, each accommodating nine men, three from each phratry.[196]

Further indications of the sacred character of the number nine in Minoan religion have been perceived in the terrace of nine steps outside the temples of Demeter at Pergamon and Lykosoura. Another, at Lato in Crete, is in the market-place. Similar terraces in Minoan Crete were near the palaces, which usually faced the market-place, like the palace of Priam at Troy and the *stoa basileios* or Royal Porch at Athens.[197]

We do not know how these terraces were used. It has, however, been suggested that they accommodated groups of priests at choral performances, like the nine *aisymnetai*, or umpires, who supervised the dance in the market-place of Phaiacia.[198] Although there is no direct proof that such officials were definitely related to the kingship, the inference is that, in Minoan times, their number did have some functional value. For they seem to be paralleled by the nine *hellanodikai*, or judges, of the Olympic Games, and the nine *archontes*, or magistrates, to whom high

[194] *Od.* 3.5–8. The people would probably meet, in the ordinary way, outside the palace of Nestor.
[195] Cf. Thomson SAGS 1.361–2, *ib.* 2.129; Glotz CG 44.
[196] *SIG* 1025; Ath. 141e–f; Willetts ASAC 220–1.
[197] *Il.* 2.788–9; Tritsch AE 18, 98, 100, 102.   [198] *Od.* 8.256–67.

authority was delegated after the Athenian kingship had ceased to exist. The *hellanodikai* are described as *epoptai* ('overseers') of the Games.[199] If the primitive basis of the Olympic Games was an initiation ceremony of some kind, then the description of the 'overseers' as *epoptai* is significant. For *epoptai* was a term applied to those initiated to the highest grade of mysteries; having been thus initiated themselves, they then supervised the initiation of others.[200]

We have seen reason to accept the possibility of a formal system of initiation of the youth in the Minoan Age, developed from a primitive basis in association with the rise of the religious conception of the armed god, as the Minoan youth adapted their arms from hunting to warfare.[201] The Kouretes of Crete were guardians of the infant god and attendants on the Mother-goddess. They were initiated young men.[202] According to Hesiod, they were also 'lovers of sport and dancing'.[203] They are likened by Strabo to similar bands, such as Korybantes, Kabeiroi, Daktyloi and Telkhines. Strabo also refers to the tradition that, of the nine Telkhines who lived in Rhodes, those who accompanied Rhea to Crete and nourished the young Zeus were named Kouretes.[204] Moreover, one Kyrbas, a comrade of these, was the founder of the Cretan city of Hierapytna—hence the saying that the Korybantes were *daimons*, 'spirits', and sons of the goddess Athene and the sun-god, Helios. A variant account of the Korybantes, cited from Pherekydes by Strabo, again associates the number nine with the sun-god. For Pherekydes said that nine Korybantes were sprung from Apollo and Rhetia. Demetrios of Skepsis considered it probable that the Kouretes and Korybantes were the same, namely unmarried *kouroi*, 'youths', chosen for the war dance connected with the rituals of the Mother of the gods, known also as Korybantes because they walked with a butting of their heads, in dancing style. These were called by Homer *betarmones*, 'dancers' (lit. 'going in harmony', according to the scholiast), in that same context of the *Odyssey* where the Phaiacians appointed nine *aisymnetai* after the best *betarmones* were invited to dance.[205] Now Eustathius de-

---

[199] Paus. 5.9.5.

[200] LSJ s.v. ἐπόπτης; cf. Thomson AA 125–6, WC 10, SAGS 2.129.

[201] P. 81.   [202] Cf. Harrison T 27.

[203] *Fr.* 198 *ap* Str. 10.471.

[204] καὶ τὸν Δία κουροτροφήσαντας Κουρῆτας ὀνομασθῆναι. Str. 10.472.

[205] Str. 10.472–3; cf. *Od.* 8.250. Korybantes is derived, according to Demetrios, from *koryptein*, 'butt with the head', and *bainein*, 'walk', 'go'.

rived the word *kouros* from *keirein* ('to cut'), implying one who had shorn his hair on emerging from boyhood.[206] Though Eustathius might have been arguing from false etymology,[207] he was right to associate shorn hair with youths—a rite, as we have seen, apparently known to the Minoans.

Strabo adds that there was a general assumption that the Idaian Daktyloi (of the Troad) were wizards and attendants of the Mother of the gods. It was suspected that both Kouretes and Korybantes were offspring of the Idaian Daktyloi. For there was a tradition that the first hundred men born in Crete were called Idaian Daktyloi. To them were born nine Kouretes; and each of these had ten children called Idaian Daktyloi.[208]

Strabo admits that he was not in the least fond of myths, but emphasizes that enigmas can be solved only by examining them, even if they are confused.[209] We can conclude from his account that tradition associated the Kouretes (*a*) with the number nine, (*b*) with the Mother-goddess and the Sun-god, (*c*) with the initiation rites of youth.

In other cases, the number nine may have had traditional, rather than functional, associations, but sometimes it is difficult to draw the line between function and tradition. For example, nine boys and nine girls headed the procession when the bull was presented to Zeus Sosipolis at Magnesia perhaps because, as we shall see, of the association between the bull and the octennium.[210]

Hence the octennial cyclical reckoning acquired profound significance in the religious sphere. It is a more abstract, highly developed successor of the earlier totemic cycle and the later vegetation cycle, reflecting a more mature social system with its increased knowledge of natural forces. At the same time it is the mythological ancestor of the cyclical theories developed by ancient historiography. The culmination of the cycle is also its time of dramatic renewal, and the concept depends on ordered reckoning; thus the octennial period, or 'great year', became a symbol of universal renewal and regeneration.[211]

---

[206] 582.20, *al.*

[207] κόρ(ϝ)ος (masc. of κόρη) is perhaps cognate with Latin Ceres, Cerus, cresco: LSJ s.v.

[208] Str. 10.473.   [209] *Ib.* 474.

[210] *SIG* 589.

[211] By way of illustration it may be remarked that Herakles laboured for eight years to expiate the murder of his children (Apollod. 2.5.11); Kadmos served a penance of eight years for the slaughter of the Theban dragon (*Ib.* 3.4.2, cf. Serv. *ad* Verg. *A.* 7.761, Hes. *Th.* 801); in the ninth year Persephone released the souls of

We have seen that the cult of the moon must have been an early element behind the conception of the Cretan goddess. Our examination of the myth of Glaukos showed its links with the totemic cycle of birth and death, which, though embracing plant, animal and man, is prior to any ideas of anthropomorphic deity. At this stage the waxing and waning moon symbolizes fertility, death and renewal, and is also the means of reckoning time. As agriculture develops and attention is directed to the seasons, the solar year begins to take precedence over the lunar month. The concept of fertility and of cyclical renewal undergoes parallel change. The new phenomenon which had to be explained in the tale of Glaukos was the appearance of a cow with three different colours. The Kouretes (or Apollo) required this novelty to be explained in terms of something already known. The enigma was solved when the cow was compared with the mulberry.[212] With reference to this comparison, A. B. Cook commented as follows: 'Now a common folk-lore explanation of the moon's spots is that they are a thorn-bush carried by a man in the moon. It might be maintained that the bramble-bush or mulberry-tree was a possible description of the moon. And, if so, then the three-coloured cow, or calf that changed its colour three times a day, was merely another way of describing the moon. I am the more disposed to advance this view because Io, who was so often identified with the moon, became according to one account now a white cow, now a black, now a violet, and because Bacis or Bacchis the sacred bull at Hermonthis, which is known to have been consecrated to the sun, was said to change its colour every hour.'[213]

As the cow became a symbol of the moon, so the bull became a symbol of fertility identified with the sun, in Crete, as in Egypt.[214] This explains the dazzling white bull shining conspicuously in the herd of Minos, described by the first Vatican mythographer.[215] The association of the bull and the sun is testified from other sources which also indicate the development of an anthropomorphic conception of a sun-god.[216] The Cretan Talos, 'the bronze man', was described as a bull.[217] He was also the sun.[218]

---

the dead, who were born again to be exalted as wise men, athletes, kings and sanctified heroes. (Pi. *fr.* 133, cf. Orph. *fr.* 295; Rohde 2.211.)

[212] See p. 66. [213] Z 1.470; cf. *ib.* 454 ff., 441; Suid. s.v. Isis.
[214] *Id.* 1.468; cf. *ib.* 430 ff.
[215] *Myth. Vat.* 1.47. Cf. *Myth. Vat.* 2.120; Lact. Plac. *in* Stat. *Theb.* 5.431.
[216] Cook Z 1.719. Cf. Frazer GB 3.74 ff.
[217] Apollod. 1.9.26. [218] Hsch. Ταλῶς. ὁ ἥλιος.

He belonged to a bronze generation;[219] and he was given by Hephaistos to Minos;[220] or was made by Hephaistos and given by Zeus to Europa.[221] He was a guardian, running round the island of Crete three times a day;[222] or, as Plato fancied, he went the round of the Cretan villages three times a year with the laws of Minos inscribed on tablets of bronze.[223] A single vein extended from his neck to his ankles and the vein was stopped by a bronze nail.[224] This detail has been interpreted as a mythological reflection of the *cire-perdue* method of bronze-casting. Bronze rods, stuck through the wax coating, projected like pins and were cut smooth after the heating process. The interpretation is supported by the statement of Simonides that Talos sprang into a fire.[225] Talos was also sometimes identified with the Phoenician Kronos, a form of the Semitic deity El, who, like the Cretan Minotaur, was described as having a bovine head.[226] At Athens Talos was identified as, or closely associated with, the partridge,[227] which was regarded as sacred to Aphrodite,[228] because of its fertility.[229] Since the sun is a source of fertilizing power, the partridge may have become associated with Talos as sun-god.[230] According to Latin authors, Talos was changed by Athene into a partridge.[231] In Crete he became, inevitably, Zeus.[232]

Talos was also regarded as the mythical inventor of such devices as the compasses and the potter's wheel.[233] This is in keeping with his character of 'bronze man', who, like Daidalos, personifies the technical advances of the Bronze Age. We have

[219] Apollod. 1.9.26; A.R. 4. 1639 f. and Sch. *ad loc.*; Zen. 5.85.
[220] Apollod. 1.9.26; Simon. *ap* Sch. Pl. R. 337a; Zen. 5.85.
[221] Sch. *Od.* 20.302; Eust. *ad* Od. 1839.9; A.R. 4.1641.
[222] Apollod. 1.9.26; Zen. 5.85.   [223] Pl. *Min.* 320c.
[224] Apollod. 1.9.26; Zen. 5.85. Cf. A.R. 4.1643 ff.
[225] Suid. s.v. Σαρδάνιος γέλως; cf. Sch. Pl. R. 337a.
[226] M. Mayer in Roscher *Lex.* 2.1504 f.; E. Mayer *ib.* 1.1228; Cook Z 1.722; Frazer GB 3.75. See further p. 165.
[227] Cook Z 1.726 and nn. 4 and 5.
[228] Lyd. *Mens.* 4.64 p. 117, 20 ff. (Wünsch); cf. Ael. *NA* 10.35, Roscher SV 97, LGRM 2.3171.
[229] Ael. *NA* 3.5, 3.16, 4.1, 7.19, 17.15, Antig. *Mir.* 81, Ath. 389a ff., Plin. *NH* 10.101.
[230] Cook Z 1.728.
[231] Ov. *Met.* 8.251 ff., Lact. Plat. *Narr. Fab.* 8.3.
[232] Hsch. Ταλαιός· ὁ Ζεὺς ἐν Κρήτῃ.
[233] D.S. 4.76, Ov. *Met.* 8.247 ff., Hyg. *Fab.* 274, Serv. *ad* Verg. *Georg* 1.143, *id. ad* Verg. *A.* 6.14, Sidon *Epist.* 4.3.5. Cf. Cook Z 1.725: '. . . a contrivance for describing a circle on a machine consisting in a rotatory disk was naturally attributed to one who, as the Sun, was himself at once circular and discoidal'.

seen that the pivoted disk and the foot-wheel were possibly in use in Crete from 1800 B.C.[234] If we are right to assume[235] changes in methods of cultivating arable land designed to increase the production of corn, and also of stock-raising, parallel with the technical advances of the Middle Minoan period, there must have been, in the economic sphere, as there certainly was in the religious sphere, an increasing importance attached to the bull. We have discussed the requirement of bulls' hides for military purposes and we have seen that their provision for these purposes was not devoid of sacral associations.[236] In Phrygia, and elsewhere in antiquity, it was a capital offence to kill a plough-ox.[237] Such a regulation is a sign of the sanctity attaching to both cow and bull as they acquired a special importance in the developing agrarian economy of the Bronze Age, an importance amply confirmed by their special importance likewise in the representations of cult practices and in the mythological tradition.

The cow and bull became such integral factors in the life of the community that they figure in myths as guides in the founding of cities by those who follow the advice of the sun-god. The story of Kadmos who, in obedience to the Delphic oracle, followed a cow until it lay down on the site of Thebes, is familiar.[238] On each of the cow's flanks was a white mark like the circle of the full moon.[239] Less familiar is the lexical gloss of the 'Adiounian bull' as the Cretan name for the sun, because when he changed the site of his city he led the way in the likeness of a bull.[240] The growth, decay and renewal of crops and cattle is bound up with the cycle of the seasons; and the measurement of the cycle is a social task dependent on the observation of sun and moon. The identification of bull and cow with sun and moon is the means whereby the related dependence of the earthly and the heavenly orders of nature is identified.

Since the sun was conceived as a bull, it seems likely that the Labyrinth at Knossos was an arena or *orchestra* of solar pattern designed for the performance of a mimetic dance, in which a

---

[234] P. 14.

[235] Cf. pp. 19–20.

[236] Cf. pp. 85–7.

[237] Ael. *NA* 12.34, Nic. Dam. *fr.* 128, Varro RR 2.5.4, Colum. *De re rust.* 6. praef., Cook Z 1.469 and n. 4.

[238] Sch. *Il.* 2.494; Hellanic. *fr.* 8, Apollod. 3.4.1, f.; see further pp. 157–60.

[239] Paus. 9.12.1.

[240] *AB* 344, Phot. s.v.v. ἀδιούνιος ταῦρος, Cook, Z 1.468 and n. 8, who asks if ἀδιούνιος may not be a dialect form of Adonis.

dancer masqueraded as a bull and represented the movement of the sun. The arena may well have been the Theatral Area at the north-west corner of the palace.[241] The Labyrinth built by Daidalos was recognized in antiquity as an imitation of the Egyptian Labyrinth, which, in turn, was generally believed to be sacred to the sun. [242] The dances in the Labyrinth were connected in antiquity with the Roman Game of Troy, performed by bands of armed youths on horseback. Surveying the evidence for labyrinths and mazes elsewhere, in relation to the Cretan Labyrinth, Frazer wrote:

'A dance or game which has thus spread over Europe and survived in a fashion to modern times must have been very popular, and bearing in mind how often with the decay of old faiths the serious rites and pageants of grown people have degenerated into the sports of children, we may reasonably ask whether Ariadne's Dance or the Game of Troy may not have had its origin in religious ritual. The ancients connected it with Knossos and the Minotaur. Now we have seen reason to hold, with many other scholars, that Knossos was the seat of a great worship of the sun, and that the Minotaur was a representative or embodiment of the sun-god. May not, then, Ariadne's dance have been an imitation of the sun's course in the sky? and may its intention have been, by means of sympathetic magic, to aid the great luminary to run his race on high? We have seen that during an eclipse of the sun the Chilcotin Indians walk in a circle, leaning on staves, apparently to assist the labouring orb. In Egypt also the king, who embodied the sun-god, seems to have solemnly walked round the walls of a temple for the sake of helping the sun on his way. If there is any truth in this conjecture, it would seem to follow that the sinuous lines of the labyrinth which the dancers followed in their evolutions may have represented the ecliptic, the sun's apparent annual path in the sky. It is some confirmation of this view that on coins of Knossos the sun or a star appears in the middle of the labyrinth, the place which on other coins is occupied by the Minotaur.'[243]

[241] Not the palace itself, as Evans argued. Cf. Cook Z 1.473.
[242] D.S. 1.61 and 97, Plin. *NH* 36.84 ff.
[243] GB 3.77. Supported by Cook Z 1.491, with this proviso: 'From the concluding sentences of this paragraph I should dissent. The fact that the earliest known form of the Labyrinth is a derivative of the *swastika* leads us to believe that the dance represented the revolving sun rather than the ecliptic. But that the Minotaur . . . was engaged in a piece of mimetic ritual seems to me highly probable.'

8(b). THE HISTORICAL CALENDAR

One of the characteristics of the independent *polis* of the historical period was its individual calendar. The calendar governed the cycle of festivals and was thus the means whereby the state officially ordered the cults of its community. Much of the evidence relating to the Cretan calendars will be mentioned incidentally, wherever this evidence had a bearing upon a cult, a festival or the nature of a specific deity. This evidence is so piecemeal, both in time and place, that nothing like a systematic account of the history of the Cretan calendars can be attempted. But if the arguments advanced above[244] have substance, this history must be supposed to have begun in the Minoan Age.

It may be profitable to set out here the evidence, fragmentary though it is, for the calendars of the historical period, with some additional comment. First, it should be mentioned that, although we have references to August and October at the temple of Diktynna as early as 6 B.C.,[245] the bulk of the evidence for the Julian calendar falls between the second and the fifth centuries A.D.;[246] and that the Julian calendar was preceded by a Cretan calendar of the Imperial epoch, as we know from the *Florentine Hemerologion*.[247] The evidence can be readily assessed from the following tables.[248]

A. THE EVIDENCE BY DATE

Date	Place	Name	Festival	Time of Year
7th–6th cent. B.C.	Gortyna	Welkhanios	[Welkhania]	Spring assumed
c. 4th cent. B.C.	Gortyna?	Leskhanorios	—	—
	Gortyna	[Thermoloios]	Thermoloia	—
3rd cent. B.C.	Aptera	Diktynnaios	—	—
	Gortyna	Amyklaios	—	—
	Praisos	Dionysios	Dionysia assumed	Spring assumed

[244] Pp. 92–103.
[246] IC *passim*.
[247] Hoeck K 3.444; Paton-Hicks 332.
[245] IC 2.XI.3.
[248] Collected from IC *passim*. Cf. Bischoff in RE s.v. Kalender; Deiters 38 f.; Kubitschek *Wiener Denkschr.* 62.104 ff.; Guarducci *Epigraphica* 7.72 ff. Table C, with slight variation in the arrangement, as proposed by Guarducci *ib.* 79.

Date	Place	Name	Festival	Time of Year
3rd–2nd cent. B.C.	Dreros	Haliaios	Cf. Rhodian Halieia?	—
		Komnokarios		—
	Gortyna	Kanneios = Karneios	—	—
2nd cent. B.C.	Aptera	Phthinoporios?	—	Autumn assumed
	Biannos	Eleusinios	Eleusinia assumed	Autumn assumed
	Gortyna	Amyklaios	—	Nov.–Dec.?
		Ionios	—	Aug.–Sept.?
		Kanneios = Karneios	Karneia assumed	July–Aug.?
		Leskhanorios	—	Oct.–Nov.?
		—nios	—	—
		—thios	—	Sept.–Oct.?
		Weukhanios = Welkhanios	[Welkhania]	Spring assumed
	Hiera-pytna	[Heraios]	Heraia	—
		Himalios	—	—
		Theodaisios	Theudaisia	—
	Knossos	Agyios?	—	July–Aug.?
		Elkhanios =Welkhanios	[Welkhania]	Spring assumed
2nd cent. B.C.	Knossos	Karneios	Karneia assumed	Aug.–Sept.?
		Karonios	—	Oct.–Nov.?
		Nekysios	Nekysia assumed	Nov.–Dec.?
		Spermios	—	Sept.–Oct.?
	Lato	Bakinthios =Hyakin-thios	Hyakinthia assumed	—
		Khartiobiarios?	—	Oct.–Nov.?
		Thermolaios	[Thermolaia]	—
		Thesmophorios	Thesmophoria assumed	Nov.–Dec.?
		Thiodaisios	Thiodaisia	Sept.–Oct.?
	Lyttos	Panamos	Cf. Panamia at Thespiai	—
	Malla	Bakinthios = Hyakin-thios	Hyakinthia assumed	—
	Olous	Agrianios?	—	—
		Apellaios	—	Nov.–Dec.?
		Delphinios	—	Oct.–Nov.?
		Eleusynios (Elousinios)	Eleusinia assumed	Sept.–Oct.?
		Heraios	Heraia assumed	—
		[Thiodaisios]	Thiodaisia	—

Date	Place	Name	Festival	Time of Year
	Priansos	Dromeios	Dromeia? assumed	—
		[Heraios]	Heraia	—
2nd–3rd cent. A.D.	Lyttos	[Belkhanios] =Welkhanios	Belkhania = Welkhania	May
		Theodaisios	Theodaisia	—

B. THE EVIDENCE BY MONTHS

Name	Place	Comment
1. Agrianios?	Olous	Doric. Known elsewhere.
2. Agyios?	Knossos	Cretan in *Hemerolog. Flor.* Also Aitolian, Lokrian, Argive.
3. Amyklaios	Gortyna	Only in Crete at Gortyna.
4. Apellaios	Olous	Doric. Known elsewhere.
5. Bakinthios	Lato Malla	= Hyakinthios. Doric. Known elsewhere.
6. Delphinios	Olous	Also at Aigina, Thera.
7. Diktynnaios	Aptera	Only known here. Presupposes a festival.
8. Dionysios	Praisos	Only in Crete at Praisos.
9. Dromeios	Priansos	Only here.
10. Eleusinios	Biannos Olous	Spelling varies. Known elsewhere.
11. Haliaios	Dreros	Only here.
12. Heraios	[Hierapytna] Olous [Priansos]	Known elsewhere.
13. Himalios	Hierapytna	Only here.
14. Ionios	Gortyna	Only here.
15. Karneios	Gortyna Knossos	Doric. Known elsewhere.
16. Karonios (Koronios)	Knossos	Only here.
17. Khartiobiarios?	Lato	Only here.
18. Komnokarios	Dreros	Only here.
19. Leskhanorios	Gortyna	Known elsewhere.
20. Nekysios	Knossos	Cretan in *Hemerolog. Flor.*
21. Panamos	Lyttos	Only in Crete at Lyttos. Known elsewhere.
22. Phthinoporios?	Aptera	Only here.
23. Spermios	Knossos	Only here.
24. Thermolaios	[Gortyna] Lato	Only in Crete.
25. Thesmophorios	Lato	Cretan in *Hemerolog. Flor.* Known elsewhere.
26. Thiodaisios	Hierapytna Lato [Lyttos] [Olous]	Known elsewhere.

Name	Place	Comment
27. Welkhanios	Gortyna	Only in Crete.
	Knossos	
	[Lyttos]	
28. —nios	Gortyna	
29. —thios	Gortyna	

C. LIKELY CORRESPONDENCES IN SECOND CENTURY B.C.

Place in Calendar	Knossos	Lato	Olous	Gortyna	(Attic)
11th (Aug.–Sept.)	Karneios	—	—	Ionios	(Metageitnion)
12th (Sept.–Oct.)	Spermios	Thiodaisios	Eleusinios	—thios	(Boedromion)
1st (Oct.–Nov.)	Karonios	Khartiobiarios?	Delphinios	Leskhanorios	(Pyanopsion)
2nd (Nov.–Dec.)	Nekysios	Thesmophorios	Apellaios	Amyklaios	(Maimakterion)

It should be explained that Agrianios at Olous cannot be regarded as certain because the middle letters are supplied, viz. A[gria]nios,[249] that Agyios at Knossos is a plausible conjecture;[250] that there is uncertainty about Khartiobiarios at Lato and especially about the initial letter;[251] and that the ending of Phthinoporios is supplied, viz. Phthinop[orios].[252]

The evidence from the second century B.C. indicates that it was still usual for the new year to begin in Crete with the autumnal equinox; and it seems entirely fitting, considering its etymology,[253] that the administrative year should begin at Gortyna, for example, with the month Leskhanorios.

But more important conclusions follow if we bring under review the evidence from inscriptions regarding the annual oath of the citizen novices before the magistrates of various cities. This evidence—from Dreros, Lato, Lyttos, Malla, Olous and Hierapytna[254]—consists, with the exception of the Drerian oath, of treaties. (The Drerian oath, promising loyalty to Dreros and the allied Knossos, but enmity to Lyttos, is, in some respects, similar.) Hence it is common to find an injunction that festivals in one city should be visited by officials and citizens of an allied city.

At Lato it seems that the last month was Thiodaisios; and in the treaty between Lato and Olous the annual oath is to be taken at the festival of the Thiodaisia. (The name of the corresponding festival at Olous is missing, but, since we know that the Thiodaisia was celebrated at Olous, it has been suggested that the Thiodaisia was intended here also.) At Hierapytna the Thiodaisia is again

[249] IC 1.XVI.3.4.
[250] Cf. IC 1 pp. 52 and 55 with ib. 4.197.11.
[251] IC 1.XVI.4 A 22.
[252] Ib. 2.III.17.2.
[253] P. 266.
[254] IC 1.IX (third to second century B.C.); ib. XVI.5 (second century B.C.); ib. XVIII.9 (second century B.C.); ib. XIX.1 (third century B.C.); ib. 3.III.1 B (third century B.C.). Cf. ib. 1.VIII (Knossos) 13 (second century B.C.).

mentioned; at Malla the Hyperboia; at Lyttos the Periblemaia or Periblemata. At Dreros the initiative for impeachment of the magistrates, in case of future failure to preserve the continuity of the oath, is made binding on those who have just taken the oath. Impeachment, if necessary, would follow after the magistrates had retired from office, in the months of Komnokarios or Haliaios. It follows that these two months were probably the first and second of the calendar year at Dreros.

Autumn then was a time when the new citizens were inaugurated, when old officers retired and new ones took over, when the fruits of the year, following the order of nature, were accounted for.

The diversity regarding the beginning of the calendar year in the various parts of Greece has not been explained. In Sparta, Rhodes and Miletos, just as in Crete, the year began with the autumnal equinox; in Chios with the vernal equinox; in Athens and Delphi at the first new moon after the summer solstice; in Boiotia and Delos after the winter solstice. If the diversity was not due to local factors, it was possibly inherent in the Greek calendar from the beginning. This possibility is linked with the traces which can be found in Greece of a bipartite year divided, as in Babylonia, at the equinox. Hence the further possibility that there was, in various Greek cities, an ancient co-ordination of equinoctial rites corresponding with the Mesopotamian New Year Festival, which was observed in Nisan (March–April) and again in Teshrit (September–October). On the fifth day of this festival the kings performed a ceremony, which signified the victory of Marduk over his enemies, in the presence of a white bull, addressed by the king as 'divine bull of Anu, glorious light which illumines the darkness'. The presence of the bull was an ancient and characteristic feature of the festival; and if the various Greek festivals, associated alike with the sacrifice of a bull and with priestly functions derived from the prehistoric kingship, were of Mesopotamian origin, the likelihood is that they were brought into Greece by way of Crete in Minoan times.[255]

In the light of these considerations, it is significant that the Cretan new year should begin in the autumn. The arguments which will be advanced later concerning the nature of the festival known as the Periblemaia or Periblemata are strengthened.[256] For this festival, with its complementary festival, the Ekdysia, is at

[255] Thomson SAGS 2.111–14.   [256] P. 294.

once brought into relation with the Hyperboia and the Thiodaisia. The Hyperboia, it will be suggested, was a festival which took its form from the celebration of a god in the form of a bull.[257]

We shall also see that the special deity honoured at the Thiodaisia originated with the Minoan bull-god and became allied with the 'Cretan-born' Zeus; that foot-races must have formed part of the *agon* of the festival; and that the sacrifice of a bull was probably a prominent feature.[258] These conclusions will be partly derived from a comparison with the Athenian Dionysia, the comparison being based on general grounds. But a discrepancy here seems to arise. For, whereas the Cretan Thiodaisia is to be associated with the ritual graduation of the youths from the *agela* in the autumn, the Athenian Dionysia took place at the beginning of spring, in the month Elaphebolion (March–April).

But the discrepancy can be discounted if it is accepted as a further indication of an original bipartite year. The Athenian *Dionysia* (which we know was reorganized at the end of the sixth century B.C.), taking place in March–April, and the Latian (and presumably other Cretan) Thiodaisia of September–October can be regarded equally as equinoctial festivals of the old bipartite year.

That Eleusinios at Olous should apparently coincide with September–October is of interest, because, as we shall see, the Eleusinian Mysteries were performed in September, and because the time of the celebration had once been the sowing-time, although in the historical period it was a month later, in October.[259] The connexion with the sowing-time appears again with the equation of Olountian Eleusinios and Knossian Spermios. Latian Thesmophorios would not exactly coincide with the time of the Attic Thesmophoria, which took place towards the end of October, but it is near enough to suggest that a Cretan festival involved similar rites.[260] Its corresponding Knossian month Nekysios was presumably associated with a festival of the dead, Nekysia.[261]

Some light is thrown upon the name Himalios by glosses of Hesychios indicating a connexion with the harvest.[262] Phthin-

[257] P. 239.
[258] P. 206.
[259] P. 150.
[260] Cf. pp. 151–2.
[261] Cf. PLond ined. 2309ʳ 21; Bull. Soc. Arch. Alex. 7.67; Artem. 4.81; Eust. 1615.2.
[262] Hsch. s.v.v. ἱμαλιά, ἱμάλιος, ἱμαλίς.

oporios would indicate autumn. Haliaios at Dreros is presumably to be associated with the mention of Halios among the deities of the oath. As in Sparta and Argos, the Knossian Karneia, to judge from the month-name, would fall in August–September. This would not apply, however, to a Gortynian Karneia—a reminder that, although our evidence is fragmentary, it is not without its testimony to the diversity of the Cretan calendar. Even so, the surviving terminology is sufficient proof that the emphasis repeatedly placed here upon the abiding influence of the vegetation cycle in Cretan religious ideas and customs is not exaggerated.

9. THE SACRED MARRIAGE

According to Pausanias, Pasiphae ('She who shines on all') was the moon.[263] In myth, Pasiphae, wife of Minos, conceived a passion for a bull, which had been sent in answer to the prayers of Minos. Instead of sacrificing the bull as he had promised, Minos sent it away among his herds and sacrificed another. The unnatural passion of his wife was the punishment. Daidalos made for Pasiphae a wooden cow on wheels, hollowed it out, sewed it up in the hide of a cow which he had skinned, and put it in the meadow where the bull grazed. He put Pasiphae inside this image, and the bull coupled with it. In consequence Pasiphae gave birth to Asterios ('Starry One'), who was called the Minotaur ('Minos bull'); he had the face of a bull, but the rest of him was human. Minos, obeying certain oracles, shut him up under guard in the Labyrinth—also made by Daidalos. It was a building whose intricate windings led astray those seeking to escape from it.[264]

Frazer and Cook agreed that this myth reflected a sacred marriage of sun and moon at Knossos.[265] The ritual pairing of solar bull and lunar cow would have been enacted by a man and woman masked as bull and cow. 'When we remember,' wrote Frazer, 'that at the court of Egypt the king and queen figured as god and goddess in solemn masquerades, where the parts of animal-headed deities were played by masked men and women, we need have no difficulty in imagining that similar dramas may have been performed at the court of a Cretan king, whether we suppose

---

[263] 3.26.1. Cf. Cook Z 1.521 ff.; Persson RGPT 131.
[264] Apollod. 3.1.1 ff.; cf. D.S. 4.77, Tz. H. 1.473 ff.
[265] Frazer GB 3.71; Cook Z 1.521 ff.

them to have been imported from Egypt or to have had an independent origin.'[266] It is reasonable to suppose that the sacred marriage of solar bull and lunar cow took place at Knossos as part of the palace-cult ritual in the 'great year' which marked the octennial period.[267] In this ritual, we may further suppose, the part of the solar bull was enacted by the 'priest-king' Minos himself; and the part of the lunar cow by the Knossian priestess of the Moon-goddess.

In later cult the ritual became a sacred marriage of Zeus and Hera, or of Zeus and some other female personage. Hera was originally a cow-goddess.[268] Her priestess at Argos was Io, who was ravished by Zeus when she had been changed by him to a cow. The myth of Io also reflects a sacred marriage. The bride is the priestess of Hera, the bridegroom the priest of Zeus disguised as a bull. The ox-herd Argos who watched over Io was *panoptes* ('all-seeing'); and *panoptes* was an epithet of Zeus and the sun. Argos wore a bull's hide.[269]

It has been suggested that the priestesses of Hera were descended from the women of a cow clan, who had expressed their sense of affinity to the sacred animal in the form of the belief that they were cows, and in this guise performed a traditional dance designed to promote the fertility of their herds by means of mimetic magic.[270] It is at least certain that the connexion of Zeus with the sacred marriage of solar bull and lunar cow is late and superficial.[271] Similarly, the association of sun and moon may well be an accretion dating from the reorganization of the calendar on an octennial basis. If there was a calendar in use at Knossos by *c.* 1400 B.C., it is unlikely that this was an innovation introduced at this time by the Mycenaeans. We should rather suppose that the calendar, based on the octennial cycle, had been introduced into Crete at some time during the Middle Minoan period.[272] When it was introduced, or so we may surmise, so too was the octennial ceremony which confirmed either the renewed tenure of office of the old 'priest-king' or his replacement by a new official. Since, so far as the evidence goes, Minos is always young, the latter alternative is the more likely. But, prior to this reorganization, we can

[266] *Ib.* 3.72.　　　　　　　　　　　　　[267] Cf. Frazer *ib.* 3.71.
[268] Cook Z 1.444–7; In the *Iliad* she is described on fourteen occasions as 'cow-eyed lady Hera'. *id. ib.* 444 n. 5.
[269] A. *Supp.* 291–325. Cf. Apollod. 2.1.3; Cook Z 1.453–64.
[270] Thomson AA 148.　　　　　　　　　　[271] Cook Z 1.543–4.
[272] Cf. p. 94.

suppose that the ritual dance of the pairing of bull and cow already existed.

At an earlier stage the original ceremony may not have been restricted to a single pair. It may have been celebrated by the youthful initiates of both sexes to ensure the reproduction both of the human community and of the community's crops and cattle. For Strabo informs us that it was still the custom for all those who were promoted from the *agela* ('herd') of the youth to marry at the same time; and the Gortynian Code of the fifth century B.C. contains a provision which is likely to mean that certain exceptions to this general and ancient custom were henceforth to be sanctioned.[273] The hypothesis of an original collective union of young men and women of the same age-grade, still attested for young men in the historical period, strengthens the possibility that the institution of the '*agela*' (with which we may also compare the Spartan *boua*,[274] 'herd of oxen'), has direct connexions with Minoan Crete.[275] The *agela* in historical Crete was restricted to young men, because initiation had become restricted to them, as a social institution. This process of exclusion may also date from Minoan times, when, in fact, the sacred marriage replaced primitive collective union—at least as a palace cult.

When initiation does become exclusive in this way, there is a tendency for it to assume the form of an ordeal, especially among the men.

There is some indication that, in historical times, such an ordeal took the form of a race.[276] In Minoan times, the ordeal may have been connected with the bull-games. Reichel, in his discussion of the evidence, suggested that the bull-grappling had some religious significance, but did not specify the cult or its meaning.[277] If it did form part of the Minoan initiation ceremonies, it is clear that girls had not yet been excluded. For the statuettes, reliefs, paintings and seal-stones which supply our evidence show that male and female toreadors took part. Reichel concluded that, in the earliest form of the bull-games, the bull was captured by one or more unarmed men, who clung to its horns. Out of this developed the various Minoan acrobatic feats, in one of which the athlete rushed towards the charging bull, grasped it by the horns,

---

[273] Str. 10.482; Willetts ASAC 7–10.
[274] Hsch. βοῦα. ἀγέλη παίδων.
[275] Cf. p. 66.
[276] Willetts ASAC 122–3.
[277] SKMC; cf. Cook Z 1.497.

turned a somersault over its head and was then projected over its back to the ground.[278]

Much of the further evidence for the sacred marriage in Crete is post-Minoan and, as we should expect, often involves Zeus. This evidence will be reviewed at a later stage. But there is one other older version of the Cretan sacred marriage which clearly connects it with that stage in agriculture when the introduction of the cattle-drawn plough implies a fresh division of labour, when men are brought increasingly into agricultural work.[279] According to this myth, Iasion embraced Demeter in a thrice-ploughed field, that is, in a field prepared for sowing.[280] The sacred marriage is bound up with the fertility of the crops.

Now Korybas, eponym of the Korybantes, was said to have been a son of Iasion by Kybele, the Asiatic mountain-goddess.[281] We have seen that the Korybantes may have been synonymous with the Kouretes.[282] They are alike presumably because they were initiates who danced with a butting of their heads—like bulls. This dance was designed to make the bull leap, like its successor the Dithyramb—if that was designed to make Zeus leap or beget.[283] But Zeus had not yet succeeded to the bull.

Although the ritual of the festival of Zeus Polieus at Athens, known as the Bouphonia ('The Ox-slaying') or Dipolieia, lasted to the time of Theophrastos, it already represented all that was archaic and practically obsolete by the time of Aristophanes.[284] Moreover, although a sacrifice was presumably made to Zeus, in the extant detailed accounts mention of Zeus is conspicuously absent.[285] At the festival,[286] barley mixed with wheat—or cakes made from them—was laid on the bronze altar of Zeus Polieus. Oxen chosen for the purpose were then driven round the altar, and the ox which went up to the altar and tasted the offering

---

[278] Doubt has been cast upon the possibility of the genuineness of this feat. But cf. Spanish *trascuerno*.

[279] Cf. pp. 19–20.   [280] *Od.* 5.125–8. Cf. D.S. 5.49, Hes. *Th.* 969 ff.

[281] D.S. 5.49.   [282] Pp. 98–9.

[283] A. B. Cook cited by Harrison T 204 n. 1. Rejected by Pickard-Cambridge DTC 14.

[284] Harrison T 142; Ar. *Nu.* 984.   [285] Cf. Harrison T 144.

[286] The ritual of the festival is described in passages of Porphyrios (*Abst.* 2.29 ff.), who appears to be quoting directly from Theophrastos's treatise *On Piety* (*c.* 322 B.C.) and Paus. 1.24.4. Cf. Ael. *VH* 83. Cook's account (Z. 3.577 ff.) is, in the main, based on these sources. Cf. Harrison PSGR 111 ff. and T 141 ff., following Frazer's earlier summary. Robertson Smith (RS 304 ff.) explained the Bouphonia as a typical case of totemic ritual. He was followed by Farnell, S. Reinach and Harrison. For criticisms and other views see Cook Z 3.598 n. 6.

was slain. Regulations governing the slaughter were carefully observed. The axe and the knife were whetted by certain men with water brought by virgins, called *hydrophoroi* ('water-carriers'). Another man handed over the axe. Another struck the ox. Another slit its throat with the knife.[287] It was then flayed; and its flesh was distributed and tasted by all. The hide was then stuffed with straw and sewn up. The stuffed animal was raised to its feet and yoked to a plough, as if it were ploughing. Meanwhile, the man who had struck the beast dropped the axe beside the altar and fled. A trial to determine guilt then took place and the axe was tried and acquitted. All who had participated were charged and obliged to defend themselves. The water-carriers blamed the men who had whetted the axe and the knife; these blamed the man who handed over the axe; he blamed the man who had used the knife on the ox; he, in turn, blamed the knife. The knife was then condemned and thrown into the sea.

There is reason to suppose that the Bouphonia was introduced from Crete.[288] Its origin as a yearly communal tribal or clan feast is indicated by the ritual prescription that the flesh should be distributed and tasted by all. Moreover, those taking part in the ritual belonged to three groups, known respectively as *Boutypoi* ('Ox-strikers'), *Kentriadai* ('Goad-men') and *Daitroi* ('Carvers'), whom Theophrastos apparently described as 'clans' (*gene*).[289] The scholiast on the *Peace* of Aristophanes explains that the festival was 'an imitation' (*apomimema*), that is to say, the resurrection is 'a mimetic representation of the new life of the new year and this resurrection is meant to act magically. The worshippers taste the flesh to get the *mana* of the ox, and to do that they must slay him. To taste the flesh is good, but best of all is it that the ox himself should on his resurrection renew his life and strength.'[290] The trial ritual following upon the slaughter suggests that the taboo which had been broken may have been the ancient but presumably familiar ban on the slaughter of plough oxen.[291] But the rite of expiation may have been, originally in this case, such as is

---

[287] Cf. *Od.* 3.447 ff.

[288] Cook Z 3.593 on Thphr. *ap.* Porph. *Abst.* 2.29.

[289] Photios (s.v. Κεντριάδαι) speaks of the *Kentriadai* as a *patria* of *Kerykes* ('heralds'). Mommsen (FSA 521) contended that the *Boutypoi*, *Kentriadai* and *Daitroi* were three families all belonging to the clan of *Kerykes*. He was supported by Cook Z 3.585.

[290] Harrison T 143–4.

[291] Ael *VH* 5.14; Arat. 132 sch.; D.L. 8.20; Philostr. *Im.* 2.24. Cf. p. 102.

common when a totemic taboo is infringed,[292] with the taboo operating, not against the ox, but the cow-totem. For the scholiast on Aristophanes' *Clouds* explains the festival as a representation of what happened about 'the cakes and the cows'.[293] Finally, we should note that, as late as the decade 190–200 A.D., a certain Lakrateides, the son of Eutykhides the Azenian, is three times recorded as *Boutypos* priest and *Kosmetes* ('Marshal') of the Athenian *epheboi*.[294]

The details of the annual sacrifice of a bull to Zeus Sosipolis at Magnesia on the Maeander are known to us from an inscription of the third century B.C.[295] The bull was dedicated at the new moon of the month Kronion, at the beginning of seed-time. It was led in a procession headed by priests and officials. In the procession were two bands of youths and maidens whose parents were still alive.[296] A prayer was offered on behalf of the safety of the city, the land, the citizens, the women and children, for peace and wealth, for the bringing forth of grain and all other fruits and of cattle.

The bull was sacrificed on the 12th of Artemision (late spring or early summer). On the day of the sacrifice there was another procession. Behind the priest and priestess of Artemis came other city officials and priests, and also certain chosen *epheboi*, youths (*neoi*)[297] and children, the victors in the games of the goddess, and other victorious competitors.

The sacrificial bull had to be the finest possible, bought by the city stewards. Similarly, at the sacrifice of a bull to Zeus Polieus at Kos, each ninth part of the three Dorian tribes drove up a bull to the sacrificial table, and the finest was chosen by some special test.[298] The 'butting bull' features on the coins of Magnesia. In one such illustration,[299] the bull figures on a Maeander pattern, behind him a symbolic ear of grain. In another,[300] a bull is driven by a youth to the mouth of what appears to be a cave. He kneels 'as though in willing acceptance of his fate'.

[292] Frazer TE 1.18-20, 2.156-8, 160, 3.67, 81.
[293] Sch. Ar. *Nub.* 984; cf. Harrison PSGR 111 n. 4.
[294] IG²2–3, 2 no. 2291 a, 1 f., *ib.* no. 2128 2 f., *ib.* no 2129, 2 f. Cf. Cook Z 3.586.
[295] O. Kern *Inschriften v. Magnesia* no. 98; *Arch. Anz.* (1894) 78; Nilsson GF 23; Harrison T 150.
[296] 'Where fertility is magically invoked there must be no contagion of death.' Harrison T 151.
[297] Presumably older than the *epheboi*. Willetts ASAC 188–92.
[298] Paton and Hicks no. 37.
[299] Harrison T 151 n. 4 and fig. 28 a.
[300] *Ib.* 152 n. 1, fig. 28 b.

It is clear that, by the fourth century B.C., the Cretan institution of the *agela* was partly of a private character, since the organization was now dependent on the influence of a social *élite*.[301] For the leaders of the *agela* were generally the fathers of their organizers, who were the most conspicuous and influential boys of their generation. The love affairs of the young Cretans were likewise peculiar, involving a mock 'marriage' by capture—of an older with a younger boy, whose friends were warned three or four days beforehand that the abduction was to take place. If the abductor was the younger boy's equal or superior in rank or other respects, the boy's friends pursued him and seized him, but only in a gentle way, to satisfy custom; he was then handed over to the abductor. The pursuit was considered to end when the boy was taken to the Men's House of the abductor. He was then given presents and taken away into the country. Those who were present at the abduction followed, and after feasting and hunting with them for two months they returned to the city. The boy was then released after receiving the presents which custom required. Aside from other things so numerous and costly that all the friends made contributions to defray the expenses, particular mention is made of three presents. These were a military costume, a drinking-cup and—an ox. The young initiate then sacrificed the ox to Zeus and gave a feast to those who had accompanied him. It was considered a disgrace for those who were handsome in appearance or of distinguished ancestry to fail to obtain lovers, since their characters would thus be considered impugned.

The abducted boys were called by a special name, *parastathentes* ('those set beside') and they continued to receive special favours. They had the positions of highest honour in dances and races, were allowed to dress in better clothes than the others, the clothes presented by their lovers. Even when they had grown to manhood they wore a distinctive dress, intended to mark the wearer as one who had become *kleinos* ('famous', 'renowned'). For 'those set beside' were called 'renowned'.

Of course this custom does recall the common theme of the youth who is abducted from his parents by jealous divinities when he is to be initiated.[302] But does it not also hide, beneath its idealization of sodomy, a perverse reminiscence of the Cretan sacred marriage? The aristocratic *élite* who practised the custom may have derived their ultimate origin from the chosen band of

[301] Ephor. cited by Str. 10.483–4.   [302] Jeanmaire CC 455.

youths whom Evans supposed to exist at the court of Minos.[303] The myth of Ganymede, according to Plato,[304] was said to have originated in Crete; and there was a tradition that Minos, and not Zeus, was the ravisher.[305] But all this later sophistication must be set beside the original form of the myth, where Ganymede is not the bedfellow but the cup-bearer of Zeus. He was chosen by the gods; he was blessed with immortality; his father was compensated for his loss.[306] He was the young initiate chosen for special office.

Side by side with the historical Cretan custom of choosing the *kleinos*—whose sacrifice of an ox must surely derive from Minoan ritual—there was preserved, as we have seen, an earlier custom still. The *kleinos*, when he left the *agela*, like all others of his age, married at the same time.

We can then suppose an early cult of cow and moon, celebrated in a clan feast, followed by collective marriage. The custom of collective marriage persists. Other features undergo marked change. The sun enters with the bull. The collective marriage produces also a sacred marriage of a chosen pair. Later, perhaps, these are in fact chosen from a pre-selected group of specially privileged young persons attached to the palace. Marriage, collective and sacred, is combined with initiation. Initiation, for the sacred pair, is also a kind of coronation.[307] Since the young Cretan god is an annually dying god, perhaps the sacred pair were chosen annually. Did the male partner, the original of the 'priest-king', die, if only a mimic death, at the end of his annual tenure? Frazer's comparative evidence might suggest the possibility. It is perhaps worth recalling that Plutarch, who tells us that he spent a considerable time in Crete, mentions the celebration of an extraordinary festival there. An image of a man without a head was exhibited at the festival. The man was said to be Molos, the father of Meriones. It was said that he had violated a young woman, and when discovered was without a head.[308] Since Molos was a son of Deukalion the inference is that the myth behind the festival was of considerable antiquity.

But whatever may have happened to the male consort at the end of his period of office originally, we are on firmer ground in supposing that, as the sun-bull becomes more dominant, the 'priest-

---

[303] PM 4.397-9. Cf. p 84.   [304] *Lg* 636d.
[305] Ath. 13. 601f.
[306] *Il.* 5.265, 20.232. Cf. *h. Ven.* 203-12; also Jeanmaire CC 454.
[307] On coronation as a specialized rite of initiation see Hocart 77-98.
[308] *De defect. orac.* 417.14e.

king' holds sway throughout the octennial period. The time of his choosing becomes also probably an occasion of ritual ordeal. The young try their strength against the bull, from whom in turn that strength, especially the strength of the 'priest-king', derives.

10. THE MYCENAEAN PANTHEON

There is good reason to suppose that the hierarchical organization of the deities of the Homeric poems reflects the social conditions of the Mycenaean period.[309] Under the monarchical hegemony of Zeus, the gods and goddesses are gathered together in a single heavenly stronghold. Their dwellings, built by Hephaistos, surround the central palace of Zeus. The authority of the supreme male deity is now fairly stable, but still by no means unchallenged. The lady Hera, wife of Zeus, is among those who resort to intrigue against his pre-eminence.

The Homeric poems, however, do not present a uniform picture of the Olympian system. There are two passages of the *Iliad*[310] in which Zeus lives alone on Olympos. In one passage he hurls a thunderbolt, in the other he sends a storm. Olympos itself must be considered, in all probability, as a generic term for 'mountain'. The mountains of this name in Greece itself and in Asia Minor did not all derive from the Thessalian Olympos. In one passage of the *Odyssey* the celestial Olympos is described in legendary terms more reminiscent of the Minoan Fields of the Blest than the mountain centre of storm, rain and lightning.[311] It is here 'the steadfast abode of the gods, never shaken by winds, wetted by showers or approached by snows, where the cloudless air is outspread and a white radiance is diffused'.

The Olympian pantheon was established in a different way from the pantheons of Egypt and Babylonia, where the local god of a city which subjugated other cities became supreme over the gods of the subordinate cities. In Egypt and Babylonia the pantheon is organized in such a way that it closely reflects the economic and political centralization of the Oriental despotism. The Mycenaean pantheon is, however, much less urbane—in the strict sense of the term. It rather reflects the process whereby tribal federation has been achieved and leads to military kingship. A weather-god, lord

---

[309] Cf. Nilsson MOGM Ch. 4, HM 266–72, HGR 158–9.
[310] 13.243, 16.364.
[311] 6.42–5: ὅθι φασὶ κτλ. Cf. Nilsson MOGM 250, HM 272.

of storms, of rain, lightning and thunder, acquires supremacy in his lofty stronghold. His earthly prototype is the Mycenaean Great King. Other deities with other functions at first reside elsewhere: Hera in Argos, Poseidon in the sea, Aphrodite in Paphos, Artemis in field and forest, Athene in the house of Erekhtheus. Eventually, whilst preserving their functions, they live with the Olympian in his stronghold, subordinate to his will.

The Mycenaean pantheon, we may assume, spread its influence as the Mycenaean social and economic system became dominant elsewhere. The ensuing social conflict and fusion is paralleled by an increasing complexity in cult, mythology and the composition and organization of the pantheon. In its most dramatic form this process assumed the character of a struggle between the older conception of the Aegean goddess and a newer conception of a dominant male god, Zeus. Crete had been the centre of Minoan civilization and had now become part of the fringe of the Mycenaean. The social and economic consequences have been considered. The religious consequences are, in a general sense, the theme of the rest of this work.

But before we embark upon the task of analysing the process whereby, and in what diverse forms, the Minoan religion, with its prime allegiance to a Great Goddess (though already familiar with the growing power of its own Cretan male god), became reconciled with the Mycenaean pantheon, it will be profitable to see how Crete is featured in the Homeric poems. Since the *Iliad* and the *Odyssey* are the literary memorials of that heroic age which sundered the age of bronze from the age of iron, the references and allusions to Crete, as it appeared to the bards who hymned the glories of the mainland Mycenaeans, are not without their special significance.

CHAPTER 4

Homer on Crete

W E have seen that the Parian Marble preserves the record of two distinct bearers of the royal title of Minos, one belonging to the fifteenth, the other to the thirteenth, century B.C., or, respectively, to the period of the supremacy and to the period of the subordination of Knossos. In Homer, Minos is compounded of myth, saga and tradition; and he is successively presented in the following ways:

Idomeneus boasts of his descent from Zeus, who made his son Minos the *epiouros* ('guardian', 'watcher') over Crete. Deukalion was the son of Minos, and Idomeneus himself the son of Deukalion, whom he succeeded as the *wanax* ('lord') over many men in spacious Crete.[1]

Zeus himself supplies further details of this pedigree when he refers to the far-famed daughter of Phoinix (Europa) who bore to him Minos and god-like Rhadamanthys.[2]

Among the heroines seen by Odysseus in Hades were 'Phaidra, Prokris and fair Ariadne, the daughter of ill-designing (*"oloophron"*) Minos, whom Theseus once upon a time tried to carry off from Crete to the fruitful land of sacred Athens, though he had no joy of her. For, before that could happen, Artemis killed her in sea-girt Dia, on the testimony of Dionysos.'[3]

Odysseus also saw Minos in person, here described as the 'splendid son of Zeus, seated, holding a golden sceptre, ordaining righteousness among the dead, who were sitting or standing around the lord (*"wanax"*), questioning him about their rights, within the wide gates of the House of Hades'.[4]

Crete is once referred to as the place of Minos' kin.[5] Finally, in

[1] *Il.* 13.449–52.
[2] *Il.* 14.321–2. On the mingling of Greek and Phoenician elements in Crete see pp. 152–68.
[3] *Od.* 11.321–5.
[4] *Od.* 11.568–72.
[5] *Od.* 17.523.

the passage already discussed, Minos is described as the *oaristes* ('familiar') of mighty Zeus.[6] If we bear in mind all that has been said concerning the development of the role of the 'priest-king', it seems clear that the conception of Minos as the *oaristes* of Zeus must precede the more common Homeric description of him as (in accordance with normal Achaean pedigree) the *son* of Zeus.[7]

With Idomeneus, however, the case is different and there is no element of uncertainty about his status. In his person the now subordinate, though by no means unimportant, role of Crete is fixed. The Achaean prince of Knossos, like other leaders of the Heroic Age, has a short pedigree which goes up to a god in the third generation before the Trojan War.[8] His first cousin, Aerope, is linked by marriage with the family of his great allies, the Atreidai. She married Atreus and was herself a granddaughter of Minos. This Minos of the Achaean pedigrees must be the 'second Minos', who headed the 'divine-born' dynasty of Knossos *c.* 1250 B.C.[9] Of the strife which accompanied the founding of the Achaean dynasty at Knossos there is perhaps an echo in the *Iliad*, where Idomeneus kills Phaistos, son of the Maionian Boros from Tarne.[10] For this Phaistos may well be the eponymous hero of the great Cretan city of that name, implying that a tradition of a Cretan battle has been transferred to Troy—with an appropriate Lydian pedigree for Phaistos.[11]

Phaistos is not the only 'Creto-Asiatic' opponent of Idomeneus. There is Asios, also from Lydia, and Othryoneus (a name from *othrys*, the Cretan word for a *hill*).[12] On the other hand, his opponents Oinomaos and Alkathoos have associations with Pelops and the Peloponnese. His father Deukalion has Thessalian associations. The implication is that he is a northerner by extraction, an intruder in Crete before he becomes an intruder at Troy.[13]

If, as seems likely, the armed might of the Achaean Empire was naturally estimated in terms of warships, which served equally as transports for fighting men, then the Cretan entry in the Catalogue of Ships[14] reveals the extent to which the considerable resources

---

[6] *Od.* 19.179. The significance of the use of the adjective Μινώϊος in *h. Ap.* 393 with reference to Knossos is discussed later. See. p. 262.

[7] Perhaps he became the *oaristes* of Zeus because he had formerly been the lover of the Mother-goddess. Cf. the use of ὀαρίζω in *Il.* 22.126–8.

[8] Cf. Myres WWG 308.   [9] Cf. p. 89.

[10] *Il.* 5.43 ff.   [11] Murray RGE 221; Nilsson HM 264.

[12] Hsch. s.v. ὄθρυν.   [13] Murray *ib.* 221.

[14] *Il.* 2.645–52.

of the island had now been exploited to the advantage of the Achaeans. For Idomeneus and Meriones head a contingent of no less than eighty ships (compared, for example, with the hundred ships under command of Agamemnon himself, the ninety under Nestor, the sixty under Menelaos, the twelve under Odysseus). Crete is described as having a hundred towns, of which seven are mentioned by name. They are Knossos, Gortyna, Lyktos, Miletos, Lykastos, Phaistos and Rhytion, all of them from central Crete, the principal area of Achaean occupation.[15] Hence, although they do not emerge as principal agents in the *Iliad*, the importance of the Cretan captains is clearly portrayed,[16] and bears a close relation with the contribution of Crete itself to the sum total of the armament of the expedition to Troy.

All this lends some plausibility to the traditions reported by Herodotos.[17] When the Cretans were approached to take part in the struggle against Persia, they sent for advice to Delphi. 'Fools!' replied the Pythoness, 'do you find anything to complain of in the woes brought upon you by Minos in his anger for the help you gave to Menelaos?' The cause of this anger was that the Cretans had helped the Achaeans to avenge the carrying-off of a woman from Sparta, although they had received no aid themselves to avenge the death of Minos at Kamikos.

Minos, according to tradition, continues Herodotos, went to Sicily in search of Daidalos and perished by violent death. After a time the Cretans (with the exception of the Polikhnites and the Praisians) made a great expedition to Sicily and besieged Kamikos for five years. Unsuccessful in their efforts, they called off the siege and departed. They had reached Iapygia on the voyage home when their ships were broken in pieces by a storm. Having no means of returning to Crete, they founded the town of Hyria and changed their name to Messapian Iapygians. After this disaster, according to Praisian (i.e. Eteocretan) tradition, Crete was stripped of inhabitants and people of various nations and— above all—Greeks, flocked there. Three generations after the death of Minos the Trojan War took place (Herodotos here agrees with the evidence of the Achaean pedigrees), and the Cretans were not the least distinguished among those who came to the aid of Menelaos. But, when they returned from Troy, men and cattle were destroyed by famine and pestilence. Crete was stripped of

---

[15] Cf. Lorimer 47.

[16] See e.g. *Il*. 4.250-71.

[17] Hdt. 7.169-71.

inhabitants for a second time. Only a remnant was left, who formed, with new settlers, the later inhabitants of the island. This third population was, presumably, the Dorian. The real substance of the remainder of this account is difficult to assess. There may be truth in the suggestion of conflict between Cretan and Achaean interests. It may also be not unlikely that the older 'Minoan' population was drastically reduced as a result of various expeditions overseas.[18]

As for information of a more general kind concerning Crete, the *Iliad* is less revealing than the *Odyssey*. Apart from the few passages mentioned already, with specific reference to Minos and Idomeneus, the only other passage of the *Iliad* which need concern us here is from the description of the Shield of Achilles, whose connexion with the traditions of the Labyrinth has already been mentioned.[19] Hephaistos, says Homer, 'wrought a dancing-floor like that which Daidalos once fashioned in spacious Knossos for Ariadne of the lovely hair. Youths and courted maidens were dancing on it, their hands on each other's wrists. The girls were wearing dresses of fine linen, the youths well-woven tunics with a faint gloss of oil; and the girls had lovely garlands, the youths golden daggers attached to their silver belts. Now they ran ever so lightly with cunning feet, as when a potter sits gripping his wheel with his hands and tries it out to see how it spins. Now again they ran in lines opposite to each other. A big crowd stood around enjoying the passionate dance; and two tumblers spun around in their midst setting the rhythm of the performance.'

It is likely, as we saw, that we have here a reference to the Labyrinth, perhaps to be identified with the Minoan 'Theatral Area', an *orchestra* or 'arena' designed for the performance of a mimetic dance.[20] It may have been worked out with mazy lines, to help the movements of the dancers, according to the practice known in later times.[21] The simile of the potter's wheel, turning now this way, now that way, in its trial runs, would be an apt illustration of the labyrinthine progress of the lines of dancers, rushing forward and then doubling back on their tracks, following the intricate course marked out for them on the dancing-floor.

---

[18] Cf. How and Wells *ad. loc.*   [19] *Il.* 18.590–606.
[20] Cook Z 1.479 ff.; Leaf ed. *Il.* 1 pp. 609–10; cf. p. 103.
[21] Cook *ib.* 479, citing Hsch. γραμμαί. ἐν τῇ ὀρχήστρᾳ ἦσαν, ὡς τὸν χορὸν ἐν στοίχῳ ἵστασθαι.

The dance is an accompaniment to some kind of pantomime or dramatic performance acted by the two tumblers.

The scholiast on the passage in question thought that the dance was at least not secular. He explains that Theseus, after escaping from the Labyrinth by means of Ariadne's clue, together with the rescued youths and maidens wove a circling dance for the gods that resembled his own entrance into and exit from the Labyrinth, Daidalos showing them how to dance it.[22] Lucian, too, describes as Cretan dance-themes 'Europa, Pasiphae, both the Bulls, the Labyrinth, Ariadne, Phaidra, Androgeos, Daidalos, Ikaros, Glaukos, the seer-craft of Polyidos, and Talos the bronze-sentinel of Crete'.[23]

A similar sort of dance was performed at Delos and is expressly associated by Plutarch with the same cycle of tradition. According to Plutarch,[24] when Theseus sailed away from Crete, he put in at Delos. He sacrificed to the god, dedicated the image of Aphrodite that he had received from Ariadne, and danced a dance with the young men which apparently still survived among the Delians. This dance imitated the circuits and exits of the Labyrinth by means of a certain measure involving turnings and returnings. It was called the Crane Dance,[25] and Theseus danced it round the Horned Altar.[26] It was also said that Theseus instituted a contest in Delos and was the first to award a palm to the victors.

This aspect of contest may serve to remind us that the youths and maidens who accompanied Theseus underwent an ordeal. After the ordeal Theseus married the king's daughter. This union may have signified the union of *kouros* and *koure*—pre-eminent youth and pre-eminent maiden. That the dance was in some sense designed as a prelude to marriage can be inferred from its description by Homer as *himeroeis* ('exciting desire'). It was a love-dance. Those who took part are expressly described as bachelors and virgins. The virgins moreover are *alphesiboiai* (translated above as *courted*, but properly signifying *yielding, bringing in oxen*). This

---

[22] Sch. A.B. *Il*. 18.590, cited by Cook *ib*. 481, who points out that Eust. (*ad Il*. 1166.17 ff.) adds that this was the first occasion on which men and women danced together, that Sophocles had referred to the 'dances of Knossos' (*Aj*. 700) and that old-fashioned people in his own time, especially sailors, performed a dance with many twists and turns intended to recall the windings of the Labyrinth.

[23] *Salt*. 49, cited by Cook *ibid*.   [24] *Thes*. 21.

[25] Cf. Poll. 4.101; Call *Del*. 312 f.

[26] On the association between bull and crane see Cook *ib*. 482.

epithet is sometimes understood as meaning maidens *who yield their parents many oxen as presents from their suitors*.[27] But the cattle are more likely to have been the wedding-gifts made to the bride by those of her own household and therefore of advantage not to her parents but to her suitors.[28] Female inheritance normally precedes the custom of the dowry, which represents the economic perquisite originally bestowed on her husband by a matrilocal wife. Female inheritance precedes the dowry in historical times in Crete, and matrilocal custom survives in a number of forms.[29] Both are likely to have been more marked in earlier times.

Since the custom of collective marriage was also perpetuated in Crete into the historical period,[30] and since, again, this custom is likely to have been more flourishing in earlier times than otherwise,[31] it is likely that Homer's Knossian dance was part of the ritual of such collective marriage, following upon the graduation of the youthful initiates from the *agela*, or its equivalent. Homer's dance has, in fact, been properly compared with the dance described by Lucian as the *hormos* ('ring-dance'), whose participants were *epheboi* and maidens.[32] The context indicates that the word *epheboi* is used, not of adolescents in the general sense, but in the technical sense of those undergoing ephebic training in the *agela*—dancing being as much studied as fighting under arms. This Spartan *hormos* is compared by Lucian with their choral dances dear to Dionysos and Aphrodite. That is why, he explains, the song they sing during such dances is an invocation of Aphrodite and the Loves, so that they may join their revels and dances. After describing the *hormos*, Lucian then refers to what Homer has to say about Ariadne, refraining from detailed discussion on the ground that the matter is already familiar to his readers. For Lucian the Spartan *hormos* and Ariadne's *choros* are love-dances. Elsewhere, too, performances of this kind are described as being regarded as incentives to marriage in Sparta in historical times. Now when Telemachos visits the palace of Menelaos in Sparta, the king is celebrating the double wedding of his son and daughter. On this

---

[27] L.S.J. s.v.

[28] LSJ s.v. ἕδνον. In *Od.* 1.277 and 2.196, οἱ δὲ γάμον τεύξουσι καὶ ἀρτυνέουσιν ἔεδνα, cannot be the suitors, but οἱ ἀμφὶ τὸν πατέρα, as Eust. explained.

[29] Willetts ASAC 99 *et passim*.   [30] Str. 10.482.

[31] For the evidence of change in the historical period see Willetts ASAC 8.

[32] *Salt.* 11: ὁ δὲ ὅρμος ὄρχησίς ἐστι κοινὴ ἐφήβων τε καὶ παρθένων κτλ. The comparison was made by Leaf *ad. loc.* Its validity is strengthened by the evidence of the Hsch. gloss: χορός· κύκλος, στέφανος, from which it is possible to infer that Homer's χορός was a floor on which the 'ring-dance' was performed. Cf. Plu. *Lyc.* 15.

occasion too the whirling tumblers dance in and out among the crowding guests; and the same descriptive formula is used of their performance in Sparta as in Crete.[33]

The first certain reference[34] to Crete in the *Odyssey* forms a grim corollary to what Herodotos has to say concerning the fate of those who returned from Troy.[35] According to Nestor, Idomeneus brought all his men back to Crete—all who escaped from war. The sea robbed him of none.

In answer to further inquiries from Telemachos concerning the fate of those who returned from Troy, Nestor later describes how it came about that Menelaos was absent when Agamemnon was murdered.[36] He and Menelaos were sailing together from Troy and had reached Sounion, the southern headland of Attica. Here Menelaos was detained, while Nestor continued his journey. His steersman, Phrontis, had died and had to be buried with the proper rites. Menelaos afterwards sailed away with his ships, but suffered mishap at the treacherous Cape Malia, the south-eastern promontory of Laconia. He ran into a gale so severe that he was obliged to divide his ships. Menelaos himself, with five ships, was driven by wind and wave to Egypt. The other ships made for Crete, or that part of it 'where the Kydonians lived, round about the waters of the Iardanos. At the border of Gortyna, in the murky sea, there is a smooth rock that runs sheer into the water, where the south wind thrusts the mighty swell upon the headland on the left, towards Phaistos, and a tiny stone wards off the mighty swell.' The details of this description, exact as they appear to be, are not easy to interpret. They are best discussed in conjunction with a later passage which is our main Homeric source for the ethnography of Crete.[37]

The Phaiacian episode of the *Odyssey* is constructed with delicate skill and haunting charm. Odysseus, it has been said, 'except at the court of Phaiacia, belongs to the realist school of fiction'.[38] The archaeological discoveries of the past half-century and more have taught us to be wary of the view that apparent lack of

---

[33] *Od.* 4.18–19.
[34] At *Od.* 1.93 (πέμψω δ'ἐς Σπάρτην τε καὶ ἐς Πύλον ἠμαθόεντα) there is, for Σπάρτην, the v.l. by Zenod. Κρήτην. Some MSS add after 93: Κεῖθεν δ'ἐς Κρήτην τε παρ' Ἰδομενῆα ἄνακτα· ὃς γὰρ δεύτατος ἦλθεν Ἀχαιῶν χαλκοχιτώνων. Cf. *ib.* 285: κεῖθεν δὲ Σπάρτηνδε παρὰ ξανθὸν Μενέλαον, where cf. Sch. HMQR on *Od.* 3.313, who says that Zenod. wrote: κεῖθεν δὲ Κρήτηνδε παρ' Ἰδομενῆα ἄνακτα.
[35] *Od.* 3.191.
[36] *Ib.* 276–300.
[37] P. 134.
[38] Lorimer 93.

realism may be due to the elaboration of boundless fancy.[39] The appearance of the Phaiacians in what may have been the earliest form of the *Odyssey* has been explained as based upon their ultimate identity with those familiar characters of folklore, the Ferrymen of the Dead. It is true that the magic ship of the Phaiacians brings Odysseus to his home wrapped in a sound, sweet sleep that is very like death.[40] But it does not necessarily follow that 'it is altogether appropriate that Odysseus as Eniautos Daimon should be ferried between the shores of Life and Death by mysterious Grey men'.[41] For it is also true that a very wakeful Odysseus has but recently returned from a visit to the underworld, where death is by no means presented as being like sound, sweet sleep, but rather as a nightmare travesty of mortal life. The image of death applied to the sleeping Odysseus is more proper, not to the traveller to the underworld, but rather to those Blessed Fields which seem to have belonged to Minoan folklore.

The Skheria of the Phaiacians can, in fact, be connected with Crete in one certain detail. Its king, Alkinoos, promises a safe return home for Odysseus even if that home be more remote than Euboia. Euboia, he explains, is said to be the farthest away of all places by those Phaiacians who travelled there with Rhadamanthys.[42] Rhadamanthys is certainly Minoan and Euboia would represent, for a Minoan, a known limit of his geographical world. It is then possible that Phaiacia represents the faded Minoan world imaginatively recalled.[43]

Unlike the normally isolated Homeric palace, the magnificent palace of Alkinoos, though conspicuously finer than other dwellings,[44] is built near to them.[45] Far from being isolated, it has to be approached by walking through the town. Its splendours are such, however, that even Odysseus hesitates in wonder before crossing its bronze threshold.

---

[39] Cf. Rhode *Psyche* 1.81 n. 2. [40] *Od.* 13.79.
[41] J. A. K. Thomson 97; cf. Welcker *Kl. Schr.* 2.1–79. [42] *Od.* 7.317–24.
[43] Frost JHS 33.189; Leaf 184; cf. Page, on the *Iliad*: '. . . these systems (of formular phrases) must be the product of a long process of poetic creation and selection, and it is within them that we should look for relics of the very remote past. . . . Poetry of this type was continuously composed and recited in Greece from (at latest) the fifteenth century B.C. onwards, the period of the boar's-tusk helmet and the shield of Ajax. It was from the beginning, and remained to the end, oral poetry, composed in the mind and preserved in the memory, without the aid of writing': Page 258–9. Cf. Thomson SAGS 1.418–20, 435–82.
[44] *Od.* 6.301. [45] *Ib.* 7.29.

'For a gleam, as of the sun or moon, played over the high-roofed dwelling of mighty Alkinoos. Bronze walls ran this way and that, from threshold to inmost part, with their coping of dark-blue enamel. Doors of gold confined the compact structure. Door-posts of silver stood in the bronze threshold, running up to a silver lintel; the door-handle too was of gold. Of gold and silver were the dogs on either side, forged by Hephaistos with a subtle skill, to guard the dwelling of mighty Alkinoos, deathless as they were, and ageless all their days. Inside, chairs were set around the wall, on this side and on that, from threshold through and through to inmost part; they were draped with lovely, fine-woven covers, work of the women. There sat the leaders of the Phaiacians, drinking and eating. They had an abundance. Of gold again were the youths standing on their well-built pedestals, with flaring torches grasped in their hands to give light for the guests about the halls by night.

'There are fifty bond-women of the household; some of them grind the apple-coloured corn in the mill, some weave at the loom or sit twisting the wool—just like leaves on a tall poplar—while soft olive-oil runs down off the close-woven cloth. Just as Phaiacian men surpass all others in their skill in driving a swift ship on the sea, in the same way their women excel at the loom. For Athene has endowed them with a ripe under-standing of works of beauty and has blessed them with fine minds.'[46]

Reminiscences of Egyptian, even Assyrian, prototypes have been considered as, in part at least, responsible for the admittedly foreign, Oriental splendours of this palace.[47] But Crete was, so to speak, the nearest available centre of the summary of such Oriental influences, the sharp point of contact with an older civilization with stable roots in the culture of the ancient East. The description of the palace of Alkinoos may then be an artistic memorial of this contact, preserved by the Homeric bards. This is not to deny that imagination has worked upon the original materials. In the same way, but probably to a lesser degree, the process of imaginative change has been detected at work upon the genealogy of Alkinoos and his wife Arete. For what appears to have been a marriage of brother and sister is presented in the form of marriage between uncle and niece. The familiar type of marriage according to the rules of patriarchal endogamy is

[46] *Ib.* 84–111.   [47] Lorimer 97, 429 and n. 1.

imposed upon a traditional, but unfamiliar, relationship sanctioned by the rules of matriarchal endogamy.[48]

Hence something more than a simple fiction may underlie the tale told by Odysseus to the disguised Pallas Athene when he wakes up on the soil of Ithaca after his voyage from the country of the Phaiacians.[49] He heard of Ithaca, he explains, even in spacious Crete, far away over the sea. Yet, if Phaiacia can in some sense be plausibly identified with Minoan Crete, the Crete that features in the tale that he proceeds to concoct is implicitly post-Minoan, where feuds and quarrels arising from a weakness of central authority can be imagined as part of the natural order of things. Odysseus represents himself as a petty chieftain who scorned to win the favour of Idomeneus by serving under him at Troy, but preferred to keep independent command over his own troops. The consequence was that Orsilokhos, son of Idomeneus, tried to rob him of the spoils he had won at Troy. In revenge, he and a friend had killed Orsilokhos from ambush. He had then decided to become a fugitive. Placing himself at the mercy of the crew of a Phoenician ship, he persuaded them to put him down in Pylos or Elis. Driven off their course, however, they had eventually put him down in Ithaca.

This story is of a piece with that other Odyssean travellers' tale with Cretan background which is a recurrent theme of the second half of the *Odyssey*.[50]

In its first version the tale is told by Odysseus to Eumaios, after he has left Pallas Athene.[51] He is a Cretan, he explains, and the son of a rich man and a concubine. His father, Kastor, son of Hylax, held him in the same regard as his many other, legitimate, sons. After the death of Kastor, his sons divided up his estate among themselves by lot and assigned only a meagre portion to the illegitimate son. Yet this did not prevent him from marrying into a well-endowed family—such were his natural gifts of intelligence and courage. Work he had not liked, nor the home-life that fosters a fine family. His real prowess showed itself in war; and his love was all for ships, battles, javelins and arrows—baneful things that made others tremble. Even before the Achaeans went to Troy he had nine times commanded expeditions against peoples overseas. His estate benefited from the great quantity of booty that came his way in consequence. He was both feared and

[48] Cf. Murray RGE 125–6.
[49] *Od.* 13.256–86.
[50] *Ib.* 14.199–359; 16.60–7; 17.512–27; 19.164–348.
[51] *Od.* 14.199–359.

respected among the Cretans. Hence, when the Trojan War did occur, he and Idomeneus were prevailed upon to lead the Cretan contingent.

After the sack of Troy in the tenth year of the war he returned to Crete. But, after only a month of the pleasures of home-life, he equipped a fleet to sail to Egypt. Arrived in Egypt, and before he had had time to make the proper reconnaissance he had planned, his men began to plunder farms, kill the men and carry off the women and children. The alarm was raised in the neighbouring city and the Cretan force was overwhelmed by superior numbers. Many of his men were killed, the rest enslaved. He himself surrendered to the king and his opponents, asked for mercy and was spared.

He then sojourned for seven years in Egypt, acquiring much wealth from the Egyptians. In the eighth year he made the acquaintance of a Phoenician who persuaded him to voyage home with him. After a year in Phoenicia his host took him on a ship bound for Libya, ostensibly as his partner but really intending to sell him for a large sum. When they had reached and passed by Crete on their voyage, the plot was foiled by a storm which wrecked the ship. The Cretan was the only survivor and was eventually cast up on the coast of Thesprotia. There he was hospitably received by the king, who later sent him away on a ship bound for Doulikhion, bidding the crew take care of him and escort him to the king of Doulikhion. But once at sea the crew planned to enslave him instead. On arriving at Ithaca they tied up their prisoner and left the ship to take their meal on the beach. The Cretan, however, managed to free himself, swam ashore, and lay in hiding until his captors gave up their search for him.

Eumaios accepts this story without question and briefly repeats its essentials, first to Telemachos and then to Penelope.[52] It features again at greater length when Penelope presses the still-disguised Odysseus to give a fuller account of himself. Complying with this request,[53] he introduces certain changes of detail into the account of his fictitious career, and also some actual details from the wanderings of the real Odysseus, including mention of the visit to Phaiacia. His name, he says, is Aithon, younger brother of Idomeneus, son of Deukalion, grandson of Minos. Odysseus had put in at Amnisos (the harbour of Knossos) some nine or ten days after Idomeneus had left for Troy. To him, therefore, fell the

---

[52] *Od.* 16.60–7; 17.512–27. [53] *Od.* 19.164–348.

responsibility of entertaining Odysseus. He had by no means lacked the resources of ample hospitality for his guest in his own household. The followers of Odysseus had been well provided for by a levy of corn, wine and cattle from among the people.[54]

The changes of detail in this yarn of the wandering Cretan are of less concern than the unchanging substance. Disguised Odysseus represents himself as a prominent Cretan chief, in some kind of relationship with, and subordinate to, Idomeneus, the Achaean with the conventional short pedigree of three generations before the Trojan War. Raiding and piracy are natural means of adding to the wealth acquired from landed estates; and generally unsettled conditions apply not only in a Crete prone to rivalry and vendetta, but also overseas, where the freebooter may be kidnapped and sold into servitude, or, in different circumstances, with luck and determination acquire fortune. The hero of this fiction has had much practice in raiding before the Trojan War. He is in fact the kind of person who is likely to have been a common enough type in the age of the Aegean sea-raiders who actually harassed Egypt and other centres in the decades of the twelfth century B.C. which preceded the Trojan War.[55] Eumaios, the swineherd, had good reason to know the times and the type and to listen with sympathy to the account of the supposed Cretan's wanderings. For he had himself been kidnapped from his father's palace and eventually sold to Laertes, the father of Odysseus.[56]

Crete itself, says Odysseus to Penelope, by way of prelude to his story, is 'fair and fertile, sea-girt. Therein are many men, countless men, and ninety cities. They have a mixture of languages. For there are Achaeans, stout-hearted Eteocretans, Kydonians, Dorians with their three tribes, god-like Pelasgians. There too is Knossos, a mighty city, where Minos used to be king for nine years, a familiar of mighty Zeus.'[57]

To what extent can these details of Cretan ethnography be plausibly assigned to the early decades of the twelfth century, in

---

[54] δημόθεν ἄλφιτα δῶκα καὶ αἴθοπα οἶνον ἀγείρας/καὶ βοῦς ἱρεύσασθαι, ἵνα πλησαίατο θυμόν, *ib.* 197–8. This reference to a tribute system is paralleled by the reference to the levy on the Phaiacian people proposed by Alkinoos to defray the expense of the presents given to Odysseus on his departure from Phaiacia: ἡμεῖς δ᾽ αὖτε ἀγειρόμενοι κατὰ δῆμον/τισόμεθ᾽. *ib.* 13.14–15. Δημόθεν is found only here in Homer; but cf. A.R.1. 7.

[55] Myres WWG 123, 131.   [56] *Od.* 15.403–84.

[57] *Od.* 19.172–9.

the same way as we have attempted to assign the social conditions inherent in the fiction of the Cretan adventurer to the same period?

Evans[58] took the view that the name of Idomeneus, the Achaean leader, seems to point to early settlement in the land round Ida; and that the account of the Achaean dominion over central Crete, according to the Catalogue of Ships in the *Iliad*[59] (which need not exclude the participation of other Hellenic elements such as the Dorian), seems to offer a real glimpse of historic conditions in Crete at the beginning of the Iron Age. On the other hand, he argued, the endeavour to annex Minos and to thrust back Achaean or Dorian dominion in Crete into the glorious days of Minoan history was but part of a process of which other traces are perceptible. One such trace he found, following Beloch,[60] to be supplied by an interpolation in the passage of the *Odyssey* cited above. 'The interpolator—regardless of the order of composition or even of the most obvious grammatical requirements—has broken into the sentence "Ninety cities and among them Knossos" to insert a brief summary of the later ethnography of the island—including an allusion to the three Dorian tribes.'

Lorimer,[61] however, agreeing that the Cretan entry in the Catalogue contains nothing which suggests interpolation, found the Crete mirrored in the Catalogue's selection from her hundred towns to be the Crete of the Achaean occupation in LH III. The situation of these seven towns of central Crete is the region which contains the road that links the ports of her northern and southern coasts. That it was occupied by the Achaeans is plain from the lines in the *Odyssey* (mentioning Achaeans, Eteocretans and Kydonians) which give the main division into centre, east and west.[62] 'They are not necessarily interpolated as 177 certainly is, but even if they are, their evidence is none the worse for that.' (Line 177 contains the reference to Dorians and Pelasgians.)[63]

The interpolation—to quote Evans[64]—'recently exposed by Professor Beloch, but which, when once attention has been called to it, must command general recognition', now commands, owing to the advance in our knowledge since Evans wrote, much less general recognition. Until we know far more about the early

---

[58] Evans PM 1.10–12.
[59] Cf. pp. 27–8.
[60] *Origini Cretesi. Ausonia* 4 (1910) 220–1.
[61] Lorimer 47.
[62] *Od.* 19.175–6: ἐν μὲν ᾿Αχαιοί, ἐν δ᾿Ετεόκρητες μεγαλήτορες, ἐν δὲ Κύδωνες.
[63] *Ib.* 177: Δωριέες τε τριχάϊκες δῖοί τε Πελασγοί.
[64] PM 1.12.

Dorian occupation both of Crete and the mainland, it would perhaps be wiser to withhold even partial recognition. But this is not to deny that the mention of the Dorians in the passage causes most difficulty.

No difficulty is now presented by the mention of the Achaeans, and of their dominion over central Crete. In this respect at least Strabo's views accord with the modern.[65] For, when commenting upon the *Odyssey* passage, Strabo cites Staphylos to the effect that the Dorians occupied the part towards the east, the Kydonians the western part, the Eteocretans the southern—whereas the other peoples, since they were more powerful, lived in the plains. It is likely, he continues, that the Eteocretans and the Kydonians were autochthonous, and the others (i.e. the Dorians, since he singles out these three peoples for special comment) were foreigners, who, according to Andron, came from Thessaly, from the country which in earlier times was called Doris.

We can undoubtedly infer from Strabo that the Eteocretans represented the now reduced elements of the earlier pre-Greek inhabitants of Crete.[66] He tells us, moreover, that the town of Praisos (in the centre of the eastern tip of the island) belonged to them. It seems that the Praisians preserved their separate language at least until the third century B.C. For we have a number of inscriptions from Praisos in which the 'Eteocretan' language is written in the Greek alphabet.[67] Their decipherment could possibly help us to gain a clearer conception of that common non-Greek tongue which was once spoken in Greece, Crete, the other islands and (in a different form) in the south-west of Asia Minor.[68] It is furthermore clear from what Herodotos has to tell of the Praisians[69] that their links with the old Minoan stock were close. They may thus represent a remarkable survival into the late historical period of that Cretan affinity with Asia Minor which is a major characteristic of Cretan institutions in the Bronze Age.[70]

The Kydonia (modern Khania) of historical times was situated on the north-west coast, facing the Peloponnese.[71] Its eponymous hero was one Kydon.[72] But the Kydonians had an older history than this hero; and indeed much older than that foundation of the city by Samians in 524 B.C. which is reported by Herodotos, with

[65] 10.475.   [66] Cf. Nilsson HM 67.
[67] Guarducci IC 3.VI.1–6; cf. *Rev. Phil.* (1946) 131–8.
[68] Cf. Lorimer 1–3.   [69] Hdt. 7.170.
[70] Cf. Guarducci IC 3 p. 135.   [71] Str. 10.479; Guarducci IC 2 p. 104.
[72] Paus. 8.33.4.

the further information that these Samians were reduced to slavery after a period of five years.[73] The name of the people, rather than the name of the city, is likely to have been applied to the quince which has an early and continuous place in literature.[74] The later prominence of the people is indicated by the use of their name as an ethnic synonym for Cretan.[75] Their earlier importance is emphasized by Strabo, and confirmed by Homer.

According to Strabo, the greatest and most famous of the Cretan cities were Knossos, Gortyna and Kydonia.[76] Minos—presumably the second, 'Achaean', Minos of tradition—gained the mastery of the sea, divided the island into three parts and founded a city in each part: Knossos in that region of the island facing towards Asia, Phaistos on the sea, turned towards the south, Kydonia in the western part.[77] Both Kydonia and Knossos lie to the north.

The fame and importance of Knossos do extend, of course, continuously from Minoan times throughout the historical period. The importance of Phaistos declines after Minoan times and becomes subordinate to that of Gortyna in the historical period. Mycenaean remains have been found at Kydonia,[78] and the Homeric record agrees with this impression of the early significance, if not of Kydonia, certainly of the Kydonians, in the west.

The place where disaster overtook the ships belonging to Menelaos is, as we have seen, exactly described.[79] Though certain details of this description have long been disputed, it seems probable that the wreck occurred outside the port of Komo, at the terminus of the great road running southwards from Knossos, through which trade passed to and from Egypt in the Bronze Age.[80] It appears from the description that the port was situated in the territory of the Kydonians, but was also near the fringe of Gortynian territory. Phaistos, Gortyna's eastern neighbour, is also mentioned. But it can be inferred that Gortyna was now, as compared with Minoan times, both more extensive and more important.

[73] Hdt. 3.59.

[74] Stesich. 29, cf. Alcm. 143; Canthar. 6; Phylarch. 10 J; Ibyc. 1.1; Dsc. 1.115.

[75] Call. *Dian.* 81, 197; *id. Jov.* 45; Theoc. 7.12; Verg. *A.* 12.858; Nonn. *D.* 8.119, 13.226, 47.298, cf. 33.374.

[76] Str. 10.476.

[77] *Ibid.*, supplied from D.S. 5.78. Cf. IG 5.444.21 f.

[78] Guarducci *ad* IC 2.104.   [79] *Od.* 3.276–300. See p. 126.

[80] Lorimer 93. Cf. Evans PM 2.86; Pendlebury *Aegyptiaca* xviii–xix; Wainwright JHS 52.127.

Historical Kydonia lay on the north-west coast. But the ships were running along the south coast when they were wrecked. The Kydonians therefore must be supposed as occupying the whole breadth of the western part of the island, including the south coast as far as the cape on which Komo was situated, and which was also the border fringe of Gortyna. They are described as living round about the 'streams of the Iardanos'. This river cannot be identified with certainty.[81] There was a river of the same name in Elis, according to the *Iliad*.[82] The identity of names may indicate close relations in Achaean times between western Crete and the Peloponnese,[83] and, if the *Iliad* passage is genuine,[84] we must suppose that the name was brought from Crete to the Peloponnese. For this name appears to be Semitic, that is, equivalent to 'Jordan'.[85] If that is the case, we have some confirmation of the non-Greek origin of the Kydonians, implied in Strabo's account. At the same time we should note that both Homer and Strabo distinguish Kydonians from Eteocretans. Though, for Strabo, both were autochthonous, these Kydonians who had spread over western Crete in Achaean times may have derived from Bronze Age immigrants from Asia Minor, who were, however, of a rather different and later ethnic stratum than the Eteocretans.[86]

Of the presence of Pelasgians in Crete we have independent testimony from the mention of their characteristic place-name, Larisa. According to Strabo, Cretan Larisa was absorbed by Hierapytna.[87] There was a tradition that Gortyna had, at one time, been called Larisa.[88] Apart from Crete, the name is found in several parts of Thessaly, Attica, Argolis, Elis, the Troad, Aiolis and Lydia.[89] Judging from survivals in his own time, Herodotos concluded that the Pelasgian language was not Greek.[90] The Pelasgians themselves seem to have been closely related to Lydians and to Etruscans.[91] The languages of all three peoples

---

[81] Guarducci *ad* IC 2.106; cf. Malten in RE. s.v. Iardanos.

[82] *Il.* 7.135; cf. Paus. 5.5.9.   [83] Cf. Guarducci *ad* IC 2.106.

[84] See Leaf *ad loc.*

[85] 'Yardēn' from yārad, 'to flow'. Leaf *ad Il.* 7.133.

[86] See further pp. 156-8. Cf., however, Beloch GG 1.1.99 n. 1, *Ausonia* 4.221. Also Meyer 1.2.505, 514; Bürchner in RE s.v. Κύδωνες.

[87] Str. 9.440.   [88] St. Byz. s.v. Γόρτυν.

[89] *Il.* 2.841; Str. 9.430, 440, 13.620-1; Paus. 2.24.1, 7.17.5. According to Paus. (2.24.1) Larisa was a daughter of Pelasgos. Larisa Kremaste was also known as Pelasgia (Str. 9.435).

[90] 1.57.

[91] Hdt. 1.57, 94; Th. 4.109; Str. 5.221; A. *Supp.* 246-7, *Pr.* 860; Hecat. *fr.* 334.

were probably similarly related.[92] The main provenance of the Pelasgians was the north Aegean, particularly the Macedonian coast, the islands of Samothraike, Lemnos and Imbros. They can be traced through the Hellespont and Propontis along the north coast of Anatolia.[93] They may therefore have derived ultimately from the far side of the Black Sea. There is some possibility that they did not arrive in Crete before the beginning of the second millennium B.C.[94]

If then we are to admit that the population of Crete could have included, by the early part of the twelfth century, Achaeans, Eteocretans, Kydonians and Pelasgians, can we exclude the Dorians? If we do not, we are merely admitting the possibility that some explanation may yet be found for their presence at this early period. Meantime, conjecture is not bound to start from the unlikely premise that the original Dorians were a Cretan people.[95]

The problem is complicated, if only for the simple reason that Homer presents us with a picture of a pre-Dorian Greece. Dorians are admitted alongside the Achaeans only in Crete. Homer's consistency can be preserved entirely if we banish Dorians from Crete on grounds of later interpolation. But this solution, we have seen, is not so easy as it was.

The Dorian migration into southern Greece occurred at the end of the second millennium B.C. The fall of Mycenae, coinciding with the collapse of the Achaean hegemony, presumably under pressure from the Dorians, has been dated, with some confidence, to the last third of the twelfth century.[96] It was the habit of the Dorians, as Nilsson observed, to possess 'themselves only of provinces and islands already inhabited by Greeks, and . . . in contrast to the earlier invasions, they did not conquer land inhabited by an earlier indigenous population'.[97] Can we suppose that, upwards of a century before they achieved dominance in their mainland areas, a contingent of Dorians had followed the Achaeans into Crete?

The possibility is not entirely without ancient authority.

[92] Cortsen DLI; Kretschmer SLS 28.108; R. S. Conway in CAH 4.408.
[93] Myres WWG 96.
[94] If the so-called 'Minyan ware' did reach Greece from Troy and was developed in Thessaly and central Greece by immigrants from north-west Anatolia who may have been Pelasgoi; Forsdyke PMW; Heurtley PM 118–23; Thomson SAGS 1.193, 278, 375.
[95] Leaf 331.   [96] Lorimer 39.
[97] HM 239.

According to Diodoros,[98] Tektamos, son of Doros, came from Thessaly, with Aiolians and Pelasgians, and founded a new regime in Crete. Myres, who stressed the importance of this pedigree, placed Tektamos in the generation of 1330 B.C.[99] Strabo too, after stating his view that the Eteocretans and Kydonians were autochthonous, goes on to consider Andron's statement that the others (i.e. the Dorians) were foreigners who came from Thessaly, from the country which in earlier times was called Doris.[100]

The references to Crete in the Homeric Hymns[101] have a special value for the understanding of Cretan cults. They cannot profitably be discussed in isolation at this stage. The purpose of this survey of the Homeric evidence will have been served if it has focused attention on its special significance for establishing a partial—even though often problematic—picture of Crete in an age of transition. It can at least be said in conclusion that this record confirms that of Herodotos in portraying a period of hazard and stress, of an intermingling of peoples. The consequences in terms of cult practice remain to be assessed in what follows.

[98] 4.60.2.
[99] Myres WWG 346, adding: 'What is significant is the tradition that a "son of Dorus" was concerned in an otherwise Aeolian aggression in Crete, contemporary with Aeolian aggression in Lesbos.'
[100] Str. 10.475. Cf. Hdt. 1.56.
[101] *h.Cer.* 123; *h.Ap.* 30, 393, 463, 470, 517–18, 525.

Part Two

TRANSITION AND CONTINUITY

"Ὅμως αὐτοὶ εἶναι θεοί, καὶ κατοικοῦν ἀπ' ὅπου
Βλέπουνε μὲς τὴν ἄβυσσο καὶ στὴν καρδιὰ τ'ἀνθρώπου,
Κ'ἔνοιωθα πὼς μοῦ διάβαζε καλύτερα τὸ νοῦ μου
Πάρεξ ἂν ἤθελα τῆς πῶ μὲ θλίψη του χειλιοῦ μου.

SOLOMOS

CHAPTER 5

The Caves

IN any inquiry into the elements of continuity which can be traced in religious cult, despite repeated modifications in the process of transition from more archaic to later forms, the evidence supplied by caves and rock shelters offers an obvious starting-point. Although the links between the traditions of the earliest inhabitants of Crete and those of the palaeolithic hunters, which are so intimately associated with cave-cults, must remain conjectural, the caves of Crete have yielded much evidence of their sacred character from neolithic times until the historical period.[1] So much so that it has been inferred that the cave-cult of Minoan divinities was the chief characteristic of popular religion.[2] It is agreed that, in Crete as elsewhere in Europe, the use of caves as sanctuaries must have depended upon the original use of cave-mouths and rock shelters as places of human habitation.[3] The Cretan archaeological record confirms the Greek tradition[4] that caves were both the earliest shrines and the earliest homes of men. The dead were often buried in caves used as dwelling-places and this practice continued after the people had moved to huts and houses.[5] Alternatively, it prompted the custom of burying the dead beneath the floor of the house, a custom which persisted in Greece to late Mycenaean times.[6] The cave of Miamu well illustrates this process of development from dwelling to burial-place.[7] Below the burial stratum (indicated by human bones and vase fragments) an intermediate layer

[1] Cf. p. 59. On recent surveys of Cretan caves see the important articles by P. Faure in BCH 80.95–103, 82.495–515, 84.189–220.
[2] Marinatos 130; Nilsson MMR 56 n. 11.
[3] Hawkes 36–7; Nilsson MMR 56.   [4] Porph. *Antr.* 20; Ps. Luc. *Am.* 34.
[5] Hawkes 126, 130, 172–3, 261, 309; Childe DEC 4, 6, 17, 23, 61, 214, 222, 226, 235, 260, 270, 293, 300, 302; Nilsson MMR 53; Faure BCH 80 *passim*.
[6] Nilsson *ibid.* n. 1. Cf. ABSA 6.77; Pl. *Min.* 315d.
[7] Taramelli in AJA 1.287, cf. MA 9.301; Nilsson MMR 53.

of hardened earth and stones indicated some lapse of time before the cave was used for burials after it had been abandoned by the human families whose lengthy occupation was attested by an extensive lower deposit. This contained several hearths at different levels; fragments of charcoal; animal bones; claws of crabs and lobsters; bone implements; a hand-mill; and fragments of pottery, indicating occupation in subneolithic (EM I) times.

Human remains were found in a cave near Praisos together with fragments of pottery from the neolithic to the Geometric period.[8] In another, near Zakro, were five graves, with vases mostly dating from EM I; and human remains with hand-made vases of neolithic (or a little later) date were found in a cavern and in two rock shelters near Palaikastro.[9] Other rock shelters and caves yielding evidence of habitation or burial practices, in neolithic or Minoan times, have been found at Magasa, near Gournia, Hierapytna and in the Lasithi plain.[10] The cave at Pyrgos, north-east of Knossos, with hundreds of interments, warrants special mention.[11] It contained stone idols, bronze daggers and other bronze objects, obsidian flakes and more than 150 vases from the whole of the Early Minoan period. There is clear evidence that both caves and rock shelters continued to be used for burial purposes into Late Minoan times.[12]

Many caves have yielded evidence, in the form of votive offerings, of their use as shrines. The natural cavern near the southern summit of Mount Juktas contained terracotta figures of animals and fragments of pottery.[13] What Evans assumed to be the sacred cave of Knossos (at Skoteino, west of the palace) has winding galleries and broken stalagmite columns. It contained many Middle Minoan sherds and at least one fine double-axe.[14] The cave at Phaneromeni,[15] among the foothills of Lasithi, continued in use until Roman times. In addition to Hellenistic and Roman pottery and lamps, bronze statuettes of Geometric style, together with Geometric and Orientalizing pottery, have been found. In the forepart of the cave Minoan objects were discovered (none of them earlier than LM I) and some bronze statuettes of wor-

---

[8] ABSA 8.235.   [9] ABSA 9.339.
[10] ABSA 11.260; AJA 40.371; ABSA 36.13, 38.6, 9, 14; JHS 47.140.
[11] Evans PM 1.59; Xanthoudides, 'Αρχ. Δελτ. 4.136.
[12] ABSA 11.293, 12.1; 'Αρχ. Δελτ. 4. Appx. 2.17.
[13] Taramelli MA 9.356; Cook Z 1.160.
[14] Evans PM 1.163; AJA 5.442; Faure BCH 80.96, 82.508–11; cf. p. 180 n. 268.
[15] BCH 61.475; JHS 57.139; Arch. Anz. 222 and fig. 324.

shippers, probably post-Minoan. The cave at Arkalokhori,[16] near Lyttos, was used from Early Minoan until at least the end of the Minoan period. It has yielded a great quantity of votive double-axes, of gold and of silver, knives, swords and other objects. It was clearly an important cult centre.

The cave of Eileithyia at Amnisos, the ancient harbour of Knossos, is mentioned in the *Odyssey*.[17] A cave near the river Karteros, four miles east of Herakleion, was identified in the last century as that of Eileithyia.[18] This identification was confirmed by the exploration of Marinatos,[19] who found much pottery, especially neolithic pottery, but also from all Minoan and later periods. The evidence pointed to the conclusion that there was a revival of the cult in Roman times, since late Roman and also Christian lamps were found.[20]

The name of Mount Ida, like that of other mountain-names, means 'forest', 'wood'.[21] Its cypresses and oak-trees were well known.[22] The mountain was said to see the sun before the sunrise.[23] Naturally it became associated with Zeus. But this association followed upon an earlier Minoan association with a goddess. Such, apparently, is the conclusion to be drawn from the evidence of the exploration of the oldest cult-cave on the mountain. Known locally as Maurospelaion, this cave, on the southern summit facing Phaistos, is now familiar as the cave of Kamares, the name given to the pottery first found there. Explored by Taramelli in 1894,[24] it was excavated by the British School in 1913.[25] Objects discovered included two neolithic sherds, one Early Minoan vase and a few sherds, many fine pieces of Middle Minoan ware and a few Late Minoan specimens. Among the pottery in one place was a mass of what appeared to be the remains of wheat or other grain. Bronze votive objects familiar from similar sites were not found. Yet the cave must have been a

---

[16] ABSA 19.35; Evans PM 1.59, 4.846; *Arch. Anz.* (1934) 252 and fig. 3, (1935) 245, 249 and figs. 3–5; AJA 39.134 and figs. 5–6 and pl. xxiv; *Praktika* (1935) 212 and figs. 12–20; Nilsson MMR 60–1, 74, 197, 459–60.

[17] *Od.* 19.188.

[18] Hazzidakis in *Parnossos* 10 (1886–7) 349; Halbherr in *Antiquary* 27 (1893) 112.

[19] *Praktika* (1929) 94, (1930) 91; cf. BCH 53.520 n. 5, *Arch. Anz.* (1930) 156.

[20] Cf. Hirschfeld in R.E. s.v. Amnisos; Nilsson MMR 58; Guarducci IC 1.2.

[21] Boisacq s.v.; Cook Z 2.932.

[22] Thphr. *H.P.* 3.2.3, 4.1.3; Nic. *Ther.* 585; Verg. *Georg.* 2.84; Pl. *NH* 16.142; D.P. 503.

[23] Solin. 11.6; Prisc. *Per.* 527 f.   [24] AJA 5.437–51.

[25] ABSA 19. 1–34.

sanctuary rather than a dwelling, since it is blocked by snow for a good part of the year. The inference is therefore that only vases and perhaps grain were deposited as offerings in the cave, which, little frequented in Late Minoan times, flourished as a cult-centre in the Middle Minoan period. Hence there is no ground for connecting this cave with Zeus, as Taramelli supposed. It must have been sacred to the Minoan goddess, more specifically, as Cook argued, the mountain-goddess Rhea.[26]

At the time that the cave of Kamares was ceasing to be used as a sanctuary, the famous cave of Zeus below the summit of Mount Ida began to be frequented. This Idaian cave[27] was systematically explored in 1885.[28] On the south side of the entry is a large fallen rock shaped into an altar. In front of the cave many objects of bronze, silver and gold were discovered. Below it are the foundations of a Roman house which belonged to the custodians of the sanctuary. In addition to the entrance, the cave further consists of two chambers. The first, and larger, contained patches of black carbonized matter and here were found most of the plate-bronze objects. The floor of the second, and very dark, chamber was covered to a depth of several feet with a layer of ashes and charcoal, where fragments of half-burnt animal bones were found, together with several ox-skulls with horns attached and many terracotta lamps.

Votive objects discovered included convex circular shields of thin bronze, with central bosses representing a lion's head, an eagle, a hawk and so on; a bronze drum with Assyrianized representation of Zeus and the Kouretes; bronze cymbals, bowls, vessels for pouring wine, and basins; archaic groups in cast bronze, such as a warship with rowers, chariots, warriors, hounds, a man milking a cow; bronze votive animals, such as bulls and goats, and ornamental figures such as sphinxes, doves, snakes, a horse and a lion; objects in terracotta and iron arrow-heads and lance-heads. Thus Zeus was worshipped on Ida for more than a thousand years, well into Roman times. A hitherto unknown part of the cave, recently explored, may have been the centre of a secret cult, associated with initiation.[29]

---

[26] Cook Z 2.934; Nilsson MMR 65–7, 73, 458.

[27] Cook Z 2.935–9; Nilsson MMR 64–5, 458, 461, 514 n. 17, 534 n. 3, 578; Guarducci IC 1.96; JHS 77 (Sup.) 23.

[28] Halbherr in *Mus. It.* 2.689–768; Orsi *ib.* 769–904. Cf. Fabricius in AM 10.59–72, 280 f.; Frothingham in AJA 4.431–49; Thiersch in *Arch. Anz.* (1913) 47–53; Bürchner in R.E. s.v.v. Ida, Idaion.

[29] Faure in BCH 80.97.

The cave of Psychro,[30] near Lyttos, was partially explored by Halbherr and Hazzidakis in 1886,[31] by Evans and Myres in 1894–6,[32] by Demargne in 1897,[33] and fully by Hogarth in 1899–1900.[34] It was at first assumed that this cave of Psychro was the Diktaian Cave,[35] but this assumption was later refuted.[36]

This cave has an upper chamber and a steep slope of about 200 feet which leads down to a pool and a series of stalactite halls. There was a structure like an altar three feet high, built of roughly squared stones, round which were fragments of libation-tables, including one of steatite inscribed with three linear signs; and also small cups, fragments of fruit-stand vases, lamps and ashes. In the top strata of this upper chamber were found swords, knives, axes, and bracelets of iron, together with early Hellenic pottery. In the lower strata were objects chiefly of bronze. These included a model of a two-wheeled cart drawn by an ox and a ram, intended to carry at least one small figurine; images of bulls, knives, ornaments; earthenware cups for food or incense; a small mask of clay, with its lips, eyelids and lashes painted with ochre. A paved *temenos*, surrounded by a wall, produced many sherds of Minoan pottery and the remains of animal sacrifices—the skulls and bones of oxen, wild goats, sheep, deer, swine and dogs. Bronze statuettes, male and female, nude and clothed, were recovered from the pool. They had arms folded across the chest or one hand raised in a gesture of adoration. In the crevices of the stalactite columns were many votive bronzes, including double-axes.

The cave of Psychro was frequented from the Middle Minoan until the Geometric period; and the cult there practised was most flourishing in the Late Minoan period. Presumably this was a cult of the Minoan goddess in one of her familiar forms. One of the most important objects recovered from the cave is a bronze votive tablet (perhaps belonging to LM I) which represents a cult scene, apparently that of a goddess closely associated with the sacred tree. A votary stands on the right, with the tree in the middle and the sun's orb and the moon sickle at the upper edge. A pair of horns of consecration is in the left corner with a bough between

---

[30] Cook Z 2.925–7; Nilsson MMR 61–4, 73, 458–60 *et passim*; Guarducci IC 1.1.
[31] Halbherr-Orsi in *Mus. It.* 2.905–10; Taramelli MA 9.411.
[32] Evans JHS 17.350–61.   [33] Evans PM 1.629.
[34] ABSA 6.94–116. Cf. Boardman 1 ff.   [35] See p. 215.
[36] Aly 47; Beloch K 11.435; Toutain RHR 64.277–91.

them. On this bough is perched a bird, a ring-dove, to represent the epiphany of the goddess.

Another sacred cave of Mount Ida, near the village of Patso, is of special interest.[37] An inscription of *c.* first century B.C. indicates that it was, in historical times, sacred to Hermes Kranaios.[38] Besides this inscription, Greek votive objects have been found. But other objects indicate that the cave had also been a centre of Minoan cult. These include human and animal figurines, of bronze and terracotta, and three small terracotta birds. Some of the figurines are painted in the last Minoan style. One human head had a peculiar headdress. Two pairs of horns of consecration were also found.

In the Tallaian range, between Axos and the sea, there is a stalactite cave at Melidoni, where Hermes was worshipped in historical times.[39] The epithet Talaios or Tallaios was certainly applied to Zeus. Whether Hermes was worshipped under that same title in this region is, as we shall see,[40] not clear from the available evidence.

Human remains and sherds of neolithic pottery have been found in a cave in the western part of Crete, on the peninsula of Diktynnaion;[41] and also at Hellenospelio farther south.[42] Faure's recent survey has added to our knowledge of the topography of the west and its caves from Minoan times onward.[43]

It must be conceded that this evidence provides us with scanty information concerning the actual cults of the caves and the deities worshipped there. Nor can the continuity of a single cult in a particular place be demonstrated except in a few instances.[44] But this concession must be set beside the clear proof that, from the earliest times until the Roman period, strong religious associations endured at such sites. When new deities superseded older ones, the new cults must have incorporated traditions firmly established in the Bronze Age, and to that extent must have modified Cretan religion of the historical period in specific forms. The evidence of continuity drawn from other sources—idols, cult objects and

[37] Halbherr *Mus. It.* 2.913; Nilsson MMR 67, 335, 460; Guarducci IC 2.102; Faure in BCH 80.98.
[38] Guarducci *ibid.*; see further p. 289.
[39] Guarducci IC 2.302; Cook Z 2.948; Pashley 1.126 ff.; Faure *ibid.*
[40] P. 249. [41] Nilsson MMR 67.
[42] Faure in BCH 80.99. [43] BCH 84.202–20.
[44] Cf. Nilsson MMR 458, 462. One particularly interesting instance, relating to the cult of Artemis, will be discussed later, p. 275.

buildings—strengthens this assumption.[45] But the most certain proofs of the interrelation between transition and continuity from the Bronze Age until the historical period are to be found in the evidence relating to certain Cretan goddesses and also in the traditions of an infant god.

[45] Cf. Nilsson *ib.* 447–57; Alexiou KK (1950) 441–62; Platon *ib.* (1954) 428–83.

CHAPTER 6

The Cretan Goddesses

I N this chapter will be discussed those goddesses who, though
they may not all be restricted to Crete, yet have specific
Cretan associations of prehistoric origin. They must therefore
be distinguished in various respects from the conventional
goddesses of the later Olympian pantheon—even though some of
these too have their Minoan roots.

I. DEMETER

As has been mentioned already, Demeter is said to have reached
Greece from Crete,[1] and again, in our oldest literary authority, the
sacred marriage is restricted to Crete, in the form of the myth of
Demeter and Iasion.[2] The sacred marriage is an inherent part of
the vegetation cycle, of the death and revival of the crops, and
Cretan Demeter thus had associations in common with the
Oriental rituals of Magna Mater and Attis, Ishtar and Tammuz,
Aphrodite and Adonis.[3] Through Triptolemos she instructed
mankind in the art of agriculture.[4]

In historical times her cult was not restricted to any particular
region of Crete. For in western Crete she was worshipped at
Axos,[5] at Hyrtakina,[6] and perhaps also at Kydonia;[7] in central
Crete at Knossos,[8] at Gortyna[9] and perhaps also at Rhaukos;[10] in
eastern Crete at Hierapytna.[11]

---

[1] *h. Cer.* 123; p. 20. [2] Homer *Od.* 5.125–8; p. 113.
[3] Persson RGPT *passim*; Nilsson MMR 403. [4] P. 20.
[5] Petrulakis 'Αρχ. 'Εφ. (1915) 43 ff.; Guarducci IC 2. pp. 42, 47.
[6] Guarducci *ib.* 184–5. [7] Guarducci *ib.* 113–14.
[8] Guarducci IC 1. p. 54 and VIII.16 (*c.* first century B.C.). Cf. Halbherr *Mus. It.*
3.683 f. n. 114.
[9] Guarducci IC 4. p. 13 and p. 45 *ad* 3.3 (a–c), seventh–sixth century B.C.
[10] Guarducci IC 1. p. 291.
[11] Guarducci IC 3. p. 23 and III.12 (first century B.C. or first century A.D.).

At Hierapytna, either in the first century B.C. or in the first century A.D., after some calamity which had befallen the city, a girl made a dedication to Demeter and to Persephone, who is called the 'Maid'.[12] The title 'Demeter and the Maid' recalls the double aspect of the Minoan goddess as Mother and Maid. Their continuing close identity is further indicated by our inability to decide whether Demeter or Persephone is portrayed on coins of Kydonia (*c.* 400–300 B.C.) and Rhaukos (*c.* 300–*c.* 165 B.C.).[13]

The same uncertainty exists with coins of Knossos (*c.* 400–350 B.C.),[14] where Persephone is again referred to as the 'Maid' in a dedication of the first or second century A.D.[15] At Eleutherna (second century B.C.?) and at Lappa (*c.* second century A.D.) in western Crete she is called Phersoponē.[16]

Of more interest in connexion with this long-standing cult of Mother and Maid are some verses from Kydonia of the Imperial Age.[17] They mourn the sudden ravishing away by Hades of the fair Mattia. 'I die,' the memorial continues, 'at twelve years of age, unmarried . . . I have left the light and lie in the depths in Persephone's murky chamber.' Her parents have been abandoned to eternal sorrow.

The word translated above as 'chamber' (*thalamos*) also means 'store-room'.[18] Its frequent Homeric sense is of an inner room or chamber, surrounded by other buildings. Similarly the word *megaron* is applied by Homer to a house or a palace. But it is also the term regularly used of caves sacred to Demeter and Persephone;[19] and the chasm into which Hades disappeared with Persephone was also a *megaron*.[20] The myth of the rape of Persephone has been interpreted[21] as being symbolic of the practice of storing the seed-corn from harvest-time to sowing-time in underground pits, that it might be fertilized by contact with the dead.

[12] Τὰν Δάματρα / καὶ τὰν Κώραν κτλ. Guarducci *loc. cit.* = CIG 2567, Blass 5047. The form Κώραν is from the older Κόρϝαν: Bechtel 2.690 f., Thumb-Kieckers 1.153, Buck GD 29 and 50. κόρ(ϝ)ος is perhaps cognate with Latin Ceres, Cerus, cresco; LSJ cf. Boisacq s.v. κόρος. On the other hand, the Arcadians worshipped Demeter under the name Despoina, 'Mistress': Seltman GC 97.

[13] Guarducci IC 1. p. 291, 2. p. 114. Cf. Head 464, 477.

[14] Guarducci IC 1, p. 55. Cf. Head 461.   [15] IC 1.VII.21.

[16] IC 2.XII.31 *bis*, *ib.* XVI.10. On the form see Bechtel 2.712–13. Cf. Phersephona IC 2.V.49.5 (Axos, epigram *c.* first century B.C.) and *ib.* X.20.8 (Kydonia, Imperial Age).

[17] IC 2.X.20.   [18] *Il.* 24.191; *Od.* 21.8; X. *Oec.* 9.3, etc.

[19] Luc. *DMeretr.* 1 sch.; Plu. *M* 378e; Paus. 1.39.5, 3.25.9, 8.37.8, 9.8.1; Clem. *Pr.* 2.14; Eust. *ad Od.* 1.27; Phot. μάγαρον.

[20] Hom. *h. Cer.* 379.   [21] Cornford AEM 157–91.

Like the corn-seed, Persephone the Corn-Spirit dies and is born again. She is ravished away by Hades, mourned by her mother, and is restored to life again, but only on condition that she goes below the earth to rejoin Hades for a third part of every year.

The Eleusinian Mysteries were performed, in honour of Demeter and Persephone, in September. The time of the celebration had once been the sowing-time,[22] although in the historical period it was a month later, in October. Since the harvest-time was June, the seed-corn had been stored for four months, a third part of the year.

The date of the Mysteries is not their only link with ancient practice. They included a sacred marriage, celebrated by hiero- phant and high-priestess.[23] Although we have no information about this ritual of the sacred marriage at Eleusis, we know that the Phrygian Mysteries of Sabazios—which probably derived from the Mysteries of the Hittite Mother-goddess—included the ritual of the 'god through the bosom'. That is to say, a priestess slipped a gold snake down through her clothes to the ground.[24] Since Persephone, like Demeter, was originally fatherless, it has been argued that the background of her myth was originally matriarchal; and that the ritual of the 'god through the bosom', was once enacted, not with a gold snake in a temple 'but in one of those prehistoric cave sanctuaries in which real snakes abound'.[25]

Coins of the Cretan Priansos (*c.* 430–200 B.C.) represent a goddess enthroned beneath a palm-tree, caressing the head of a snake with her hand. Lenormant,[26] Gardner,[27] and Wroth[28] argued that the goddess was Persephone, Svoronos[29] that she was Hygieia. If we cannot be absolutely certain about the name of the goddess in the historical period, her association with the snake gives the clue to her ultimate origin. 'Whatever her name, she could doubtless claim kinship with the snake-goddess of Knossos, Gournia and Palaikastro.'[30] In the same way, Demeter's familiar

[22] Plu. *fr.* 11.23; Procl. *ad* Hes. *Op.* 389=*Carm. Pop.* 50.
[23] Aster. *Hom.* 10=Migne 40.323; Ps. Orig. *Philos.* 5.1=Cruice 170; Clem. *Pr.* 2.13. In the cult of Demeter at Sikyon the women's rite was performed in a 'bridal- chamber': Paus. 2.11.3.
[24] Clem. *Pr.* 2.14. [25] Thomson SAGS 1.236.
[26] *Gaz. Arch.* (1879) v. 24. [27] TGC 162 pl. 9, 5.
[28] *Brit. Mus. Cat. Coins*, Crete etc. p. XXXII f.; cf. JHS 5.87.
[29] Svoronos 1.295 f. pl. 28, 21–3.
[30] Cook Z 1.402; cf. Head 476, Guarducci IC 1.280.

attributes of snakes, trees, poppies and small animals lead us back to the Minoan goddess.[31]

Though the ultimate origin of the Eleusinian Mysteries may have to be sought in the East, there can be little doubt that they were brought into mainland Greece from Crete.[32] Such is the testimony not only of the Homeric Hymn to Demeter, but also of an important passage of Diodoros,[33] who says:

'As what they consider to be the chief proof of their contention that divine honours, sacrifices and rites involved in the Mysteries were transmitted from Crete to other peoples, the Cretans advance the following argument. The rite celebrated by the Athenians at Eleusis, perhaps the most remarkable of all, the one in Samothraike, and that in Thrace among the Kikones, whence came Orpheus who introduced them—these were all transmitted in secret forms: at Knossos in Crete, however, it was customary, from ancient times, for these rites to be transmitted to all quite openly; and such things as are elsewhere transmitted in secret are there not concealed from anyone who wishes to know about them. They declare that most of the gods proceeded from Crete to many parts of the inhabited world conferring benefits upon the races of men and sharing among each of them the advantages of their own discoveries. Thus Demeter passed over into Attica and from there to Sicily and, later on, to Egypt. In these places especially she received great honours among those she benefited in transmitting the fruit of the corn and in teaching them about the sowing of the seed.'

At Athens there was, from early times, a cult of Demeter Thesmophoros; and Herodotos says that the ritual of the Thesmophoria was brought from Egypt.[34] Since this ritual was similar to the Eleusinian Mysteries,[35] our knowledge of it throws light not only on the Eleusinian festival, but also on those more public festivals of Crete which, in one form or another, had been attached to the worship of the Minoan goddess.

The festival of the Thesmophoria[36] was performed by women. The rites were of great antiquity, and, as Jane Harrison pointed out, 'owing to the conservative character of women and the mixed contempt and superstition with which such rites were regarded by

[31] See Cook Z *passim* s.v. Demeter.
[32] Cf. Persson DUEM, RGPT 149–50. [33] D.S. 5.77.3–5.
[34] Hdt. 2.171. It was brought, presumably, by way of Crete.
[35] Nilsson HGR 211.
[36] The chief sources are Luc. *DMeretr.* 2.1 sch., 7.4 sch.; Deubner 43–66.

men, they were preserved in pristine purity down to late days'.[37]
The purpose of the festival was to fertilize the crops. It took place
towards the end of October—the sowing-time.[38]

Thesmophoria means 'carrying of *thesmoi*', i.e. of what has been
stored away. At some time prior to the festival the women had
sacrificed pigs to Demeter and thrown them into caverns. During
the Thesmophoria, certain of the women, who were obliged to
keep themselves in a state of ritual purity (including strict chastity)
for three days beforehand, brought up the rotting remains of
these sacrificed pigs. As they did so they made a din to drive away
the guardian snakes who were supposed to eat of the flesh, which
was now replaced by images of paste. The pigs were regarded as
symbols, presumably, of the fertility both of crops and human
beings, and their decomposed flesh was mixed with the seed to
ensure a good harvest.

2. EUROPA

An archaic Europa, riding on her bull, is featured on the earliest
(fifth century B.C.) coins of Gortyna and also of Phaistos.[39] The
type persists on coins of Gortyna throughout the fifth century.
The pictorial character of these coins suggests a derivation from
local frescoes, and it is even more pronounced in the fourth-
century coins both of Gortyna and of Phaistos. On a Phaistos type
Europa sits on a rock and welcomes with her raised hand the bull
who approaches her. A coin series from contemporary Gortyna
tells the story of the marriage of Zeus and Europa. 'At first she
sits pensively in her willow while the bull, upon the reverse,
skilfully foreshortened, licks his flank. Next Zeus has changed
into an eagle perched on a branch beside her, while she lifts her
veil with the gesture of a bride; on the reverse, since the god has
passed into an eagle, the bull is mortal once more and is startled
by a teasing gad-fly. In the third stage there is the embrace,
Europa and the eagle grouped like a Leda and swan; and the poor
bull maddened by the fly. This is surely the story told by some
painter and translated to a series of coins, a weird myth full of
lost or faintly discerned links with the beliefs of Minoan Crete,
its sacred trees and birds and bulls, and its all-powerful goddess,

---

[37] PSGR 120. [38] Corn. *ND* 28.
[39] Seltman GC 169. Cf. Head 465, 467, 472; Guarducci IC 4, p. 37; Svoronos 153.

sunk now to the rank of a nymph though bearing the name of a continent.'[40]

Coins of Knossos, probably struck in 220 B.C., when the city was in close alliance with Gortyna, are similar to the Gortynian type featuring Europa.[41] Europa or the bull remained one of the chief coin-types (probably struck at Gortyna between 66 and 31 B.C.) of the Roman province of Crete.[42]

Outside Crete, persistence of the motif of Europa or the bull is indicated by coins of Hadrianopolis in Thrace, by a fifth-century B.C. type at Kyzikos, and by a type from Seleukeia in Cilicia, whose coinage began in the second century B.C. But the most significant coin-types with a bearing on the legends of Europa, although late in date, come from Tyre and Sidon. The Phoenician standard coins of Tyre (c. 126–5 B.C. to 195–6 A.D.) include the following types: Zeus as a bull approaches Europa; Kadmos starts on a voyage, fights a serpent, joins hands with Harmonia, founds Thebes or gives the alphabet to the Greeks.[43]

Sidon was the ancient metropolis of Phoenicia. It possessed the most important coinage of its part of the world down to the time of Alexander. Of the Phoenician standard, this coinage began to be issued about the end of the fifth century B.C. In the period 202–111 B.C. there was a small autonomous bronze coinage which included among its types Europa on a bull.[44] A similar type persisted during the autonomous era of Sidon from 111 B.C. to Imperial times, as also from the time of Augustus to Severus Alexander. A type portraying Kadmos also occurs at Sidon in Imperial times.

The evidence of coin-types thus indicates that in Asia Minor the two Phoenician cities of Tyre and Sidon and in Crete the city of Gortyna in particular fostered the traditions of Europa.

According to Stephanos, the city of Gortyna had had four names.[45] The first of these names, he explains, was Hellotis, which was how Europa was known among the Cretans. It was then called Larisa, then Kremnia and finally Gortys.

Gortys was traditionally the name of a hero-founder. It occurs in a Gortynian inscription of the first half of the first century B.C.,[46] and also at Lebena, the port of Gortyna, in a document of

---

[40] Seltman GC 170–1.
[41] Head 461; Guarducci IC 1. p. 55.
[42] Head 479.
[43] Head 287, 525, 728, 797–8, 801.
[44] Cf. Luc. *Syr.D.* 6.
[45] St. Byz. s.v. Γόρτυν
[46] IC 4.252.

about the same date.[47] According to Pausanias,[48] a Tegean claim to the founder was disputed by the Cretans themselves in favour of a Minoan connexion. Plato offers supporting evidence for the view that Gortyna was founded by Achaeans from the Peloponnese, but says they were, not Tegeans, but Arcadians.[49] The Cretan Arcadians of historical times were in fact settled not far to the east of Gortyna. Konon, however, says that some emigrants from Amyklai who broke with the Dorian Spartans and settled in Melos also occupied Gortyna with the help of neighbouring Cretans.[50]

Amyklai had remained in Achaean hands for some time after the Dorian conquest,[51] and it is therefore likely that a relationship between the Peloponnesian and the Cretan Amyklai would antedate a Dorian hegemony at Gortyna. These various traditions link the mainland settlers of Gortyna, or of its neighbourhood, with the Arcadian area where the Achaean dialect survived,[52] or with Achaean Amyklai.

The 'walled' city of Gortyna mentioned in the Catalogue of Ships must be associated with the period of Achaean domination of Crete.[53] It therefore seems reasonable to assign approximately to this same period Achaean pedigrees, cults, cult-names and cult modifications, such as appear in later Gortynian tradition. So too with the name 'Gortys' or 'Gortyna', pre-Greek though it may be.[54] For, although it has Etruscan, Thessalian and Macedonian connexions, the most significant parallel is the Arcadian town 'Gortyn' (or 'Gortys' or 'Gortyna') and the tributary of the Alpheus, 'Gortynios'.[55] The name could have been brought by Achaean settlers from Arcadia. We shall see how Minoan tradition could have been adapted to fit such a change. But the persistence

---

[47] IC 1.17.21.   [48] 8.53.4.

[49] Lg. 4.708a.   [50] Narrat. 36. Cf. ib. 47.

[51] Paus. 3.2.6. The name is pre-Greek: Haley 145; Fick VO 91, 113. The relationship is well supported by evidence. There is the gloss of St. Byz.: Ἀμύκλαι—ἔστι καὶ πόλις Ἀμύκλαιον ἐν Κρήτῃ καὶ ὅρμος; the cult of Apollo Amyklaois (to be inferred from Leg. Gort. III.5–9); the month Ἀ]μυκλα[ί]ω in the Gortynian calendar (IC 4.182.23 and perhaps ib. 173.12); and the important inscription of the third–second century B.C. (ib. 172), recording a decree of the Gortynians concerning the people of Amyklai, reduced now, it seems, to perioecic subjection. For Apollo Amyklos in Cyprus, see Schaeffer Enkomi-Alasia I (1952) 6 ff. (Dussaud). See further below pp. 260–1.

[52] Buck GD 7–8

[53] Il. 2.646. Eust. (ad. loc.) explains that the epithet 'walled' (τειχιόεις) is used, as it is used of Tiryns earlier (Il. 2.559), to connote a fortified city.

[54] Haley ibid.   [55] Guarducci IC 4, p. 14.

of Minoan tradition despite Achaean (and, later, Dorian) modifications, is attested by very late authorities.[56]

The precise origin of the name Kremnia is doubtful.[57] But Larisa is certainly 'Pelasgian', and it is found in several parts of Thessaly, Attica, Argolis, Elis, the Troad, Aiolis and Lydia, as well as Crete.[58] The Cretan Pelasgoi were clearly distinguished from the Eteocretans,[59] and it may be that they did not arrive in Crete before the beginning of the second millennium.[60] It may then be the case that the name Hellotis can be associated with the Eteocretans, going as far back as Early Minoan if not to neolithic times,[61] Larisa with Pelasgian, and Gortys, Gortyn and Gortyna with Achaean immigrants.

So far then it seems that Stephanos may well have correctly reported the chronological order of at least three names for sites at, or near, the site of historical Gortyna, presumably based on the traditions of actual settlers in the neighbourhood. If so, Kremnia (and associated Kartemnides)[62] could then be linked with other immigrants who arrived after the Pelasgoi and before the Achaeans, that is to say, in the earlier second millennium and before c. 1450 B.C. There is evidence to suggest that such new arrivals may well have been Kadmeioi from Phoenicia.

According to Herodotos, some Greeks, who were probably Cretans, landed on the Phoenician coast at Tyre and carried off the king's daughter, Europa, in retaliation for the earlier seizure of Io.[63] Though he did not know how women's names came to be applied to Libya, Asia and Europe, he admitted the possibility, though with no great conviction, that Europe might have derived its name from the Tyrian Europa. But he *was* convinced that Europa was Asiatic; and that she never reached Europe, as it was

---

[56] Kedren. *Hist. Comp.* in Migne 121.65 D; Eust. *ad* D.P. 88.

[57] Cf. Bürchner in RE s.v.v. Gortyn and Κρημνία. The meaning of the Hsch. glosses Καρτεμνίδες. οἱ Γορτύνιοι. Κρῆτες and Κορύστιοι. οἱ Γορτύνιοι is almost equally doubtful. Κορύστιοι may be connected with the Gortynian Arcadians, since the name Κόρτυς was applied to Arcadia (cf. Guarducci *ibid.*). Relying on another Hsch. gloss (viz. κάρτην. τὴν βοῦν Κρῆτες, καὶ τὸν οἰκέτην οἱ αὐτοί) and the occurrence of the word καρταῖπος = 'large cattle' in archaic Gortynian inscriptions, Cook (Z 1.471) interpreted Καρτεμνίδες as 'Cow-men' or 'Cow-herds'.

[58] *Il.* 2.841; Str. 9.430, 440, 13. 620-1; Paus. 2.24.1, 7.17.5.

[59] Pp. 132-6. [60] See p. 136 and n. 94 above.

[61] Soundings on the north slope of the Acropolis at Gortyna have proved that occupation here goes back to neolithic times: JHS 76 (Sup.). 31.

[62] See n. 57 above. [63] 1.1-2.

defined in his time, but only came as far as Crete, and then from Crete to Lycia.[64]

Herodotos also believed that the Lycians derived from Crete at a time when the island was wholly occupied by 'barbarians'. For when the sons of Europa, Sarpedon and Minos, quarrelled about the kingship, Minos was able to banish Sarpedon and his followers, who went to Asia and settled in the Milyan district, where they were known as Termilai. Their customs were partly Cretan, partly Carian. One of their customs Herodotos thought sufficiently remarkable to distinguish them from every other nation: they took the mother's and not the father's name. If a free woman married a slave, her children were free.[65] (Herodotos was apparently unaware that, in his own time, the children of a free Gortynian woman and a serf were legally free provided that the marriage was matrilocal).[66]

According to the familiar myth, Belos and Agenor were the sons of Poseidon and Libya. Belos became king of Egypt, but Agenor settled in Phoenicia. His children were Europa, Phoinix, Kilix and Kadmos, whom the Greeks considered a Phoenician. Zeus, disguised as a bull, carried off Europa to Crete, where she became the mother of Minos. Kilix and Kadmos went in search of their sister, Kilix staying in Cilicia and Kadmos travelling to Delphi by way of Rhodes and Thasos. At Delphi he was told by the oracle to give up the search and to follow a cow to the place where it sat down. This place became the site of Thebes.[67]

A cult of Demeter Europa was established at Lebadeia, near Thebes,[68] and the Theban temple of Demeter Thesmophoros was said to have been the palace of Kadmos.[69] It has been inferred that the mainland Kadmeioi were immigrants from Crete who brought a cult of the Minoan Mother-goddess.[70] But myth and the father of history alike agree that Europa came to Crete from Phoenicia. Hence the possibility that the myth of Zeus and Europa ultimately derived from the Phoenician myth of the bull-god El and the Mother-goddess Asherat.[71]

---

[64] 4.45. Europe appears as a geographical name first in Homer *h. Ap.* 251, Pi. *N.* 4.70, A. *fr.* 191. In Hes. *Th.* 357, she is a daughter of Ocean.
[65] 1.173. [66] *Leg. Gort.* VII.1–10.
[67] Apollod. 3.1.1, 3.4.1. [68] Paus. 9.39.5.
[69] Paus. 9.16.5. Cf. X. *HG.* 5.2.29.
[70] Thomson SAGS 1.124. Cf. *ib.* 376 and the criticism of the view that Kadmos was a Phoenician only in the sense of being a red-skinned Minoan from Crete.
[71] Schaeffer CTRS 39. Cf. Persson RGPT 132–6.

In the Middle Minoan period, Ugarit was one of the most important centres of Cretan trade in Syria.[72] The oldest of the many Minoan and Mycenaean objects found there date from the seventeenth century B.C.[73] There is good reason to suppose, as we have seen, that Middle Minoan culture was dependent on this area for some of its features.[74] Partly for these reasons, and partly because Proto-Phoenician was among the different languages spoken in Ugarit, there exists the possibility that the Kadmeioi were Phoenicians who reached Greece by way of Crete some time in the Middle Minoan period.[75] The implications of this possibility are important. For an approximate date is thus provided for the fusion of the cult of a bull-god[76] and Mother-goddess with an indigenous cult of the Mother-goddess—one of whose names was reputedly Hellotia.

Support for the dating of the arrival of the Kadmeioi to the Middle Minoan period can be derived from the connexions between the legend of Io (and her descendants) and the history of Egypt in the second millennium. It has been argued that, on archaeological, linguistic and religious grounds, this complex of legend cannot be assigned to any other period of Egyptian history than that of the Hyksos; and, furthermore, that the arrival of Danaos and Kadmos in Greece corresponds with the expulsion of the Hyksos by Ahmosis, c. 1580 B.C.[77] The hypothesis that official, peaceful relations existed between Crete and the Hyksos Pharaoh Khyan was originally suggested with confidence by Evans. It was based on the discovery of the alabaster lid bearing the name of Khyan which was found in a Middle Minoan III(a) deposit by the North Lustral Area at Knossos. Evans suggested that the deposit may well have dated from shortly after the middle of the seventeenth century B.C.[78] His view that the Hyksos were predominantly of Semitic stock appears to be firmly established.[79] The three major deities of the Hyksos pantheon were those of the Canaanite pantheon, namely, El, Baal and Anat.[80]

It is, however, open to doubt whether the travels of Kadmos towards Greece can be so firmly equated with the dispersal of the

---

[72] Schaeffer *ib.* 12.　　　　[73] Gaster in *Ant.* 13.204.
[74] Pp. 16–18.　　　　[75] Schaeffer *ib.* 39; Thomson SAGS 1.376.
[76] 'In Crete itself the motive [of a galloping bull] already appears in MM II.' Evans PM 2.649.
[77] Bérard HLI.　　　　[78] PM. 1.419. Cf. Pendlebury 172.
[79] Bérard *ib.* 13–14. Cf. Evans *ib.* 420.
[80] Bérard *ib.* 23, citing Dussaud in RHR 109, 119.

Hyksos. The possibility that Phoenicians, who were later identified with Kadmos and the Kadmos legends, could have brought their cults from Syria directly to Crete at an earlier date in the Middle Minoan period than *c.* 1580 B.C. cannot be excluded. The date *c.* 1580 B.C. may possibly be better taken as an approximate lower limit.

Is it likely that Europa journeyed later from Crete to Lycia, as Herodotos says? There is no reason to doubt the connexion between the Minoan Cretans and the Lycians.[81] According to what may be regarded as the Minoan tradition, Sarpedon was the brother of Minos. But in the *Iliad* Sarpedon is a grandson of Bellerophon, and since Apollodoros[82] reports that he lived for three generations, we naturally suspect that the Greek tradition involved some alteration of older genealogies. It seems therefore likely that Herodotos was correctly reporting that Sarpedon established himself in 'Lycia',[83] at a time when Greek was not yet spoken in Crete. If we assume that the Achaeans introduced Greek speech, this event cannot have taken place later than *c.* 1450 B.C., and can perhaps be roughly assigned to the sixteenth century B.C.

If there were Eteocretan, Phoenician and Achaean contributions to the complex of Gortynian culture for well over a thousand years before the region became 'Dorianized', it is natural to look for traces of these successive influences in the cult of Europa. Cook[84] agreed with Frazer that 'ultimately both Europa and Diktynna came to be regarded as moon-goddesses—the former through the influence of Phoenician religion, the latter by assimilation to the lunar aspect of Artemis'. He denied however that 'originally and essentially either Europa or Diktynna stood for the moon', and preferred to regard Europa as a 'Cretan earth-goddess responsible for the vegetation of the year'.[85] But others have recognized an earlier stratum than is represented by Europa, indicated by the name Hellotis and the associated festival of the Hellotia. Thus Lesky[86] inferred a sacred marriage between the

---

[81] Cf. Rose in OCD s.v. Sarpedon.   [82] 3.6.

[83] It is doubtful if the region occupied by the immigrants was the historical Lycia.

[84] Z 1.524. Cf. Frazer GB 3.73; Hoeck K 1.90 ff.; Roscher SV 128–35.

[85] *Ib.* 526.

[86] WS 45.152–3, 46.48–67, 107–29. Lesky found traces of similar beliefs at Dodona in the Helloi and their eponym Hellos, at Corinth and Marathon in Athene Hellotis, and perhaps in Helle of the Hellespont. Cf. also Aly *Philol.* 25 (N.S.) 472, Guarducci IC 4, p. 35.

earth-goddess Europa, originally called Hellotis in Crete, and the sky-god Zeus, who in pre-Greek times had the form of a bull. This clear distinction between the earlier Hellotis and the later Europa was, in fact, already made in antiquity, both in definitions of nomenclature[87] and in descriptions of cult.

The most important piece of evidence about the primitive goddess and her festival of the Hellotia is given by Seleukos[88] who explains that a garland of myrtle, thirty feet in circumference, was carried in procession; and that the bones of Europa, who was called Hellotis, were carried in the garland.

Now if, as we have already seen reason to believe, and as the epithet Φοινικογενής, applied to her by Euripides,[89] confirms, Europa was indeed a later arrival than the indigenous goddess whom she at least partly replaced, her bones could not have been carried in the garland of myrtle by those who formed the procession in the original Hellotia. Before asking what, if anything, had been carried in the garland instead of the bones of Europa, in earlier times, and who formed the procession, we must note that the cult was not confined to Gortyna. It was observed at Argos[90] and was attached to the cult of Athene at Marathon and Corinth.[91]

These cults could have reached the mainland from Crete, through the agency of the Kadmeioi, when Europa had already become fused with Hellotia, herself an emanation of the Minoan Mother-goddess. Europa was a parallel figure to Demeter, yet another emanation of the same archetype.[92] We have seen that there was a cult of Demeter Europa at Lebadeia, while at Thebes itself the temple of Demeter Thesmophoros was said to have been the palace of Kadmos.[93] It has been argued that Demeter reached Greece by two main routes, the first passing through Euboia to Boiotia, the second through Argos to the Peloponnese. They converged in Attica, Demeter Achaia coming from Boiotia and

---

[87] That the cult of Hellotis was an ancient and distinctive cult of Gortyna can be inferred from the statement of St. Byz. that the earliest home of Gortyna was Hellotis. Cf. EM s.v.v. 'Ελλώτια and 'Ελλωτίς.
[88] Ap. Ath. 15. 678b. Cf. Hsch. s.v.v. 'Ελλώτια and ἑλλωτίς.
[89] Cret. fr. 472.
[90] Vollgraff M 47.162 n. 7; Guarducci IC 4, p. 35.
[91] Sch. Pi. O 13.56 a, d; EM s.v. 'Ελλωτία; Seleukos ap. Ath. ibid.; Cook Z 1.526.
[92] Nilsson MOGM 33; Farnell CGS 2.479; Roscher LGRM 1.1417; Persson UEM 303–8; Picard PPD 336.
[93] P. 156.

Demeter Eleusinia from the Peloponnese.[94] If we bear in mind the extremely conservative character of the cult of Demeter, it is hardly surprising that the mainland cults of the primitive Hellotia should be found along Demeter's two main routes. If their common archetype is the Minoan goddess, it is logical to look for the explanation of the cult of Hellotia in the cult of Demeter. It is important to bear in mind that the information we have about the Hellotia lacks mention of any male deity or principle. Even when Europa's bones are involved, there is no bull. This negative testimony is in keeping with our knowledge of the Minoan goddess. The male partner, son or consort or both, of the goddess, whose status, though still subordinate, rises in the Middle and Late Minoan periods, does not appear in the Neolithic Age at all.

These various considerations justify the hypothesis that the Hellotia was a women's festival, analogous to the Thesmophoria, whose object was to fertilize the crops. The hypothesis can be supported by a number of inferences derived from the ancient evidence relating to the Hellotia. We saw that the chief Minoan deity, in her capacity as moon-goddess, was associated with herbal magic, which is older than agriculture and is everywhere the province of women.[95] In Greece, the root of the peony, the dittany, the withy, the galingale, the pomegranate, the lily and the myrtle had special associations with childbirth and menstruation.[96] The lily and the myrtle were both sacred to Aphrodite,[97] the lily checking menstruation and the myrtle preventing premature delivery by closing the uterus.[98] At Boiai, in Laconia, the myrtle was sacred to Artemis Soteira who aided women in childbirth.[99] Just as the statue of Artemis at Agra, in Attica, was decorated with garlands of withy,[100] and wreaths of helychryse and galingale were made by Spartan girls for Hera,[101] so crowns of myrtle were

---

[94] Thomson SAGS 1.132, on the basis of evidence from Hdt. 2.171; Paus. 1.14.2, 38.1–3, 39.1, 43.2; 2.14.1–4, 18.3, 34.6, 35.4–8; 7.3.9, 27.9; 8.4.1–2, 15.1–4, 45.1; 9.8.1, 33.5; 10.32.3; Hom. *h. Cer.* 105–10, 161, 184–7, 206–7; D.S. 4.29; Cornford AEM 161; Plu. *M* 378e, cf. *EM* Ἀχαία; Polem. 65; Str. 9. 398; IG 2.785; Apollod. 3.9.1; Hyg. *F.* 147; St. B. Ἐλευθεραί and Ἀζανία.

[95] P. 79.

[96] Peony: Dsc. 3.157; Plin. *NH.* 26.151. Dittany: Thphr. *HP* 9.16.1; Arat. 33 sch. Withy: Dsc. 1.134; Plin. *NH.* 24.59–60. Galingale: Plin. *NH.* 21.118. Pomegranate: Plin. *NH.* 23.107, 112.

[97] Paus. 6.24.7; Ov. *Met.* 10.512.

[98] Plin. *NH.* 23.159–60, 24.50, 21.126.

[99] Paus. 3.22.12.

[100] E. *Hipp.* 73 sch., reading λύγῳ for λόγῳ.

[101] Plin. *NH.* 21.148; Ath. 15. 678a; Alc. 24.

used by Eleusinian hierophants.[102] Like *kokkos* (pomegranate-seed), the word *myrton* (myrtle-berry) was used to mean *pudenda muliebria*.[103] It seems safe to infer that the myrtle garland of the Hellotia was also associated with herbal magic and therefore represents a primitive stratum of cult practice confined to women.

The starting-point of the Hellotia, as of the Thesmophoria, could well have been the ancient practice of secretly disposing of the *katharmata*. According to the oldest and most reliable of several explanations of the Hellotia of Athene Hellotis at Corinth, a certain Hellotis flung herself and her little sister Khryse on to a fire.[104] 'And so,' concludes this account, '*Katharsia* (cleansings) are brought to the goddess . . . and they are called Hellotia.' Nilsson[105] inferred that a large puppet called Hellotis was burnt (or two large puppets, Hellotis and another sister Eurytione), together with a small puppet called Khryse. He doubted whether actual bones were carried at the Cretan Hellotia and suggested that a puppet called Hellotis was concealed in the wreath, which was later regarded as the relic of a dead heroine. Cook[106] agreed that this enormous wreath was clearly some sort of May-garland with a puppet inside it, and, since in modern Greece such garlands were burnt on the midsummer bonfire, considered the fire on which Hellotis and Khryse were burnt at Corinth to be a noteworthy feature of the ancient tradition.

The aetiology is an invention but the possibility that a puppet called Hellotis was carried in the myrtle in the Corinthian Hellotia cannot be dismissed. If such were the case, then, as Nilsson suggested, the puppet was probably a substitute for Hellotis. But who was Hellotis? The pigs of the Thesmophoria were symbols of fertility: for pigs were believed to be most prolific.[107] Before the bones of Europa were carried in the myrtle wreath at Gortyna, it is possible that the remains of smaller animals, like the pig, were carried instead—since sacrificial animals offered by women universally belong to small species.[108] If the Hellotia was essentially like the Thesmophoria, the *katharmata* would have been mingled with these remains. The aetiology relating to Athene Hellotis would thus be an invention in so far as it inverts the truth, giving

[102] S. *OC* 683 sch. Cf. Ar. *Ra.* 330 sch.   [103] Ar. *Lys.* 1004.
[104] Pi. *O.* 13.56 sch.; Nilsson GF 96; Cook Z 1.525 n. 5.
[105] GF 95–6.   [106] Cook Z 1.525, cf. *ib.* 338.
[107] Luc. *DMeretr.* 1 sch.   [108] Cf. p. 78.

a myth first and a cult to follow. But some truth would still remain, even though distorted. What is given as the consequence would really be the cause. If Hellotis was a woman personified before she became a goddess, since *katharsia* were brought to the goddess which were called Hellotia, the practice would have begun before there was even a rudimentary goddess. The Hellotia would have been there from the beginning as the basis of the ritual.

Can it be supposed that the bones of Europa, despite Nilsson's doubts, were actually carried in the wreath, perhaps replacing the bones of smaller animals, after Europa arrived in Crete from Syria? There are indications in the religious texts of Ugarit[109] which allow of the possibility. The idea of force, more especially the force of procreation, was symbolized, to the Canaanites of Ugarit, by a bull. In some of the texts the god El appears as Shor-El or the Bull-El. In this form of a bull El forms a union with Asherat-of-the-Sea. Asherat was the chief goddess, the mother and the counsellor of the gods. Consequently she held a primordial place in the Canaanite pantheon of Ugarit. After El and Asherat the most important deity was Baal. This god can be identified with the Phoenician Hadad, the Syrian-Hittite Teshub and the Egyptian Seth or Sutekh—different names for a god of heights, storms and rains. The voice of Baal is heard in the clouds, he sends forth the lightning and the rain and he carries a thunderbolt. He has the strength of a bull, destroying his enemies with his horns, and horns rise from the front of his helmet. A bull's head was his symbol and in several monuments priests are shown dressed in animal masks and horns. Baal hunts on the edge of the desert, meets monsters with a human body and the head of a bull, fights and falls 'like the bull under the sacrificer's knife'. He also fights with Lotan, the seven-headed serpent, the Biblical Leviathan.

In the Ugaritic poems Baal is sometimes accompanied, sometimes replaced, by his son Aliyan. While Baal is the god of storms and rains, Aliyan safeguards springs and underground waters, and represents the growth of plants in the rainy season. Their rule endures through autumn, winter and spring. In the summer the god Mot, spirit of harvest, replaces them, to rule over the parched earth. Each spring Mot begins his fight with Baal and Aliyan, and in summer, when the fruit is ripening, they are overcome. The

[109] Schaeffer CTRS 60–72; cf. Pritchard 129 ff.

rains cease, and Baal disappears. But while water remains in the springs and river-beds, Aliyan lives on.

As the hot season advances, however, Aliyan must leave the earth. Before he takes his departure, he obeys his father's command and assures the increase of the cattle by entering into symbolic union with a heifer:

> Aliyan-Baal obeys his father,
> He loves the heifer in the pasture,
> The cow in the field.
> He makes love seventy-seven times,
> He makes love eighty-eight times.

The heifer is the hypostasis of the goddess Anat, Aliyan's sister, who has now become his lover. When Aliyan dies, Anat goes in search of him. She finds his body in the home of the dead inside the earth, and carries it on her shoulder up to the heights of Saphon, where she buries him and sacrifices hecatombs of wild bulls, oxen, sheep, deer, wild goats and wild asses. She then pleads with Mot for her lover to be restored. When he refuses, she kills him:

> Anat seized Mot, the divine son,
> With a sickle she cut him,
> With a winnow she winnows him,
> With a fire she scorches him,
> With a mill she crushes him,
> She scatters his flesh in the field to be eaten by birds,
> So that his destiny may be fulfilled.

'In sacrificing Mot,' Schaeffer explains, 'Anat performs the harvest rite, which consists of taking from him his sacred character to allow of his profane usefulness. By dispersing Mot's flesh, that is by scattering corn, the goddess restores to the fields the spirit of vegetation and so assures crops in the coming year. This ritual, called the last sheaf, is common to all ancient civilizations. Many isolated traces of it linger in the cults of the anthropomorphic gods of antiquity, from Osiris, Tammuz and Adonis to Dionysos and Bacchus. They have survived even down to the present day. Although Mot, in the Ras Shamra ritual, is already an anthropomorphic spirit, he is cooked and treated like the last sheaf at harvest-time.'

The documents on which this account is based are dated to the middle of the second millennium, and it is quite likely that, at the time when the Kadmeioi arrived in Crete, the essential and certainly the more primitive features of the cult were already present.

In the story of the founding of Thebes as it is told by the scholiast on the *Iliad*,[110] Kadmos, having journeyed to Delphi to consult the god, was advised to trouble no more about Europa, but to take as his guide a cow and to found a city when the cow became tired and lay on its right side. He followed a cow from the herds of Pelagon through Boiotia to the site of Thebes. Kadmos wished to sacrifice the cow to Athene and sent some of his men for lustral water from the spring of Ares. Most of these men were killed by a snake, the child of Ares, which guarded the spring. The angry Kadmos killed the snake and, on the advice of Athene, sowed its teeth. Ares, in turn, was about to destroy Kadmos but was restrained by Zeus, who gave Harmonia to Kadmos as his wife.

Cook detected Phoenician and lunar elements in this version and wrote: 'The whole story gains immensely in coherence and significance, if we assume that the guiding cow was none other than Europa in animal form. The lost sister is thus recovered at the last, and the Pythian oracle is vindicated from the charge of irrelevance. Besides, it was, to say the least of it, appropriate that Zeus as a bull should mate with Europa as a cow.'[111] According to Pausanias, the place where the cow lay down was still shown, with its open-air altar and an image of Athene dedicated by Kadmos—an Athene with the Phoenician title of *Onga*;[112] and, according to a scholiast on Euripides,[113] the actual oracle delivered to Kadmos instructed him to sacrifice the exhausted cow to Earth.

Just as Athene became involved with Hellotis at Marathon and Corinth, so Athene became involved with Europa at Thebes. The fight with the snake and the union of brother and sister recall the Ugaritic myths. But there is a significant difference. In the Ugaritic myths it is the cow-sister who searches for her brother

---

[110] Sch. *Il.* 2.494, citing the *Boiotiaka* of Hellanikos (*fr.* 8) and the *Bibliotheke* of Apollod. 3.4.1 f.

[111] Cook Z 1.540. Cf. Frazer (GB 3.87–9) who, arguing that the marriage of Kadmos and Harmonia at Thebes may have been a dramatic representation of the marriage of the sun and moon at the end of the octennial cycle, put forward the hypothesis that Harmonia, the wife of Kadmos, was only another form of his sister Europa, both of them being personifications of the moon.

[112] Paus. 9.12.2. Cf. Frazer *Paus.* 5.48 f.   [113] Sch. E. *Ph.* 638.

and the male deity who dies. Modifications in the form of crossing of the sexes could have occurred in Crete, if we grant that the Kadmeioi reached the mainland by way of Crete—and may perhaps be due to differing conceptions of gender of cosmic phenomena.[114] In Crete, tradition certainly remembered the bones of Europa; and the Minoan goddess did not become subordinate to the male deity who grew in stature in the Middle and Late Minoan periods. At Knossos, this male deity appears to have been identified with the bull, just as the Phoenician Shor-El is a bull-god, apparently connected with the solar year.[115]

The independent behaviour of Asherat in one of the Ugaritic texts lends support to matriarchal theory; and the 'conception of her as counsellor of the gods, together with that of mother goddess or "creator of the gods", evidently confers on Asherat-of-the-Sea a primordial place in the Canaanite pantheon of Ugarit. It would be unfair to deny her such a position.'[116] In Crete the traditions present us with a primordial deity, Hellotis, who is later joined by Europa. But there is no male deity in these traditions; there is not yet even a bull. Before the earth of Crete was tossed on the horns of a bull, it is likely that the fertility of its fields was promoted by the magic offerings of its women and that Hellotis took shape as their goddess. Her early rites may have included the sacrifice of small animals. It would be after the arrival of Europa with the Kadmeioi that the bones of a sacrificial cow were carried in magic myrtle to help the crops to grow.

It was earlier conjectured that the larger populations, the higher levels of economic and social achievement, of the Middle Minoan period, were accompanied by a more efficient exploitation of

[114] Comparing a glass plaque from Dendra-Midea showing Europa, or her counterpart, with an Egyptian design on papyrus showing the Moon God on a cow, Persson points out that 'in Egypt, the moon is a male god, Thot, the firmament is pictured as a star-bedecked woman; in Greece, the moon is a goddess, Selene, and the sky is Uranos. It therefore seems justifiable to regard Europa as a moon heroine': RGPT 134–5. Cf. Levi GC 280: 'I do not believe we can admit for the period of our signets direct communication between Egypt and Crete; in my opinion, relations between the two civilizations developed through coastal navigation along the shores of Syria and Asia Minor. But on these shores the influence of Asiatic civilizations and art was not less active and fecund than that of Egypt. . . . Minoan art in the signet of a riding woman used a Mesopotamian subject with the same freedom with which it interpreted every foreign loan, according to its own spirit and its own formulas. It connected the dragon with its chief goddess, in her luxurious garments, rather than with the more usual male Mesopotamian deities.' Cf. also Banti MPA 310.
[115] Shor-El corresponds to the Greek Kronos. See Schaeffer CTRS 60, Pl. 31.
[116] Schaeffer ib. 62–3.

agricultural resources, with the introduction of better methods of tillage and of stock-raising on a relatively large scale. Such advances, it was suggested, may have been due to Asiatic influences along the trade routes and to the arrival of Asiatic immigrants. These immigrants may have included the Kadmeioi, who would therefore have played their part in a tendency for the work of agriculture to be transferred from women to men, with an accompanying gradual transition from matrilineal to patrilineal descent.[117] Such innovations could have been sufficiently important to be marked by the attribution of the title 'Cow-men' or 'Cow-herds' to the ancestors of the historical Gortynians.[118]

It seems likely that the final evolution of the male deity from a bull into the anthropomorphic Zeus who later became so closely associated with Europa must have occurred in the Mycenaean period.[119] Animal sacrifices continued to be a major characteristic of the ritual of Zeus.[120] His sacrificial victims were usually either rams or more often oxen, both animals being associated with sky-gods in general and with Zeus in particular.[121] They were the most precious victims that pastoral peoples could offer and, at the same time, in their view, were most possessed of fertilizing power, and therefore most essential to their economy and survival.[122] In view of what was said earlier about the connexions between Arcadia and Gortyna, it is noteworthy that the Gortynian Zeus shared the title of Hekatombaios with the Arcadian Zeus.[123]

A celestial Zeus of Gortyna (Zeus Asterios) is mentioned by Byzantine writers,[124] and he is associated with Europa. Earlier writers, including Hesiod and Bakchylides, say that Zeus, after his association with Europa, gave her in marriage to the Cretan king Asterion[125] or Asterios[126] or Asteros.[127] He was childless himself and reared the children of Europa and Zeus. According to Tzetzes, Sarpedon, Minos and Rhadamanthys were the sons of

---

[117] Cf. pp. 19–20. [118] See n. 57 above.

[119] Zeus features as the partner of Europa in literature, not only in Hes. *fr.* 309 but already in the *Iliad*, 14.321 f.

[120] Farnell CGS 1.101. [121] Cook Z 1.712 n. 2 *et passim*.

[122] Cook *ibid.* [123] Hsch. s.v. Ἑκατόμβαιος.

[124] Kedren. *Hist. Comp.* in Migne. 121.252 A; Io. Malal. *Chron.* in Migne. 97.180 C; Tz. *Antehom.* 99 ff., H. 1.473 ff., *ad* Lyc. *Al.* 1301.

[125] Hes. *fr.* 209; B. *fr.* 47; Apollod. 3.1.2; Nonn. *D.* 1.353 ff., 2.693 ff.; *EM* 588. 24 ff.

[126] D.S. 4.60; Nonn. *D.* 13.222 ff., 35.384 ff., 37.46 ff., 81 ff., 724 ff., 40.284 ff.; Hieron. *Chron. ann. Abr.* 570, cf. 527.

[127] Lyc. *Al.* 1301. See Cook Z 1.547 n. 2.

Zeus Asterios. [128] The Knossian Minotaur was also called Asterios or Asterion,[129] and there were sacred herds of cattle of the sun-god at Gortyna.[130] Here too there was a cult of a solar deity called Atymnos, brother of Europa, whose early death was mourned;[131] and an inscription of the early fifth century B.C. testifies to the worship of the sun.[132] Cook was of the opinion that there occurred what he described as the 'solarization' of the Gortynian Zeus on the basis of this evidence—although admitting that it took place at a comparatively early date: 'It looks as though the contamination of the Gortynian Zeus with the solar cycle had begun as early as *c.* 700 B.C.'[133] But if, as we have seen reason to suppose, the solar cycle goes back to Minoan times, it is logical to interpret the evidence in the opposite way and to argue that Zeus supplants the solar 'priest-king'. In other words, Zeus Asterios was in origin a Phoenician solar deity, the male counterpart of Astarte.[134] This goddess, who is pictured riding on a bull in Sidonian coins of 111 B.C. to 117 A.D., is no different from Europa in the Gortynian coin-series.[135]

That the sacred marriage of Zeus and Europa united Mycenaean with Minoan and with neolithic cult traditions is indeed clear from the art and from the literary and numismatic evidence of historical times. In art Europa is frequently shown on the bull, holding his fertilizing horn in one hand and in the other the flower, at once the symbol of her own fertility and the sign of her origin in herbal magic before agriculture and cattle-raising deified the bull.[136] The marriage of Zeus and Europa was said to have taken place in or under an evergreen plane-tree near a stream at Gortyna.[137] Fifth-century B.C. coins of Gortyna, as was mentioned earlier, show a goddess in a tree, generally agreed to be Europa.[138] She is possessed by Zeus in the form of an eagle, and so becomes identified

---

[128] Tz. *H.* 1.473, *ad* Lyc. *Al.* 1301.　　　[129] Cook Z 1.492, 495, 546.
[130] Serv. *ad* Verg. *Ecl.* 6.60.
[131] Solin. 11.9; Nonn. *D.* 19.179 ff.; Guarducci IC 4, pp. 33–4.
[132] IC 4.65.　　　[133] Cook Z 1.547.
[134] Robertson Smith RS 310; Farnell CGS 1.44; Cook Z 1.546. Textual evidence now shows that the goddess Astarte of Ugarit was a huntress, as Baal was a hunter. Also, that in Ugaritic mythology there was a moon-god and a sun-goddess (cf. n. 114 above). But, again, one text makes mention of a tribute paid to a sun-king, either Hittite or Egyptian: Virolleaud in CRA (1956) 60–3. Cf. Levi GC 279.
[135] Persson RGPT 133.
[136] Cf. Cook Z 1.526 and pl. xxxii (The Europa-kylix at Munich).
[137] Thphr. *HP.* 1.95; Varr. RR 1.7.6; Pl. *NH* 12.11; Antig. *Mir.* 163 (179). Cf. Sot. *Flum.* 4.
[138] Cook Z 1.526 and n. 1. Cf. Guarducci IC 4, p. 34.

with Hera.[139] But a bull's head is often apparently fixed to the trunk of the tree.

The coins show, however, not a plane-tree but a pollard willow.[140] Cook observed that there was special cause to connect Zeus with the willow in the neighbourhood of Gortyna.[141] He asked if it was 'over-rash to conjecture that the name *Europe* or *Europeia* was a cult-title rightly or wrongly taken to mean the goddess "of Flourishing Willow-withies" '.[142] Arguments derived from etymology alone are always dubious, but since Europa took over from Hellotis, who had such strong associations with herbal magic, Cook may not have been over-rash. But there is no need to suggest, as Cook did, that Europa was a willow-goddess and that Zeus, 'as a nurseling of the willow might naturally be mated with a willow-bride'.[143] The willow—or at least the plant—associations were there before Zeus or Europa. We must suppose that Zeus became connected with the willow at Gortyna because he entered into a sacred marriage with a goddess who had grown out of herbal magic. The role of Hellotis was concealed in the mention of the tree where the sacred marriage took place, and the stream near by where she bathed.[144]

3. EILEITHYIA

The links between the goddess Eileithyia, the Minoan goddess, and a still earlier neolithic prototype are very firm in comparison with the conjecture surrounding the origin of Europa. The explanation is as simple as it is important. The continuity of her cult depends on the unchanging concept of her function. Eileithyia was the goddess of childbirth. The divine helper of women in labour has an obvious origin in the human midwife. To Homer she is *mogostokos*, 'goddess of the pains of birth'.[145] When Leto

---

[139] Hsch. s.v. Εὐρωπία. Cf. Cook Z 1.532 and figs. 391–9, 528–9.

[140] Cook Z 1.527–32. 'Yet we need not tax Theophrastos, who spoke of a plane, with blundering. Both trees grow in damp, marshy soil and probably flourished side by side at Gortyna'; *ib.* 529.

[141] *Ib.* 528. Cook pointed out that, although Theophrastos (*HP* 3.3.4 cf. 2.2.10) mentions a fruitful poplar growing in the mouth of the Idaian Cave, Pliny apparently thought it was a willow: *HP* 16.110. On Mount Ida, Zeus had been nursed by Helike, 'Willow': Thphr. *HP* 3.13.7.

[142] On the supposed etymology see further Cook Z 1.531; Persson RGPT 135.

[143] Cook Z 1.530.

[144] Cf., for the sacred significance of such localities: Th. 2.15.5; Poll. 3.43; E. *Ph.* 344–8; Harp. λουτροφόρος; Plu. *M.* 772b; Nonn. *D.* 3.89; E. *Ph.* 347 sch.

[145] *Il.* 11.270, 16.187, 19.103.

gave birth to Apollo in Delos, *mogostokos* Eileithyia was in attendance, and so were a number of other goddesses who bathed the god-child and wrapped him in his swaddling-clothes.[146] Leto adopted the kneeling position to deliver the child. She must have been supported by midwives—Eileithyia and her companion goddesses. Such is the practice among many primitive peoples; and Greek statuettes of kneeling women have thus been interpreted as goddesses of childbirth, Eileithyiai.[147]

The mention of the cave of Eileithyia at Amnisos, in the *Odyssey*,[148] indicates that the Homeric tradition derives from the Minoan Age.[149] Exploration of the cave itself has established the continuity of the cult from neolithic times and even points to a revival in the Roman period.[150] The name Eileithyia is not Indo-European, which strengthens the possibility of a direct descent from a Minoan goddess of childbirth.[151] The cult of the goddess was widespread,[152] the forms of her name various,[153] but in Crete, where her cult was more prominent than anywhere else, the common form was Eleuthyia.[154]

Other forms of the name can be explained from the Cretan.[155] On etymological grounds it is possible to suppose a connexion between the Cretan goddess Eleuthyia and the Cretan city of Eleutherna,[156] though there are no traces of her cult here. Of more importance, however, is the occurrence of the name of the month

---

[146] *H.Ap.* 115-22.

[147] Earthy 69, 71; Roscoe B 51, BB 242, BTUP 24; Allen 219; Thomson SAGS 1.245; Baur *Philol.* 8 *Sup.* 481 f.; Farnell CGS 2.613-14. For the plural Eileithyiai see *Il.* 11.270, 19.119.

[148] *Od.* 19.188. [149] Nilsson MMR 73.

[150] P. 143.

[151] Malten *Jahrb.* 28-39; Wilamowitz *Berl. Sitzb.* (1908) 331; Wackernagel, reported by Nilsson, MMR 521.

[152] It is attested at Athens, Megara, Corinth, Achaia, Arcadia, Messenia, Sparta, Delos, Tenos, Paros, Naxos, Thera and Astypalaia: Jessen in RE 5.2101; Nilsson MMR 518.

[153] Ἐλείθυια Pi. P. 3.9, N. 7.1, SIG 602 (Delph.), IG 3.1320. Ἐλέθυα IG 12(3).192 (Astypalaia). Εἰλήθυια IG 12(5).197 (Paros prob.), Call. *Del.* 132, *AP* 6.200 (Leòn.), Paus. 2.5.4. Ἐλευθία(-ίη) SGDI 4584 (Hippola), IG 12(5).187 (Paros). Laconian Ἐλευσία IG 5(1).236. Boiotian Εἰλείθεια(-ια) IG 7.2228, 3410. For other variations cf. Nilsson MMR 519 n. 43.

[154] IC 1.XVI (Lato) 2.31, 3.18, 4A.13, 5.48, 75, 15.35, 26.8 (cf. 27.3 Ἐλουθύα, explained by the common Cretan change of ευ to ου: Bechtel GD 2.661 f.); IC 2.III (Aptera).22; IC 4 (Gortyna) 174.60, 76.

[155] Wackernagel, reported by Nilsson, MMR 521.

[156] Nilsson MMR 519, 521. The termination -ρνα occurs in other pre-Greek place-names: Kretschmer EGGS 405, Fick VO 87.

Eleusynios or Elousinios at Olous,[157] or Eleusinios at Biannos.[158] The same month-name (in the form Eleusynios) occurs in Thera.[159] Eleusinios is the regular epithet meaning 'of Eleusis'.[160] An epithet of Zeus in Ionia, of Artemis in Sicily and Antioch,[161] it is most commonly used, as we might expect, of Demeter.[162] Similarly, Eleuseiniai is used of Demeter and Kore,[163] Eleusinion of their temple at Eleusis,[164] and Eleusinia of their festivals.[165]

Apart from Crete and the islands, Eileithyia also had a flourishing cult in Laconia. She had two temples at Sparta, according to Pausanias, who also mentions the sanctuary of Demeter Eleusinia, the Eleusinion, near Taygeton.[166] Votive inscriptions to Demeter and Kore have been found at a village near Sparta;[167] and in one inscription of the Roman Age they are called Eleusiniai.[168] We also know that there was a Laconian festival called the Eleuhunia (i.e. Eleusynia) in the fifth century B.C.[169] Because the month-name occurs in Crete the same festival was presumably celebrated there.[170] If this Cretan month Eleusinios coincided with Boedromion, the month in which the Eleusinian Mysteries were celebrated,[171] we have a further indication, in addition to the philological evidence,[172] of a close connexion between the Cretan goddess Eleuthyia, a Cretan, Theran and Laconian festival of the Eleusinia, the place-name Eleusis and also for the Cretan origin of the Eleusinian Mysteries.[173]

With one exception, the Cretan cities linked with Eileithyia, either by the testimony of inscriptions or by evidence of other kinds, belong to the centre of the island, between Eleutherna to the west (where the assumed connexion is based on purely philological grounds) and Lato to the east. The exception is

---

[157] IC 1.XVI.4A.8, 5.3. On the change from ευ to ου see n. 154 above.
[158] IC 1.VI.2.39.
[159] *Test. Epict.* 2.7, 3.3.
[160] *H. Cer.* 266, Hdt. 9.57.
[161] Hsch. s.v.; Lib. *Or.* 11.109.
[162] Antim. 63.
[163] IG 4.955.14 (Epid).
[164] And. 1.110; IG 1².6.129.
[165] IG 1².5, 2².847.24; Hyp. *fr.* 112; Paus. 4.33.5.
[166] 3.14.6, 17.1, 20.5.
[167] Von Prott AM 29.8; ABSA 16.12; Nilsson GF 334, MMR 520 n. 50.
[168] IG 5(1).607.28.
[169] IG 5(1).213.11. On the assimilation of ι to υ in 'Ελευhύνια = 'Ελευσίνια (cf. also the month 'Ελευσύνιος) and the change of intervocalic s to spiritus asper, see Buck GD 26 and 55.
[170] Nilsson MMR 523.
[171] So Guarducci, *Epigraphica* 7.72.
[172] This evidence is considerable but not accepted as conclusive by Wackernagel: Nilsson MMR 522.
[173] Cf. p. 151.

Aptera, in the western part of the island, where a single votive inscription, offered by a woman to the goddess, was reported by Wescher in 1864, which was not found again by Haussoullier in 1878.[174] In the case of Olous and Biannos, though no mention is made of the goddess by name, a strong connexion is established by the month-name discussed above, occurring twice at Olous in inscriptions of the second century B.C., once at Biannos in an inscription of the late third century B.C.[175]

Though it can only be assumed that the city of Eleutherna drew its name from Cretan Eleuthyia, the city of Lato is certainly named after the goddess Leto (Doric Lato),[176] to whose assistance came the goddess of childbirth when Apollo was born. By coincidence, the cult of Apollo enjoyed some distinction at Eleutherna,[177] and Lato provides most of the inscriptional evidence in Crete for Eleuthyia.

Decrees of 201 B.C. concerning Teos have to be published in the temple of Eleuthyia.[178] So do the joint decrees of Lato and Olous concerning negotiations, with Knossos as arbitrator, of about the time 120–116/15 B.C.,[179] and the treaty between Lato and Olous in the second half of the second century B.C.[180] In this same treaty Eleuthyia is among the deities invoked in the oath by which the treaty-makers bind themselves.[181] In or about the year 116/15 B.C., either a new temple was built to the goddess or an old one rebuilt.[182] Coins of the period 200–67 B.C. confirm the evidence supplied by these inscriptions that Eleuthyia was the principal deity worshipped at Lato.[183]

In the treaty which the Gortynians and Hierapytnians made with the Priansians at the beginning of the second century B.C., among the deities invoked in the binding oath is listed Eleuthyia Binatia,[184] that is to say Eleuthyia Inatia, of Inatos. This reference confirms other indications that the city of Inatos was under the power of Priansos and probably served as its port.[185] We know from other sources that the epithet Inatia was associated with Eleuthyia[186] A hill and a stream were especially sacred to Eleuthyia Inatia,[187] and traces of a shrine probably belonging to the

[174] IC 2.III.22 and Guarducci *ad loc.*
[176] Guarducci IC 1, p. 107.
[178] IC 1.XVI.2.31, 15.35.
[180] *Ib.* 5.48.
[182] *Ib.* 26.8. Cf. 27.3.
[184] IC 4.174.61, 76.
[186] *EM* s.v. Εἰνατία; Call. *fr.* 168.

[175] See n. 157 and n. 158 above.
[177] Guarducci IC 2, pp. 141, 145.
[179] *Ib.* 3.18, 4A.13.
[181] *Ib.* 5.75.
[183] *Ib.* p. 108; cf. Head 470.
[185] IC 1, pp. 98, 280; IC 4, p. 244.
[187] St. Byz. s.v. Εἴνατος.

goddess have been found on high ground near a stream on the site of Inatos.[188]

Near Knossos there was a stream known as Amnisos.[189] At its mouth was the town of the same name which served as the harbour of Knossos. For, as Strabo expresses it, 'Minos is said to have used Amnisos as a seaport, where there is a temple of Eileithyia'.[190] This association between Amnisos and Eileithyia is also mentioned by Pausanias and Hesychios.[191] The importance of the cult in Homeric times is clear from the mention of the cave in the *Odyssey*. The continuity of the cult from the earliest times is confirmed by inscriptional evidence and traditional associations elsewhere. For the hill shrine and the stream at Inatos, the cave and the stream of Amnisos, with its nymphs, the Amnisiades,[192] remind us that this continuity implies the retention of the most primitive elements which underlie the making of a goddess.[193]

4. LETO

The cult of Apollo[194] and of his mother Leto originated in Asia Minor. The importance of their association with Crete has long been recognized, together with the signs of a more marked survival of the cult of the goddess in Crete as compared with Greece itself, where, as Nilsson remarked,[195] her cults are very few and their age uncertain. Investigation along these lines has made it possible to clarify the distinction between the cult of the son and the older cult of his mother, whom he sometimes quite supplanted.[196] But the relevance of the Cretan evidence (as substantial, in its way, as that relating to Eileithyia) to the argument for a separate worship of Leto is still perhaps not fully appreciated. This evidence indicates that the cult of Leto separately survived on Cretan soil far into the historical period, within the general framework of Hellenic religion. But where and when did it originate?

---

[188] Guarducci IC 1, p. 98.   [189] A.R. 3.876, Nonn. *D.* 8.115, 13.251.

[190] Str. 10.476.

[191] Paus. 1.18.5; Hsch. s.v. Ἀμνησία. ἡ Εἰλείθυια. Also, as an epithet of Eileithyia, Ἀμνιάς (Ruf. *Onom.* 229), with which cf. ἀμνειός or ἄμνιος, ἀμνεῖον or ἀμνίον = inner membrane surrounding the foetus: Sor. 1.58; Gal. *UP* 15.4; *Hippiatr.* 14; Emp. 71. In *Od.* 3.444 ἀμνίον = a bowl in which the blood of victims was caught.

[192] St. Byz. s.v. Ἀμνισός.

[193] Cf. pp. 78–9. Even at Paros, where Eileithyia was not a goddess of childbirth, but a healing goddess, she had a sacred well: Nilsson MMR 518.

[194] Cf. p. 256.   [195] MMR 517.

[196] Cf. Nilsson MMR 517 with Thomson SAGS 1.294.

Personal names compounded with Leto occur only in south-west Asia Minor; and Leto (Doric Lato) has been connected with the Carian word *lada* 'woman'.[197] There was a time, according to Cretan tradition, as we saw,[198] when the Carians were subjects of Minos, paid no tribute, but manned Minoan ships whenever they were required. But, according to Thucydides, Minos drove the Carians out of the islands. These two accounts can be reconciled if we suppose that the first of them relates to the period *c.* 1600–*c.* 1400 B.C., the second to a later Minos who may have driven the Carians out of the islands *c.* 1250 B.C. It is unlikely that these aggressors from Crete would have adopted a Carian goddess. The Cretans would have been more likely to introduce such a goddess when their relations with the Carians were on a more friendly basis and at a time when the male element in their own religion was still markedly subordinate. The Carian cult was probably not, in any case, very different from the cult of their own major goddess, and even the name of the Carian goddess could hardly be less specific.

The Cretan evidence is, as we might indeed expect of the survivals of a Minoan goddess-cult, concentrated in the central and eastern parts of the island. At Lato, the city which derived its name from the goddess, there are three epigraphical references. She is mentioned (between Pythian Apollo and Artemis) in the list of deities to whom the Latians take the oath in the treaty concluded by themselves and Olous, in the second half of the second century B.C.[199] At this time, as is clear from a whole group of inscriptions,[200] there was considerable building, or rebuilding, of temples. A temple of Lato is twice specified.[201]

In the oath of the Drerians (end of the third to early second century B.C.), the young candidates for initiation into citizenship swear by a number of deities, including Lato.[202] Here again she is included between Pythian Apollo (as compared with Apollo Delphinios, already separately mentioned)[203] and Artemis.

In the treaty made by Lyttos and Olous of 111/10 B.C., Lato is included among the deities of the Lyttian oath, and once more by the same formula between Pythian Apollo and Artemis.[204]

---

[197] Nilsson MMR 516.
[199] IC 1.XVI.5.75.
[201] *Ib.* 21–2.
[203] *Ib.* 20–1.

[198] P. 88.
[200] *Ib.* 21–34.
[202] *Ib.* IX. 1A 24–6.
[204] *Ib.* XVIII. 9 c, 6.

Part of the evidence from Gortyna is of a peculiarly interesting kind. Two inscriptions of the first half of the fifth century B.C. indicate that there was a special region of the city, reserved for metics and freedmen, called Latosion.[205] Its inhabitants, Latosioi, though of subordinate status as compared with the free Dorian citizen class, were relatively privileged, perhaps because of their artisan status.[206] The worship of Pythian Apollo was of especial importance at Gortyna,[207] and his temple was situated in the old city-centre, a district which was therefore named Pythion and its inhabitants Pythieis.[208] In the same way, the names Latosion and Latosioi probably derived from a sanctuary of Lato situated in a *temenos* over which the state exercised special rights.[209]

It is then not surprising to find a strong possibility of yet another example of the formula including Lato between Pythian Apollo and Artemis in the list of deities of the oath binding the treaty of the Gortynians and the Hierapytnians with the Priansians, at the beginning of the second century B.C.[210]

The formula appears also at Hierapytna in a treaty of the second half of the second century B.C.[211] But in a treaty concluded between Hierapytna and Lyttos, at the beginning of this century, Pythian Apollo and Lato are mentioned, but Artemis is excluded, both in the oath of the Hierapytnians and of the Lyttians.[212] An inscription found in 1907, a mile to the north-west of the site of the cult of Zeus Diktaios, which had come under the control of Hierapytna, commemorates the restoration by that city, round about the period 145–139 B.C., of some statues in the temple. Plausible emendations of mutilated passages suggest that perhaps Lato, less certainly also her children, Apollo and Artemis, were among the deities specifically mentioned.[213]

Arguing that the Delphic Apollo images the social changes which had created him, Thomson pointed out that, when the Carian Apollo came to Delos, his mother, the Woman, was still strong enough to secure a place there for herself and her daughter; whereas, at Delphi, in myth and ritual alike, the mother and sister

---

[205] IC 4.58, 78; perhaps also *ib.* 79 (*c.* 480–*c.* 450 B.C.) and *ib.* 144 (*c.* mid-fifth to early fourth centuries B.C.).

[206] See further Willetts ASAC 40–1, 43–4, 53, 110. [207] Cf. pp. 267–9.

[208] St. Byz. s.v. Πύθιον.

[209] Cf. DHR 1.492; Kahrstedt GS 1.345; Guarducci IC 4, p. 181.

[210] IC 4.174.59. [211] IC 3.III.5.13–14.

[212] *Ibid.* 3 B. 14, 20.

[213] *Ib.* II.1; Guarducci *ad loc.*; Willetts ASAC 143; cf. Cook Z 2.930–1.

dropped out.[214] Moreover, though Apollo's birth was located in Delos,[215] the Ephesian origin of the Delian cult is indicated by the old name of the island, Ortygia.[216] This was the name of the grove in which Apollo was said to have been born at Ephesos.[217] There are indications of the original connexion of the cult with childbirth and initiation, especially the initiation of girls.[218]

It was suggested earlier[219] that the hypothesis of an original collective union of young men and women initiates of the same age-grade (still attested for young men in the historical period) strengthens the possibility that the institution of the *agela* can be connected with Minoan Crete; and, further, that the process of excluding girls may also date from Minoan times.

These general considerations have a bearing on the unique evidence of the historical cult of Lato at Phaistos, a city whose links with the Minoan Age need no emphasis. Here too Lato was accompanied by, but apparently not directly linked with, Pythian Apollo[220] and Artemis.[221]

It seems likely, from epigraphic evidence, that the Cretan youths, when they took part in the ceremony of graduation from the *agela*, having now reached the final stage of their initiation into manhood, laid aside their boyhood garments before assuming the warriors' costumes which each had received as a gift after his period of seclusion.[222] Confirmation of this formal ritual derives from our knowledge of a festival at Phaistos, known as the Ekdysia, during which the youth put aside his boy's clothes. This festival was connected with the local cult of Lato Phytia, and with the myth of Leukippos, who was changed from a girl to a boy. According to the myth,[223] Galatea, daughter of Eurytos and wife of Lampros, gave birth to a daughter. She persuaded Lato to allow the girl to change her sex when she was grown up.[224] To

---

[214] SAGS 1.294; cf. Farnell CGS 2.465.

[215] Call. *Del.* 36–58; Simon. 26 b Bergk.

[216] Ath. 9.392d. The Ephesian cult of Artemis originally belonged to Lato: Picard EC 13–21.

[217] Tac. *Ann.* 3.61.

[218] Hdt. 4.34–5; Call. *Del.* 255–7, 296–306; Paus. 1.18.5, 8.21.3.

[219] P. 112.

[220] IC I XVII 1.18 (third century B.C.); *ib.* XXIII 2.6 (third–second century B.C.); Guarducci *ib.* p. 270.

[221] *Ib.* XXIII 6 A (first century B.C.–first century A.D.).

[222] Willetts ASAC 120.   [223] Ant. Lib. *Met.* 17.

[224] Cf. Ov. *Met.* 9.666 (Galatea=Telethusa; Lampros=Ligdus; Leukippos=Iphis).

commemorate the change the Phaistians celebrated their festival of the Ekdysia; and, when they married, lay down beside the statue of Leukippos.[225]

The festival and the myth combine elements of fertility, initiation and marriage ritual; and in the tradition as we have it there is some suggestion of a change from a female to a male cult.

The Phaistian youth were apparently initiated into manhood, citizenship, and also marriage, at the same period of life.[226] Phytia, like Physkoa[227] at Olympia, perhaps also like Orthia at Sparta, is the one who promotes growth, including the growth of fertility in the young.[228] When this growth has been achieved the boy dies as a boy and is born again as a man. This crucial change is marked by the casting-away of boyhood costume and the assumption of a costume appropriate to adult status.

Lato Phytia and her Phaistian festival clearly have roots in the earliest stratum of Cretan religion. If the festival was at one time restricted to (or at least included) girl initiates, their later exclusion would have been part of the process whereby the sacred marriage replaced primitive collective union, and whereby coronation becomes a specialized form of initiation, following on a pre-nuptial ordeal.[229] Such an ordeal may lie behind the festival of Molos, mentioned by Plutarch, whose headless image was exhibited in token of his violation of a young woman.[230]

A similar fate befell that Leukippos who was the son of Oino-maos, prince of Pisa, and who fell in love with Daphne.[231] Because she avoided male company, he despaired of winning her by open courtship, and gained her friendship by disguising himself as a woman and joining her female band. Apollo, also in love with Daphne, became jealous and prompted a desire in Daphne and her friends to bathe naked in the Ladon. The deception of Leukippos was thereupon discovered and the women killed him. The myth is similar to others where the practice of

---

[225] Presumably the statue was in the sanctuary of Lato: cf. Guarducci IC 1 p. 270.
[226] See further Willetts ASAC 120–3. [227] Paus. 5.16.6.
[228] With Lato Phytia cf. Λατὼ κουροτρόφος: Theoc. 18.50. Artemis too was κουρο-τροφος: Farnell CGS 2.577. Several statuettes of the *kourotrophos* type, a woman nursing an infant, have been found on the site of the Ephesos temple. The oldest represent Lato and Artemis as mother and child: Picard EC 455–6, 479–81. For other examples of the *kourotrophos* type see Hansen 69, Nilsson MMR 304.
[229] Cf. pp. 112–18. [230] P. 117.
[231] Paus. 8.20.3.

bathing in streams indicates an origin in the initiation rites of marriageable girls.[232]

Cook, following up yet another suggestion of Plutarch, came to the conclusion that the Laconian Pasiphae of Thalamai was an ancient oracular goddess, whose nature had been so far forgotten that she had become identified with a number of better-known mythological characters—including Daphne.[233] Her sanctuary is described by Pausanias,[234] who says that two bronze statues stood there in the open air, one of them a statue of Pasiphae,[235] the other of Helios; and there was a sacred spring of water that was sweet to drink. In his opinion Pasiphae was not a local deity of Thalamai but an epithet of Selene. These statues of moon-goddess and sun-god recall the ritual performance in which the Cretan Pasiphae, representing the moon, within the wooden cow was united in a sacred marriage with the solar bull.[236]

These are tenuous links with Phaistian Lato and the Ekdysia. But slightly firmer ground can be reached with the further aid of Plutarch and Cook, who combine to prove that the sacred marriage of Zeus and Hera on Mount Kithairon replaced an earlier union of Zeus with Lato Mykhia or Nykhia—'Lato of the Nook' or 'Lato of the Night'.[237] Because the cock was dear to Lato, as to all women in childbirth, since he stood by to lighten her labour,[238] Cook further suggested that Lato Phytia of Phaistos stood in some relation to Zeus Welkhanos of Phaistos, whose sacred bird was the cock.[239] Coins of Phaistos from c. 430–300 B.C. show Welkhanos as a youthful, beardless god sitting in the branches of a leafless tree, his right hand caressing a cock. On the reverse is a bull.[240]

Cook and Atkinson jointly reached the conclusion that the meaning of Welkhanos is 'god of the Willow-tree' and Cook further announced: 'My contention that Zeus at Phaistos, as at Gortyna, was the consort of a willow-goddess is thus strikingly confirmed. Instead of his usual eagle he has a cock, because that bird as the crest of the Phaistian Idomeneus had a long-standing

---

[232] Cf. the streams called Parthenia or Parthenios: Paus. 6.21.7; Str. 8.357, 10.457; Hom. *h. Cer.* 99 etc.; and for the connexion with initiation cf. Earthy 167 and Nic. Dam. 110.

[233] Cook Z 1.522; Plu. *Agis.* 9.

[234] 3.26.1.

[235] See Cook Z 1.522 n. 4.

[236] Cook Z 1.522.

[237] *Ib.* 3.1042.

[238] Ael. *NA* 4.29.

[239] Cook Z 3.1042 n. 9.

[240] Head 473; Cook Z 2.946; Guarducci IC 1. p. 270.

mythical connexion with the town.'[241] For Pausanias had reported the tradition that Idomeneus was descended from the Sun, who was the sire of Pasiphae, and that the cock is sacred to the Sun.[242]

There is one other strand of evidence which connects the myth of the Ekdysia with a sacred marriage of sun and moon. The names Lampros and Galatea suggest that they can be identified with the sun and moon and from the genealogy of this pair we can infer that the identification may not be fanciful.

Galatea was the daughter of Eurytos. Now Eurytos is else-where[243] described as a son of Molione, daughter of Molos. He and his twin brother Kteatos had two heads, four hands, four feet and one body. They were like the bisexual creatures that Plato identifies with sun and moon.[244] Their descriptive epithet in the sixth century B.C. was the equivalent of the name of the bisexual offspring of Lampros and Galatea, *leukippos* ('riding or driving white horses').[245]

Lampros was the son of Pandion. This name too connects with the sun and moon. The Attic festival of the Pandia seems to have been celebrated at the time of the full moon.[246] In Greek belief this was the time when dew fell thickest.[247] The festival was said to have derived its name either from Pandia, the daughter of Selene, or from Pandion, the eponym of the tribe Pandionis, being held in honour of Zeus.[248] A not uncommon form of the sacred marriage is that between Zeus and Selene. This marriage, for example, produced Nemea[249] and also, in one tradition, Diony-sos.[250] The union produced an even more interesting offspring. For, in the seventh century B.C., Alkman refers to flowers and plants which are nourished by the dew—daughter of Zeus and Selene.[251] This reference must derive its origin from the traditions of herbal magic, from the time when moon-worship and the tending of plants were the province of women.[252] Hence, as Roscher suggested,[253] Pandia was probably an epithet belonging originally not to Selene's daughter, but to Selene herself. It is the

---

[241] Cook Z 2.947.   [242] 5.25.9.
[243] Pherecyd. 36 *ap.* sch. *Il.* 11.709.
[244] Cook Z 1.310–11 on Pl. *Smp.* 189d–190c. Cf. *ib.* 2.1015 n. 8.
[245] Ibyc. 16.
[246] Mommsen FSA 432 n. 4, 441; Gruppe 938 n. 1.
[247] Cook Z 1.733.   [248] Phot., *EM* s.v.
[249] Sch. Pi. *N* 425. Boeckh.
[250] Ulp. *in Mid.* 174; cf. Cic. DND 3.58; Cook Z 1.457 n. 5.
[251] Alcm. 48.   [252] P. 79.
[253] SV 100; cf. *id.* LGRM 2.3172.

sacred marriage of Zeus with Selene that transfers the epithet to the offspring and may well have been responsible for a metamorphosis of that offspring from a female to a male—Pandia to Pandion.

Here, for the time, we must leave Zeus, in his Phaistian form Welkhanos[254] and return to Lato. We must note in conclusion that she does enjoy a measure of independence still in historical Crete. Pythian Apollo accompanies her, but Artemis is also closely linked. Finally, her festival at Phaistos is of particular importance in establishing her relationship to Minoan and even pre-Minoan cults and institutions. In fact, the close relationship of this festival with the institution of the *agela* probably accounts for its survival, because the state authorities were concerned to foster archaic practices in their own interests.[255]

5. BRITOMARTIS AND DIKTYNNA

Other considerations apart, the cult of Britomartis has a peculiar interest because there is little doubt that it concerns a deity with a Minoan name which we can understand—'sweet maiden'.[256] In myth she is associated with Minos and has begun to be assimilated to Artemis. She is said to have escaped the attentions of Minos by disappearing in a grove at Aigina, where she was worshipped as Aphaia.[257] In another version of the story she is the companion of Artemis, is pursued by Minos for nine months, and escapes by throwing herself in the sea.[258] There is an element here common to initiation myths.[259] What prevented Britomartis from degenerating into a mere epithet of Artemis was the persistence in Crete itself of both her name and her cult in a number of places.[260]

In the Drerian oath she is distinguished from Artemis.[261] Here she was known as Britomarpis.[262] That this was the Cretan form as opposed to the Greek form Britomartis is indicated by the epigraphic evidence elsewhere: that is to say, in the treaty between Lato and Olous (second century B.C.);[263] in the treaty between

---

[254] See further pp. 250–1.   [255] See further Willetts ASAC 123, 243–4.
[256] Hsch. βριτύ. γλυκύ. Κρῆτες; EM 214.29 βρίτον. τουτέστιν ἀγαθόν; Solin. 11.8: Britomartem, quod sermone nostro sonat virginem dulcem.
[257] Ant. Lib. 40; cf. Paus. 2.30.3.   [258] Call. *Dian.* 189–203.
[259] P. 176.
[260] Cf. Hsch. Βριτόμαρτις. ἐν Κρήτῃ ἡ Ἄρτεμις; D.S. 5.76; Paus. 3.14.2.
[261] IC 1.IX.1 A 29, cf. 26.   [262] See further Guarducci IC 1 p. 36.
[263] IC 1.XVI.5.75–6.

Lyttos and Olous (second century B.C.);[264] and in an inscription from Khersonesos (second century B.C.).[265] We cannot be certain of the spelling in the single fragmentary inscription from Gortyna (third to second century B.C.),[266] which confirms other evidence of her worship here.[267]

This distribution of epigraphic evidence indicates that the worship of Britomartis survived from early times in central Crete, especially along the northern coast. We know further that, at Khersonesos, the port of Lyttos, the goddess had a temple;[268] and her head is represented on coins of the period 370–300 B.C.— perhaps a copy of an actual cult-statue.[269] In the treaty between Lato and Olous, Britomartis is again distinguished from Artemis;[270] and her festival at Olous, the Britomarpeia, is mentioned.[271] This festival was presumably the equivalent of the Britomartia at Delos, which followed immediately on the festival of Artemis.[272] At Olous also her head is portrayed on coins, of the period 330–200 B.C.[273] Here too she had a temple, reputed to contain a wooden statue of the goddess made by Daidalos.[274]

The close relationship between Britomartis and Diktynna is generally recognized, but has not been satisfactorily explained. The same remark applies to the association between Diktynna and Artemis.[275] Yet there are indications in the evidence that the relationship is the old and familiar one of Mother and Maid; and that Diktynna is to Demeter as Britomartis is to Persephone.

The pursuit of the virgin Britomartis by Minos was compared by Cook to the rape of Persephone: she was 'borne off to become queen of an underground king'.[276] Yet Cook could not agree with Frazer (who followed Hoeck and Roscher)[277] that the myth of Minos and Britomartis or Diktynna was a case of sun-and-moon

[264] *Ib.* XVIII 9 c. 7.
[265] *Ib.* VII. 4.
[266] *Ib.* 4.237.
[267] Call. *Dian.* 189 f.; Guarducci IC 4. p. 34; cf. Nilsson MMR 510 n. 99.
[268] Str. 10.479; Marinatos *Arch Anz.* (1930) 163; Faure suggests that she had a cult also in the neighbouring cave of Skoteino: BCH 82.511.
[269] Guarducci IC 1. p. 34; Head 460; Cook Z 1.542.
[270] IC 1.XVI.5.75–6.
[271] *Ib.* 43.
[272] IG 11 (2).145.34; Nilsson GF 209.
[273] IC I p. 244; Head 472.
[274] Paus. 9.40.3.
[275] 'It appears that [Diktynna] was a Cretan goddess very much resembling Artemis and parallel to Britomartis, but venerated in western Crete, whilst Britomartis was worshipped in eastern Crete': Nilsson MMR 511; cf. Persson RGPT 129, LSJ s.v. Δίκτυννα.
[276] Cook Z 1.623 n. 6.
[277] Frazer GB 3.73; Hoeck K 1.90 ff., 2.170; Roscher SV 45 f., 116 ff., 128 ff.

marriage, on the grounds that Britomartis or Diktynna were not identified with the moon until Roman times—'and even then no hint is dropped that the consort of Diktynna or Britomartis was solar'.[278] But since it is generally agreed that Britomartis and Diktynna are old Cretan goddesses, it is unlikely that their association with the moon was solely invented by late mythography, since, as we have seen,[279] moon-worship played a conspicuous part in the development of the Minoan goddess. Cook may have been right, however, to this extent—the myth may reflect, not a developed sacred marriage of sun and moon, but an earlier kind of marriage, the collective marriage of initiates.

For the matriarchal elements in the myth and the associated evidence are, if anything, more strongly marked than in the case of Demeter–Persephone.[280] Zeus is apparently the father of Britomartis in one tradition where, significantly, Hekate is her mother.[281] But in the main tradition she is fatherless and her mother is Leto. Persephone's father was said to be Zeus,[282] but this is not apparent in the Homeric Hymn to Demeter; and it therefore seems that Persephone also was originally fatherless.[283] But Persephone's lover was more successful than Minos. The rape of Persephone is described by Homer as a patriarchal marriage by capture. The bride went to live with her husband for at least part of the year, spending the rest of it with her mother.

Britomartis, however, did not live with Minos. According to Kallimachos,[284] she hid away from him at first in oak-groves in the meadows; then he pursued her for nine months until she threw herself into the sea and was saved by the nets of some fishermen. In consequence, she was afterwards known as Diktynna (since *diktyon* = 'net'). According to the other version,[285] mentioned above, she escaped from Minos by hiding herself in a grove at Aigina and was afterwards worshipped as Aphaia. According to the gloss of Hesychios, Aphaia is Diktynna, or Artemis.[286] Britomartis is thus mythologically represented as a marriageable girl who undergoes a transformation and a change of name as a result

---

[278] Cook Z 1.543. cf. 524.   [279] P. 78.
[280] P. 150.
[281] Neanth. *fr.* 23; Cook Z 1.543 n. 1. But cf. Paus. 2.30.3.
[282] Hes. *Th.* 912–13.
[283] As was Demeter, whose mother Rhea gave her her name and the promise to found her Mysteries: Hom. *h. Cer.* 122, 459–69.
[284] *Dian.* 189–203.   [285] Ant. Lib. 40; cf. Paus. 2.30.3.
[286] Hsch. s.v. Ἀφαία. ἡ Δίκτυννα, καὶ Ἄρτεμις.

of the attentions of Minos. We are not told specifically that she had intercourse with him. But presumably he found her in her hiding-place, or she would not have fled. It may be significant that she was in flight for nine months—time enough to become a mother. For the initiation of the maid into mother, into nurse and guardian of the young, seems to continue as the basic conception of Britomartis-Diktynna.

Whatever may have been the intentions of the mythographers who connected Diktynna with *diktyon* and (apparently) Aphaia with *aphanes* ('unseen')[287]—an epithet applied by Sophocles to Persephone[288]—the associations are based on more than etymological fancy.[289] We now know from epigraphic evidence[290] that an impressive temple in Aigina was actually the seat of the worship of Aphaia. On the east terrace of the temple were discovered many Mycenaean remains. They included more than 150 clay bulls and a large number of female idols.[291] Moreover, four idols of women with a child and one with two children were also discovered.[292] These *kourotrophos* images are of special significance in view of the ancient association, recorded by Hesychios, of Aphaia with Diktynna and Artemis, and of the original nature of the cult of Leto, mother alike of Artemis and Britomartis.

But this aspect of the matter must not be pursued before we have dealt with the difficulties presented by the association of Diktynna with *diktyon*, which Strabo[293] commented upon as follows: 'And they say that Kallimachos is not correct either in asserting that Britomartis, in flight from the violence of Minos, leaped from Dikte into fishermen's nets (*diktya*), and because of this she herself was named Diktynna by the Kydonians and the mountain likewise Dikte. For Kydonia is not in the neighbourhood of the places referred to, but lies near the western extremities of the island; and the mountain of Kydonia is Tityros, on which there is a temple; but this is the *Diktynnaion*, not the *Diktaion*.'

The learned Kallimachos could have made a mistake, in too readily identifying *Diktynnaion* with *Dikte*. But modern scholars

---

[287] The original name of the goddess may have been Ἄφα, as in IG 4.1582. In that case Ἀφαία could be an adjectival form derived from Ἄφα, as Ἀθηναία from Ἀθήνη: Wilamowitz *Berl. Sitzb.* (1921) 952 n. 1. Holland derives Ἀφαία from ἅπτειν—'the shining one'. H 60.59.

[288] *OC* 1556.

[289] Cf. Nilsson MMR 511–12; Persson RGPT 129–30.

[290] IG 4.1580 ff.

[291] *Aegina* 1.370 and pl. CIX.

[292] *Ib.* 373, pl. CVIII, 3, 4 and CIX, 4.

[293] 10.479.

have been unwilling to identify themselves with the ready pedantry of his ancient detractors.[294] They have come to his rescue by assigning the myth of the leap from Mount Dikte to Britomartis, despite the obvious rejoinder that it is wrong to isolate the myth from the etymology of Diktynna. Or *Diktaion* hill is supposed to be a shortened form of *Diktynnaion* hill. Or (on the principle that if Mahomet will not come to the mountain, the mountain must be brought to Mahomet) the possibility has been recognized, in the turmoil of Cretan history, of a movement of the cult from east to west of the island, where it preserved the name of the mountain.[295]

There is something of value in all these rescue-attempts and particularly in the last. They are based on a premise which no amount of pedantry, ancient or modern, can remove. Despite objections, as Nilsson has observed, 'the affinity between Mt. Dikte and the goddess Diktynna is so striking that it is hard to get rid of it'.[296] Though it be true that Britomartis is venerated east of Knossos and Diktynna to the west, their cult association obviously defies any distinction based on such nicely defined boundary lines; and, in any case, the cult of Lato Kourotrophos is concentrated in the central and eastern parts of the island,[297] which perhaps is not, as we shall see, irrelevant in this connexion. Nor can we ignore that the same (presumably pre-Greek) root is common to the mountain and the goddess.[298]

A reference by Euripides[299] and one by Aristophanes[300] have been interpreted to mean either that assimilation of Diktynna to the huntress Artemis can be traced back in literature to the time of Euripides;[301] or that, in Athens, as compared with Crete, Diktynna had apparently been fused with Artemis by the fifth century B.C.[302] What is more important, however, than the evidence of formal identification, is that both references indicate the reason for the tendency to fusion. The names of Artemis and Diktynna invoke the conception of a mountain-mother and a huntress.[303] Such an underlying conception is a pre-condition,

---

[294] See Nilsson MMR 511 and Persson RGPT 129.
[295] Mingazzini in *Religio* (1919) 276.   [296] MMR 512.
[297] P. 173.   [298] Guarducci IC 3. p. 5.
[299] *IT* 126; ὦ παῖ τᾶς Λατοῦς, Δίκτυνν' οὐρεία.
[300] *Ra.* 1359 f.; ἅμα δὲ Δίκτυννα παῖς Ἄρτεμις καλὰ τὰς κυνίσκας ἔχουσ' ἐλθέτω. Aristophanes conceives of Diktynna elsewhere as watching over hunters' nets: *V.* 368: ἢ δέ μοι Δίκτυννα συγγνώμην ἔχοι τοῦ δικτύου.
[301] Cook Z 1.542.   [302] Guarducci IC 2 p. 130.
[303] Cf. Cook Z 1.541–2.

rather than a consequence, of literary allusion. In the same way, when Herodotos tells us that the Samians who founded the city of Kydonia in 524 B.C. also built the temple of Diktynna—which is very probably correct—we are not to infer that no shrine of the goddess previously existed near by.[304]

When this passage of Herodotos was discussed earlier in conjunction with other relevant evidence, the following conclusions were drawn: (1) the Kydonians had a much older history than the foundation of the city of Kydonia on the north-west coast in 524 B.C.; (2) in Mycenaean times they occupied the whole breadth of the western part of the island; (3) they may have derived from Bronze Age immigrants into Crete from Asia Minor.[305] Evidence from the historical period makes it appear likely that the cult of Diktynna should be related to these Kydonians who had occupied the western part of the island in earlier times. For, apart from the main centre of her worship at the Diktynnaion itself, on the promontory between Phalasarna and Kydonia, this evidence is also distributed along the north-west coast from Phalasarna (to the westward) to Kydonia (eastward of the Diktynnaion) and Aptera (eastward of Kydonia); it includes Polyrhenia (to the south-east of Phalasarna); and also Lisos (on the south-west coast).

Outside Crete, Diktynna's cult-centres include Astypalaia,[306] Las, on the Laconian gulf,[307] Sparta,[308] Phokis,[309] Athens;[310] and her worship seems to have stretched westward as far as Marseille.[311] Only by regarding Diktynna as unique, as specifically Cretan in origin, would it be possible to agree with the conclusion that her worship was carried to these places by Cretans.[312] But such a view would have to ignore the close relations of Diktynna with Britomartis, of Britomartis-Diktynna with Artemis and with Leto.

The cult of Diktynna, though widespread, falls within the limits of the old Carian domain.[313] This suggests the possibility that it belongs to a religious substratum which cannot be localized in Crete. In seeking for an explanation of the characteristics of the

---

[304] Hdt. 3.59; Guarducci *ib.* pp. 128–9.
[305] Pp. 133–5.
[306] IG XII. 3.189.
[307] Paus. 3.24.8.
[308] Paus. 3.12.8.
[309] IG IX.1.5.
[310] IG II–III².4688.
[311] CIG III.6764.
[312] Guarducci IC 2 p. 130.
[313] Bounded by a line drawn from Leukas to Lamia and thence across to Chios: Thomson SAGS 1.171, after review of the ancient evidence.

cult of Cretan Leto, reference was made both to her Carian name and to the nature of the Ephesian cult.[314] This topic must now be pursued in more detail.

The cult of Artemis Orthia (despite our ignorance of the meaning of the epithet Orthia) was of the same nature as the cult of Artemis Limnatis, goddess 'of the marshes', and of Artemis Agrotera, goddess 'of the wild'. These three cults are so characteristically Peloponnesian as to make it possible to consider that they were introduced from Anatolia by Carians or Leleges, in some cases by way of Crete, since in several places they are identified with Cretan Britomartis-Diktynna.[315] Moreover, the northward extension of the titles Orthia, Limnatis and Agrotera coincides with the limits of the old Carian domain.[316]

The ceremony of initiation of the Spartan youths included an ordeal of flagellation. They were scourged in the presence of the priestess of Artemis Orthia, holding the sacred image of the goddess.[317] Similarly, the *epheboi* held races and processions in honour of Artemis Agrotera of Agra near Athens.[318] The presence of the priestess of Orthia at an initiation rite of males is a feature so unusual as to suggest the explanation that the priestess had originally officiated over an initiation rite of girls.[319] A similar ordeal is at least attested at Alea in Arcadia, and there women were actually involved.[320]

The temple of Artemis Orthia was in the marshes of the Eurotas. The image of the goddess was said to have been found in a bed of withies and the goddess herself was called Lygodesma, 'withy-bound'; or, alternatively, Orestes is said to have brought back the image from Tauris.[321] This detail of the image evokes such a close parallel with the traditions of the image at Ephesos that it has been suggested that 'the Spartan Artemis was an offshoot of the Ephesian'.[322] The Ephesian cult of Artemis, if it was founded by the Hittites, must date at least as far back as the thirteenth century B.C.[323] But it belonged originally to Leto, who was represented by a wooden image, reputedly found in the swamps of the Kaÿstros. This was hung on a sacred tree. The

[314] Pp. 172–5.
[315] Paus. 3.14.2 (Sparta), 10.36.5 (Phokis), E. *Hipp.* 145, 1130 (Troizen), Homolle 23 (Delos).
[316] Thomson SAGS 1.276.
[317] Plu. *Lyc.* 18; Paus. 3.16.11.
[318] IG II.467–71.
[319] Thomson SAGS 1.273.
[320] Paus. 8.23.1.
[321] Paus. 3.16.11, 3.16.17.
[322] Thomson SAGS 1.271.
[323] Lethaby ETA.

earliest shrine was a courtyard around the sacred tree; and below the tree stood a small altar.[324] These elements—of goddess, shrine and sacred tree—are also common features in the scenes portrayed on Minoan rings.[325] The shrine became a temple for the goddess and her image in the early archaic period, eventually becoming one of the largest of Greek temples. The annual spring festival lasted for a month and opened with sacrifices and dances which were followed by athletic contests, the winners being enrolled in a sacred college.[326] The Ephesian goddess was conceived as presiding over the whole realm of nature: the elements, the fertility of the soil, the life of beasts, the life of human beings.[327]

The sacred tree marked her birthplace: for Leto had leant against it when the birth-pangs came upon her.[328] This was the origin of the cult. For several statuettes of the *kourotrophos* type—a woman nursing an infant—have been found on the site. The oldest of these represent a mother and child, that is to say, Leto and Artemis. In some of the later specimens, however, there are two children. The daughter now has an infant brother. But, although Artemis eventually grew up to supersede her mother, Ephesian Apollo remained a child.[329]

At the sacred grove of Klaros near Kolophon, however, twenty miles north of Ephesos, where there had also been an original cult of Leto, she was succeeded by Apollo and not by Artemis. Picard explains that, since Klaros was more resistant than Ephesos to the East and its traditions, a god such as Apollo, celestial ruler of a patriarchal society, was naturally likely to receive a more favourable reception at Kolophon.[330]

Some of these old traditions in the East died hard. We now know that the goddess Astarte of Ugarit was a huntress, as Baal was a hunter.[331] Baal was also the god of storms and rains.[332] Now Zeus Kretagenes or Kretogenes, 'Zeus the Cretan-born', was likewise a hunter.[333] His birth was first of all located in a cave on Mount Dikte.[334] He was identified, farther east, with a local rain-

---

[324] Picard EC 13–19.
[325] Persson RGPT *passim*; Nilsson MMR 268, 275, 278, 280 n. 61, 333, 343.
[326] Picard EC 20-1, 28, 104, 328, 332; CIG 2954. The month was Artemision.
[327] Picard EC 377.   [328] Tac. *Ann.* 3.61.
[329] Picard EC 455-6, 479-81.   [330] Picard EC 455-7.
[331] Virolleaud in CRA (1956) 60-3.   [332] P. 162.
[333] Cook Z 1.157 n. 3, 645, 652, 663 n. 2, 2.522, 727, 3.550.
[334] See further pp. 216-17.

god, the Philistine Marna or Marnas,[335] who had a temple at Gaza. The eponymous founder of Gaza was Minos, who may be featured as a helmeted warrior holding the branch of a sacred bay-tree on coins of the town.[336] The name Marnas was understood to be Cretan, meaning 'virgin'.[337] It is tempting to suppose that Britomartis ('sweet maid') is derived from the same root.[338] Bronze coins of Gaza, struck by Hadrian, Faustina Iunior and Lucilla, Septimius Severus, Caracalla, Plautilla and Geta, show the façade of a temple within which two young deities stand, apparently Apollo with his bow and Artemis as a huntress.[339] The male figure, however, appears to be named Marnas or, more commonly, Marna. Hence the possibility that Marnas and Britomartis, hunter and huntress, are featured.[340]

The Marneion of Zeus Kretagenes was the most famous of the eight pagan temples of Gaza.[341] These were all demolished as a result of Christian pressure on the authorities and with the aid of troops, between 401 and 402 A.D. An initial attack on the Marneion was repulsed by the priests, but the other temples were destroyed and plundered. Finally, in June 402, the Marneion was burnt down by the Christians and a Christian church was then built on its site. The story of the destruction of these pagan temples and of how it was engineered by the Christian leaders survives.[342] The description of the Marneion itself, a circular structure with concentric colonnades and inner shrine, has suggested a resemblance to the Cretan Labyrinth.[343]

When the Marneion had been destroyed, the houses of the devotees of the cult were searched for sacred books of magic which were used in their rites of initiation.[344] These rites of initiation must have played a major part in the cult of Marnas, the deliberate desecration of which by the Christians outraged his worshippers, especially the women.[345] Similar rites of initiation must have belonged to Zeus Kretagenes in Crete.[346] Although the cult of Artemis succeeded that of Leto at Ephesos, and although

---

[335] Cook Z 1.149 n. 1, 3.549; Preisendantz in RE s.v.; S. A. Cook 180–6; Baudissin 2.38 ff., 4.5, 186 f.; Bethe in H. 65.204, cf. Nilsson MMR 535 n. 4.
[336] St. Byz. s.v. Γάζα; Cook Z 1.235.   [337] St. Byz. ibid; Cook Z 3.550.
[338] Cf. Cook Z ibid.   [339] Ibid.
[340] Ibid. and n. 8.
[341] Viz., in addition to the Marneion, those of Helios, Aphrodite, Apollo, Kore and Hekate, the Heroeion and the Tykhaion.
[342] Markos Diakonos v. Porphyrii episcopi Gazensis 19 ff.
[343] Cook Z 1.478, 3.555; S. A. Cook 180.   [344] Mark. Diak. 71.
[345] Ib. 76.   [346] See further pp. 199–220.

the cult of Apollo succeeded that of Leto at Delos (as at Klaros), the original connexion of the cult with initiation is apparent.[347] The Peloponnesian Artemis continued to be associated with initiation.[348] In Crete, Lato, Artemis and Apollo, Britomartis and Diktynna, all continued to flourish side by side. We have seen that at Phaistos the cult of Lato was certainly connected with initiation, though it appears to reflect its more developed form of the sacred marriage.[349] Can it be that the cult of Britomartis-Diktynna reflects the more primitive stage of collective initiation —in keeping with the survival of the custom of collective marriage, in something more than a formal sense?[350]

Certainly the Mycenaean Aphaia was, like the early Ephesian goddess, *kourotrophos*.[351] A survey of the epigraphic and numismatic evidence relating to Cretan Diktynna will show that she continued to preserve similar characteristics of the maid become mother, of Britomartis become mature.

The evidence from Aptera is of the utmost interest, though tantalizingly slight. Connexion with Diktynna is established by a decree of 201 B.C., which makes reference to the month Diktynnaios, known to us only from this single instance.[352] From the single evidence of another inscription (third or second century B.C.) we also know that games were celebrated in which the prize was a crown.[353] Yet another (second century B.C.) makes it clear, firstly, that the temple of Artemis was of prime importance and, secondly, that she was worshipped here as Artemis Aptera.[354]

It seems then that we have another example of the naming of a city after the principal deity worshipped by the inhabitants. The parallel case of Cretan Lato immediately springs to mind. But there is a significant difference. The town is not called after Artemis, but after the specific local epithet attaching to her cult. The inference is that Aptera was there before Artemis and that the two cults became fused because of their similar characteristics.[355]

But this inference seems to involve us immediately in contradictions. There is no doubt that Aptera is the common Greek word meaning 'wingless' and Artemis Aptera must have signified

---

[347] P. 175.

[349] Pp. 175–6.

[351] P. 182.

[353] *Ib.* 4 C 9, cf. 11.

[355] Cf. Kretschmer EGGS 419; Meister *Indogerman. Forsch.* 18.150,

[348] P. 185.

[350] P. 181.

[352] IC 2.III.1.13.

[354] *Ib.* 2.56.

188

'Wingless Artemis'. Indeed, the 'wingless' conception seems to lie at the root of the myth of the contest between the Sirens and the Muses which was supposed to have taken place at Aptera.[356] The victorious Muses plucked out the feathers of the Sirens, who thereupon became white and threw themselves into the sea. In consequence the town was called Aptera and some neighbouring islands Leukai ('white'). The myth in its literary form may be late, but it is unwise to dismiss its connexion with Aptera as 'due to a mistaken etymology'.[357] For the content betrays some familiar archaic features. The leap into the sea is a Minoan religious feature involved with initiation myths.[358] It must, in the present context, recall the leap of Britomartis to escape the pursuit of Minos. Glaukos of Anthedon also performed a ritual leap into the sea before undergoing metamorphosis. He and his counterpart and namesake, the son of Minos, have a name which probably alluded to the first stage of an initiatory rite.[359]

Were the Leukai, the 'White Girls' of Aptera, the female counterparts of Glaukos, female initiates? The winged Sirens were originally parentless and when, later on, they were given a pedigree, their father is a river-god, Acheloos, and their mother is the Muse Terpsichore.[360] They are linked with the Muses through music, and through music of a particular kind—the dirge.[361] Helen, in Euripides' play, prays for Persephone to send the Sirens to weep with her, conceiving them as daughters of Earth, winged girls, virgins.[362] In Greece, as elsewhere, the dirge was sung and accompanied with an ecstatic dance in which the women beat their breasts and tore their hair.[363] The mythology then, though late, has matriarchal and collective associations. It is also based upon a contest between rival choirs of females, a contest which ends with the ritual ordeal of the leap into the sea. The victors in the contest wore crowns made from the feathers of the vanquished. Were the games at Aptera based upon an actual ritual which gave rise to this mythology? The evidence is too fragmentary for the possibility to be seriously tested. But it can be

[356] Sch. *ad* Lyc. 653; Paus. 9.34.3; Jul. *Ep.* 40.3; St. Byz. s.v. Ἄπτερα.
[357] Harrison MO 176.
[358] P. 179, cf. Guarducci IC 2 p. 130. The representation of a Siren on a fragment of a large vase from Praisos shows interesting archaic features which may have perpetuated a pre-Hellenic tradition: Levi GC 280–93.
[359] P. 64.
[360] A.R. 4.893–4.
[361] Cf. Harrison MO 146–82.
[362] E. *Hel.* 167.
[363] *Il.* 18.50–1; A. *Ch.* 423–7, *Pers.* 123–8, 1039–77, *Supp.* 126–8; cf. Th. 2.34.4; Bücher 442.

more certainly suggested that the cult of Artemis Aptera involved originally a rite of initiation and purification performed by female *agelai*.

There is also a patriarchal tradition associated with the name of the city, preserved by Pausanias.[364] According to one version, the second temple of Apollo at Delphi was built by a Delphian whose name was Pteras. It was said that the Cretan city Aptera was named after Pteras—with the addition of the letter 'A'. This tradition is useful confirmation of friendly relations between Delphi and Crete;[365] and also for the spread of the Leto-Artemis-Apollo cult from the East to the mainland by way of Crete.[366] But it is the insertion of the letter 'A' that brings us to the heart of the contradiction represented by the cult of Wingless Artemis.

The contradiction is, however, not new. Thus, although the sanctuary of Artemis Orthia cannot be dated back beyond the Iron Age, some of the cult objects and offerings indicate that Orthia had Bronze Age associations.[367] They are sometimes connected with the archaic so-called 'Persian Artemis' or Mistress of Animals, familiar in the whole Aegean area, including Minoan Crete. This Mistress of Animals in Greek art survives from Minoan times, but, as Nilsson observed, with a difference.[368] 'The Mistress of Animals in archaic art is often, but by no means always, winged; whereas the Minoan goddess has no wings . . . in Asia Minor and in the region north of the Black Sea, which was dependent on Ionian art, only the winged type appears; the Mistress of Animals without wings is missing here, though this type on the contrary was found in Greece; this means that the Minoan prototype was preserved in Greece.'

The most likely solution of the problem therefore is that the survival of the cult of Artemis Aptera is a further demonstration of the Minoan origin of Artemis as Mistress of Animals. There is no essential difference between (sometimes) winged Orthia and wingless Artemis of Aptera. Winged or wingless, she is *kouro-trophos*. But in Aptera she was nearer her Minoan origin: Diktynna in all but name. For coins of the city (*c.* 400–300 B.C.) show the head of Artemis Aptera with ornamented crown. On the reverse, an armed warrior stands with his right hand raised to salute a sacred tree.[369] We recall that, at Dreros, where Britomartis retains

---

[364] Paus. 10.5.10.
[365] Guarducci IC 2 p. 9.
[366] Pp. 172–9.
[367] Dawkins, *passim*; Nilsson MMR 505.
[368] MMR 507.
[369] Head 458.

her individuality beside Artemis in the oath of the citizen-initiates, the members of the *agela* were obliged to plant olive-trees.[370] Coins of Aptera of a later period (*c.* 250–67 B.C.) show the head of Artemis Aptera and a warrior advancing.[371]

Diktynna is featured on coins of Kydonia, Polyrhenia, perhaps of Phalasarna, and of the Roman province. At Kydonia (200–67 B.C.) coins have the head of Diktynna, with bow and quiver; and also Diktynna standing in a hunting-dress, holding a long torch, a dog beside her, with the whole in an olive-wreath.[372] At Polyrhenia (400–330 B.C.) coins show a head of Diktynna, her hair rolled (sometimes in coif); and later (200–67 B.C.) a bust of Diktynna facing, with bow and quiver, and male figure (Apollo?) advancing, with a bow.[373] At Phalasarna (*c.* 400–300 B.C.) the head of a goddess on coins, with hair bound with a crossing cord, or rolled, may perhaps be that of Diktynna.[374] Coins of the Province of Crete of the time of Domitian feature Diktynna hunting, with the title Diktynna Sebaste. Most interesting of all, coins of the time of Trajan have Diktynna seated on rocks between two Kouretes, nursing the infant Zeus.[375]

The cult of Diktynna at Lisos is attested by coins (*c.* 400–250 B.C.) with head of the goddess. That the cult was especially important here is apparent from an inscription of the third century B.C., recording a treaty between the Oreioi and King Magas of Cyrene.[376] The inscription is highly important for a number of reasons. It establishes the existence of a temple of Diktynna at Lisos, thereby also proving that the Diktynnaion was not the only temple of the goddess in western Crete. Since the treaty has to be deposited in the temple, the importance of the cult at Lisos is clear. Moreover, the goddess heads the list of deities in the oath. She is followed by the deities who shared her sanctuary—who, unfortunately, are not named; and then the deities of the neighbouring city of Poikilasion—also not specified. Then, before the conventional final mention of 'all gods and goddesses', Zeus Kretagenes is included. The juxtaposition of

---

[370] Willetts ASAC 122 and H. 85.381-4; see further pp. 201-2; 306-7.
[371] Head 458; Seltman 171-2. [372] Head 464.
[373] Head 474-5; cf. Guarducci *ad* IC 2 p. 241.
[374] Diktynna: Head 474; perhaps Aphrodite: Guarducci IC 2 p. 220.
[375] Head 479; Cook Z 1.541; Guarducci IC 2 p. 129.
[376] IC 2.XVII.1; Willetts ASAC 226. The Oreioi ('People of the Mountains') were a group of cities, centred on Lisos, with common religious and political ties and a common coinage.

Diktynna and Zeus Kretagenes in this oath has an obvious bearing on what has been said before about Marnas. For not only have we here the earliest reference to Zeus Kretagenes in Crete; it is early enough to invalidate the proposition[377] that the cult of Zeus Kretagenes has a purely Hellenistic origin. The precedence of Diktynna over all other deities, including Zeus Kretagenes, is a reminder both of her antiquity and of her continuing eminence in this region. Finally, the existence of a temple of Diktynna at Lisos opens up the possibility that there were still more temples to the goddess, besides the Diktynnaion, in the west of Crete—for example, at Polyrhenia and Phalasarna.[378]

There is no reason why we should not accept as genuine the story, reported by Herodotos, that the Samians who were at Kydonia between 524 and 519 B.C. built the various temples that he says could still be seen there, including the Diktynnaion. It follows that the temple was under the jurisdiction of Kydonia at this period. By the end of the fourth or beginning of the third century B.C., it appears that control had passed to Polyrhenia.[379]

Since Diktynna is featured on coins of Kydonia between 200 and 67 B.C., it can be inferred that control reverted to Kydonia during this period.[380] After the Roman occupation the Polyrhenians again took over, as appears from a reference in Strabo and from an inscription dated 6 B.C.[381] The latter is a fragment of the temple accounts. The revenues of the temple were drawn from slaves and cattle let out for hire, from the sale of cattle, wool, cheese and other commodities. Expenses included wine and oil for the temple officials and the wages of a slave and a freedman. Other inscriptions make it clear that, in the times of Hadrian and other emperors, the revenues of the temple of Diktynna were regarded as belonging to the public treasury and were used to finance public works (including roads) for the whole of the Province of Crete.[382]

The inference is that the temple enjoyed increasing power and affluence. Confirmation of the wealth it possessed is forthcoming in the account of the miraculous end of Apollonios Tyanensis at the Diktynnaion. He found, on his arrival, that savage dogs were

---

[377] As advanced by Fehrle in Roscher LGRM s.v. Zeus; cf. Guarducci *ad loc.*
[378] Guarducci IC 2 pp. 220 and 241.   [379] IC 2.XI.1.
[380] Guarducci *ib.* p. 129.   [381] Str. 10.479; IC 2.XI,3.
[382] IC 2.XI (Dictynnaeum) 6; *ib.* 4 (Gortyna) 333 and 334.

kept at the temple for the express purpose of guarding its wealth.[383]

Just as Diktynna was etymologically connected with Mount Dikte, so the name Diktynnaios was applied to the mountains of the north-west in the region of Kydonia.[384] But the mountain on which there was a shrine of Diktynna, long before the Diktynnaion was built by the Samians, was known as Tityros.[385] Tityros was supposed to mean 'satyr'.[386] According to Strabo, Tityroi were like the Korybantes.[387] They belonged to that cycle of Cretan-Phrygian tradition which was bound up with the sacred rites of the rearing of the child Zeus in Crete and in honour of the mother of the gods in Phrygia and in the region of the Trojan Ida.[388] In Crete, such rites were performed with orgiastic worship and with such ministers as served Dionysos—the Satyrs. These the Cretans called Kouretes, the armed young men who danced the story of the birth of Zeus.[389] The Dikytnna represented on the coins of Trajan's time therefore still retains her archaic aspect of mountain-mother, *kourotrophos*, guardian of initiates.

6. ARIADNE

It is now generally agreed that Ariadne was a vegetation-goddess of Minoan origin, a type of the Minoan goddess—like Britomartis. The comparison holds good in several respects. Just as Britomartis means 'Sweet Maid', so Ariadne (or Ariagne) means 'Very Holy Maid'.[390] Like Pasiphae, she had old associations with the moon,[391] and therefore with fertility. It was suggested earlier that the Knossian dance in her honour was part of the ritual of collective marriage, following on the graduation of the initiates: it was a love-dance.[392] This partly explains her association with Dionysos

---

[383] Philostr. *VA* 8.30.

[384] Plin. *NH* 4.12.59; Solin. 11.6; Mart. Cap. 6.659; Dion. Calliph. 129; Guarducci IC 2 p. 128.

[385] Str. 10.479; Guarducci IC 2 pp. 128–9.

[386] Ael. *VH* 3.40; Dor. acc. to Eust. 1157.39; Sicilian for Σιληνοί or Σάτυροι or τράγοι acc. to Sch. Theoc. 3.2 (dub. l.).

[387] Str. 10.470.   [388] *Ib.* 466.

[389] *Ib.* 468.

[390] Hsch. ἀδνόν· ἀγνόν· Κρῆτες. On 'Αρι—Boisacq s.v.; Brugmann in *Indogerman. Forsch.* (1895) 379. The form 'Αριάγνη occurs on vases: Roscher LGRM 1.539.

[391] As the 'very visible one': Hsch. 'Αριδήλαν· τὴν 'Αριάδνην. Κρῆτες.

[392] P. 125.

and with Aphrodite. Again, just as we compared Britomartis with Persephone,[393] so we may compare Ariadne with both. She too is carried off and mourned. Finally, just as there is another side to the concept of Britomartis which is represented by Diktynna, and of Persephone represented by Demeter, so there is another side to Ariadne. But Ariadne has no other name to represent this ambivalence. At Naxos, however, she had two festivals, really perhaps two parts of the same festival.[394] The one was a festival of rejoicing in honour of Ariadne, bride of Dionysos, the other a festival of sorrow for the Ariadne who died on Naxos, abandoned by Theseus.

'No other heroine suffered death in so many ways as Ariadne,' comments Nilsson, 'and these different versions can only be explained as originating in a cult in which her death was celebrated.'[395] He continues: 'The Naxian rite gives us the clue. It closely resembles a type of vegetation-festival, well known from the Oriental religions but foreign to the true Greek religion. The death of the god of vegetation is celebrated with sorrow and lamentations; his resurrection with joy and exultation. In these cults it is a god who is worshipped; here it is a goddess, and this seems to make the originality of the cult certain. As far as I know, the death of such a goddess is unique, although it may seem that the idea of the death of vegetation may be applied not only to the god but also to the goddess of fertility. . . . The idea that the goddess of fertility also dies may be understood. Her death was celebrated annually, for she dies every year. But this idea is un-Greek; moreover, it does not occur in Asia in this form, and must therefore be considered as an original product of Minoan religious genius.'[396]

Yet Ariadne is not so different from Britomartis or Persephone. We have seen reason to believe that the concept of the disappearing virgin was linked with the initiation of girls. This social

---

[393] P. 180. [394] Plu. *Thes.* 20; Nilsson MMR 525.

[395] MMR 527. She was supposed to have hanged herself when she was abandoned by Theseus; she came to Naxos, after she had been carried off and abandoned by Theseus, accompanied by a nurse named Korkyne, whose tomb was at Naxos, and Ariadne also died there: Plu. *Thes.* 20. She was buried in the temple of the Cretan Dionysos at Argos: Paus. 2.23.7. She died in childbirth at Amathos in Cyprus, in the absence of Theseus, who, however, returned and gave orders for a sacrifice to Ariadne; here her tomb was in a grove called after Ariadne Aphrodite: Plu. *Thes.* 20. Artemis killed her on the island of Dia at the instigation of Dionysos: *Od.* 11.324.

[396] *Ib.* 527–8.

custom may rather be held to account for the cult of Minoan Ariadne than the Minoan religious genius. If she represented the girl initiate who suffers death at puberty and is born again, she was a social symbol as much as she was a personification of the processes of nature. She would also have been older than the goddess with a daughter or a son; which may explain why there is such a paucity of other than mythological evidence about Ariadne in Crete.

This evidence can be briefly summarized. A female head in a maeander frame on coins of Knossos (400–350 B.C.) may be that of Ariadne.[397] The island of Dia, which features in the myth, near Herakleion, the port of Knossos, is the modern Standia.[398] Very little—other than the various forms of its name—is known about the ancient town at the site of the modern village of Aradena, on the south-west coast. These forms of the name are Araden, Eraden, Aradena or Ariadne, perhaps a combination of Phoenician *Arvad* and Cretan termination –*en*.[399]

The most illuminating mythological evidence in support of the argument advanced here is forthcoming from Athens, in the information we have concerning the festival of the Oskhophoria ('The carrying of vine-shoots laden with grapes'). The information comes chiefly from Plutarch and is supplemented by details from other sources.[400] It was analysed by Jane Harrison, who concluded: 'With the Staphylodromoi of the Karneia in our minds the main gist of the Oskhophoria is clear. It is like the race of Olympia, a race of youths, *epheboi*, *kouroi*, with boughs. It has two elements, the actual *agon*, the contest, in this case a race, and then, second in time but first in importance, the procession and the *komos*. The somewhat complicated details of the race seem to have been as follows. Two *epheboi* chosen from each of the ten tribes raced against one another. The ten victors, after being feasted, formed into procession, one of them leading the way as *keryx*, two following, dressed as women and carrying branches, the remaining seven forming, as at Delphi, the *choros*.'[401]

According to Plutarch, the festival was instituted by Theseus.

---

[397] Head 461; Guarducci IC I p. 55; Seltman 171. Ariadne perhaps also featured on coinage *c.* 500–400 B.C.: Guarducci *ibid.*
[398] Str. 10.476 and 484; *Od.* 11.325; A.R. 4.434; St. Byz. s.v. Δία; Guarducci IC 1 p. 94. The name Standia may derive from εἰς τὰν Δίαν.
[399] Guarducci IC 2 p. 39, citing Hierokl. *Synecd.* 651.1; St. Byz. s.v. Ἀραδήν; *Not. Graec. episc.* 8.230, 9.139. *Cf. Fick VO* 35 f.
[400] Plu. *Thes.* 22–3; Ath. 11.495–6; Procl. *Chr.* 28.   [401] Harrison T 321–2.

In reality, he is a late element in the story. For, as Plutarch himself mentions, the two young men carried the vine-branches in honour of Dionysos and Ariadne, the vine-god and his bride.[402] The form of the festival as it can be reconstructed from our authorities can be no older than the democracy. Under the democracy the number of tribes was raised from four to ten. The dominance of the national hero Theseus in the mythology attaching to the festival presumably dates from the beginning of the democratic period, when an old clan-cult, we may assume, was reorganized as a state-cult, to conform with the new tribal system. Even so, there remained some traces of its former character. The old tradition of the communal clan feast, which must have formed the climax of the original ritual, was preserved. For Plutarch tells us that women called Deipnophoroi ('Meal-bringers') took part in the Oskhophoria. They shared in the sacrifice, 'in imitation of the mothers of those on whom the lot fell', i.e. those who were to accompany Theseus to Crete. Stories were told at the festival because these same mothers had told stories to encourage and console their children. Jane Harrison commented: 'We have then as an integral part of the ritual just the two factors always present in matriarchal mythology, the Mother and the Son. The mother brings food, because like Mother-Earth she is essentially the feeder, the Nurturer; the mother speaks words of exhortation and consolation such as many a mother must have spoken in ancient days to a son about to undergo initiation. Such words spoken aloud may have actually been a feature in initiation ritual.'[403]

This comment, however, overlooks the important point that as many daughters were chosen as sons to undergo the ordeal with Theseus. Virgins and bachelors, presumably initiates, danced in honour of Ariadne at Knossos.[404] We have found, moreover, much evidence of the factors of Mother and Daughter, or Woman and Maid, in matriarchal mythology. The mothers remained in the ritual of the Oskhophoria. Their title, Deipnophoroi, indicates that they supervised the old communal feast. Have the daughters disappeared without trace? Perhaps not.

In the reorganized festival there seem to have been ten *epheboi* from each of the ten tribes. Seven of these formed a chorus and presumably this number corresponded with the number of young

---

[402] Cf. Harrison *ib.* 322 and n. 3.
[404] Pp. 123–6.

[403] *Ib.* 323–4.

men chosen as tribute for Minos for ritual reasons.[405] One of them acted as herald. But the two who actually led the procession and carried the vine-branches were dressed as women. This detail has evoked a variety of explanation, ancient and modern.[406] Plutarch's explanation is patently aetiological. Two of the seven girls who went with Theseus to Crete were really young men dressed as girls. On their return they headed the original procession with Theseus himself.[407] But the origin of the festival did not concern Theseus. It probably did concern a group of initiates, male and female, who celebrated games, sang and danced, and carried the harvest-bough as symbol and source of their own newly announced maturity.

Plutarch has preserved the name of the hereditary clan which had charge of the festival.[408] They were the Phytalidai ('Growers'). Their eponymous ancestor, Phytalos, was taught by Demeter the art of cultivating figs.[409] With Demeter, as with Ariadne, we are led back to Crete, where the art of orchardist cultivation was early developed; and so to the conclusion that the basic elements of the Oskhophoria are ultimately inherited from Minoan Crete. These elements are (a) initiation of the youth and (b) cultivation of the sacred tree, emerging as a combined fertility-cult.

7. THE ERINYES

Illustration of the persistence of old ideas in Cretan popular religion is provided by two sepulchral inscriptions which invoke the *katakhthonioi theoi* ('subterranean deities'). The first is from Lappa, probably of the Roman Age.[410] The tomb is given over to Pluto, Demeter, Persephone, the Erinyes and all the other subterranean deities to guard. A curse is invoked against anyone violating the tomb, either personally or through the agency of others. The curse is that such a person shall not be able to escape by land or sea and that he should be uprooted with all his kith and

---

[405] P. 96.   [406] See Harrison *ib.* 324.

[407] *Thes.* 23. They carried branches to do honour to Dionysos and Ariadne 'on account of the legend', or because they came back when the fruit-harvest was being gathered in.

[408] *Ibid.* Cf. Harrison T 326.

[409] Paus. 1.37.2. Cf. Harrison *ibid.*: 'Translated into the language of fact, this means that the group of the Plant-Men at one time or another began cultivating the fig, a tree which seems long to have preceded in Greece the culture of the vine.'

[410] IC 2.XVI.28. Cf. the two similar Athenian examples of the Roman period: IG 3.1423 f.

kin. He should then become the victim of all kinds of plagues and diseases.

The tomb of the dead becomes the prerogative of the *katakhthonioi theoi*. An offence against the tomb becomes an offence against them, violating the first of the three 'unwritten laws': honour gods, honour parents, honour strangers.

There is reason to believe that these sanctions, associated with the Eleusinian and Orphic Mysteries, were a legacy from Minoan times. So too, presumably, were the Erinyes, the female deities charged with upholding the unwritten laws and with avenging their transgression. Their association with Demeter and Persephone is traditional and is a further indication of their Cretan origin. So is their part in the ordeal by oath, said to have been instituted by Rhadamanthys, and still prominent in the Gortynian Code of the fifth century B.C.[411] The traditional formula of such an oath embodied the primitive principle of collective responsibility: the prayer of the accused was that, if he broke the oath, he should not only perish himself but all his clan with him. We have a relic of this formula in the inscription under review. For any violator of the tomb is cursed *pangenei* ('with all his clan', 'kith and kin'). In the case of the ordeal-oath, the taker of the oath puts a spell upon himself. Here, of course, the guilty person has undertaken no responsibility. The spell is put upon him, responsibility is attached to him and his kith and kin, as it were by the sanction of custom which is degenerating into superstition.

The Erinyes originated as ancestral spirits, avenging ghosts. In the second inscription, from Lyttos of the third century A.D.,[412] a curse is again invoked against the violator of a tomb. Again the *katakhthonioi theoi* are called upon to avenge. But so are the spirits of the dead—'provoked to anger'. That is how the Erinyes started, before they became merely partners of the *katakhthonioi theoi*.

[411] Pl. *Lg.* 948; Willetts ASAC 212 and n. 3.   [412] IC I.XVIII.64

CHAPTER 7

The Birth and Death of a God

W E have seen that the Minoan male god was a secondary deity. He represents the element of discontinuity, of growth, decay and renewal in the vegetation cycle, as the goddess represents continuity. Because he shares in the mortality of the seed, he is an annually dying god. He is involved in the same essential pattern of Oriental ritual which gave rise to the myths of Ishtar and Tammuz, Isis and Osiris, Venus and Adonis. It was not until after the Minoan period that the youthful god pushed his way to the fore in a variety of forms and under a variety of names.[1]

1. CRETAN ZEUS

The most important eventual manifestation of this young god is as the Cretan Zeus. His Cretan characteristics and the Oriental connexions of his mother Rhea have won increasing recognition since Welcker, nearly a century ago, concluded that he was a god of the Eteocretans and therefore different from the Greek Zeus, while Rhea should be identified with the Phrygian Great Mother.[2] Yet his mother's acknowledged similarity with an Oriental prototype has not inhibited a tendency to rest content with an emphasis upon the uniquely Cretan character of her son.[3]

There is no doubt that the name Zeus is Indo-European. We must therefore conclude that the Achaeans who came into Crete gave the name of their sky-god to a Minoan deity whose original ritual and character can be discerned from the evidence of later times. But we shall see that the cult of Cretan Zeus, like the cult

---

[1] Pp. 79–81. If the figure on the Late(?) Geometric lid from Knossos is one of the earliest representations of Zeus, he is of particular historical interest for my argument. See pp. 315–16.

[2] GG 2.218. [3] E.g. Nilsson MMR 533–56.

of Diktynna, belongs to a substratum which should not be localized in Crete.

The legends surrounding the birth of Cretan Zeus were responsible for the specific epithet Kretagenes. We have already noticed that the earliest epigraphic reference to Zeus Kretagenes occurs in a third-century B.C. context from Lisos which disposes of the possibility that the cult of a deity thus specifically invoked was of purely Hellenistic origin.[4] The other epigraphic evidence may then serve, quite apart from its intrinsic importance, to illustrate the widespread provenance of a cult whose undoubted antiquity is mythologically so well substantiated.[5]

While the mythological evidence is closely associated with the Diktaian Cave, the epigraphic evidence for Zeus Kretagenes comes from cities of central and especially western Crete—a distribution similar to that for Diktynna.

From central Crete we have three inscriptions, one from each of the cities of Gortyna, Lato and Lyttos. At Gortyna Zeus Kretagenes is listed among the deities of the oath appended to a treaty with Sybrita, drawn up at Gortyna. It appears that the oath, only a fragment of which survives, had to be recited before the time of the new moon in some particular month.[6] That this specification was probably not without its ritual significance is indicated by other evidence.

For in a treaty between Lato and Olous,[7] reference is made to an annual oath of the young citizen-initiates before the *kosmoi* of each city, one city being represented at the ceremony in the other. The purpose of the oath was to ensure the continuity of the treaty. Heavy penalties were therefore incurred by the *kosmoi* if they failed to administer it. The provision for such penalties appears to have been normal.[8] For example, the importance of the oath of the Drerian youth[9] and the continuity of that oath is marked by the penalty laid down for the *kosmoi* in case of neglect. In such a contingency, action against the *kosmoi*, when they have laid down their office, has to be initiated by those who took the

---

[4] P. 192.
[5] Cf. Nilsson MMR 535: 'This myth earned for Zeus the epithet Κρηταγενής which reflects the taste of an age that took pride in the old myths and felt the necessity of asserting its claims.'
[6] IC 4.183.19 (*c.* second century B.C.).
[7] IC 1.XVI.5 (second century B.C).
[8] See further Willetts ASAC *passim*.
[9] IC 1.IX.1. See further Willetts ASAC 119–23.

oath. At the accompanying ceremony at Dreros, we seem to have direct evidence for that change of costume in the final stage of initiation into manhood which we have seen to be confirmed by our knowledge of the festival of the Ekdysia at Phaistos, connected with the local cult of Lato Phytia.[10]

The Drerian oath concludes with an obscure and archaic passage: 'The victor of the *agela* . . . and each shall plant an olive-tree and show it when it has been grown. Whoever does not plant an olive shall pay fifty staters.' The name of the victor is missing and we do not know by what means he came to be considered as a victor. But, as I have maintained elsewhere,[11] we can infer that he was the victor in an ordeal of initiation, an ordeal that took the form of a race, the winner and his competitors being under an obligation to cultivate the olive. This inference, plausible on general grounds, can be supported by a number of specific considerations. Firstly, there is the significant form of a gloss of Hesychios.[12] Again, the victor at Olympia was crowned with olive; and, moreover, according to local tradition, when Rhea gave birth to Zeus, she entrusted the child to the Kouretes, who came from Crete to Olympia and amused themselves by running a race, the winner being crowned with wild olive, which was so abundant that they slept on its leaves while they were still green.[13] Again, the calendar at Priansos included a month Dromeios, implying a festival Dromeia, analogous to the Ekdysia.[14] At Sparta, in fact, the term *staphylodromos* was applied to a runner at the Karneia, which fell at the same time as the Hyakinthia and also the Olympic festival.[15] Finally, the verb *egdramein* was used at Lato of those who left the *agela*, as we know from the text of the treaty between Lato and Olous now under discussion. This word *egdramein*[16] means to leave the *agela* of the youth and so qualify as a *dromeus*, 'runner' or 'citizen'.

These strands of evidence supported the conclusion 'that the

---

[10] Pp. 175–6.   [11] ASAC 122.

[12] νικατῆρες· οἱ ἀκμαιότατοι ἐν ταῖς τάξεσιν. For the respect paid to leaders of the *agela* see the inscription from Axos or Eleutherna (IC 2.XII.26, second century B.C. Cf. Willetts ASAC 17).

[13] Paus. 8.2.2. Since the leaves were still green, the practice had a ritual significance. 'The magical virtue of these leaves, for living and dead alike, was newness of life.' Thomson AA 115. It is of interest to recall that olives stood at the end of the Athenian race-course; and that old men carried young olive-shoots at the Panathenaia: Ar. *Ra*. 995, *V*. 544.

[14] Guarducci IC 1 p. 280, citing Brause in H 49.106.

[15] Hdt. 7.206, 8.72, 9.7,11; Th. 5.75.   [16] Line 21.

Cretan terms *dromeus* and *apodromos* are to be referred ultimately to
the cult practices of an agricultural community which had linked
the death and the rebirth of initiation with the fertility of the
crops, with marriage, and later with citizenship and even with its
calendar; and furthermore, that these archaic practices were
fostered and controlled by the leading magistrates in order to
ensure the legality of the new citizens in circumstances which . . .
demanded that such control be intensified'.[17]

Now the oath-taking at Lato, as at Dreros, was connected with
a festival, this time the Thiodaisia. Thiodaisios was the name of a
month at Lato[18] and also at Hierapytna.[19] The same month-name
is found in various centres outside Crete.[20] We can infer from the
name that there was a feast at a fixed time in the year, at which
there was supposed to be an epiphany of 'the god' in whose
honour the feast was held.[21] Who was the god? According to
Hesychios, Theodaisios was an epithet of Dionysos.[22] Outside Crete
the festival was certainly associated with Dionysos.[23] Hence no
doubt there is good reason to describe the Thiodaisia as the Cretan
name for the Dionysia.[24] But the reality behind this comparison
only becomes clear when it is set beside Nilsson's observation that
the cult of Dionysos is conspicuously absent in Crete and his
explanation: 'The reason why Dionysos does not appear in Crete
can only be that he was not needed there, the religious ideas of
which he was the herald having already been applied to the Cretan
Zeus.'[25] A further reason why these religious ideas had been
already applied to the Cretan Zeus is suggested by Guthrie:
'Historically, if the supreme chthonian deity of Crete is called

---

[17] ASAC 123. On the circumstances leading to intensified control see *ib.* 119, 184,
243–4.
[18] IC 1.XVI.4A.7: μηνὸς Θιοδαισίω (117–116 B.C.); cf. *ib.* 5.2 (second century B.C.).
[19] IC 3.III.7.20: μηνὸς Θεοδαισίου (second century A.D.)
[20] Kalymna: SGDI 3593, 70.71.76; 3603; 3599.2. Kos: *ib.* 3634a 14. Rhodes: *ib.*
4232; 4245, 33.66.188.246.399.466.514; IG 12(1).4. Mytilene: IG 11(4).1064a 2
(Delos).
[21] Cf. Hsch. ἡρόχια· τὰ Θεοδαίσια· οἱ δὲ ἑορτήν, οἱ δὲ ἱερά.
[22] S.v.
[23] Cyrene: Suid. s.v. Ἀστυδρόμια. παρὰ Λίβυσιν οἱονεὶ τῆς πόλεως γενέθλια καὶ
Θεοδαίσια ἑορτή, ἐν ᾗ ἐτίμων Διόνυσον καὶ τὰς Νύμφας. Andros: Pl. NH 2.231. Cf.
Gruppe GM 736 n. 3. Lesbos: BCH 4.425–6. Rhodes IG 12(1).791–804; SI G1035c.
Cf. Nilsson GF 280. The festival is also mentioned at Anaphe: IG 12(3).249.
[24] LSJ s.v., citing Call. *Aet. Oxy* 2080.88.
[25] MMR 579. Add to the qualification made by Nilsson *ibid.* ('Dionysos is rare
on Cretan coins, occurring only at Sybrita and sometimes at Kydonia') the single
epigraphic reference at Allaria: IC 2.I.1.19–20 (201 B.C.).

Zeus in the fifth century, it is most likely that he is called by this name because he has borrowed it from the supreme god of the Hellenes. What his name was in the days of King Minos we cannot say for certain, but it is most likely to have been the name which was Hellenized into Zagreus. This is a name at whose origin we can only guess, and which whenever we meet it clearly signifies a purely chthonian deity. . . . It was an Oriental name which travelled to Crete *via* Phoenicia.'[26] As Guthrie remarks, the most convincing theory of the origin of the name Zagreus makes it an ethnic from Mount Zagron, between Assyria and Media.[27]

What is most important is to realize, as Guthrie insists, that the name was Cretan before it was Greek.[28] It follows that, although the association of the Thiodaisia outside Crete with Dionysos is an invaluable clue which helps us to identify the nature of the festival of the Thiodaisia, the association should not be allowed to obscure the primary association of the festival with a god who was born in Crete. The papyrus fragment which has enabled the Thiodaisia to be equated with the Dionysia belongs to the Second Book of the *Aetia* of Kallimachos. It confirms that a prominent topic of this book was the foundation of cities. The poet is aided in his inquiry by the Muse of History herself, who tells the story of the foundation of Drepanum. 'Thus it was that at Drepanum a nameless founder was summoned to partake of the sacrificial feast. The curiosity of Kallimachos was, however, still not satisfied, and he was anxious to put further questions to the Muse concerning the observance in Boiotia and Euboia of certain Cretan customs. Here the column ends, and there is a gap of nine lines before the exiguous remains of the next one begins; if a reference to Knossos is rightly recognized in l.108, Crete was the subject of consideration at least as far as that point.'[29] Further light is thrown on the reference to the Cretan festival of the Thiodaisia at the spring of Kissousa by a passage of Plutarch:[30] 'Here [i.e. at Kissousa] as the story goes, his nurses bathed the infant Dionysos after his birth, since the water has the glistering colour of wine, is clear and very sweet to drink. Not far off grow the Cretan storax-shrubs, which the Haliartians take as evidence that Rhadamanthys once lived there; and they show his tomb, which they call Alea.' All of

[26] OGR 112–13, cf. *id* GG 45.
[27] The theory was first put forward by Miss G. Davis and adopted by Cook Z 1.651 and n. 1.
[28] OGR 113. [29] Hunt *ad POxy.* 2080.
[30] *Ib.* 11.88–9; Plu. *Lys.* 28.

which must indicate that we have here a legacy of ritual about the birth (perhaps also the death?) of a god brought into Boiotia by the Kadmeioi from Crete.

Before investigating further the nature of the Thiodaisia we must look at the evidence for its occurrence in Crete itself. The treaty between Lato and Olous makes it clear that the festival was celebrated in both of these cities in the second century B.C.[31] We have two references to its celebration at Hierapytna. A badly mutilated fragment of a treaty between the Hierapytnians and the Cretan Arcadians, to be assigned perhaps to the latter part of the third century B.C., makes it clear that the Arcadians are to attend the Thiodaisia at Hierapytna.[32] It also seems clear that the *kosmoi* were penalized if they neglected to perform certain prescribed sacrifices; and that they were responsible for the ceremony of the oath taken by the young men leaving the *agela*. The second reference occurs in another mutilated inscription, of the second century B.C., recording a treaty between Hierapytna and Knossos, deposited in the temple of Zeus Diktaios.[33] The Knossians are to attend the Thiodaisia at Hierapytna;[34] and there is some indication that the youth recited an annual oath before leaving the *agela*.[35] Finally, there is evidence for the survival of the festival at Lyttos until the second or third century A.D.[36]

From the epigraphic evidence we can gather then that the Thiodaisia was a prominent festival in certain of the most important cities of central and eastern Crete; that, if it did not flourish, it at least survived over a period of at least five hundred years; that it served as an occasion to renew the bonds of alliance between cities; and, finally, that so long as the institution of the *agela* was in being, the ritual graduation of the youth from the *agela* as citizens was bound up with the celebration of the festival in the cities where it was established, and also with the ritual continuity of an oath of alliance between that city and another. It seems as if the oath, like the citizen body, has to be annually renewed. It was a time of birth and rebirth, initiation and renewal, a time to celebrate the city's birthday[37] and the continuity of its life and functions.

We are entitled to use our information about the Athenian Dionysia to give us some idea of what took place at the Cretan

[31] IC 1.XVI.5.42–3.
[32] IC 3.III.1.B.8.
[33] IC 1.VIII.13, cf. *ib.* 3.II.6; Cook Z 2.931.
[34] L.9.
[35] L.16.
[36] IC 1.XVIII.11.
[37] Cf. Suidas cited in n. 23 above.

204

Thiodaisia.[38] The festival in Athens lasted for five or six days. On the first day the image of Dionysos Eleuthereus was carried from the city to a shrine on the road to the village of Eleutherai, on the frontier between Attica and Boiotia, reputedly its original home. It was escorted by the armed *epheboi* of Athens. The accompanying procession included sacrificial animals, unmarried girls with baskets on their heads containing sacrificial implements, as well as the ordinary participants. After the procession had stopped in the market-place, while a chorus performed before the statues of the Twelve Gods, it continued on its way to the shrine. Here the image was placed on a low altar. Hymns were then sung in praise of the god and the animals were sacrificed. The most important of these animals was a bull, sacrificed on behalf of the state. The bull was chosen as 'worthy of the god'.[39] After being sacrificed the bull was presumably roasted and the meat then shared among the state officials. The procession returned to the city by torchlight in the evening, when the feast was over, and the *epheboi* took the image of Dionysos to the theatre. Here it remained, on an altar in the middle of the orchestra, until the festival concluded.

Three features here call for our special attention: the procession itself, the sacrifice of the bull and the presence of the *epheboi*. The latter of course correspond with the members of the Cretan *agela*. We have seen that the *parastathentes*, the Cretan boys who were abducted, together with their fellow-initiates, went away from the city, feasted and hunted for a definite period in the country and then returned to the city. An abducted boy then received presents, which included a military costume, a drinking-cup and an ox. He sacrificed the ox to Zeus and gave a feast to his companions.[40] This Cretan custom follows a familiar threefold pattern of tribal initiation, in which the initiate is taken away from his settlement, undergoes an ordeal and then returns as a man. These three stages appear in Greek as *pompe* ('send-off'), *agon* ('ordeal' or 'contest') and *komos* ('triumphal return'). The first day's events at the Athenian Dionysia seem to have followed the same ritual sequence in Classical times.[41] In fact the procession from the city is called a *pompe* and the return a *komos* in an Athenian law.[42] If, as seems likely, the bull who was 'worthy of the god' was actually the

[38] For the general reasons suggested here and for the more particular reasons suggested later, pp. 213–14.

[39] CIA 2.470.

[40] P. 116.

[41] See the discussion of evidence in Pickard-Cambridge DFA 55 f.

[42] D.21.10.

incarnation of the god, then the sacrifice of the bull corresponds to the *agon*—the ordeal of the god.[43]

The Olympian festival exhibits the same three basic stages of *pompe*, *agon* and *komos*, the *agon* being represented by athletic contests, whose basic feature, the men's foot-race, was itself an *agon* or ritual ordeal of initiation, to decide who should be the *kouros*, the pre-eminent youth of the year, invested with magical powers which persisted from seed-time to harvest.[44] We recall the local tradition at Olympia, according to which the Kouretes travelled there from Crete and ran a race; and also that the running of races by the men in Crete must have been sufficiently important for the citizen to be distinguished by the title of *dromeus* ('runner').

It is likely then that the Thiodaisia was a festival closely associated with the annual graduation of the youths from the *agela* and (on Strabo's evidence) their collective marriage. The special deity honoured had his origin in the Minoan bull-god and later became allied with Zeus—the 'Cretan-born' Zeus. Foot-races must have formed (though perhaps not exclusively, as we shall see) the *agon* of this festival and the sacrifice of a bull was probably a prominent feature.[45] A clear trace of the magical virtues attaching to the victor of the *agon* survives in the Drerian oath.

In the treaty between Lyttos and Olous of 111–110 B.C. the name of Zeus Kretagenes has been restored in the list of deities of the Lyttians.[46] It is also possible that a badly mutilated section of the inscription not only contained a reference to the administration by the *kosmoi* of an annual oath of those leaving the *agela* in each city, but that this ceremony was connected with the celebration of the Thiodaisia both at Lyttos and at Olous.[47]

The oath-formulae of the treaties between Cretan cities provide an obviously valuable source of evidence about local cults. The order of precedence of deities listed in these oaths must also be regarded as a significant testimony to their relative importance in particular localities. In the oaths of the documents discussed earlier (which presumably follow a traditionally archaic pattern) a high priority indeed attaches to Zeus Kretagenes.

In the Gortynian inscription, although the list of deities in the oath appended to the treaty is mutilated, it is at least clear that (*a*)

---

[43] Thomson AA 167–8.   [44] Cf. Cornford in Harrison T 212–59.
[45] Suid. s.v. Ἀστυδρόμια (Cyrene); Βουκόπια at Lindos: IG 12(1).792, *al.*; Nilsson GF 280.
[46] IC I.XVIII.9 c 4.   [47] *Ib.* b 8 ff.; cf. Deiters 51.

Zeus Kretagenes came very high in the list; (*b*) he preceded Pythian Apollo and Athene Poliokhos and also the Nymphs; to judge merely from the archaic form of the latter word[48] in a Hellenistic context, the whole oath-formula is confirmed as archaic.

In the oath of the Latians,[49] Zeus Kretagenes comes second after Hestia, and those who follow are Hera, Zeus Tallaios, Poseidon, Amphritite, Pythian Apollo, Lato, Artemis, Ares, Aphrodite, Eileithyia, Britomartis, Hermes, the Kouretes, Nymphs 'and all the other gods and goddesses'.

In the oath of the Lyttians, Zeus Kretagenes again comes second after Hestia, but takes precedence over Zeus Tallaios, Idaian Zeus, Zeus Monnitios, Hera, Athene Polias, Pythian Apollo, Lato, Artemis, Ares, Aphrodite, Hermes, Helios(?), Britomartis 'and all the other gods and goddesses'.

In western Crete, in addition to the important reference in the inscription from Lisos,[50] we also have evidence from Kydonia, Polyrhenia and Kisamos. In the oath appended to the treaty from Lisos, between the Oreioi and King Magas, Zeus Kretagenes is named after Diktynna, patron goddess of Lisos and the deities who shared her shrine, and also after the deities of Poikilasion. The likely explanation is that he was included at all only as a god of the Gortynians, who played a prominent part in the negotiations.[51] Hence, although he is the last deity to be singled out before the conventional conclusion ('and all the gods and goddesses'), this has little significance in comparison with the simple fact that he is singled out to represent the Gortynians.

That there was probably a cult of Zeus Kretagenes at Kydonia can be inferred from the coin-types of the period 200–67 B.C.;[52] and at Polyrhenia from coin-types of the Augustan age.[53] From Kisamos we have a mention of the god in an inscription of the second century A.D.[54]

In eastern Crete the 'Cretan-born Zeus' was specifically associated with Dikte by the epithet Diktaios. We have inscriptions from the cities of Hierapytna, Itanos and Praisos which make reference to Zeus Diktaios.

In the treaty between Hierapytna and one of her colonies, of

---

[48] I.e. Νύμφανς.
[49] The deities of both Lato and Olous are listed.
[50] See pp. 191 and 200.
[51] Guarducci *ad. loc.*
[52] Svoronos 'Εφ. 'Αρχ. (1893) 5; Guarducci IC 2 p. 114.
[53] Guarducci *ib.* p. 241.
[54] IC 2.VIII.1.5.

about the second century B.C.,[55] the order of the deities listed in the oath is: Hestia, Zeus Oratrios and Zeus Diktaios,[56] Hera, Athene Oleria, Athene Polias, Athene Samonia, Pythian Apollo, Lato, Artemis, Ares, Aphrodite, the Kouretes, Nymphs and Kyrbantes (= Korybantes) and 'all gods and goddesses'. The precedence of Hestia over Zeus in such oaths is, of course, normal,[57] and the precedence of Zeus Oratrios ('Protector of Treaties')[58] over Zeus Diktaios is natural in this context. The high priority of Zeus Diktaios is therefore comparable with that of Zeus Kretagenes in the examples previously cited.

The great importance of the cult of Zeus Diktaios in the east could not be more clearly attested than it is in the Itanian oath of about the beginning of the third century B.C.[59] For here Zeus Diktaios heads the list, taking precedence over Hera, 'the gods in Dikte',[60] Athene Polias, 'all the gods to whom sacrifice is made in the temple of Athene', Zeus Agoraios and Pythian Apollo. Another Itanian inscription,[61] of the second half of the second century B.C., shows that the precincts of the temple of Zeus Diktaios featured in the territorial disputes between Hierapytna and Itanos which were a characteristic of Cretan internal politics at this period.

In the oath appended to the important decree from Praisos of the third century B.C., concerning the Stalitai,[62] Zeus Diktaios heads the list of deities;[63] he is followed by Poseidon, Athene, Pythian Apollo and 'all gods and goddesses'.

Before beginning the discussion of the evidence from the temple of Diktaian Zeus itself, it will be convenient to mention here first of all the evidence, such as it is, for the Kouretes and for Rhea, from the rest of Crete; since this evidence naturally has a bearing on the diffusion of the cult of the 'Cretan-born Zeus'.

The evidence for the Kouretes is restricted to central and eastern Crete. There was a legend that the Kouretes and Korybantes founded Knossos and instituted the cult of Kybele.[64] It is

[55] IC 3.III.5.
[56] Actually Τῆνα 'Ορἀτριον and Τῆνα Δικταῖον. On Cretan Τῆνα, Ττῆνα = Ζῆνα see Buck GD 72, 93.
[57] Cf. p. 304.
[58] Cf. p. 247.
[59] IC 3.IV.8. Willetts ASAC 126–9, 182, 184–5, 226.
[60] Who they are is made clear in IC 3.II.1. See p. 210.
[61] IC 3.IV.9.
[62] Ib. VI.7. See further Willetts ASAC 129–30.
[63] Viz. ὀμνύω Δῆ/να Δικταῖον. For Δῆνα cf. IC 1.IX (Dreros) 1.17 f.
[64] Eus. Hieron. Chron. 22, 26, 42. Cf. Nonn. D. 13. 137 ff.

clear from the treaty between Lato and Olous[65] that there was a sanctuary of the Kouretes in the territory of Lato, perhaps at a point not far from the junction of the boundaries of Lato, Lyttos and Hierapytna, from all of which 'the snowy ridges of Dikte are the most conspicuous features of the landscape'.[66] The sanctuary must have been sited on the north-east flank of Dikte in just such a terrain as is described by Diodoros, who explains that the Kouretes 'used to dwell on the mountains, in wooded places and glens and in general where there was natural cover and shelter, because the art of building houses had not yet been discovered'.[67]

From country districts near Gortyna we have three inscriptions to the Kouretes as 'guardians of kine', which show how their cult persisted to a late date in such localities.[68] One of these dedications was made by Ertaios, son of Amnatos, who may have belonged to the same family as (and if so, was perhaps the grandson of) the *kosmos* of Gortyna who features in the second-century B.C. decree of Gortyna relating to the Kaudians.[69] If so, the cult cannot have been restricted to country-folk. At Gortyna itself the Kouretes may well feature in the oath-formula of the treaty of the Gortynians and Hierapytnians with the Priansians.[70]

At Hierapytna, farther east, the Kouretes feature in the oath-formulae of two inscriptions of the second century B.C.[71]

For Rhea, the evidence is much more slight. We can infer, from a passage of Diodoros,[72] that there was some kind of shrine to Rhea and the Titans at Knossos; and the temple of Asklepios at Lebena, the port of Gortyna, was apparently also associated with Rhea.[73] She is, however, mentioned by name epigraphically only once, in the Hymn of the Kouretes.[74]

Now we must turn our attention to the temple of Diktaian Zeus and the various myths and legends associated with the birth of Zeus and the sacred cave in which the birth was supposed to have occurred.

Strabo expressly associated the temple of Diktaian Zeus with the Eteocretans and particularly with the Praisians.[75] Although

---

[65] IC 1.XVI.5. Cf. p. 204.
[66] Bosanquet in ABSA 15.352.
[67] D.S. 5.65; Bosanquet *ibid.*
[68] IC 1.XXV.3 (*c.* first century B.C.); *ib.* XXXI.7 and 8 (second–first century B.C.). Spelling Κωρῆτες.
[69] IC 4.184; Willetts ASAC 138.
[70] IC 4.174.
[71] IC 3.III.3, 5.
[72] D.S. 5.66.1.
[73] Philostr. *VA* 4.34.
[74] See p. 212.
[75] 10.475; cf. 10.478.

the Hellenic temple which stood on the site of the Minoan town of Palaikastro had been destroyed, during the course of the archaeological excavations at Palaikastro sufficient numbers of votive offerings, including architectural terracottas and bronze shields, were found near the surface to define its position; and the actual site of the altar was fixed by a bed of ashes. The discovery of the Hymn of the Kouretes, addressed to Zeus of Dikte, confirmed with absolute certainty that the temple was that of Diktaian Zeus.[76]

The votive offerings, bronzes and terracottas, belong mostly to the archaic period and indicate that the temple was at its most influential from the seventh to the fifth centuries B.C. The epithet Diktaios derives from Dikte. Hence the same pre-Greek root serves for the mountain Dikte, the goddess Diktynna and the epithet Diktaios.[77] The use of the epithet by Antimachos serves to show that it could be considered synonymous with 'Cretan'; and that the early prominence of the Diktaian temple-cult in the historical period had become familiar outside Crete itself in Classical times.[78]

A verse of the Hymn of the Kouretes apparently indicates that, at the end of the fourth century or beginning of the third century B.C., the temple did not belong to any single city but was a common centre of worship for the citizens of several towns of eastern Crete.[79]

It seems, however, that the temple was under the control of Praisos for some time.[80] But there is epigraphic evidence to show that it was controlled by Hierapytna in the second half of the second century B.C., in the inscription which was found in 1907, a mile to the north-west of the site, and which commemorates the restoration by Hierapytna of some statues in the temple, round about the period 145–139 B.C.[81] We can conclude that the site was controlled by Hierapytna during a period of its political ascendancy in eastern Crete. This would not, however, have prevented the inhabitants of other neighbouring states, particularly those of Praisos and Itanos, from continuing to frequent the temple.

Two sets of statues are distinguished in the inscription. First,

---

[76] Bosanquet in ABSA 15.339; cf. *ib.* 8.286, 9.280, 10.246, 11.298.
[77] Cf. p. 183; Fick VO 32; Haley 145.   [78] Antim. *fr.* 174 Wyss.
[79] L 29: θόρε κὲς] πόληας ἁμῶν. Cf. Guarducci IC 3 p. 6.
[80] Str. 10.475; Guarducci *ibid.*
[81] IC 3.II.1. On the association of the inscription with Hierapytna, see Willetts ASAC 143; Guarducci *ad loc.*

'old statues' are mentioned, which must presumably have been already in the temple at its most flourishing period before the fifth century B.C. They may well have been statues not only of Zeus himself but also of Rhea and of the Kouretes.[82] The statue of Zeus Diktaios himself in all probability represented a youthful, beardless god.[83]

The other statues, which had become settled in the temple by the second century B.C., included those of Athene, Artemis, Atlas, the Sphinxes, Hera, Victory and a second Zeus, and also several others which cannot with certainty be identified. These (with the exception perhaps of the Sphinxes and Atlas) were probably the 'gods in Dikte' referred to in the Itanian oath.[84]

The fragment of the treaty between Hierapytna and Knossos found near Palaikastro was probably also originally deposited in the temple of Zeus Diktaios during the same period.[85]

That the territory near the site of the temple was the subject of fierce dispute at this period between Hierapytna and Itanos is clear from Itanian inscriptions.[86] From one of these we learn that the pasturing of flocks, cultivation of land and cutting of wood were forbidden in the precincts of the temple.[87]

But it is the Hymn of the Kouretes in honour of Zeus Diktaios which far transcends in importance any other epigraphic evidence connected with the temple.[88] Although the inscription was made c. third century A.D., as is indicated by the lettering, the original is agreed to be much older; for, since it was inscribed twice on the same stone, at first badly and then more correctly, we infer that it was copied from a MS. or from oral tradition. The metre would

[82] Cf. Guarducci ad loc.
[83] Cf. EM s.v. Δίκτη: ἐνταῦθα δὲ Διὸς ἄγαλμα ἀγένειον ἵστατο.
[84] See p. 208; cf. Guarducci ad loc.
[85] Guarducci IC 3.II.6, cf. ib. 1.VIII.13; Cook Z 2.931; Tod ABSA 9.337.
[86] IC 3.IV.9-10.   [87] Ib. 9.81 f.
[88] Edited by Bosanquet and Murray ABSA 15.339, accompanied by Jane Harrison's paper The Kouretes and Zeus Kouros (ib. 308) presenting the ideas later fully developed in her Themis. See also ABSA 10.246; Jebb JHS 24.61; Kretschmer Gl. 3.305; Wünsch Arch. f. Religionswiss. 14.552; id. in RE s.v. Hymnos; Reinach REG 24.331; Xanthoudides Kretike Stoa 3.10; Aly Philol. 25 (N.S.) 469; Latte Religionsgesch. Versuche u. Vorarbeiten 13.3.43; Cook Z 1.15, 2.931; Poerner De Curetibus et Corybantibus 264; Powell CQ 9.143; Mingazzini Religio 1.256; Murray ap. Powell-Barber New Chapters in the History of Greek Literature 50; Schwenn in RE s.v. Kureten; Wilamowitz Griech. Verskunst 499; Levi Sill. cors. 385 n. 30; Diehl Anth. Lyr. Graec. 2.279; Powell Collect. Alex. 160; Ransome 95; Nilsson GGR 1.299; id MMR 546; Guarducci Studi e Materiali di Storia delle Religioni 15.1; id. ad. IC 3.II.2; Picard EC 424; Harris B. 353; Jeanmaire CC 430; Thomson AA 109; SAGS 1.467; Cornford PS 216, 249; Guthrie GG 46.

suit any date between the sixth and fourth centuries B.C., but the style indicates a date at the end of the fourth or beginning of the third century B.C. In the following translation,[89] the portions in parentheses indicate conjectural restorations of the damaged text.

> O hail, thou Kronian,
> O welcome, greatest Kouros,
> Almighty of Brightness,
> Here now present, leading thy Spirits,
> O come for the year to Dikte,
> And rejoice in this ode,
>
> Which we on the strings strike, as we
> Blend it with the pipes' sounds, as we
> Are chanting our song, standing round
> This thy altar, walled so well.
>
> O hail, etc.
>
> Since (the Kouretes), taking thee,
> Child immortal, (with their shields),
> There from Rhea, (kept thee away)
> (With circlings of) feet, (well-hid).
>
> O hail, etc.
>
> .   .   .   .
> .   .   .   .
> .   .   .   .
> .   .   .   .   . of the fair Dawn.
>
> O hail, etc.
>
> (And Seasons began to teem) from
> Year to year and Justice gained a
> Hold on man and Peace that loves wealth
> (Now attended all) creatures.
>
> O hail, etc.
>
> (Into cattle herds leap then) and
> Into fleecy (flocks) leap also,
> And leap into (the fields) of corn,
> (Into households bearing) increase.
>
> O hail, etc.

---

[89] I have followed the text of IC 3.II.2. This does not imply, however, that I endorse it at all points.

Also leap into our cities
And into our sea-borne ships,
And into our (youthful citizens),
Into Themis, (well-renowned).

O hail, etc.

In its form this hymn, consisting of a series of stanzas interpolated with a recurrent refrain, closely resembles 'what, in the light of other evidence, the primitive dithyramb appears to have been'.[90] In this respect it is similar to the hymn of the women of Elis, sung at a festival of Dionysos, apparently while waiting for the arrival of a procession. The bull which is addressed in this hymn was presumably ready to be sacrificed; and it is identified with Dionysos.[91] Perhaps then the Hymn of the Kouretes was sung by *epheboi* as part of the *agon* of a festival very like the Thiodaisia, celebrating the epiphany of Zeus Kretagenes. We know that the *parastathentes* sacrificed oxen to Zeus;[92] and a bull-sacrifice may therefore have formed part of the festival. For, since Kouretes derives from *kouros*, 'boy' or 'young man', there can be little doubt that, as Jane Harrison concluded:[93] 'The Kouretes are Young Men who have been initiated themselves and will initiate others, will instruct them in tribal duties and tribal dances, will steal them away from their mothers, conceal them, make away with them by some pretended death and finally bring them back as new-born, grown youths, full members of their tribe'.

[90] Thomson AA 169–70, cf. SAGS 1.467; Pickard-Cambridge DTC 5–53. The latter, discussing the important early fragment of Archilochos which mentions the dithyramb, wrote: '[The lines] do not suggest a literary composition, but rather the singing or shouting of some well-known traditional words, or perhaps some improvisation by the ἐξάρχων, with a traditional refrain in which the band of revellers joins, as the mourners join in the θρῆνος in the last book of the *Iliad* (24.720)': *ib.* 18–19. He further remarked that the later literary composition (like the music of the flute which accompanied it) seems to have been at first specially cultivated in Dorian lands. Even when it attained its full literary development in relation to the Dionysiac festivals at Athens, 'It is noteworthy how many of the composers of dithyrambs for the Athenian festivals, including all the most famous, were of non-Athenian birth—by no means all Dorians, but composing in a dialect containing Dorian elements, though always to music of the Phrygian type, and with the flute as the accompanying instrument': *ib.* 47–8, cf. 146 ff.
[91] The 'worthy bull' addressed in this hymn reminds us of the Athenian inscription recording that the bull sacrificed at the city Dionysia was a bull 'worthy of the god': n. 39 above.
[92] Pp. 116, 205
[93] T 19. Jane Harrison was presumably unaware that it was actually the custom in Crete for boys to be stolen from their homes and secluded in the countryside by initiated men.

Zeus is invoked as 'greatest Kouros' by these Kouretes, as the personification not so much of the whole group of *epheboi* as of a *kleinos*, a young initiate chosen for special office.[94] Yet, although his birth is naturally mentioned in the hymn, it is his rebirth as a youthful god, as Zeus Kretagenes incarnate,[95] that is especially celebrated here. Just as Kouretes must be annually created anew, so the god's annual return must be invoked by his special worshippers. Until they become initiated themselves, until the god's return as a mature youth has been accomplished, nothing can be renewed. We have seen that, in the spring festivals of Crete of the kind at which this hymn was probably sung,[96] the ritual graduation of the youth from the *agela* coincided with a time of general birth and rebirth, a time to celebrate the city's birthday and the continuity of its life and functions. Even in the age of the city-state, the old fertility magic to which the ritual belonged is not forgotten. That is why the words θόρε ἐς occurring in the last two stanzas of the hymn must not be translated 'leap for' (so Murray)[97] but 'leap into'. For, as Nilsson has pointed out:[98] 'Behind this there is certainly a yet more literal and realistic sense, that of "begetting". In this hymn, which was composed at a fairly late date of remnants of much older conceptions,[99] the words are taken metaphorically, or it would have been impossible to say: "Leap into our towns and into our seafaring ships, leap into our young citizens and a lawful order," or, to put it still more correctly, they were an old and venerable, but only half understood, sacred formula. But in the expressions: "leap into the fleecy flocks and the crops of the fields", which certainly are the oldest, the sense here suggested is the most primitive and natural.'

The story of the actual birth of the Cretan Zeus was familiar

[94] P. 116. Cf. Harrison T 46–7.

[95] The image of Diktaian Zeus was beardless: *EM* s.v. Δίκτη. ἐνταῦθα δὲ Διὸς ἄγαλμα ἀγένειον ἵστατο.

[96] Cf. Nilsson MMR 549 and n. 56.   [97] Cf. Harrison T 8.

[98] MMR 550.

[99] This attitude is oddly at variance with Nilsson's remarks just before (*ib.* 549): 'But I must express my doubts whether a god or daemon of the kind so graphically described in the Greek phrase coined by Miss Harrison (i.e. ἐνιαυτὸς δαίμων) belongs to the same cultural stage as the tribal initiation of the young men; he seems much more consistent with the life of herdsmen and agriculturalists than with that of savages; for only the former are able to attain to a notion of the year in the primary sense here required, namely the products being brought by the year in a certain established order.' The point is that, just as the original content of the hymn was supplemented, so initiation continued, but in a changed form.

to the ancients in the account given by Hesiod.[100] Before the age of supremacy of the Olympians, the children of Heaven and Earth (Ouranos and Gaia) were paramount. These were the Titans. The youngest of them, Kronos, married Rhea. Their first children, Hestia, Demeter, Hera, Hades and Poseidon, were swallowed by Kronos. For Kronos was afraid that he would be deprived of his kingship by one of them. When Rhea was about to give birth to Zeus she sought the advice of Ouranos and Gaia as to means of concealing the birth. She was brought to Lyttos in Crete, in consequence; and Gaia took the baby Zeus from Rhea to rear him and hid him in a deep cave on the wooded mountain Aigaion ('Goat-mountain'). Instead of the baby she gave Kronos a stone wrapped in swaddling-clothes. Kronos swallowed the stone which he later vomited up together with the children he had previously swallowed.

The cave to which, according to Hesiod, the baby Zeus was brought may have been either the cave of Psychro or of Arkalochori, respectively five and one and a half hours distant from Lyttos.[101] The stone substituted for the baby is the thunder-stone and obviously represents a feature of great antiquity of special relevance to Crete.[102] The 'Goat-mountain' bears an obvious relation to the story that the baby was fed with the milk of the goat Amaltheia. The myth too shares an important feature with similar folk-tales, namely that the child is abandoned by its mother and is reared by others.[103] This latter feature recalls the continuing Cretan practice among the *epheboi* of secluding themselves in the country for two months prior to the initiation ceremony. It is natural therefore for the Kouretes to be closely associated with the birth and nurture of Zeus.

The cave to which Zeus was transferred after his birth in the story of Hesiod was not only naturally identified with the Psychro Cave but it was at one time widely assumed that the Psychro Cave was also the Diktaian Cave in which Zeus was reputedly born. This assumption was then refuted, largely because it did not take account of the evidence of ancient topographers and the provenance of the inscriptions relating to the cult of Zeus Diktaios.[104]

[100] *Th.* 453 ff.

[101] Archaeological evidence equally supports either: Nilsson MMR 459.

[102] Harrison T 56; pp. 67–71.   [103] Nilsson MMR 537.

[104] Str. 10.478 f.; Ptol. 3.15.3, 6; Agathocl. *ap.* Ath. 9.375 f.; sch. Arat. *Phaen.* 33 f.; A.R. 4.1653 ff.; Luc. *DMar.* 15.4; Aly DKA 47; Beloch K 11.433–5; Toutain RHR 64.277–91; p. 207 above.

Consequently, we must conclude that the site of the Diktaian Cave is still unknown but that it was probably not far from Itanos and Hierapytna.[105]

Zeus Kretagenes undoubtedly assumed the epithet Diktaios[106] from the Diktaian Cave on Mount Dikte where the birth supposedly occurred.[107] Here too it was said that he was reared[108] and fed either by bees;[109] or a goat;[110] or a pig;[111] or doves;[112] and entrusted to the Kouretes (or to the Korybantes, later identified with them) who danced around the baby, beating drums and clashing shields and spears so that its cries should not be heard by Kronos.[113]

There were other stories attached to the Diktaian Cave. There Ankhiale bore the Idaian Daktyloi;[114] Zeus lay with Europa;[115] their son, Minos, used to descend into the cave and return with the laws of Zeus;[116] Epimenides slept for several years there and had visions;[117] and there are other references.[118]

But the legends of the nurture of Zeus in the cave cannot be left without further mention of two aspects of special interest, of which the first concerns the bees. Further information of a mythical nature is forthcoming in the story (presumably referring to the

---

[105] If a single precise centre ever in fact existed. P. Faure, after his recent survey, writes (BCH 84.193–4): 'Concluons donc provisoirement, après plusieurs campagnes de recherches, que, si cette région n'a révélé qu'une caverne archéologique certaine d'époque minoenne, et plusieurs établissements classiques, on peut se demander *si le Zeus Diktaios qui s'y trouvait invoqué ne recevait pas uniquement un culte de hauts lieux*, comme son prédécesseur minoen.' Cf., with Faure's detailed evidence, N. Platon in KK (1951) 120–40.

[106] Call. *Jov.* 4; *Anecd. Stud.* 1.266; Mart. *Ep.* 4.1.2; Min. Fel. *Oct.* 21.1; cf. Verg. *Georg.* 2.536; Stat. *Theb.* 3.481.

[107] Agathocl. *ap.* Ath. 9.375 f.; Apollod. 1.1.6; sch. Arat. *Phaen.* 33; D.S. 5.70; *EM* s.v. Δίκτη.

[108] A.R. 1.508 f.; sch. *ad loc*; Arat. *Phaen.* 30 ff.; sch. *ad loc*; Lucr. 2.633 f., cf. Sil. It. 17.21; D.H. 2.61; Arr. *ap* Eust. in D.P. 498; Serv. *ad* Verg. *Georg.* 2.536.

[109] Verg. *Georg.* 4.149 ff.; Colum. 9.2; Serv. *ad* Verg. *A.* 3.104, cf. Lact. Plac. *ad* Stat. *Ach.* 387, *Myth. Vat.* 1.104, cf. 2.116.

[110] Melisseus or Melissos, king of Crete, was father of the nymphs Adrasteia and Ide or Adrasteia and Kynosoura or Amaltheia and Melissa who reared the baby Zeus on the milk of a goat: Apollod. 1.1.6; Zen. 2.48; Orph. *fr.* 109; Hyg. *Fab.* 182; sch. E. *Rh.* 342; Did. *ap.* Lact. *Div. Inst.* 1.22; Parmenisk. *ap.* Hyg. *Poet. Astr.* 2.13.

[111] Ath. 9.375f–376a; Eust. *ad Il.* 773.14 ff.   [112] Moero *ap.* Ath. 11.491a–b.

[113] Call. *Jov.* 52 ff.; E. *Ba.* 119 ff.; Str. 10.468; D.S. 5.20.2–4; Hyg. *Fab.* 139; Cook Z 1.150, 530, 534, 659, 709.

[114] A.R. 1.1129 ff.; sch. *ad loc.*; and cf. Guarducci IC 2. p. 43.

[115] Luc. *DMar.* 15.4.   [116] D.H. 2.61.

[117] Max. Tyr. 16.1.

[118] Nonn. *D.* 8.178; Suid. s.v. Δικταῖον σπήλαιον; cf. A.R. 2.434.

Diktaian Cave) cited from the *Ornithogonia* of Boios[119] and illustrated on a black-figured *amphora* from Vulci of *c.* 550 B.C.[120] Tradition said that in Crete there was a cave sacred to bees, where Rhea gave birth to Zeus, and neither god nor man might enter it. Every year at a definite time there was seen a great glare of fire from this cave. This happened when the blood from the birth of Zeus boiled out. The cave was occupied by sacred bees, nurses of Zeus. Four men, Laïos, Keleos, Kerberos and Aigolios, dared to enter the cave to get as much honey as they could. They encased their bodies in bronze, collected the honey and saw the swaddling-clothes of Zeus. Their bronze armour thereupon burst asunder and Zeus raised his thunderbolt. But Themis and the Moirai intervened to prevent the death of the intruders, since the cave-sanctuary could not thus be defiled. So Zeus turned them into birds. From them came blue thrushes (*laioi*), green woodpeckers (*keleoi*), an unknown species (*kerberoi*) and owls (*aigolioi*). Because they saw the blood of Zeus these were good birds to appear, and reliable beyond all others.

In conjunction with the other relevant evidence, the above legend has helped to suggest the hypothesis[121] that the Kouretes represented primitive bee-keepers who attracted bees into their hives when they swarmed by their rude music of drums and clashing shields and spears. This interpretation would equally apply to the Korybantes as variants of the Kouretes, or when Kybele is substituted for Rhea. Not only caves but also hollow trees were used as beehives and this gives further motivation to the idea of the sacred tree. To this cycle of myth is also attached the concept of Zeus as 'Thunder-man' and 'Bee-man'. The story that Zeus was fed by bees on honey would be the earlier version, replaced later by a variation, as nymphs, who nevertheless retain the title of 'Bees' (Melissai), are substituted for bees. And, finally, if we grant the possibility that knowledge of bees' 'dances' can be even more than 2300 years old,[122] then we may suppose that the dance formed a part of the ceremonies of initiation into a bee-cult associated with the ancient art of bee-keeping—and with Zeus Kretagenes.

Some of the characteristics of Zeus indicate a very old and

---

[119] Ant. Lib. 19. [120] Cook Z 2.929; Ransome 92.
[121] Harris B 322, 326–32, 348–53; Ransome 84, 92–5.
[122] Cf. Arist. *HA* 9.624b and Haldane *Aristotle's Account of Bees' 'Dances'* JHS 75.24.

perhaps even an original association with the oak-tree. Since a hollow oak would commonly serve as a nest for bees, it may be that the bees who fed the infant Zeus, like the goat and the pig, represent totemistic survivals from more primitive religious strata which anthropomorphic Zeus gathered about himself as he developed.[123] These survivals are, however, perhaps most apparent in the case of the pig.

The Cretans continued to have a taboo on sow's flesh, for the reasons explained by Athenaios, citing the fifth-century B.C.(?) historian Agathokles and the third-century B.C. historian Neanthes.[124] According to this account, the sanctity of swine among the Cretans was to be referred to the myth of the birth of Zeus on Mount Dikte, where also a sacrifice that was not to be mentioned took place.[125] A sow was supposed to have suckled Zeus and, grunting as it trotted round the baby, made its whimpers inaudible to passers-by. Consequently, all regarded this animal as very holy and would not eat of its flesh. The Praisians actually made offerings to a pig and this was their regular sacrifice before marriage.

The variety and frequency of this legendary material relating to the birth of Zeus in Crete leave no doubt of its pre-eminence compared with other birth-stories of Zeus. Naturally, however, the very existence of a birth-story and attached cults meant that other places than Crete and other mountains than Dikte later laid their claims.[126] They included Sipylos, Tmolos and Messogis in Lydia;[127] possibly also the mountains of Phrygia;[128] Pergamon;[129] possibly Mount Ida in the Troad;[130] Naxos, where there was a birth-story perhaps connected with Mount Drios;[131] Chaironeia and Thebes in Boiotia;[132] Messenia, where on Mount Ithome Zeus was reputed to have been reared by the nymphs Ithome and Neda;[133] Arcadia, which, next to Crete, laid the strongest claims, with the legend that Kronos had swallowed the stone on Mount Thaumasion and that Zeus was born and reared on Mount Lykaion;[134]

---

[123] Cf. pp. 59–67, 71–4.   [124] Ath. 9. 375f–376a.
[125] Interpreted as a possible allusion to human sacrifice by Cook Z 1.653.
[126] Paus. 4.33.1; Nilsson MMR 535 and n. 5; p. 186.
[127] Lyd. Mens. 4.71.123.14 ff.; Aristid. Or. 22.270; Cook Z 2.956–61.
[128] Cook Z 1.151.   [129] Ib. 953 n. 3.
[130] Prop. 3.1.27 cf. Cook ib. 1.154 n. 2.
[131] Aglaosthenes Naxiaca frs. 1, 2; D.S. 5.51; Cook ib. 1.163–4.
[132] Paus. 9.41.6; Tz. ad Lyc. 1194; Aristodem. ap. sch. Il. 13.1 cf. Paus. 9.18.5.
[133] Th. 1.103; Paus. 4.3.9, 4.12.7 ff., 4.27.6, 4.33.1 f.
[134] Clem. Al. Protr. 2.28.1.20, 30 ff.; Cic. ND 3.53; Ampel. 9.1; St. Byz. s.v. Θαυμάσιον; Paus. 8.28.2, 8.36.2,3; Call. Jov. 44 ff.; Str. 8.348; EM 227.44 f.

and finally, Olympia, where the birth was transferred in the legend of the founding of the Olympic Games.[135]

It is consistent with his embodiment of the human, social and natural cycle of birth and death, renewal and decay, that the annually reborn Zeus of Crete should not only have his marriage commemorated,[136] but that his death too should be mourned. Hence the legend of the tomb of Zeus has persisted from ancient to recent times, being variously located at Knossos (by Ennius), Mount Ida (by Varro and Porphyrios) and on Mount Dikte (by Nonnos).[137] This belief in a dying Zeus brought upon the Cretans the censure of Kallimachos as being liars and worse, a censure that is echoed by St. Paul and other early Christian writers.

There was an inscription on the tomb of Zeus, different versions of which were reported.[138] This evidence suggests that the old name Zan for Zeus was especially familiar in Crete and that the cult of Zeus was at least associated with, if it did not grow out of, an earlier cult of Minos; and that the common link continued to be an annual festival in celebration of a god like Adonis or Tammuz, at which this god was eaten in the form of a bull.[139] For, although the evidence for tomb and epitaph is late, it proves that Cretan Zeus was conceived as a dying god; and it also carries the implication that this god was one who died annually and was born again.[140] Finally, there is a growing body of opinion for the view

---

[135] Paus. 5.7.6.

[136] Cf. pp. 110–18, 166–8.

[137] Call. *Jov.* 8 f.; sch. *ad loc.*; Enn. *Sacr. Hist. ap.* Lact. *Div. Inst.* 1.11, *Oracl. Sibyll. b.*; Varr. *ap.* Solin. 11.7; Cic. *ND* 3.53; D.S. 3.61; *AP* 7.275.6; Luc. 8.872; Mela 2.112; Stat. *Theb.* 1.278 f.; Tatian. *Or. Adv. Graec.* 44; Luc. *JTr.* 45, *Sacr.* 10, *Philopatr.* 10, *Philops.* 3, *Tim.* 6; Athenag. *Supp. pro Christ.* 30.40 f.; Theophil. *Ad Autol.* 1.10; Clem. Al. *Protr.* 2.37.4; Philostr. *VS* 2.4; Orig. *Cels.* 3.43; Min-Fel. *Oct.* 21.8; Porph. *VP* 17; Arnob. *Adv. Nat.* 4.14, 4.25; Firm. Nat. 7.6; Serv. *ad Verg. A.* 7.180; Epiphan. *Adv. Haer.* 1.3.42; Rufin. *Recognit.* 10.23; Nonn. *D.* 8.114 ff.; Migne 4.567 A, 26.573 A–C, 38.992, 61.515, 62.676 f., 76.1028 B, 82.861 B, 103.244 C; sch. Bern. Lucan. 8.872; Suid. s.v. Πῆκος ὁ καὶ Ζεύς cf. Cook Z 2.693 n. 4; Kedren. in Migne 121.57D; Cramer *Anecd. Paris.* 2.236.15 ff.; *ib.* 257.33 ff.; Io Ant. *frs.* 5,6.4; *Chron. Pasch.* 44 B–C; Psell. Ἀναγωγὴ εἰς τὸν τάνταλον 348 Boissonade; Buondelmonti *ap.* Legrand 1.20 f., 148 f.; Belon 1.17 p. 31; Pashley 1.211 ff.; Polites 1.97 no. 174; Evans MTPC 23 n. 8.

[138] Enn. *loc. cit.*: ZAN KPONOU; Chrisost. *in Ep. Paul ad Tit.* 3.1 (Migne 62.676 f.): ἐνταῦθα Ζὰν κεῖται ὃν Δία κικλήσκουσι; Porph. *loc. cit.*: ὧδε θανὼν κεῖται Ζάν, ὃν Δία κικλήσκουσιν; Kyrill. Al. *c. Iulian.* 10.342 (Migne 76.1028 B): ὧδε μέγας κεῖται ZAN, ὃν ΔIA κικλήσκουσιν; sch. Call. *Jov.* 8: Μίνωος τοῦ Διὸς τάφος; Kedren. *loc. cit.*: ἐνθάδε κεῖται θανὼν Πῖκος ὁ καὶ Ζεύς cf. Suid. Πῆκος.

[139] Cf. Evans MTPC 21–4; Cook Z 2.344–5; and the suggestive variant of the epitaph cited in the margin of *AP* 7.746: ὧδε μέγας κεῖται βοῦς, ὃν Δία κικλήσκουσι.

[140] Aratos (*Phaen.* 32) says that the infant Zeus grew up in a year; and Kallimachos (*Jov.* 1.57) also mentions his rapid maturity.

that this whole cycle of myth concerning the life story of Zeus may have had its origin in the Babylonian Hymn of Creation (*Enuma elish*), reaching Crete by way of Ugarit.[141]

2. DIONYSOS

Dionysos was also a bull-god, a dying god and a child-god not reared by his mother. It is generally agreed that he is so similar to Cretan-born Zeus in all major respects that there could be little place for him in Cretan cult. The evidence that we have surveyed hitherto certainly supports this conclusion. Nevertheless, the specific evidence for a separate cult of Dionysos in certain areas is somewhat larger than is commonly supposed[142] and deserves to be reviewed.

We need not exaggerate the importance of the references of mutual respect for Dionysos in the decrees relating to Teos from a number of cities in the Hellenistic period.[143]

The numismatic evidence covers Kydonia, Polyrhenia and Sybrita in the west and perhaps Hierapytna in the east. Coins of Kydonia of the period *c.* 200–67 B.C. show the head of a young Dionysos.[144] Coins of Polyrhenia, of the period *c.* 330–280 B.C., show a head of Dionysos with horns.[145] Coins of Sybrita, of the period *c.* 400–300 B.C. or later, show a bearded Dionysos, seated and holding a *kantharos* and *thyrsos*; a head of Dionysos, bearded and wreathed with ivy, and with grapes in front; a young Dionysos holding a *thyrsos*, riding on a galloping panther; and a head of a young Dionysos, wreathed with ivy and with grapes behind.[146] Coins of Hierapytna, of the period 200–67 B.C., show the head of a youth with a fillet or crown of ivy, which is conceivably a representation of Dionysos.[147]

---

[141] Cf. Cornford PS 239–49 and note by Dodds *ib*. 249; Barnett in JHS 65.100 f.; Thomson SAGS 2.140–55.

[142] Cf. e.g. Nilsson MMR 579.

[143] IC I.V (Arkades) 52.11, 29 (201 B.C.), 53.12, 23, 40 (after *c.* 170 B.C.); *ib*. VI (Biannos) 2.12 (after *c.* 170 B.C.); *ib*. XIV (Istron) 1.10, 28 (201 B.C.); *ib*. XVI (Lato) 2.9, 20 (201 B.C.), 15.9 f., 23 (201 B.C.); *ib*. XXVII (Rhaukos) 1.13 f. (201 B.C.); *ib*. 2.I (Allaria) 1.19 f. (201 B.C.); *ib*. III (Aptera) 2.12 f., 20, 31, 51 (after *c.* 170 B.C.); *ib*. V (Axos) 17.19 f. (201 B.C.); *ib*. X (Kydonia) 2.9, 17 (201 B.C.); *ib*. XII (Eleutherna) 21.21 (201 B.C.); *ib*. XVI (Lappa) 3.11 (201 B.C.); *ib*. XXIII (Polyrhenia) 3.9 (201 B.C.); *ib*. XXVI (Sybrita) 1.8, 14 (201 B.C.), cf. 2.6 f.(?) (*c.* third century B.C.); *ib*. 3.III (Hierapytna) 2? (201 B.C.).

[144] Head 464.

[145] Guarducci IC 2 p. 241.

[146] Head 477; Seltman 173.

[147] Guarducci IC 3 p. 24.

Considering the paucity of epigraphic evidence, the mutilated inscription from Eleutherna, of early date, is important.[148] This inscription mentions *sisyropoioi* (presumably makers of goat's-hair cloaks) and may have contained regulations for their pay. Why these workers are mentioned, apparently in some kind of connexion with a cult of Dionysos, cannot be determined, but there is certainly a reference to something 'Dionysian' and in a most interesting form, viz. Διοννύσια or Διοννυσίαν (or Διοννυσιᾶν) which must be related to Διόννυσος, i.e.*Διοsνυσοs = 'son of Zeus'.[149]

Although the numismatic evidence from Hierapytna gives no certain indication of a cult of Dionysos in the east, there is firm epigraphic evidence from Praisos. Here, in an inscription of the early third century B.C.,[150] we have the only mention of a Cretan month Dionysios, which occurs elsewhere in Greece.[151] Of course, we have no means of deciding its place in the Praisian calendar, but presumably it was a spring month; and perhaps it took the place of the month Thiodaisios which occurred at Hierapytna and Lato.[152]

Finally, we have a single brief inscription from Gortyna of about the second century B.C., in the probable form of a dedication to Dionysos.[153]

That this evidence—significant as some of it is, though hardly substantial in any sense—derives, in the main, from the west of Crete may perhaps give some plausibility to the inference that historical cults of Dionysos developed under mainland influences stemming from the 'Orphic revival' of the sixth century B.C.[154] If so, they could only have amounted to a reinforcement of indigenous mystery-cults under a change of name. Such is the conclusion to be derived from our preceding discussion. It is confirmed by the familiar literary evidence of Euripides and Firmicus relating to that old Cretan Dionysos who is none other than Zeus-Zagreus, whose mystic adherents attained communion with their god by eating the raw flesh of a bull.[155]

---

[148] IC 2.XII.9 (sixth–fifth century B.C.); cf. Willetts ASAC 41, 107–8.

[149] Kretschmer *Aus der Anomia* 17; Nilsson MMR 567 and n. 19.

[150] IC 3.VI. 7 A.

[151] In Aitolia (IG 9(1).374), Chalkedon (SIG 1009.20) and elsewhere (cf. Dittenberger in RE s.v.).

[152] Cf. Hsch. Θεοδαίσιος· Διόνυσος; p. 202 above; Maiuri CC 122.

[153] IC 4.238.   [154] Cf. Guarducci IC 2 p. 113.

[155] E. *Cret. fr.* 475 *ap.* Porph. *Abst.* 4.19; Firm. *De err. prof. relig.* 6. The full discussion by Harrison PSGR ch. 10 renders detailed treatment here superfluous; and cf. Guthrie OGR 110–15.

3. HYAKINTHOS

The origins of Hyakinthos are markedly prehistoric but never-theless by no means obscured by the cult of the god who later absorbed him. This later god was Apollo who, according to the familiar myth, both loved Hyakinthos and accidentally killed him with a discus. The tomb of Hyakinthos lay below the throne of Apollo at Amyklai, south of Sparta.[156] His festival, the Hyakin-thia, continued to be one of the most important of all Spartan festivals. It was celebrated annually and lasted for at least three days. It began with solemnity on the first day and was followed by rejoicing and general celebration on the second day. Before the regular burnt sacrifice was offered to Olympian Apollo, the worshippers gave underworld offerings to Hyakinthos through a bronze door beside the altar of Apollo.[157] Thus the compromise between the Olympian and the Minoan youthful god was ritually honoured. The Minoan origin of Hyakinthos is confirmed by the form of his name.[158] Significantly, this name also denotes a flower, the wild hyacinth or iris.[159] Thus Hyakinthos was an annually dying and reborn god of vegetation, akin not only to Adonis, Attis and Osiris, but to his Cretan counterpart, Zeus Kretagenes. Like Cretan Zeus, Hyakinthos was not reared by his mother. Nor was his nurse an animal or an ordinary nymph, but the leading nymph and mistress of animals, pre-Greek Artemis.[160]

As in Sparta and other Dorian districts, where the cult of Hyakinthos was especially widespread, we find in Crete (and at Byzantium, Sparta, Gytheion, Kalymna, Knidos, Kos, Rhodes and Thera) a month called after his name. At Lato[161] and at Malla[162] this month is mentioned in the form Βακίνθιος = Ϝακίνθιος. The associated festival (Ϝακίνθια) is attested in an

---

[156] Site excavated by Tsoundas in 1890 ('Εφ. 'Αρχ. 1892.1) and by Furtwängler in 1904 (*Jahrb.* 33.107). The continuity of finds is unbroken from Mycenean times to late antiquity. There was also a tomb, variously attributed to Apollo Hyakinthos or to Hyakinthos, at Tarentum: Plb. 8.30.

[157] Paus. 3.19.3.   [158] Kretschmer EGGS 404; Fick VO 58.

[159] A survival of the herbal magic associated with the flower may underlie those passages of the *Odyssey* where the hero's hair is changed, with the help of Athene, from its normal Achaean hue (ξανθός) to a shade of blue. Cf. *Od.* 6.231 and 16.175 with 13.399.

[160] Cf. Nilsson MMR 557 and Persson RGPT 137 on Artemis Hiakynthotrophos at Knidos.

[161] IC 1.XVI.3.3.   [162] *Ib.* XIX 3 A. 40.

inscription of the fifth century B.C., a treaty between Knossians and Tylisians.[163]

We shall find other evidence of compromise between Minoan and Olympian deities, but in these cases, generally speaking, the later cults have been more successful in hiding the aspect of continuity. Though it is sometimes difficult to draw precise lines of distinction, this evidence may best be regarded as representing rather less dominating trends of survival of the older ritual forms and cult-practices.

[163] *Ib.* VIII 4 a 17.

CHAPTER 8

Asklepios

THE cult of Asklepios deserves special notice among the historical cults of Crete, if only because of its importance at Lebena, the port of Gortyna. Also, the snake, which is the constant companion of Aklepios, represents a familiar element of continuity with a much earlier phase of Cretan religion, as we recall the prominence of the Minoan snake-cult and its anthropomorphic succession.[1] This past background, moreover, helps to account for the difficulty we have in explaining whether Asklepios is god or hero. For, as a saviour and healer, he is such an indispensable survival from the distant past that his status remains vague. The truth is that he is an old magician capable of learning new arts.

The respect shown to the Asklepios cult in the Greek world in later antiquity, with its compound of superstition, miracle cures and genuine medical lore, has been rightly contrasted with the growing scepticism towards the traditional Olympian hierarchy.[2] So much so that in the late pagan period this god was looked upon as the chief opponent of Christ.[3] The major centre of his worship was Epidauros in the Argolid, though tradition traced his original home to Trikka in Thessaly. Other cult-centres of Asklepios were established and flourished. It is fortunate that the inscription has survived which records his arrival in Athens from Epidauros in 420 B.C., accompanied by his sacred serpent and his attendant goddess of Health (Hygieia).[4]

The surviving Cretan evidence is sufficient to explain that his cult there was fairly generally widespread. It was a common habit of medical practitioners from Kos to travel to various parts of

[1] Cf. p. 74.
[3] Edelstein 1.vii, 176–7, 2.132–8.
[2] Cf. Nilsson HGR 292.
[4] SIG 88.

224

Greece in Hellenistic times, including Crete.[5] The city of Aptera, in the west, recorded its gratitude for the services of such a physician in a decree of the second century B.C., deposited in the temple of Asklepios at Kos.[6] From the site of Aptera also a small marble statue of Hygieia, of the Hellenistic period, has been preserved.[7] In the east, we know that there was a temple of Asklepios at Itanos, where official records were deposited.[8]

But the bulk of the extant evidence comes from cities of central Crete. Among the Arcadians the cult of Asklepios had a place of special importance. They celebrated a festival of the god, the Asklapieia,[9] and they deposited decrees in his temple.[10] From Khersonesos, the port of Lyttos, we have an important and interesting inscription of the first century B.C., in the form of a dedication to Asklepios, perhaps made at a monthly meeting of the Assembly.[11] At Knossos, the only surviving reference is from the time of Nero, in an inscription concerning a grant of land to the local temple of Asklepios, which had probably been first made by Augustus.[12] From Lasaia there is a dedication of the first century B.C. or first century A.D.[13] At Olous there was a temple of Asklepios where decrees were deposited and where his cult was not inferior to that of Zeus Tallaios.[14] It is possible that there was also a temple of Asklepios at Pyloros(?);[15] and, notwithstanding the prominence of his cult at Lebena, there is some evidence to indicate that there was also a shrine of the god at Gortyna.[16]

Some idea of the ultimate eminence of the Lebena sanctuary can be gained from the account of the visit of Apollonios Tyanensis in 46 A.D. For we are told that, just as the whole of Asia flocked to Pergamon, so the whole of Crete flocked to this shrine; and many Libyans also crossed the sea to visit it.[17] Much of the epigraphic evidence which survives is of a fragmentary nature.[18]

---

[5] Cf. IC I.VIII.7.　　　　　　　　[6] IC 2.III.3.

[7] *Ib.* p. 13.　　　　　[8] *Ib.* 3.IV.3 and 7 (third century B.C.).

[9] *Ib.* III 1.B.9 (third century B.C.). Names of festivals of the god and their dates varied. But many were called Asklepieia. Edelstein 1.312–20, 2.195–9.

[10] *Ib.* 1.V.52 (201 B.C.); 53 (after *c.* 170 B.C.); cf. also *ib.* 20 B (*c.* second century B.C.).

[11] *Ib.* VII.5; Willetts ASAC 150–1.　　　[12] *Ib.* VIII.49; ABSA 6.92 f.

[13] *Ib.* XV.3.

[14] *Ib.* XXII 4 A I (third century B.C.) and C XIII (second century B.C.).

[15] *Ib.* XXV 2 and Guarducci *ad loc.*

[16] *Ib.* 4.239 (second–first century B.C.); 240 (*c.* first century B.C.); cf. *ib.* p. 32.

[17] Philostr. *VA* 4.34.　　　　　　[18] IC I.XVII.1–60.

But several of the more interesting inscriptions enable us to con-firm and indeed to supplement the general picture of the procedure of temple medicine which the ancient evidence as a whole relating to the cult of Asklepios, from various sources and centres, com-bines to produce.[19]

The most crucial inscriptions about cures belong to Epidauros. They were displayed for the attention of visitors and are to be regarded as an officially inspired account of the god's powers. Likewise, the Epidaurian dedications were, if not written by the priests, at least composed under their supervision. We can assume the same to be true not only of the Athenian and Roman but also of the Lebena inscriptions.[20]

To this official category we must then assign such testimonies as the two of Poplius Granius Rufus in the first century B.C., and of an unknown woman in the second to first century B.C.[21] In the first, Rufus states that he had coughed so continuously over a period of two years that he vomited bloody pieces of flesh all day long. Then the god undertook his cure, giving him rocket to nibble on an empty stomach; Italian wine flavoured with pepper to drink; starch with hot water; powdered holy ashes; holy water; egg and pine-resin; moist pitch; iris with honey; a quince and wild purslane to be boiled together; and a fig with holy ashes from the sacrificial altar. In the second, he had been suffering from an acute inflammation of the right shoulder until the god commanded him to be confident and gave him treatment. He had to apply a plaster of barley-meal mixed with old wine and a pine-cone ground down with olive-oil, with the addition of a fig and goat's fat, milk with pepper, wax-pitch and olive-oil boiled together.

The woman offers her thanks to Asklepios the Saviour. The god had healed an ulcer on her little finger by prescribing the application of the shell of an oyster, burnt and ground down with rose-ointment, and an anointing with a compound of mallow and olive-oil.

Incubation in the sanctuaries was a normal part of a cure.[22]

---

[19] Edelstein 2.139–80.

[20] *Ib.* 2.146–7, with the conclusion: 'Certainly, nothing detrimental to the dignity of the god was allowed to be mentioned in these temple reports, and on the whole they tend to glorify the greatness of the divine rather than to testify to it in simple and unadorned language.'

[21] IC 1.XVII. 17–19.

[22] On the technique of incubation see Dodds 110–16.

After bathing and offering sacrifices, the patients entered the temple and lay down. The god appeared to them in their sleep or in a waking vision, healed the disease or recommended treatment. Naturally, serpents sometimes appeared in these visions.

Thus the unknown woman, in the inscription mentioned above, saw many glorious deeds of the god in her sleep and was commanded by him to record her visions. Phalaris, the son of Euthykhion, of Lebena, who had reached the age of fifty and was still without children, was ordered by the god to send his wife to sleep in the temple. There he put the cupping instrument on her belly, told her to leave in a hurry, and she became pregnant.[23] A certain Diodoros dedicated two statues of the Dream-God, Saviour, for his two eyes, since he now enjoyed the light of day.[24] Surgery was also practised during this curative sleep, although we remain ignorant of the details of the technique. Thus, when Demandros, son of Kalabis, of Gortyna, was suffering from sciatica, the god ordered him to come to Lebena to be cured. As soon as he had arrived, the god operated on him in his sleep and he was cured.[25] So Asklepios at Lebena, as elsewhere, effected his cures amazingly quickly, literally overnight.[26]

The god appeared in visions not only to the sick. He appeared to Sosos, son of Aristonymos, in his sleep; and he also sent him as a guide, while he was awake, a holy serpent, a great marvel to all men. Likewise he appeared to Soarkhos, the son of Sosos.[27]

Whether the cult of Asklepios at Lebena arose under the influence of Epidauros or Cyrene is disputed.[28] The first buildings dedicated to Asklepios may not be older than the third century B.C.; but there are earlier buildings, indicating that Asklepios succeeded some other deity or deities.[29] Finally, we know that the temple was restored by the Gortynians in the second to first century B.C.[30]

---

[23] IC 1.XVII.9 (second century B.C.).
[24] Ib. 24 (third century A.D.).
[25] Ib. 9.
[26] Cf. Edelstein 2.151–2.
[27] IC 1.XVII.21 (first century A.D.).
[28] Guarducci IC 1. pp. 151, 158; Edelstein 2.249.
[29] Guarducci ibid.; Edelstein ib. and n. 31.
[30] IC 1.XVII.6; Willetts ASAC 142, 147.

Part Three

CRETAN OLYMPOS

And yonder all before us lie
Deserts of vast eternity.

MARVELL

Chanted from an ill-used race of men that cleave the soil,
Sow the seed, and reap the harvest with enduring toil,
Storing yearly little dues of wheat, and wine and oil.

TENNYSON

Part Three

CRETAN OLYMPOS

CHAPTER 9

Zeus

A T an earlier stage of this inquiry it was considered reasonable to assume that the Mycenaean pantheon spread its influence as the Myceanean social and economic system achieved dominance elsewhere. Likewise the ensuing social consequences were paralleled by an increasing complexity of cult, of mythology, of the composition of the pantheon.[1] This complexity is well illustrated by the evidence relating to Zeus. Part of this evidence has been already surveyed in our examination of the characteristics of the specifically Cretan Zeus who survives with such marked traces of his original nature until long after the Olympian religion has become prevalent. The Cretan Zeus is one symbol through which the old Minoan cult still exerts its influence. Enough is known about this Cretan Zeus, the vegetation-god who dies and is born again, to distinguish him from the later Olympian monarch whom we must now pursue through the Doric cities of historical Crete.

For this later Zeus, Olympian though he may be, exhibits himself in many forms. He is rarely mentioned without the addition of one of more than a score of distinguishing epithets which often reveal a pre-Olympian basis. It will be convenient therefore to assess the evidence under the headings of these different epithets. But first, by way of emphasizing a contrast, the relatively few instances where Zeus is mentioned without distinct epithet may be listed, together with the not very extensive numismatic evidence of the same order, most of which, especially when it reveals Zeus at his most familiar and conventional, is, historically speaking, rather late.

Coins of Aptera, of the period *c.* 250–67 B.C., have a head of Zeus, wreathed in laurel.[2] At Axos, the numismatic evidence indicates that the cult of Zeus superseded an earlier cult of Apollo.

---

[1] P. 119   [2] Head 458.

For, whereas the coins of the fourth century B.C. portray a head of Apollo with laurel wreath and a tripod on reverse, coins of the period 300–67 B.C. portray a head of Zeus and a thunderbolt along with a tripod, symbol of Apollo.[3] One of the symbols on the tetradrachms of the Athenian type struck at Kydonia c. 200 B.C. was Zeus hurling a thunderbolt.[4] Although Apollo is the principal god portrayed on coins of Eleutherna, one early type, of the period c. 450–300 B.C., depicts a head of Zeus.[5] The coins of Sybrita are considered to be the most attractively produced of all the Cretan cities. Although Dionysos and Hermes were most commonly featured, from c. 400 B.C. onwards, there is a type with a laurel-wreathed head of Zeus.[6]

Arcadian coins of c. 200 B.C. show a head of Zeus or a Zeus hurling a thunderbolt.[7] Coins of Khersonesos of c. 300–200 B.C. also show a head of Zeus.[8] Knossos began to issue its coinage in the fifth century B.C. and the types are particularly interesting because they so clearly portray allusions to the Minoan past—a characteristic which endured so long as Knossos retained its independence. The earliest type shows the Minotaur with a labyrinthine swastika on reverse. Later, at the end of the century, Minos is featured, sceptred and enthroned, and the head of a young goddess who may be Ariadne, within a maeander frame. A head of Demeter or Persephone is also portrayed in a maeander frame. Then, too, in this second period (c. 400–350 B.C.), appears a seated Zeus, holding phiale and sceptre, sometimes with the whole in maeander pattern. In the period c. 200–67 B.C. there is a type showing a head of Zeus, with a square labyrinth in reverse.[9] The flying eagle on coins of Lyttos in the period c. 450–300 B.C. is apparently a symbol of Zeus. Later, c. 300–220 B.C., another type shows a head of Zeus and a standing eagle.[10] From Olous there is a reference to Zeus in an inscription of the second or third century A.D.[11]

At Gortyna a coin-type of the period 200–67 B.C. portrays a head of Zeus wreathed in laurel.[12] There are also several Gortynian inscriptions which refer to Zeus. It is possible that Zeus is

[3] Head 459; Aly 7; Guarducci IC 2 p. 47. [4] Head 464; Seltman 261.
[5] Head 465.
[6] Head 478; Guarducci IC 2 p. 290.
[7] Head 459; Guarducci IC 1 p. 7. [8] Head 460.
[9] Head 460–3; Seltman 171; Guarducci IC 1 p. 55.
[10] Head 471; Seltman 172. [11] IC 1.XXII.58.
[12] Head 467.

listed among the deities to be invoked in a law relating to oaths of the early fifth century B.C.[13] Mention must also be made of a law relating to sacrifices, of the same period, where Zeus is concerned. However, in this case the reference was probably not general but was qualified by an epithet now missing from the text.[14] There is also a reference to Zeus (perhaps Zeus Eleutherios) on a tomb relief of the fourth or third century B.C.[15]

There is epigraphic evidence from the second century B.C. to indicate that a statue of Zeus stood in the Diktaian temple, in addition to an archaic statue of Diktaian Zeus himself.[16] The Zeus-head die employed at Hierapytna from c. 300 B.C., with a palm-tree and eagle reverse, is a fine example and of particular importance in the history of Cretan coinage.[17]

Finally, mention must here be made of the cases where Zeus is referred to as 'Highest God' at Sybrita, Khersonesos, Knossos and Gortyna, or, in one case at Lato, 'Highest Zeus'.[18]

I. AGORAIOS

There are epigraphic references to Zeus Agoraios in western Crete at Kantanos, in central Crete at Dreros and Gortyna, and in eastern Crete at Itanos. The epithet seems to be the only possible restoration in a dedication at Kantanos of c. second century B.C.[19] In the oath of the Drerian *epheboi* of the third to second century B.C. Zeus Agoraios is mentioned immediately after Hera in a long list of deities; and likewise in the list appended to a treaty of the Gortynians with the Arcadians, of the third century B.C.[20] But in the Itanian oath of the third century B.C., the citizens swear by deities listed in the following order: Diktaian Zeus, Hera, the gods in Dikte, Athene Polias and the gods worshipped in the shrine of Athene, Zeus Agoraios and Pythian Apollo.[21] It is not surprising to find that Diktaian Zeus takes such marked precedence over Zeus Agoraios in a city of eastern Crete, even in the

---

[13] IC 4.51.1.
[14] *Ib.* 65.2.
[15] *Ib.* 348.
[16] Guarducci *ad* IC 3.II.1.10 f.
[17] Head 468–9; Seltman 171; Guarducci IC 3 p. 24.
[18] IC 2.XXVI (Sybrita) *c.* second century A.D.; IC 1.VII (Chersonesos) 7 *c.* first century A.D.; *ib.* VIII (Knossos) 18. N.D.; *ib.* XVI (Lato) second century B.C.; IC 4 (Gortyna) 241 *c.* first century B.C.; *ib.* 242 *c.* first century A.D. On the widespread provenance and significance of the title in Hellenistic and later times see Cook Z 2.876–90; 3.945, 1162–4.
[19] IC 2.VI.1 and Guarducci *ad loc.*
[20] IC 1.IX.1.A 17 f.; IC 4.171.13.
[21] IC 3.IV.8.1–9.

third century B.C.[22] Conversely, his high place in the lists at Dreros and Gortyna must indicate that such eminence was traditionally sanctioned in these places and was probably established fairly early in the historical period.

This epithet *agoraios*, 'of the market-place', is not peculiar to Zeus. It is also applied to Hermes[23] and, in its feminine form (*agoraia*), to Artemis at Olympia[24] and Athene at Sparta.[25] The basic meaning of the epithet no doubt derived from the location in the market-place of a shrine or altar of the deity to whom it applied.[26] But functional shades of meaning must also have been derived from the various functions of the *agora*, chiefly however as the place of assembly and as a market-place. It is tempting to suppose that Hermes had some particular association with the driving of bargains in the market-place.[27] In the same way Zeus Agoraios would be the special patron of those mustered in assembly at the *agora*. Thus, at Gortyna, the word *agora* was used in the fifth century B.C., and probably earlier, to mean an assembly of the citizens. It is not replaced in this sense by the word *polis* until the fourth or even the third century B.C.[28] From this special association with the assembly Zeus Agoraios can be described as a patron of eloquence[29] or of public supplication.[30]

2. ALEXIKAKOS

It is not so surprising to find the epithet *alexikakos* ('averter of evil') applied to Zeus in the time of Plutarch,[31] when magic and superstition are commonly supposed to have been more flourishing than in Classical times. The number of leaden tablets inscribed with imprecations, many belonging to the fourth century B.C., is strong proof against the validity of this opinion.[32] Magic and superstition had their periods of recrudescence but they are survivals from pre-Olympian beliefs and practices. The strength of this surviving core in Crete is convincingly demonstrated in the imprecation from Phalasarna, of the fourth century B.C.,

---

[22] Cf. p. 208.
[23] Ar. *Eq.* 297; IPE 1².128; IG 12(8).67; Paus. 1.15.1.
[24] Paus. 5.15.4. [25] Paus. 3.11.9.
[26] A.*A.* 90; cf. Paus. 3.11.9, 5.15.4. [27] But cf. Guthrie GG 91.
[28] Willetts ASAC 115–16. [29] A. *Eu.* 973.
[30] Hdt. 5.46; E. *Heracl.* 70. [31] 2.1076b.
[32] Nilsson GPR 114.

where Zeus is invoked as *alexikakos*, together with other beneficent spirits.[33]

3. AMMON

The evidence relating to a Cretan cult of Zeus Ammon is restricted to the coinage of Arcadia, Knossos and Aptera.

The earliest coins of Arcadia (*c.* 300 B.C.) have a head of Zeus
Ammon.[34] So do the coins of Aptera of the period *c.* 250–67
B.C.[35] Coins of Knossos of the period *c.* 200–67 B.C. have a bearded
and a beardless type of the head of Zeus Ammon.[36]

This evidence, sparse and relatively late, does not allow of any
novel conclusions concerning the cult of Zeus Ammon in Crete.
But it may well be that the coin-types reflect the cult of an aspect
of Zeus which had begun to be incorporated at a much earlier
date into the Cretan heritage of the Mycenaean pantheon. Though
it may be difficult to establish the origin of the connexion between
Olympian Zeus and Egyptian Amen-Ra, the connexion itself cannot be denied.[37] When we recall the close relationship maintained
at certain periods from the earliest times between Crete and
Africa, it seems natural that parts of Crete became centres of
commemoration of a Graeco-Libyan Zeus. The finding of a small
statuette crowned with the plumes of Amen-Ra, of the period *c.*
900 B.C., in the cave of Psychro, confirms that a process of fusion
could have begun before the historical period.[38] The numismatic
evidence elsewhere is sufficient to prove the existence of a youthful Ammon by the fifth century B.C. He may have been connected
with the Libyan Dionysos.[39] The conception of a youthful Zeus
was, however, so firmly established in the Cretan tradition that no
association would have been necessary to promote his portrayal
on coins.

4. ARBIOS

There was, it seems, a Mount Arbios on the southern coast of
Crete, between Inatos and Hierapytna, near the modern village

---

[33] IC 2.XIX.7.
[35] IC 2.III.p.13; Head 458.
[37] Cf. Cook Z 1.361 ff.
[39] Cook Z 1.371–6.

[34] IC 1.V.p.7; Head 458.
[36] IC 1.VIII.p.55; Head 462.
[38] ABSA 6.107; Cook Z 2.926.

of Arvi, where there was a cult of Zeus Arbios.[40] A few finds on the site indicate that there had been a Minoan settlement here. Hence the possibility that the epithet is pre-Greek[41] is strengthened. But attempts to elucidate its meaning are frustrated by lack of other evidence. That the district abounds in trees, that we know Zeus to have been a tree-god in Crete, are considerations inadequate to justify our yielding to the temptation to compare Greek *arbios* with Latin *arbor*.[42] Two interesting glosses of Hesychios,[43] brought into relation with attempts to solve the identity of the Jupiter Laprios or Labrios mentioned by Lactantius,[44] suggest another temptation—to refer *arbios* perhaps ultimately to *labrys*, 'the double-axe'. But the gap between the Lydian prototype and the Cretan epithet is too wide. We have to remain in ignorance of the origin of *arbios*, though we may speculate more freely upon the ancestry of a story told to a traveller who was camping in the vicinity some fifty years ago:[45]

'And I am not likely to forget the story of the Hammer of Zeus, for a hammer used to illustrate the story frequently fell very near my head as I skinned a bird on an inverted packing-case. They [the villagers] said that between us and the sea was a gorge in which, in its ultimate and very narrow ravine, one heard the hammer of Zeus. They told me that when the mountain wind was well astir, blow after blow fell upon this chasm with the sound and shock of a titanic hammer. The noise of these repeated blows they said was awe-inspiring. . . .'

5. ASTERIOS

The evidence which supports the view that the Gortynian Zeus Asterios was originally a Phoenician solar deity, male counterpart of Astarte, who supplanted the solar 'priest-king', has been already surveyed.[46]

---

[40] St. Byz. s.v. Ἄρβις; Guarducci IC 1.IV.p. 5; Cook Z 2.945; Jassen in RE s.v. Arbios; Evans PM 1.630 f.; cf. JHS 14.285 f.

[41] Cf. Fick VO 24.   [42] Cook Z 2.946.

[43] Viz. ἀρβόν· διεστός, ἀραιόν, ἐλαφρόν and Ἐλαφρός· εὐβάστακτος, κοῦφος· ἢ Ζεὺς ἐν Κρήτῃ.

[44] Lact. *Div. Inst.* 1.22; M. Mayer in Roscher LGRM 2.1506; Cook Z 2.599 and n. 7.

[45] Trevor-Battye 147 f., cited by Cook Z 2.945; cf. Spratt 1.295 and Faure in BCH 82.512.

[46] P. 167.

6. BRONTAIOS

The little altar dedicated to Zeus Brontaios ('of thunder') found in the vicinity of Hierapytna, dated to first century B.C., is of importance if only because it is the sole evidence for the cult in Crete.[47] Two references occur in literature[48] and a few dedications have survived, two from the Kyzikos district, one from Paphlagonia.[49]

Zeus Brontaios, however, differed probably in nothing but the form of his epithet from Zeus Bronton ('he who thunders'), the importance of whose cult in northern and eastern Phrygia is established by the large number of inscriptions from the region.[50]

Though it is not possible to base any conclusions upon the single piece of evidence from Crete, it is worth recalling the views expressed by Cook, apparently without knowledge of the Hierapytna inscription: 'Presumably Zeus Bronton was not only a celestial but also a terrestrial power. . . . What forms his worship took we are not expressly told. But there is good reason to suppose that he was served with mystic rites in a cave . . . it is highly probable that the cult of the Phrygian cave-Zeus resembled that of the Cretan cave-Zeus. As the mystics of Zeus Idaios had themselves to make the thunders of nocturnal Zagreus before attaining the sanctity of their god, so in all likelihood the devotees of Zeus Bronton by some *mimesis* of his thunder sought to become partakers of his godhead. This assumes, no doubt, that the Phrygians, like the Greeks, recognized subterranean thunders. But it will be remembered that in Orphic, and therefore Thraco-Phrygian, story the infant Zagreus sat on a throne grasping the thunderbolt of Zeus.'[51]

7. DIKTAIOS

The evidence which goes to show that 'Cretan-born Zeus' was, in eastern Crete, specifically associated with Dikte by the epithet Diktaios has already been discussed.[52]

[47] Halbherr *Mus. It.* 3.621.n. 38; IC 3.III.13.
[48] Arist. *Mu.* 401ª17; Orph. *H.* 15.9.   [49] Cox-Cameron MAMA 5.176.
[50] Cox-Cameron *ib. passim.*
[51] Cook Z 2.833 ff. Cf. the objection of Cox-Cameron *ib.* xliii ('Still less does the scanty evidence collected by Cook seem to warrant the view that he was normally worshipped with mystic rites in a cave'), considered as perhaps valid by Cook Z 3.1160.
[52] P. 207.

8. EPOPSIOS

The epithet *epopsios* ('overlooking') as applied to gods,[53] and especially to Zeus,[54] is attested in literature. It occurs in a single inscription from Cretan Itanos, of the fourth century B.C.[55] The inscription occurs on a stone pillar found on the site of Itanos and then used as a lintel in a cottage near the lighthouse on Cape Sidero. This inscription makes it evident that the pillar was originally so placed that a line drawn from it to a small rock at sea and then projected to the horizon would mark the exact place where the sun would rise at the winter solstice.[56] The monument naturally has a place among the records of ancient time-reckoning.[57] Whether the rosette or star which is featured on coins of Itanos of the fifth and fourth centuries B.C. was a solar symbol[58] which should be brought into relation with this particular monument is uncertain. But we need have no hesitation in regarding the monument and accompanying inscription as further evidence for the Cretan association of Zeus with a solar deity.[59]

9. HEKATOMBAIOS

At the conclusion of our discussion of the nature of the Cretan Zeus, it was suggested that the historical cult of Zeus in Crete was associated with, if it did not actually develop from, an earlier cult of Minos; and that the common link between the Minoan and the later cult continued to be an annual festival to celebrate a god like Adonis or Tammuz, at which the god was eaten in the form of a bull.[60] We have also seen reason to suppose that the evolution of the male deity from a bull into the anthropomorphic Zeus, who was later associated with Europa, occurred in the Mycenaean period. The marriage of Zeus and Europa was remembered at Gortyna, where the ancestors of the historical people may have

---

[53] S. *Ph.* 1040.
[54] A.R. 2.1123, 1133; Call. *Jov.* 82; Ant. Lib. 6.2.   [55] IC 3.IV.11.
[56] Cf. sch. Ar. *Av.* 997; Ael. *VH* 10.7.
[57] Rehm in RE s.v. Horologium; Kubitschek GAZ 188 ff.; Wilhelm *Jahresh.* 30.135 ff.
[58] Cook Z 2.1130.
[59] Pp. 110–18; Cook Z *ibid.* Perhaps ἐπόψιος is related in cult to its cognate ἐπόπτης = 'one admitted to the highest grade of mysteries'.
[60] Pp. 219–20.

been known as 'Cow-men' or 'Cow-herds', and where Zeus was known as Hekatombaios, the god to whom hecatombs were offered.[61] Hesychios explains that Gortynian Zeus and Athenian Apollo were both known as Hekatombaios, but also that this was a title of Zeus in Arcadia and among the Cretans generally.[62]

It is significant that we find the same or a similar term applied elsewhere either as the name of a month or as the name of a festival, when or at which hecatombs were offered.[63]

The foregoing discussion thus renders plausible the suggestion that it is the epithet Hekatombaios which is omitted after Zeus in an inscription from Gortyna of the early fifth century B.C., which is a law relating to sacrifices to be offered to particular deities.[64] It is also tempting to suppose that the festival called Hyperboia, mentioned at Malla, Priansos and Hierapytna,[65] was a festival of the same type as the Hekatomboia; and also that the 'great hecatomb' mentioned in an early inscription from Axos, of the sixth to fifth century B.C., was intended for Zeus.[66]

10. IDAIOS

It is natural to begin an account of Zeus 'of Ida' (Idaios) with a piece of literary evidence as important and interesting as the Hymn of the Kouretes for the light it throws upon the indigenous Cretan cult of Zeus. This is the famous and much-discussed fragment of *The Cretans* of Euripides, cited by Porphyrios, who explains that it was delivered by the chorus of inspired Cretan devotees of Zeus.[67]

[61] P. 166.

[62] Hsch. s.v. Ἑκατόμβαιος. Cf. EM 321.7; Migne 103.624 B.

[63] ἑκατόμβαιος (sc. μήν) Hemerolog. Flor.; cf. ἑκατομβαίων (Athens and elsewhere) Antipho 6.44, Plu. Thes. 12, IG 11(2).203 A 31, ib. 1².76.53, ἑκατομβεύς (Sparta) Hsch., ἑκατόμβιος (Halos) IG 9(2).109 b 50; ἑκατόμβαια (sc. ἱερά Delph.) CIG 1715; cf. ἑκατόμβοια (Delph.) SIG 36.36, 82.6, (Delos) BCH 29.243, (Tegea) IG 5(2).142, Str. 8.4.11 codd., Ἑκατομβούοις (Argos) Schwyzer 91.19, ἑκατόμβη (Geronthrai) IG 5(1).1120, Ἑκατόμβια (Amorgos) IG 12(7).388.

[64] IC 4.65. The animal sacrificed to Zeus may have been a bull. Cf. Halbherr AJA 1.162 n. 1; Guarducci ad loc.

[65] IC 1.XIX (Malla) 1 (third century B.C.); ib. XXIV (Priansos) p. 280 (second century B.C.); IC 3.III (Hierapytna) 4 (second century B.C.).

[66] IC 2.V.1.

[67] Porph. Abst. 4.19, E. Cret. fr. 472 Nauck. In l.11 the MSS. of Porphyrios have καὶ νυκτιπόλου Ζαγρέως βροντάς ('thunders of night-roving Zagreus') which was retained by Cook and Murray, but I translate βούτης or βούτας, preferred by Kern, following Diels and Wilamowitz, for the reasons stated by Guthrie OGR 146. n. 34, cf. 260. For other verse translations see Murray in Harrison PSGR 479 and Cook Z 1.648; and prose translation Guthrie ib. 111 and GG 44-5.

Thou lord over Crete with her hundred
Towns, O thou son of the mighty Zan
And Europa, Phoenician-born.

To thee I have come now, since I have left
Those sanctified shrines which are roofed by the
Native beam that was cut with Khalybian axe,
Its joints of the cypress fitted
Exact with the glue from a bull's hide.

Unsullied the life I have led since
I became initiate of Idaian Zeus
And herdsman of Zagreus who wanders by night,
Accomplished the raw-flesh feasts and held high
Torches to the Mountain-mother, torches
Of the Kouretes,
Hallowed and named as a Bakkhos.

All-white are the clothes I wear and I shun
Human birth, touch no urn of the dead, have been
On guard to avoid all taste of meat
Once endowed with the breath of life.

The first point to be noticed here is that, although Euripides
may not be giving a description of a rite that can be taken as
literally correct in all its details, he should nevertheless consider
it appropriate to ascribe a mystical character to the cult of Cretan
Zeus in the fifth century B.C. There can be little doubt that this
Idaian Zeus, also honoured by the Kouretes, is essentially the
same as the god who is celebrated in the Hymn of Palaikastro.[68]
He is the old Cretan god who is so like Dionysos elsewhere that
it is natural for the initiated mystic to describe himself as Bakkhos;
who dies and is born again; and who causes the renewal of life
in the worshipper who enters into his mysteries, culminating in
the eating of the raw flesh of the animal which is the god himself made manifest—the bull, whose blood also sanctifies his
shrines.

Further evidence for this abiding characteristic of the Cretan
mystic cult is supplied in the description of a Cretan festival by
the Christian Father, Firmicus Maternus, who wrote *On the Error
of Profane Religions* between 343 and 350 A.D. for the emperors
Constantius and Constans.[69] The Dionysiac festival he describes
was trieteric, held in alternate years, and was begun to allay the

anger of a king of Crete whose son was lured to his death by treachery. All that the boy had done and suffered was re-enacted in the ritual, which, according to Firmicus, included the tearing of a *live* bull with the teeth!

The essentials of this story are of lasting importance for three reasons, as A. B. Cook emphasized.[70] It was a dramatic story, since the Cretans duly performed all that the boy had done or suffered at his death. It was sacramental, since they tore the bull in memory of the Titans feasting on the boy's flesh. It was also self-contradictory. For, although the boy was dead and buried, he was yet living and also a god. This element of self-contradiction is perhaps the most crucial, because it reflects the tragic sense of life itself, namely that life is inconceivable without death, and death without life. The tale of Firmicus Maternus reproduces a myth very like other myths which were interwoven with the festivals out of which drama developed.[71]

Thus, whether he is later conceived as Dionysos or described by Euripides as Idaian Zeus or as Zan, an older form of Zeus, this Cretan deity is he whose name was probably first Hellenized as Zagreus.[72]

After all that has been said about the nature of this old Cretan deity, we are in a better position to appreciate why a recently explored part of the Idaian Cave may have been the centre of a secret cult associated with initiation.[73] We saw that the archaeological data from the Idaian Cave indicate that Zeus was worshipped on Ida for more than a thousand years and well into Roman times. The legends attached to the spot and the evidence of the epigraphic record confirm the strength of this survival and the underlying ancient links with herbal magic, the thunder-stone and initiation rites.

In common with other names of mountains, the name Ida means 'forest' or 'wood'.[74] References to the oak-trees which flourished on Mount Ida and to the fame of its cypresses support this etymology.[75] The fragment from *The Cretans* of Euripides quoted above confirms that the cypress, like the oak, played a part in the

---

[70] Cook Z 1.663. Cf. Harrison PSGR 485, Guthrie OGR 108.

[71] Cf. p. 205.   [72] P. 203.

[73] P. 144.

[74] Cook Z 2.932, citing Schrader *Reallex*². 88 f.; Solmsen in *Indogerman. Forsch.* 26.109 ff.; Fick VO 10, HDG 11 f.; Boisacq s.v.

[75] Thphr. *Char.* 503, *HP* 3.2.6, 4.1.3; Nic. *Ther.* 585; Verg. *Georg.* 2.84; Plin. *NH* 16.142.

cult of Rhea and Zeus.[76] In the mouth of the Idaian Cave there was, according to Theophrastos, a fruit-bearing poplar, according to Pliny, a willow.[77] The iron-coloured stones found in Crete, shaped like a human thumb and called *Idaei dactyli*, were perhaps regarded as thunderbolts.[78]

Although, as we have seen, the literary evidence for the association of Mount Ida with Zeus is early, his birth-story was not transferred there. But he was reputedly transferred after his birth to a near-by cave by the Kouretes and fed by nymphs on honey and the milk of the goat Amaltheia.[79] His nurse Adrasteia made him a golden ball and put him to sleep in a golden cradle.[80]

In keeping with the early literary tradition, the cult of Idaian Zeus, when it acquired repute all over the Classical world, was centred on the Idaian Cave, about twenty miles from Knossos and connected with it by a road beside which pilgrims rested in the shade of trees.[81] It was not only the cave itself but the surrounding meadows which were sacred to Zeus; and votive offerings were placed at the entrance.[82]

Pythagoras was said to have gone to the cave with Epimenides, a Cretan and also a Koures. When the philosopher landed in Crete, he went to the mystics of Morges, one of the Idaian Daktyloi, and was purified by them with the thunder-stone. At dawn he lay prone beside the sea and at night beside a river, his head wrapped in the fleece of a black ram. When he went down into the Idaian Cave he wore black wool, passed thrice nine days in accordance with custom, offered a funeral sacrifice to Zeus, saw the throne which was spread for him every year, and inscribed an epigram on his tomb with the title 'Pythagoras to Zeus' and beginning: 'Here Zan lies dead, whom they call Zeus.' The cavern ritual was therefore one of death and rebirth. Zan/Zeus is dead, but his return to life as Zagreus is prepared for; and the initiate shares in the death and resurrection of the god.[83]

An inscription from Gortyna of the first part of the fifth century B.C. indicates that the Gortynians were responsible for an im-

[76] Cf. Cook Z 2.932.   [77] Thphr. HP 3.3.4; Plin. NH 16.110.
[78] Plin. NH 37.170; Isid. Orig. 16.15.12; Solin. 11.14; Babelon in Daremberg-Saglio 2.1465; Blinkenberg 76 f.
[79] D.S. 5.70; Ov. Fast. 5.115 f.; Juv. 13.41.
[80] A.R. 3.132 ff.; Call. Jov. 46 ff. On the cosmic significance of the ball see Cook Z 2.933.
[81] Lact. Plac. in Stat. Theb. 4.105; Pl. Lg. 625a-b.
[82] D.S. 5.70; Thphr. HP 3.3.4.
[83] D.L. 8.3; Porph. VP 17; Cook Z 1.646 f.; above p. 219 and n. 138.

portant trieteric festival at the cave of Zeus on Mount Ida.[84] It is decreed by the Gortynians that their perioecic subjects, the Rhittenians, shall send to Ida, on the occasion of the festival, three hundred and fifty staters' worth of victims, or victims and money. It is perhaps the same trieteric festival which is mentioned again in a further Gortynian inscription of the late fifth or early fourth century B.C.[85]

In the oath of the Lyttians appended to the treaty between Lyttos and Olous, of 111–110 B.C., Idaian Zeus[86] is listed after Hestia, Zeus Kretagenes and Zeus Tallaios.

The wrath of Idaian Zeus is invoked against transgressors of a decree of Axos, c. first century B.C.[87]

In a treaty between the Gortynians and Hierapytnians with the Priansians at the beginning of the second century B.C., there is certainly mention of Idaian Zeus and perhaps of his temple or shrine on the borders of Priansos.[88]

A tablet of terracotta with an inscription to Idaian Zeus was among the votive objects found in the Idaian Cave.[89] The date is second to third century A.D. and the inscription is therefore of vital importance in proving the continuity of the cult into Roman times. We may link with this inscription the copper coins of Crete issued by Titus and Domitian, having for reverse type an eagle inscribed 'Of Idaian Zeus'.[90]

II. KAUDIOS

The island of Kaudos, off the south-west coast of Crete, had close ties of a special kind with Gortyna, established probably before the second century B.C.[91] The evidence of a single mutilated inscription of the third century B.C. makes it possible, but by no means certain, that there was a cult of Zeus Kaudios on the island.[92]

---

[84] IC 4.80; Willetts ASAC 110–14.

[85] IC 4.146. In this inscription the spelling is Ϝίδα; in the earlier inscription either Βίδα or Ϝίδα. With these two forms we must compare the definite adjectival forms Βιδάτας and Ϝιδάτας of Hellenistic times = Ἰδαῖος of Roman times. See nn. 86, 87, 88 below.

[86] IC 1.XVIII.9 c 5; viz. Τῆνα Βιδάταν.

[87] IC 2.V.35.11; viz. τὸν Δῆνα τὸν Ϝιδάταν. The form Δῆνα is also found at Dreros (IC 1.IX.1.A 17 f.) and at Praisos (IC 3.VI.7 A 15 f.). Cf. Bechtel 2.732; Buck GD 71, 93.

[88] If we read with Blass ἐς τὸ ἱαρὸν τῶ before Τηνὸ[ς] τῶ Βιδάταω at IC 4.174.22 f. Βιδάταν also restored by Blass ib. 1.57.

[89] IC 1.XII.1; viz. Δὶ Ἰδαί[ῳ].   [90] Head 479; Cook Z 2.933.

[91] Willetts ASAC 138 et passim.   [92] IC 2.VII.1; De Sanctis MA 11.525 n. 71.

12. KRONEIOS AND KRONIDAS

Some of the fixed epithets of the Homeric poems betray an earlier, pre-Olympian conception of Zeus the magician.[93] One of the more recurrent of these epithets describes him as 'son of the wizard Kronos'.[94] Like Aeschylus and Pindar,[95] the Cretans continued to think of him as 'son of Kronos'. In the Hymn of Palaikastro, as we have seen, he is so invoked;[96] and also in an epigram from Kydonia of *c.* second century B.C.[97] But in Crete this epithet was but one of several, and but one of many diverse ways in which the pre-history of Olympian Zeus could be readily called to mind.

13. MAKHANEUS

A similar conception may underlie the epithet Makhaneus ('Contriver'?).[98] This was a title of Zeus at Kos, Tanagra and Argos, of a month at Corcyra and (in the form Makhaneios) at Chalcedon.[99] A Cretan context for the epithet is found only once, in the Argive draft of the treaty between Knossos and Tylisos, arranged under the auspices of Argos and dated *c.* 450 B.C.[100] The treaty contains a provision that, when sixty rams are sacrificed to Makhaneus, a leg of each victim should be reserved for Hera. Since this region of Crete had been settled by colonists from Argos, and since Argos supervised the treaty, the provision clearly owes its existence to the importance of the Argive cult of Zeus Makhaneus and also of the Argive Hera, chief goddess of the city.[101]

14. MELIKHIOS

The epigraphic evidence for a cult of Zeus Melikhios in historical Crete, though scanty, is important. It shows that he was wor-

[93] Cook Z 1.14.
[94] Viz. Κρόνου πάϊς ἀγκυλομήτεω.
[95] A. *Pr.* 577 f., Pi. *O.* 2.22.
[96] Viz. Κρόνειε.
[97] Viz. *(Z)εῦ Κρονίδα*: IC 2.X.19.7.
[98] Cf. Cook Z 3.567.
[99] SIG 1026.10 (fourth–third century B.C.); IG 7.548; SIG 56.29 (fifth century. B.C.); IG 9(1).694; SIG 1011.7 (third–second century B.C.). For Argos cf. Paus. 2.22.2.
[100] IC 1.VIII.4 b 9.
[101] Cf. Beloch GG 1.1.128 f.; Guarducci *ad loc.*; Cook *ib.* 566; Paton-Hicks 333.

shipped by those markedly religious conservatives the Latians and was remembered at Olous.[102] But the most significant link with the distant origin of the cult is provided by an inscription from Hierapytna.[103] That it is relatively late (c. first century A.D.) is less noteworthy than that it comes from an Eteocretan centre. This inscription proves that a joint cult of Zeus Melikhios and of Hera Melikhia was still flourishing at the time.

For detailed discussion of the cult of Zeus under this aspect the reader may be referred to Cook, Harrison and Nilsson.[104] When examining the results of his inquiry Cook concluded that: 'Early Greek kings, especially such as would claim descent from Aiolos, were held to be embodiments of the sky-god Zeus, and as weather-makers for the community bore a sceptre tipped with the light-ning-bird. Even when dead and buried the king continued to help his people. He preserved and perpetuated the tribe (Zeus Soter). He brought its young folk to his own state of maturity (Zeus Teleios). He watched over its interests (Zeus Epopsios). Hence, like other chthonian powers, he was fitly addressed by a coaxing appellation—"the Kindly One" (Zeus Meilikhios). Regents of this sort, at once human and divine, were, strictly speaking, *daimones* rather than *theoi*. . . . The *daimon*, in short, was the *theos* incarnate. And the Agathos Daimon *par excellence* was Zeus Meilikhios.'

Cook dissented from Jane Harrison's view that the festival of the Diasia of Zeus Meilikhios had originally nothing to do with Zeus and denoted a 'festival of curses' with 'associated rites of placation and purgation'. For Cook the scattered indications of a divine ram in the cult of Zeus Meilikhios (as of Zeus Ktesios and other Zeus-cults) confirmed other indications of a Graeco-Libyan and Thraco-Phrygian Zeus, appearing sometimes as a ram, some-times as a snake.[105]

Nilsson's conclusion was that, where Zeus appears in the shape of a snake under the names of Meilikhios, Ktesios and Philios, the name of Zeus had been added to the house deity which appeared as a snake, because Zeus was also protector and guardian of the house. A deity, male in later Greece, female in the Minoan Age,

---

[102] IC 1.XVI.29 and Guarducci *ad* IC 3.III.14. [103] IC 3.III.14.

[104] Cook Z 2.1091–1160 *et passim*; Harrison PSGR 13–28 cf. T 298; Nilsson GGR 1.385 ff.; MMR 327–8. Cf., at Athens, IG 1².866 (written Μιλίχιος), Th. 1.126, X. *An.* 7.8.4; at Orchomenos IG 7.3169; in Argolis, Paus. 2.20.1; also of Dionysos, Plu. 2.994a, cf. Aphrodite AP 5.225. The Cretan form is Μηλίχιος.

[105] Cook Z 1.427–8.

developed out of a domestic snake-cult.[106] The inscription from Hierapytna is a remarkable confirmation of this view, showing as it does how the old Minoan snake-goddess survives beside Zeus in the person of Hera, combining and transcending both by virtue of the epithet Melikhios/Melikhia.

15. MONNITIOS

Any possible explanation of the meaning of the Cretan epithet Monnitios must be cautiously advanced.

Zeus Monnitios was the chief deity of Malla. His temple there is referred to in the text of the treaty between Lyttos and Malla, c. 221 B.C., and also in the decree of the period after c. 170 B.C. relating to Teos.[107] He is also invoked by the Hierapytnians in their oath appended to the treaty with Lyttos, 200–197 B.C., being mentioned after Hestia, Zeus Oratrios, Athene Oleria, but preceding Hera and a list of other deities.[108] The Lyttians also probably (some restoration of the text is required) invoked the same list of deities.[109] The epithet is also plausibly restored in the text of the treaty of the Gortynians and Hierapytnians with the Priansians at the beginning of the second century B.C.[110]

Coins of Malla of the third to second century B.C. have a laureate head of Zeus Monnitios with an eagle and thunderbolt on reverse.[111]

Pollux perhaps gives us a clue to the etymology when he explains that the *triopis* (viz. *triottis* elsewhere), a necklace with three pendants like eyes, had also the name, especially among Dorians, of *mannos* or *monnos*.[112] If so, the epithet could well have been applied to a god whose image had originally been adorned in this way.[113]

Have we here, in the person of Zeus Monnitios, a direct link with those two Minoan representations which we have definitely accepted as those of a ruler or 'priest-king' and which share one mark of distinction—an elaborate necklace?[114]

---

[106] MMR 327–9; cf. p. 74.
[107] IC 1.XIX.1.19; *ib.* 2.14.
[108] IC 3.III.3 B.20.
[109] *Ib.* 14.
[110] IC 4.174.57, 73.
[111] Head 724.
[112] Poll. 5.99. Cf. μανιάκης, of a gold necklace worn by Persians and Gauls: Plb. 2.29.8, 2.31.5; LXX 1 Es. 3.6; Plu. *Cim.* 9; Jul. *ad Ath.* 284d; Lyd. *Mag.* 1.46; also μανιάκη *PMon.* 7.74, and μανιάκιον sch. Theoc. 11.41.
[113] Guarducci *ad* IC 1 p. 233. Cf. however Maiuri OC 2.656.
[114] P. 90. Was he a solar Zeus? Cf. Cook Z 1.298.

16. OLYMPIOS

An inscription from Soulia of *c.* first century B.C., recording a dedication by a priest and his wife to Olympian Zeus and Olympian Hera, is of special interest because the combination occurs only here in the Cretan epigraphic record.[115]

The cult of Zeus Olympios was, of course, common throughout the Greek world even where there was no mountain to establish the connexion.[116]

17. ORATRIOS

Zeus Oratrios is mentioned, second after Hestia, in the oaths of the Lyttians and the Hierapytnians in their treaty of *c.* 200–197 B.C., and again, second after Hestia, in the oath of the treaty between Hierapytna and a colony, in the second half of the second century B.C.; and also in the treaty between Gortyna and Hierapytna with Priansos.[117]

The epithet signifies that Zeus was invoked as 'guardian and patron of treaties'.[118]

18. SKYLIOS

An inscription of 120 A.D. from Rhytion concerns a letter, restored by a priest of Zeus Skylios, and an Imperial rescript relating to Gortynian trespassers on the sacred domains of the god, which had been engraved on a stele kept in his temple.[119]

There is an earlier reference in the treaty of the Gortynians and Hierapytnians with the Priansians of the early second century B.C., where both parties include Zeus Skylios among the deities of their oath.[120]

Skylios and Skyllios are apparently the same, though our source for the latter does not help in deciding the etymology.[121]

---

[115] IC 2.XXV.3 and Guarducci *ad loc.*
[116] Roscher LGRM 3.840–7; Farnell CGS 1.155 f.
[117] IC 3.III.3 B, and 5; IC 4.174.
[118] Ὁράτριος = Ϝράτριος. Guarducci *ad* IC 3.III.3 B.13; Thumb-Kieckers GD 1.155; Buck GD 25, 50–1, 64. Not to be confused with Φράτριος: Guarducci *ibid.* and cf. Willetts ASAC 67.
[119] IC 1.XXIX.1.   [120] IC 4.174.58, 73.
[121] St. Byz. Σκύλλιον· ὄρος Κρήτης. οἱ παροικοῦντες Σκύλλιοι· Σκύλλιος γὰρ ὁ Ζεὺς αὐτοῦ τιμᾶται, ἔνθα φασὶν ἀποθέσθαι τοὺς Κουρῆτας μετὰ τῶν Σπαρτιατῶν (Κορυβάντων Salmasius) τὸν Δία.

Nor does a supposed connexion with Dionysos Skyllatis of Kos give much help, since Skyllatis was probably associated with the vine.[122] There are objections to the explanation that Skylios is to be related to the words *skyllos*, *skylax* ('dog') and to the monster *Skylla*.[123] A connexion with *skyla*[124] ('arms stripped off a slain enemy, spoils') is even more unlikely.

There remains the possibility that Skylios may have been originally associated with *skylos*[125] ('an animal's skin or hide'). If so, a Minoan-Mycenaean origin of the cult may be suggested.[126]

19. SOTER

There are two Cretan inscriptions which indicate a cult of Zeus Soter ('the Saviour').[127]

A dedication by a physician to Zeus Soter, of *c.* first century B.C., may have been taken from Knossos to the place some distance away where it was found.[128]

At Itanos, in a dedication dating perhaps to the beginning of the second century B.C., Zeus Soter is coupled with Tykhe Protogeneia.[129]

20. TALLAIOS

We have seen that Talos, 'the bronze man' who was described as a bull and who was also the sun, became Zeus in Crete.[130] Several inscriptions support the testimony of Hesychios to this effect.[131]

Zeus Tallaios is mentioned third (after Hestia and Zeus Agoraios) in the list of deities of the Drerian oath, of the end of the third or early second century B.C.[132] At neighbouring Olous he had a temple, where decrees concerning Knossian arbitration between Lato and Olous, of *c.* 120–116 B.C., were to be set up.[133] The same applies to the treaty between Lato and Olous of the second half

---

[122] Hsch. σκυλλίς· κληματίς; Paton-Hicks 86.
[123] See Cook Z 3.413–16, 1148.
[124] Guarducci *ad* IC 1.XIX. Cf. *id. Hist.* 8.77.
[125] Call. *fr.* 142; cf. Theoc. 25.142, *AP* 6.35, 165.
[126] Cf. p. 86.   [127] See p. 245.
[128] IC 1.VIII.17.
[129] IC 3.IV.14. Cf. Artemis Soteira in the Itanian inscription (*ib.* 13), of the fourth or third century B.C.
[130] Pp. 100–1.   [131] Ταλαῖος· ὁ Ζεὺς ἐν Κρήτῃ.
[132] IC 1.IX.1 A.   [133] IC 1.XVI.3–4.

of the second century B.C.[134] and to the decree of the second century B.C. in honour of a physician from the island of Kasos who had helped the Olountians during a plague.[135]

Coins of Olous of the period c. 330–200 B.C. have as obverse type a head of Britomartis with a laurel wreath and quiver, and as reverse type a head of Zeus enthroned with an eagle in the right hand and a sceptre in the left.[136] Coins of Phaistos of the period 430–250 B.C. portray Talos with a hound which was the protector of Zeus.[137]

That the cult was established on Mount Ida can be inferred from an inscription concerning a dedication to Hermes 'established on the Tallaian heights'.[138] For, since Ida was sacred to Zeus, it is likely that the epithet has to do with Zeus rather than with Hermes.[139]

21. THENATAS

The location of the Cretan city Thenai and the neighbouring Omphalian plain, where the child Zeus was said to have lost his navel-string,[140] remained unknown until excavations of the area of Amnisos under Marinatos led to the discovery of the altar of Zeus Thenatas. On the neighbouring hill of Palaiokhora an extensive Minoan building was brought to light. In the archaic period its walls had been used for the building of a temple. Among many other finds were Egyptian faience objects of the archaic period. The identity of the deity worshipped was established by the discovery of two inscriptions, in 1934 and 1938, the second of which certainly bears the name of Zeus Thenatas.[141] As Nilsson

---

[134] Ib. 5.48,73 f.

[135] IC 1.XXII.4 C.59 f.

[136] Head 472.

[137] Ib. 474.

[138] IC 2.XXVIII.2.

[139] Cf. Guarducci ad loc.; and Cook Z 1.730: 'As in Crete, so in Laconia, Talos the sun-god came to be identified with Zeus. Mount Taleton, the culminating peak of Mount Taygeton, was sacred to the Sun, and amongst the sacrifices there offered to him were horses. It would appear, therefore, that the Laconians too had a sun-god akin to Talos. But Zeus, whose worship spread by degrees over most of the mountain-tops of Greece, naturally usurped the position of this ancient deity. A Spartan inscription links together Zeus Taletitas with Auxesia and Damoia. These were goddesses of fertility, and Zeus Taletitas was presumably coupled with them as being himself a fertilizing force.'

[140] Call. Jov. 42–5, sch. ad loc.; D.S. 5.70.4; St. Byz. s.v.v. Θεναί, Ὀμφάλιον; Guarducci IC 1 p. 46; Svoronos 326 f., Ἐφ. Ἀρχ. (1889) 211.

[141] Praktika (1932) 76, (1933) 98, (1934) 132, (1935) 128, (1936) 81, (1938) 128; AJA 43.345; BCH 82.502. The inscription found in 1938 reads: οἱ κόσμοι οἱ σὺν Ὑπε/ργένει τῷ Κ/οίχιος Τηνὶ Θενάται.

comments: 'Of course, it cannot be said for certain that a cult was practised in the Minoan house and continued by that of Zeus Thenatas, yet it is significant that this temple is built on ruins from the Minoan age.'[142]

22. WELKHANOS

Mention has already been made of the coins of Phaistos from *c.* 430–300 B.C., which show Welkhanos as a youthful, beardless god sitting in the branches of a leafless tree, his right hand caressing a cock, and on the reverse a bull.[143] The Cretan identification of Zeus with Welkhanos is apparently confirmed by a gloss of Hesychios.[144]

At Haghia Triada the discovery of numerous tiles bearing the name of the god Weukhanos (= Welkhanos) was noted by Halbherr.[145] For here the temple of Zeus Welkhanos was built upon the ruins of the palace of Haghia Triada.[146] An associated month-name and spring festival of the god, the Welkhania, is known from inscriptions at Gortyna,[147] Lyttos[148] and Knossos.[149] The cult was known in Cyprus;[150] and at Magnesia on the Maeander, which was colonized from Crete, the god was identified with Apollo.[151]

The conclusion of Cook and Atkinson that Welkhanos means 'god of the willow-tree' goes beyond the evidence.[152] Nevertheless, the historical provenance of the cult and the nature of the evidence do enable us to conclude that Zeus Welkhanos is another

---

[142] MMR 461. [143] P. 177.

[144] S.v. Γελχάνος (for Ϝέλχανος)· ὁ Ζεὺς παρὰ Κρησίν (so Penger for κρισίω cod.; cf. Masurus Ἀκρισίω).

[145] RL 14.381; cf. Guarducci *ad* IC 1.XXIII.4 f.

[146] Nilsson MMR 464, 550.

[147] IC 4.3.1(a–c), an archaic inscription from the Pythion: ἰα]ρὰ/τετελημέ[να . . . .] ·υι/τôι [Ϝ]ελκ<u>α</u>νί[ôι— —; and *ib.* 184.3 (early second century B.C.): μηνὸς Ϝευχάνιω.

[148] IC 1.XVIII.11.2 (second-third century A.D.) καὶ Θεοδαισίοις καὶ Βελχανίοις.

[149] IC 1.XVI.3.2 (*c.* 120–116/115 B.C.): μηνὸς Ἐλχανίω.

[150] SGDI 86. [151] Michel 438; Kern 20.

[152] Mr. W. B. Lockwood has kindly supplied me with the following note: '*Willow* is well attested in West Germanic, but cognates outside this area are in doubt. Many authorities connect it with Greek *helike*, but this is no more than a supposition, the connexion being in no sense demonstrated beyond a fair degree of similarity. *Welkhanos* could theoretically fit in with OE *welig* (willow) but until the Greek ending is cleared up we cannot seriously suppose a relationship, much less start to build any theories on such a supposed relationship. Actually a Greek form *welkh-* would also fit the Germanic, but I would hesitate to equate the words until some internal evidence is found for the meaning of *Welkhanos*.'

survival of the Minoan youthful god of fertility, associated with the vegetation cycle, naturally connected with the Cretan Zeus in particular or, like Hyakinthos, with Apollo at a later stage.

The similarity between the Phaistian coin-series showing Welkhanos with a cock in the branches of a tree, and the Gortynian series showing Zeus, Europa and the eagle, enable us further to suppose that the cock, like the eagle, illustrates a bird-epiphany; and that Welkhanos was the male partner in a sacred marriage with the Minoan Mother-goddess.[153]

---

[153] Cf. Nilsson 552. Nilsson states that the cock did not become known to the Greeks until the sixth century B.C. But we can now cite the evidence of an eighth-century hen: Kübler *Karemeikos* V. 1.178 and pl. 144.

CHAPTER 10

Hera

THE etymology of the word 'Hera' is uncertain but may have signified 'Lady' or 'Mistress'.[1] But if we suppose that the uneasy marriage relationship of Zeus and Hera reflects the intrusion of a Greek patriarchal deity (whose original partner may have been Dione) into the realm of the Minoan Mother-goddess (whose partner, supplanted by Zeus, had been 'called after Hera', i.e. Herakles), we are following a trail of evidence perhaps based on more than speculative etymology.[2] Not the least contradictory feature of the relationship of Zeus and Hera, the Olympian patrons of lawful marriage, is its lack of lawful offspring. Zeus is the father of many children, of whom Hera is not the mother. Hera has fewer children, but Zeus is not their father. Although, according to Hesiod, Hebe, Ares and Eileithyia at least were the children of Zeus and Hera, it is doubtful if this claim can be substantiated.[3] However, Eileithyia could well have been Hera's daughter, since the birthplace was the cave at the mouth of the Amnisos near Knossos.[4]

The Cretan associations of Hera are, of course, all-important for the view that she was originally a form of the Minoan goddess. We have seen reason to believe that the palace-cult of the sacred marriage has behind it, as its human reality, the process whereby primitive collective union of the sexes was replaced in the late Bronze Age by more restrictive social practices which eventually culminated in marriage proper.[5] The Greek evidence for the sacred marriage of Zeus and Hera, most of it comparatively late, partially reveals that Zeus seems to have had an older partner who was not Hera, or Hera an older partner who was not Zeus.[6]

[1] LSJ s.v.; Boisacq s.v. ἥρως; Nilsson MMR 489 n. 9.
[2] Thomson SAGS 1.255, 280–92; Cook WWZ, Z 3.1065; cf. Nilsson MMR 501–2; Guthrie GG 66–73.
[3] Cook WWZ 365.
[4] Paus. 1.18.5.
[5] P. 112.
[6] Cook Z 3.1025–65.

At Knossos we have definite grounds for the view that there had once existed a ritual marriage of a sun-god and a moon-goddess in bovine form.[7] Later this was replaced by the representation of a sacred marriage of Zeus and Hera in myth and ritual. This marriage reputedly occurred near the river Theren, where a sanctuary was built and yearly sacrifices offered with traditional wedding-rites.[8] Similarly, at Gortyna, the goddess who is possessed by Zeus in the form of an eagle becomes identified with Hera.[9]

These Cretan associations give substance to the inference that, despite, or perhaps because of, the supremacy of Argive Hera on the mainland of Greece, Hera had arrived in Greece from Crete. The oldest image of Hera in the Argive Heraion was made of pear-wood and had been brought from Tiryns. Nauplia, two miles away from Tiryns, is likely to have been a familiar harbour for Minoan traders. Here there was a cult of Hera 'The Maiden' (Parthenos). At Hermione to the south-east there was also a cult of Hera Parthenos, coupled with the tradition that it was at this point that Zeus and Hera landed when they arrived in Greece from Crete.[10]

The epigraphic and numismatic evidence of the historical period confirms the strength of Hera's hold on Cretan religious belief.

We have already noticed the Argive draft of the treaty between Knossos and Tylisos, arranged under the auspices of Argos, of c. mid-fifth century B.C., one of whose provisions is that, when sixty rams are sacrificed to Makhaneus, a leg of each victim should be reserved for Hera.[11] There is another provision that a cow should be sacrificed to Hera by the contracting parties in her sanctuary, the Heraion, i.e. presumably a Cretan Heraion, either at Knossos or Tylisos.[12] Coins of Knossos, of the period c. 350–200 B.C., show a head of Hera, wearing a crown with floral ornaments, and also a square labyrinth.[13]

In the oath of the Latians and Olountians appended to their

[7] Pp. 110–18.
[8] D.S. 5.72; G. W. Elderkin 424–5; Cook Z 3.1032.
[9] P. 168.
[10] Paus. 2.17.5, 2.38.2; St. Byz. Ἑρμίων, cf. Theoc. 15.64 sch.
[11] IC 1.VIII.4 b 9, p. 244.
[12] Cf. Guarducci *Epigraphica* 7.83 with the remarks *ad* IC 1.VIII.4 a 16, where, following Vollgraff, the view was adopted that ἐν Ἑραίοι meant 'in the month Heraios'.
[13] Head 461.

treaty of the second half of the second century B.C., Hera occurs high in the long list of deities (third, after Hestia and Zeus Kretagenes).[14] The same text indicates that the month named after the goddess, Heraios, was part of the calendar at Olous, as at Delphi.[15]

An inscription from Hyrtakina (some time after *c*. 170 B.C.) is significant for its mention of a temple of Hera, which seems to have been the most important in the city at this time.[16] The inscription to Olympian Zeus and Olympian Hera of *c*. first century B.C. at Soulia has already called for comment.[17]

The inscription which records the restoration by Hierapytna (*c*. 145–139 B.C.) of certain statues in the temple of Zeus Diktaios has likewise been mentioned.[18] These statues included a head of Hera which perhaps, like the old statue in the Argive Heraion, was made of wood.[19] It may be that the goddess who is featured on the coins of Hierapytna and Priansos is Hera.[20] In the treaty between these two cities, at the beginning of the second century B.C., the citizens are allowed to attend each other's festivals, and it is clear from the special mention of the Heraia that this festival of Hera occupied a special place in Hierapytna and in Priansos.[21] Hera is invoked in the Hierapytnian oaths of the treaties with Lyttos (end of third to early second century B.C.) and with the Hierapytnian colonists (*c*. second century B.C.).[22] In an important Hierapytnian inscription of *c*. first century A.D., as we have seen, Zeus Melikhios and Hera Melikhia are jointly invoked.[23]

The high place occupied thus continually by the cult of Hera in eastern Crete is further emphasized by the invocation of the goddess (second after Zeus Diktaios) in the Itanian oath of *c*. early third century B.C.[24]

For the earliest epigraphic mention of Hera we rely upon a reference in an archaic fragment (mid-seventh to end of sixth century B.C.) from Gortyna, apparently specifying the victims to be offered to the deities of the city, including Hera, at particular times.[25] Apart from a possible relief representation of the fourth

[14] IC 1.XVI. 5.73.
[15] *Ib*. 5.88. Cf. *ib*. XVIII. 9 c 5 (111–110 B.C.).
[16] IC 2.XV.2.10.
[17] *Ib*. XXV.3.14 f.; p. 247.
[18] IC 3.II.1.10; p. 210.
[19] Cf. Guarducci *ad loc*.
[20] Guarducci *ad* IC 3.III.4.38–40.
[21] *Ibid*.
[22] *Ib*. 3 B 14, 20; 5, 12.
[23] *Ib*. 14; p. 245.
[24] *Ib*. IV.8; cf. p. 233; Willetts ASAC 128–9.
[25] IC 4.3.3,(a–c).

254

century B.C.,[26] there is no further epigraphic evidence from Gortyna unless we accept the probable restoration of her name in the treaty of the Gortynians and Hierapytnians with the Priansians at the beginning of the second century B.C.[27]

The possibility that Hera had a cult at Kydonia depends upon the mention of the place-name Herais in an inscription of the third century B.C.[28]

We should also notice that Hera is featured on the coins of Tylisos (*c.* 400–300 B.C.), with her head wearing a crown adorned with floral devices;[29] on coins of Aptera (*c.* 250–67 B.C.), her head wearing a crown;[30] and her head is also portrayed on coins of Polyrhenia.[31]

The wooden statues of Hera, and the coin-types of the goddess with crown and floral decorations recall those more primitive associations of the old Minoan goddess with the sacred tree and with herbal magic.[32]

[26] Guarducci IC 4 pp. 35 and 37.

[27] IC. 4.174, 58, 74.

[28] IC 2.X.1.16.

[29] Head 478.

[30] Guarducci IC 2 p. 13.

[31] Guarducci *ib.* p. 241.

[32] Pp. 67–71, 78–9. Cf. Paus. 2.17.4, 7.4.4; Plin. *NH* 21.118; Alcm. 24; Varr. *ap.* Aug. *CD* 7.2; Farnell CGS 1.196; G. W. Elderkin 429–31; Bossert BKSK 327; Zanotti-Bianco 244.

CHAPTER 11

Apollo

THERE is no need to accept unreservedly the view adopted here earlier[1] that the cult of Apollo originated in Asia Minor to appreciate the special importance of Crete in the development of his cult.[2] There is a good deal of epigraphic and numismatic evidence of the historical period to substantiate the prominence of his role, whether the god be portrayed or cited plainly or referred to by one of his many special epithets. We begin by mentioning the evidence of the first and more general kind. But we should note that the cities of central Crete provide the bulk of the evidence.

Taking the cities of the west of the island first of all, we find from an inscription of the second century B.C. that Apollo had a temple at Allaria and also that he was the principal deity worshipped in the city at this time.[3] Whether another temple of Apollo reported in the west some two centuries later belonged to Phalasarna is not clear.[4] But the god is invoked as a helper in the incantation from Phalasarna of the late fourth century B.C.[5]

Coins of Aptera of the period *c.* 250–67 B.C. have a head of Apollo with laurel wreath or a nude Apollo with a lyre.[6] From the coinage of Axos, particularly that of the fourth century B.C., it can be inferred that the worship of Apollo was, at least in earlier times, conspicuous in that city, though it may have been increasingly superseded by the worship of Zeus.[7] This inference is strengthened by the tradition that the eponymous hero Oaxos or Oaxes (or even Naxos) was the son of Apollo.[8] Kydon, eponymous hero of Kydonia, was also said to have been a son of

---

[1] P. 172. Cf. Nilsson GGR 1.499, MMR 516.
[2] See e.g. Swindler 1–14, with discussion of previous literature; Levi GC 293–310.
[3] IC 2.I.2 B.23.
[4] *Stad.* 336; Guarducci *ad* IC 2 p. 219.
[5] IC 2.XIX.7.4. Cf. p. 234 above.
[6] Guarducci *ib.* p. 13; Head 458.
[7] Guarducci *ib.* p. 47; cf. Aly 7.
[8] Serv. *ad* Verg. *Ecl.* 1.65; cf. St. Byz. s.v. "Οαξος, sch. *ad* A.R. 4.1491.

Apollo, which may have contributed to the idea that Kydonia was once called Apollonia.[9] Nevertheless, coins of Kydonia of the period *c.* 200–67 B.C. have a wreathed head of Apollo, sometimes also with a quiver.[10]

We have seen that the widespread folklore motif of the exposed baby suckled by animals is especially common in Crete and particularly with reference to Zeus. The motif occurs also in the city of Elyros, where coins of the period 400–300 B.C. portray goats (sometimes with arrows, sometimes standing with forefoot planted on a tree), bees and also a head of Apollo. The bees may be connected with Zeus, but the goat seems to be connected with Apollo—a Cretan hunting Apollo. For, according to Pausanias, the Elyrians sent to Delphi a bronze goat suckling the twins Phylakis and Phylandros, sons of Apollo by Akakallis.[11]

Apollo is the chief deity represented on the coins of Eleutherna from *c.* 450 B.C., generally in the character of a hunter.[12] If the Apollo on the earliest coin-type was Styrakites we have perhaps more reason than has been supposed to connect the worship of Apollo with the so-called Ametoridai of Eleutherna.[13] It is the prominence of the cult of Apollo at Eleutherna which probably explains that one of its alternative names was Apollonia.[14]

Tetradrachms of Athenian type from Lappa of the period *c.* 200 B.C. to 67 B.C. have a head of Apollo wreathed in laurel, or standing with a lyre; and coins of the Imperial epoch also show him standing with a lyre.[15] He is also portrayed on the coins of Polyrhenia (300–67 B.C.) and Rhithymna (*c.* 400–300 B.C.). The Rhithymna type is related to the early coin of Eleutherna which will be discussed below.[16]

There is some evidence for supposing that Apollo had a cult at Kisamos;[17] but whether he is featured in the coinage of Sybrita is uncertain.[18]

Turning next to the cities of the eastern part of the island, we find that, at Hierapytna, when the temple of Apollo is referred to, in the treaty between the Hierapytnians and the Lyttians (end of third to early second century B.C.), it is Apollo Dekataphoros who

[9] St. Byz. s.v. Κυδωνία; sch. *ad Od.* 19.176; Guarducci *ib.* pp. 105, 113.
[10] Guarducci *ib.* p. 114; Head 464.
[11] Paus. 10.16.5; Head 465; Nilsson MMR 540; Guarducci *ib.* p. 176.
[12] Head 464. [13] See p. 270.
[14] St. Byz. s.v. Ἀπολλωνία. [15] Head 470.
[16] Guarducci *ib.* pp. 241, 269; Head 475, 477; p. 270.
[17] Guarducci *ib.* p. 101. [18] Head 478.

is undoubtedly understood.[19] The name of the god is twice in-scribed on a rock at the Samonian site;[20] and his head is portrayed in the coinage of Praisos from *c.* 400 B.C. to *c.* 148 B.C.[21]

Of the cities of central Crete, Gortyna provides the earliest evidence, in the archaic fragment apparently specifying the sacri-fices to be offered to deities of the city at particular times.[22] In a fragment of a law relating to oaths of obligation, of the early fifth century B.C., Zeus, Apollo, Athene and Hermes (in that order) are the deities listed by whom the persons involved in the legal undertaking bind themselves, all other deities being expressly excluded from such oaths.[23] A head of Apollo is among the types of bronze coinage of Gortyna of the period *c.* 200–67 B.C.[24]

When Apollo is mentioned in the Knossian treaty with the Milesians in the third century B.C.[25] and in the mutilated inscrip-tion recording an agreement between Knossos and Hierapytna, of perhaps the second half of the second century B.C.,[26] we are able to understand that Apollo Delphinios is meant, for his cult was especially prominent at Knossos.[27] Apollo features on coins of Knossos from *c.* 350 B.C.–67 B.C.[28]

A single inscription (fourth to third century B.C.) commemorat-ing the dedication of a sanctuary to Apollo and the sacrifice of twenty-two oxen by a certain Damokhares prove that there was a cult of the god in the city of Olous.[29] But the decree of the Latians and Olountians concerning Knossian arbitration (116/115 B.C.) indicates that the well-known Doric month Apellaios featured in the calendar at Olous.[30]

Coins of Khersonesos of the period *c.* 370–300 B.C. have a type with Apollo, naked, seated on an omphalos, holding a lyre; and coins of Tylisos, of the period *c.* 400–300 B.C., have a type with Apollo, naked, standing holding a goat's head and bow.[31]

---

[19] IC 3.III.3.B 11, 12; see p. 261.   [20] *Ib.*VII.19 A, B.

[21] Head 476.

[22] IC 4.3.2 (a–c); cf. p. 233 above. Guarducci (*ad loc.*) comments:' Ἀπ[όλōνι Com-paretti, Ἀπ[έλλōνι Blass rectius, cum haec forma ad sermonem Creticum huius aetatis accommoda sit.' Cf., on the vowel-gradation, Buck GD 46.

[23] *Ib.* 51.2: viz. Ἀπέλλōνα.   [24] Head 467; cf. Guarducci *ib.* 38.

[25] IC 1.VIII.6.8, viz. Ἀπόλλωνος.

[26] *Ib.* 13.24 (cf. IC 3 p. 17), viz. Ἀπέλλωνο[ς.

[27] See p. 263.   [28] Head 461–2.

[29] IC 1.XXII.9, viz. Φοίβωι. On the significance of the number of victims, Wilhelm *Wien. Sitz.* 180 *Abh.* 2.49.

[30] *Ib.* XVI.4 B.59.   [31] Head 460, 478.

I. AGYIEUS

Although there is no mention of Apollo under his aspect of Agyieus in the epigraphic or the numismatic record, there are good reasons for discussing the cult in a survey of Cretan religion. For we know that Agyios (with which we may compare the Argive, Aitolian and Lokrian month of the same name) was the name of a month in the Cretan calendar in Imperial times.[32] More important still, the Agyieus worship, predominantly but not exclusively associated with Apollo, developed out of the cult of the Agyieus-pillar[33] as a fertility-symbol and was thus fused with the Minoan pillar-worship. We have seen how the omphalos persists in association with Apollo in the Cretan coinage.[34] There is even some evidence to suggest that the cult of the sacred stone side by side with the cult of the guardian of gates and ways, which formed the essence of the conception of Agyieus in ancient Greece, was paralleled at an earlier date in Anatolia in a way which confirms the Oriental origin of Apollo.[35]

The term Agyieus was defined sometimes as a pointed[36] or a conical pillar,[37] sometimes as an altar,[38] standing before the doorway. For Hesychios, Agyieus was 'the pillar-shaped altar that stands before the doors'.[39] These descriptions enable us to identify

[32] *Hemerolog. Flor.*; also possibly at Knossos, depending on restoration of a mutilated portion of a second-century B.C. inscription: IC 4.197.11. Cf. pp. 105–6.

[33] On the Agyieus-monuments see Welcker GG 1.495 ff.; Saglio in Daremberg-Saglio 1.168 f.; Overbeck GK Apollon 3 ff. Münztaf. 1, 1–8; Wentzel in RE 1.909 f.; Reisch *ib.* 1.910 ff.; Wernicke *ib.* 2.41 f.; Evans JHS 21.173; Gruppe GMR 774 n. 4, 776 n. 1 f., 1232; Farnell CGS 4.148 ff., 307 f., 371 f.; Harrison T 406–15; Swindler 41–2; Nilsson HGR 109, 125, MMR 254; Cook Z 2.160 ff.

[34] Cf. p. 68.

[35] Nilsson GPR 79 (on the inscriptions on four Hittite altars at Anatolian sites published by Hrozný *Archiv Orientální* 8.171), writes: 'Among other gods there is mentioned one whose name is read Apulunas. He is a god of the gates. If this be so, then the Oriental origin of Apollo, which has often been asserted but which has also been vehemently contested, is proved beyond doubt. This Oriental Apollo was the protector of the gates; so was the Apollo of Classical Greece.' Cf. Guthrie GG 86 and n. 1.

[36] Harp. s.v. 'Αγυιᾶς = AB 1.331.32 f. = Suid. s.v. ἀγυιαί = sch. Ald. Ar. *V.* 875 = Zonar. s.v.'Αγυιεύς = Favorin. 28.27 f.; Hdn. 2.889, 27 ff. = St. Byz. s.v. ἀγυιά = AB 1.327.17 f.; sch. E. *Ph.* 631 = Eust. *ad Il.* 166.22 = Favorin. 798.5 f.

[37] Suid. s.v. ἀγυιαί = Zonar. s.v. 'Αγυιᾶς = Favorin. 28.31 f.; Hdn. 1.240.21 ff. = St. Byz. s.v. ἀγυιά; Cook Z 2.160 n. 5.

[38] Harp. s.v. 'Αγυιᾶς = AB 1.332.3 ff. = Suid. s.v. ἀγυιαί = sch. Ald. Ar. *V.* 875 = Zonar. s.v. 'Αγυιᾶς = Favorin. 28.29 ff.; Nigidius *ap.* Macrob. *Sat.* 1.9.6; Varr. *ap.* Porph. in Hor. *Od.* 4.6.28; Poll. 4.123; Hellad. *ap.* Phot. *Bibl.* 535 b 33 ff.; Phot s.v. Λοξίας; Eust. *ad Il.* 166.23 f.; S. *fr.* 370.

[39] Hsch. s.v. 'Αγυιεύς.

the Agyieus on certain Greek coins from various places which have as reverse type a pillar or baluster tapering to a point with a stepped plinth or base, a discoid capital, occasionally an extra ring or rings on its shaft and sometimes a fillet or two fillets at the apex, and also in one case a palm-branch attached to the side. The common obverse type is a head or symbol of Apollo, though this is not always the case.[40] Apollo was worshipped as Agyieus at Akharnai, Athens, Argos, Tegea, Megalopolis and Halikarnassos.[41] Although the epithet was normally regarded as proper to Apollo, it was sometimes associated also with Dionysos and with Zeus.[42] This degree of uncertainty indicates that the cult of the pillar antedates the association with Apollo or with either of the other two not very strong claimants. Hence, when Dieukhidas, the fourth-century historian of Megara, claims that the erection of Agyieus-pillars was especially a Dorian custom—a claim that is confirmed by the numismatic evidence—we are justified in supposing that by 'Dorian' we are to understand 'pre-Hellenic'.[43]

2. AMYKLAIOS

The epithet Amyklaios derives from the pre-Greek place-name Amyklai and tradition connects the mainland settlers of Gortyna, or of a region in the neighbourhood of Gortyna, with the Arcadian area where the Achaean dialect survived, or with Achaean Amyklai.[44] Excavations on the site of the old Amyklai (where Hyakinthos was succeeded by Apollo)[45] have produced many Mycenaean remains, in the form of vase fragments, terracotta figurines, human and animal, and steatite whorls; and they have also revealed evidence of a settlement going perhaps as far back as Early Helladic times, with more finds from Middle Helladic, these two layers being separated from finds of the following Late Helladic period consisting of sherds, votive gifts, idols and animal figurines. Continuity is unbroken down to Classical times and late antiquity.[46]

---

[40] Head 314 (Apollonia), 316 (Orikos); Cook Z 2.161 n. 9 (Olympe); Head 320 (Ambrakia), 269 (Byzantion), 393 (Megara).
[41] Cook Z 2.163–4 with references and discussion of the ancient sources.
[42] Harp. s.v. Ἀγυιᾶς; Anecd. Stud. 1.266; Cook Z 2.164–5.
[43] Dieukhid. 2. Cf. Cook Z 2.165–6; Harrison T 408.
[44] P. 154.   [45] P. 222.
[46] Nilsson MMR 471.

Evidence for a similar place-name in Crete is provided by the tradition that there was a sea-port town called Amyklaion;[47] and also by a decree of the Gortynians, of the third to second century B.C., only part of which survives, concerning apparently this same Amyklaion, and indicating that its inhabitants, known as Amyklaioi, now formed a perioecic community subject to Gortyna.[48]

Presumably the Amyklaioi represented a pre-Dorian element in the Cretan population. Though now reduced to a status of inferiority, their traditions continued to play a part of some importance at Gortyna. That there was a cult and a temple of Amyklaios in the early fifth century B.C. can be inferred from the Gortyn Code; and it is highly probable that the deity, like his Spartan counterpart, who was equipped with helmet, spear and bow, was an armed god.[49] Moreover, there was, in the Gortynian calendar, a month called Amyklaios, in the earlier second century B.C.[50] and perhaps also the same month-name can be read, with a fair degree of probability, in a Gortynian inscription of earlier date.[51]

3. DEKATAPHOROS

Although there was a cult of Apollo Dekataphoros (the 'Tithe-Receiver') at Megara, he was there distinguished from the ancient Megarian cult of Apollo Pythios.[52] This was apparently not the case, however, at Cretan Hierapytna, where Apollo Dekataphoros had a temple, as we learn from an inscription of the second century B.C.[53] For this tithe-receiving Apollo appears to be the same as the Pythian Apollo mentioned in the civic oaths of Hierapytna.[54] At Gortyna also, in the decree concerning the island of Kaudos, of the early second century B.C., it is implied that the tithe imposed on all Kaudian products by land and sea, excluding flocks, vegetables and harbour-dues, was dedicated to Pythian Apollo at Gortyna. The tribute was also imposed on the citizens of Gortyna.[55]

[47] St. Byz. s.v. 'Αμύκλαι; cf. Eust. ad Il. 2.584.
[48] IC 4.172; Guarducci ad loc.; Larsen PC 31; Willetts ASAC 119.
[49] IC 4.72.III.5–9; Guarducci ad loc.; cf. Paus. 3.19.1 f.   [50] Ib. 182.23.
[51] Ib. 173.12 f. Guarducci, ad loc., comments: ' 'Αμυ[κλαίω, quod Halbherr dubitanter suppleverat, Aly dubitanter probavit, mihi quidem certum videtur.'
[52] Paus. 1.42.5.
[53] IC 3.III.9, cf. 10; Dekataphoros was implied ib. 3 B.11,12; Guarducci ad loc.
[54] Guarducci ad ib. 9.1.
[55] IC 4.184; Willetts ASAC 138–40.

Since the inscription of 201 B.C., concerning Teos, had to be published in his temple, it is clear that Apollo Dekataphoros was the principal deity worshipped at Apollonia;[56] and, since the city obviously derived its name from the god, added emphasis is given to the prominence of his cult-epithet here.

This evidence concerning Apollo Dekataphoros confirms Aristotle's statement that a proportion of the tribute levied in Crete was assigned to the gods.[57]

4. DELPHINIOS

If etymological proof alone were in question, we might have stricter reservations about the derivation of the cult-epithet Delphinios from the same root as *delphis* ('dolphin').[58] But by following this etymological clue of a cult of a 'dolphin-god', and accepting that the name Delphi which superseded Homeric Pytho is derived from Delphinios, we admit also the influence of other factors which link Delphinios with Crete.

Since there has been no general agreement about the origin of Apollo, the origin of Delphinios has likewise naturally been disputed. But there has been majority agreement that the home of Delphinios was an island, or at least a maritime locality.[59]

The dolphin features in Minoan art.[60] It also features in the coinage of Crete, though not in association with Apollo.[61] But the dolphins on the coins of Delphi itself refer to the cult of Apollo Delphinios, who assumed the form of a dolphin.[62] For the first priests of Apollo Delphinios at Pytho were Cretans from Minoan Knossos, according to the Homeric Hymn to the Pythian Apollo,[63] which tells how the god in the form of a dolphin came on board a ship and brought it with its Knossian Cretans to Krisa, the harbour of Delphi. The description of the arrival has been considered appropriate to a god of light with lunisolar connexions.[64] For, as the god leaps ashore, he is likened to a star, sparks of fire flash away from him and a radiance illuminates the

---

[56] IC 1.III.1.9. [57] *Pol.* 1272a; see further p. 303.
[58] Boisacq, s.v. [59] Swindler 22–3, with refs.; cf. Fontenrose 396.
[60] Nilsson MMR 415. [61] Head 459, 461, 471–2, 474, 476–8.
[62] St. Byz. s.v. Δελφοί; Head 341.
[63] *H. Ap.* 388 ff.; cf. Nilsson GGR 521, MMR 576–7; Picard RP 207; Aly 35 ff.; Swindler 27.
[64] Swindler 28; cf. Gruppe GM 1.101.

whole scene. He then appears as Apollo and orders the Cretans to be servants in his temple.

Thus, in one form or another, the cult of Delphinios may have dated from Minoan times and have preceded the cult of Apollo proper at Delphi.[65] This conclusion is supported by the tradition of a sacred Knossian centre known as Omphalos, a tradition which probably derived from the Cretan Epimenides, and which, at least as early as the fifth century B.C., was believed to be the place hallowed by the navel-string of the infant Zeus.[66]

The cult of Delphinios outside Crete at other places, such as Miletos, Olbia, Massilia, Thera, Chios, Aigina, Athens, Chalkis, Oropos and Sparta, has more or less clearly defined Cretan associations.[67]

In Crete itself the cult of Apollo Delphinios continued to be important at Knossos. For the decree of 201 B.C. concerning Teos has to be published in his temple;[68] so does a proxeny decree at the end of the second century B.C.;[69] so do the decrees of the Latians and Olountians concerning Knossian arbitration of *c.* 120–116/15 B.C. and 117/16 B.C., and also the terms of the treaty between the same two cities of the same period.[70]

The allies of the Knossians, the Drerians, also gave a high priority to the cult of Delphinios, as is clear from the text of the Drerian oath of the later third or early second century B.C.[71] The archaic temple built for Delphinios at Dreros is of particular importance because it shows the fusion of a Greek cult with a Minoan. It is a small rectangular room with, in one corner, a bench or ledge on which archaic terracottas, vase fragments and a bronze *gorgoneion* were found. A hollow structure of vertical slabs set against the back wall had probably been covered by a board. On this altar were found a lamp and three statuettes, one male and two female, made of thin hammered bronze plates joined with short pins. In the filling were numerous horns (mostly left horns) of young goats. This was therefore like the altar at Delos, round which Theseus danced the Crane-dance, and which also consisted of the left horns of goats. In front was a square pillar which had probably supported a round table of offerings.

---

[65] Cf. Swindler 27–8.
[66] Call. *Jov.* 42 ff.; D.S. 5.70; Cook Z 2.190–1.
[67] Swindler 24–6.
[68] IC 1.VIII.8.12 f.
[69] *Ib.* 12.45 f.
[70] *Ib.* XVI.3.17, 4 A 12 f.; 5.49.
[71] *Ib.* IX A 21, C 117. Here Δελφίνιος only in Crete, except for the month-name at Olous. Elsewhere Δελφίδιος.

In the middle of the room was a four-sided pit, edged with worked stones, filled with red earth and covered by a layer of ashes 10 cm. thick. The male statuette represents Apollo, the others perhaps Artemis and Leto. Though the deities are Greek and the sacrificial pit is a sign of archaic Greek custom, the ledge for the idols and the offering table are Minoan survivals.[72]

A month Delphinios was part of the calendar at Olous.[73] Finally, the temple of Apollo Delphinios at Hyrtakina is of unusual interest. For here, as late as the second century B.C., the 'common hearth' of the city, normally situated in the town-hall, was still placed in the temple of Delphinios:[74] which indicates that the people of Hyrtakina had not built a town-hall; and also that the cult of Delphinios, still important, had once been even more important than that of Hera.[75]

5. DIDYMEUS

The epithet Didymaios relating to Zeus indicates that he was worshipped jointly with Apollo at Didyma near Miletos.[76] The related epithet Didymeus is cited in literature of Apollo.[77] The temple of Zeus and Apollo at Miletos was called the Didymaion and their festival the Didymeia.[78]

Therefore, when we find Apollo Didymeus mentioned in the fragment of a treaty apparently made by Cretan Aptera with another city (probably c. third century B.C.), the weight of general evidence is against the conclusion that this other city, presumably with a cult of Didymeus, was Cretan.[79] We must rather suppose that it was a city in Asia Minor, perhaps Miletos, perhaps Teos.[80]

6. DROMAIOS(?)

The calendar at Priansos included a month Dromeios, corresponding with the Hierapytnian Himalios, as we learn from the text of the

[72] Plu. *Thes.* 21; BCH 60.214–85; *Praktika* (1935) 203; CRA 478; AJA 40.267; *Arch. Anz.* 51.215; Nilsson MMR 455–6.

[73] IC 1.XVI.4 A 22 (117/116 B.C.). Also at Thera, Aigina (*Test. Epict.* 2.31, Pi. N. 5.81 sch.) etc.

[74] *Ib.* 2.XV.2.18.

[75] Cf. Guarducci *ad loc.*; p. 254 above.

[76] Nic. *fr.* 1; of Apollo SIG 906 A; Cook Z 2.317 and n. 2, citing Call. *fr.* 36, cf. Ter. Maur. 1885 f. and St. Byz. s.v. Δίδυμα.

[77] Orph. *H.* 34.7.   [78] Plu. *Pomp.* 24; CIG 2881, *al.* (Brankhidai); IG 3.129.8.

[79] IC 2.III.16.3.   [80] Guarducci *ad loc.*; cf. IC 1.XIX.2.8 f.

treaty between Priansos and Hierapytna at the beginning of the second century B.C.[81] The possibility of a Cretan festival Dromeia, analogous to the Phaistian festival of the Ekdysia, has also been plausibly proposed.[82]

Although Dromaios was an epithet of Apollo at Sparta,[83] as patron of racing, we should not therefore conclude that there was perhaps a cult of Apollo Dromaios in Crete.[84] The reasons for associating the Cretan terminology with Hermes rather than Apollo will be discussed later.[85]

7. ENAUROS

Hesychios is our sole authority for the epithet Enauros applied to Apollo as a god of the early morning.[86]

8. KARNEIOS

The cult-title Karneios attached to Apollo is most familiar in the Peloponnese, with the associated festival of the Karneia held in his honour, especially by the Spartans, and the name of the month, Karneios, in which the festival was held.[87]

The title signifies an ancient ram-god, derived from *karnos*, a horned sheep (cf. *keras*, 'horn').[88] Legend supports the antiquity of the cult. For, at Sparta, Karneios surnamed Oiketas was worshipped before the return of the Herakleidai, with a shrine in the house of Krios, son of Theokles, a soothsayer; Apollo Karneios was worshipped by all the Dorians from the time of Karnos, an Akarnanian, who was inspired with the gift of soothsaying by Apollo; and Karnos, as son of Europa and Zeus, foster-child of Apollo and Leto, was traced back to Crete.[89]

In Crete itself in the historical period only the month-name

---

[81] IC 3.III.4.5; cf. *ib.* 1 p. 280.

[82] Brause in H 49.106; p. 108.

[83] Plu. 2.724c; Paus. 3.14.6; IG 5(1).497.

[84] Cf. Swindler 43–4.

[85] P. 289.

[86] *Id. ἐναύρω· πρωὶ Κρῆτες:* Swindler 43.

[87] Pi. *P.* 5.80; Call. *Ap.* 71; Theoc. 5.54, 83; Hdt. 7.206; Th. 5.75; E. *Alc.* 449; SIG 735.25; IG 4.620, 1485; Head 77, 341, 434; Wide *ap.* Roscher LGRM s.v. Karneios.

[88] Hsch. s.v. κάρνος; Boisacq s.v.v. κάρνος, κεραός, κέρας, κέρασος, κορύπτω, κριός; Wide and Höfer *ap.* Roscher *ib.* 2.961 ff.; 964 ff.; Cook Z 1.351 and n. 7.

[89] Hsch. s.v. Κάρνειος; Paus. 3.13.3, 4; sch. Theoc. 5.83; Cook *ibid.*; Swindler 46.

Karneios is revealed in the epigraphic record, at Knossos[90] and at Gortyna.[91] But we can thereby infer that there was a Cretan cult of Apollo Karneios; and what we know of the Spartan festival of the Karneia,[92] which fell at the same time as the Hyakinthia, and also sometimes the Olympic festival (for example in 480 B.C.),[93] is involved with a set of religious concepts familiar in Crete.

Like the Olympic festival (if this began as an annual seasonal feast),[94] the Karneia occurred at the time of the full moon in the month Karneios.[95] The festival was managed by a group of Karneatai, young bachelors, holding office for four years, five (perhaps) from each tribe.[96] It included the race of the *staphylodromoi*,[97] a rite similar to the Athenian Oskhophoria whose basic elements were derived from Minoan Crete.[98] The *staphylodromoi*, so called because of the clustered vine-branches which they carried, were young men chosen from among the Karneatai. One of them ran, garlanded and perhaps disguised in the skin of a beast, praying for a blessing on the city. The others pursued him, and if he was caught, good luck resulted, bad luck if he was not. The vine-clusters connect the rite with the fruit-harvest, the very name of the festival calls the flocks to mind, and so the whole complex derives from the vegetation cycle. The Kouretes, who came from Crete to Olympia, ran a race and crowned the victor with wild olive,[99] were like the unmarried Karneatai of Sparta; and Cretan and Spartan *epheboi* were all alike initiates.

9. LESKHANORIOS

Leskhanorios was an epithet of Apollo, as patron of meetings in the Leskhe, apparently a Greek equivalent of the 'Men's House'.[100] At Sparta the father was obliged to bring his child to a place called the Leskhe, where it was examined by the oldest men of the tribe to see if it was strong enough to be allowed to survive

[90] IC 4.181.5 (early second century B.C.). On the form Καρνήϊω for Καρνείω see Vollgraff *Mnemos.* 44.50 n. 1.
[91] *Ib.* 172.21, viz. Καννεία[ς (third–second century B.C.); 197.8, viz. Καρ]νήϊω or Καν]νήϊω? (second century B.C.); 235.7 f., viz. Καννήϊω (early second century B.C.).
[92] Cf. Harrison T 233–5, 237, 255; Wide 73 ff.; Nilsson GF 118 ff.
[93] Hdt. 7.206; 8.72; 9.7, 11; Th. 5.75.
[94] Harrison T 237; Thomson SAGS 2.121–4.   [95] E. *Alc.* 445–51.
[96] Hsch. s.v. Καρνεᾶται.   [97] AB 305, cf. Hsch. s.v.
[98] Pp. 195–7.   [99] Paus. 5.7.6.
[100] Cleanth. *Stoic.* 1.123; Plu. 2.385c; Corn. ND 32; Harrison T 36 n. 3.

as a future tribesman.[101] Leskhanorios then may well belong to the same cycle of ideas as we have tracked down in Karneios.

There was a month-name Leskhanasios at Tegea,[102] and Leskhanorios in Thessaly[103] and in Crete. In Crete, however, it seems to have been confined to Gortyna, to judge from the epigraphic evidence. It is mentioned in a Gortynian inscription of the early second century B.C.;[104] and a mention occurs in an earlier fragment, of the fourth century B.C., which may well be Gortynian.[105] We may therefore reasonably suppose a cult of Leskhanorios at Gortyna.

10. LYKEIOS

We have seen that Apollo was associated with goats and rams. His cult-epithet Lykeios designates him also as a 'wolf-god'. This is the meaning the Greeks themselves gave to the epithet, which also serves to link Apollo with the Lycians, so named because their national god, Apollo Lykeios, was worshipped as a wolf.[106]

Apollo Lykeios is mentioned in an inscription from Knossos, c. second century B.C.[107] This evidence is much too slight for us to draw any conclusions concerning the cult of Lykeios in Crete. It is true that the epithet has ancient and firm associations with the Peloponnese. It is also true that the Argives had early ties with the Knossians and other Cretans. But, before deciding that Lykeios was derived by Knossos from Argos,[108] we must bear in mind that there were also old traditions connecting Crete with Lycia.[109]

11. PYTHIOS

The title Pythios suggests a cult that has been moved from one locality to another. But the cult-associations between Crete and Delphi are such that we cannot account for the Cretan cult of

[101] Plu. *Lyc.* 16. Cf. also S. *OT* 1035.
[102] IG 5(2).3.
[103] IG 9(2).509, *al*; Swindler 44.
[104] IC 4.181.17, 26.
[105] *Ib.* 2.XXX.1.4.
[106] *Scr. Myth. Gr.* 77, cf. Ael. *NA* 10.26, Ant. Lib. 35; Thomson SAGS 1.114, 163; Guthrie GG 82–4; Farnell CGS 4.112; Wilamowitz DGH 1.324 ff.; 2.28 ff.; Nilsson MMR 516; CAH 2.632.
[107] IC 1.VIII.15.2.
[108] Guarducci *ad loc*.
[109] Pp. 156–8.

Pythios as being due to a simple process of transference. A common early background must be postulated for both.

Pytho was the term applied to the region in which Delphi was situated or to Delphi itself.[110] Here Apollo was an intruder, usurping the oracle of an earth-goddess closely related to the Minoan goddess.[111] The Python which guarded the shrine and which was slain by Apollo was symbolic of this primitive goddess. Thus a pre-deistic snake-cult, indigenous also in Minoan Crete, was drawn into the cult of the Delphic Apollo; and, according to legend, Pytho was so called from the rotting of the serpent.[112] To this early stratum belong the rites of the Delphic festival of the Stepterion, or 'Festival of the Wreaths', held at intervals of eight years.[113] Not only the snake, but the sacred tree, in the form of the laurel, and also the goat, were associated with Apollo's predecessor. The Pythian priestess, who chewed laurel and drank from an underground spring, derived her ecstatic inspiration also from the old goddess. Hence it has been possible to suggest that, essentially, the Delphic cult was derived from Crete.[114] Archaeological investigation has, at any rate, proved that a cult was present in Mycenaean times on exactly the same spot as in the Greek period, the seat of the temple and altar of Apollo.[115]

Similarly, the temple of Pythian Apollo, which occupied the principal site at Gortyna,[116] also shows traces of an earlier origin.[117] Because the cult of Pythios was so conspicuous at Gortyna, the most important state documents were published in his temple from *c*. seventh century B.C. until the middle of the fifth century B.C., and also onward from the third century B.C.[118] In the same way, state documents were published in the Pythion of Lyttos and of Itanos.[119]

---

[110] *Il.* 9.405; *Od.* 8.80; Hes. *Th.* 499; Pi. *P.* 4.66, 10.4; Hdt. 1.54.

[111] Farnell CGS 3.8; Swindler 16; Nilsson MMR 467–8, 576; cf. Fontenrose 15, 88, 394–7, 415, 417, 426, 431, 468–9.

[112] *H. Ap.* 372; cf. Swindler 14; Nilsson MMR 577; Fontenrose 14.

[113] Plu. *Quaest. Graec.* 12.293c, *Def. Orac.* 14.418a, *De Mus.* 1136b; Ael. *VH* 3.1; Str. 9.422; Nilsson GF 150–7; Harrison T 425–9; Cook Z 2.240 and n. 1; Guthrie GG 80 and n. 2; Fontenrose 20, 87, 125, 199, 383, 400, 453–6, 458, 460–1.

[114] Swindler 14–22.

[115] Nilsson MMR 467; but cf. Fontenrose 418.

[116] St. Byz. s.v. Πύθιον.   [117] Guarducci IC 4. pp. 5, 33.

[118] Guarducci *ib.* p. 6 and *ib.* 182.19, viz., ἐμ Πυτίοι: on the form here and elsewhere in Crete, also in Arcadia and Pamphylia, Bechtel 2.794, Buck GD 60.

[119] IC 1.XVIII.8.9 f., viz. Ποιτίου: on the form, Bechtel 2.661; *ib.* 3.IV.7.14 f. 29 f.

The Gortynian decree concerning Kaudos[120] not only establishes the continuing pre-eminence of the temple of Pythian
Apollo in the city in the early second century B.C., but also proves
that the temple served as the state treasury, into which the tithes
due from Gortynian citizens and perioecic subjects were paid.[121]
Apollo Pythios is invoked in oaths of the Gortynians appended
to several treaties.[122] The first of these documents also makes
mention of an associated festival, the Pythia, at Gortyna.[123]

The cult of Pythios flourished elsewhere in Crete, but only, it
seems, in the central and eastern parts of the island. In addition
to the documents from Lyttos and Itanos, there is evidence for
the cult at Dreros, in the seventh century B.C.,[124] and the Hierapytnian Dekataphoros was perhaps synonymous with Pythios.[125]

Moreover, in addition to Gortyna, the epigraphic evidence
reveals that Pythian Apollo was invoked in the oaths of Dreros,
Lato, Lyttos, Olous, Malla, Hierapytna, Itanos and Praisos, in the
Hellenistic period.[126]

12. SMINTHEUS

Although Apollo-Smintheus shared with Olympian Apollo the
attributes of the bow and the gift of prophecy,[127] his origin is
undoubtedly pre-Hellenic and must be closely associated with
Crete. That Smintheus was a 'mouse-killer' whose role was to
protect the crops from field-mice[128] seems to be confirmed by the
tradition that *sminthoi* was the Cretan word for mice, a word
whose termination indicates that it was not Greek.[129]

The earliest record of Smintheus occurs in a passage of the *Iliad*
where Khryse, Killa and Tenedos are named as important cult-
centres.[130] Examination of the evidence based on the distribution
of these and other centres has led to the conclusion that the cult

---

[120] P. 261.　　　　　　　　　　　　　[121] Cf. Guarducci *ad* IC 4 p. 33.
[122] IC 4.171 (third century B.C.); *ib.* 174 (second century B.C.); *ib.* 183 (*c.* second
century B.C.).
[123] *Ib.* 171.39 and Guarducci *ad loc.*
[124] BCH 70.603 f., n. 6. Guarducci *ad* IC 4 p. 33.
[125] See above p. 261, and Guarducci *ibid.*　　　[126] IC 1, 3 *passim.*
[127] Swindler 32–3; Head 540–1, 546.
[128] Pp. 67 and 72 n. 82. Cf. Nilsson GF 142.
[129] Str. 13.613; sch. *ad* Lyc. 1303; Hsch. s.v.; St. Byz. s.v.; Kretschmer EGGS 308,
404. Cf. Fick VO 28, Swindler 29–30.
[130] *Il.* 1.39.

of Smintheus may have travelled from Crete to Rhodes, and from Rhodes to the Troad in early times.[131]

13. STYRAKITES

The spherical object held by Apollo on coins of Eleutherna has been variously interpreted as an apple, a disk, a sun or a stone. Cook, who considered none of these explanations free from doubt, offered another solution based on his interpretation of the earliest known coin of the town.[132] This shows on the obverse Apollo, nude except for a belt, stepping left towards a height on which grows a storax-tree, carrying a bow in his left hand, a spherical object in his right. He is accompanied by a hound and in the field behind him is a second storax-tree. On the reverse Artemis, also accompanied by a hound, shoots an arrow from a bow.

Cook thought it highly probable that this coin represents Apollo Styrakites ('god of the storax-tree') repairing to Mount Styrakion in Crete with his bow and hound,[133] and he surmised that the globe in the god's hand is a ball of resin from the bark of the storax-trees comparable with the drops of amber believed to exude from poplars. He pointed out that the balsamic juice known as 'liquid storax' is obtained by incision from a tree whose botanical name is *liquidambar orientalis*.

This plausible interpretation would not only link Apollo Styrakites with an ancient cult of the sacred tree; it makes it possible to suggest further that the Ametoridai of Eleutherna were a clan associated with the cultivation of the storax, whose special deity was Styrakites.[134]

14. TARRHAIOS

The epithet Tarrhaios derives from the town of Tarrha in south-western Crete, where there was a special cult of Apollo Tarrhaios.[135] It was at Tarrha, in the house of the seer Karmanor, that Apollo was married to the nymph Akakallis.[136] Numismatic evidence indicates that close relations existed between Tarrha

---

[131] Swindler 32.
[132] Cook Z 2.492. Cf. Head 464; Guarducci IC 2 p. 146.
[133] Cf. St. Byz. s.v. Στυράκιον; Eust. *ad Il.* 281.13.
[134] Ath. 14.638b; Hsch. s.v. Ἀμητορίδας· καθαριστάς Κρῆτες. ἢ κιθαριστάς.
[135] St. Byz. s.v. Τάρρα.
[136] Paus. 10.16.5; p. 257 above.

and the neighbouring cities of Elyros, Hyrtakina and Lisos at the beginning of the third century B.C.[137] Coins of Tarrha show the head of a goat, which probably refers to Apollo Tarrhaios.[138] For not only did Apollo marry Akakallis at Tarrha; the neighbouring Elyrians, as we have seen,[139] sent to Delphi a bronze goat suckling the twins Phylakis and Phylandros, the sons of Apollo by Akakallis.

A further ancient link with Delphi is supplied by the tradition that, after the slaughter of Python, Apollo was purified in Crete by Karmanor.[140] Karmanor, moreover, was the father of Euboulos, whose daughter Karme became by Zeus the mother of Britomartis,[141] and who himself was reputed to have won the prize in the earliest musical contest at Delphi.[142] It is of interest that Karmanor should survive as a man's name in Crete.[143]

[137] Guarducci IC 2 p. 307; cf. p. 257 above.
[138] Guarducci *ibid.*; Head 478.   [139] P. 257.
[140] Paus. 2.7.7, cf. 10.6.7, 10.7.2, 10.16.5. Or by Khrysothemis, Sch. P. *P.* 3.
[141] Paus. 2.30.3; cf. D.S. 5.76; Ant. Lib. 40.
[142] Paus. 10.7.2. On another occasion the prize was won by Eleuther, perhaps the eponym of Cretan Eleutherna: Paus. 10.7.3; Svoronos BCH 20.8; Cook Z 2.190.
[143] IC 2.III.38 (second–first century B.C.).

CHAPTER 12

Artemis

W E have earlier traced some of the interconnexions between Lato, Artemis and Apollo, Britomartis and Diktynna, whose cults all continued to flourish side by side in Crete.[1] It is the purpose of the present chapter to collect the evidence relating to the independent cult of Artemis in the historical period.

In the west of the island we begin with Axos, where a head of Artemis is featured on coins of the period c. 300–67 B.C.[2] That she had a temple here can be inferred from a single inscription of the second or first century B.C.[3]

At Eleutherna, Artemis as a huntress shooting with a bow and accompanied by a hound, is featured on the earliest coins, of the period c. 450–300 B.C.[4] Just as there seems to have been some special association at Eleutherna between the clan of the Ametoridai and Apollo, we should also presumably connect the Artemitai with the cult of Artemis at Eleutherna. The Artemitai are mentioned in a badly mutilated inscription of the third or second century B.C.[5] They were apparently a perioecic community of some kind subject to the jurisdiction of Eleutherna. Two dedications to Artemis by women, the second of which is dated to the first or second century A.D., have also been preserved.[6]

A cult of Artemis at Lappa is indicated by the portrayal of the head of the goddess on coins of the period c. 200–67 B.C., of her standing with a bow on coins of the Imperial epoch, and confirmed by the discovery of a statue of c. second century B.C.[7]

As we have seen,[8] Diktynna was worshipped at Polyrhenia and she is featured on its coins. But Artemis also appears, shooting

[1] Pp. 172–93.
[2] Head 459.
[3] IC 2.V.36.
[4] Head 464; cf. Guarducci IC 2 p. 145.
[5] IC 2.XII.22 A, B, C; Willetts ASAC 124.
[6] Ib. 23, 24.
[7] Head 470; Guarducci IC 2 p. 195.
[8] P. 191.

with a bow, on coins of the city from *c.* 200–67 B.C., in a form
apparently to be distinguished from Diktynna.[9]

But, of all the cities of the west, Soulia provides most abundant
evidence of a special cult of Artemis. On stones from her temple
there, many names, of men and women, may be read. Though
most of this epigraphic evidence probably belongs to the
Imperial epoch, there is little doubt that the cult of Artemis at
Soulia is of much earlier date.[10]

In eastern Crete there was a statue of Artemis in the temple of
Diktaian Zeus;[11] and she is invoked in the treaty between Hierapytna and her colonists, of *c.* second century B.C.[12]

In the central area, the magistrates of Arcadia were made
responsible for work done on a temple of Artemis, financed from
public funds, *c.* second century B.C.[13] A number of other inscriptions relate to the same temple, including the thank-offering
made by the grandfather, father and son of a family of Parian
sculptors, all three with the name of Timotheos, in the first
century B.C. or first century A.D.[14] Two other thank-offerings by
individuals, of approximately the same date, invite no comment.[15] But it is worth noticing that the sacrifice of a heifer
to the goddess to ensure the good fortune of the emperor Trajan
called for a special commemoration.[16]

Coins of Biannos of *c.* third century B.C. have as reverse a lily
(or a rose), as obverse a female head, perhaps of Artemis, perhaps
of Bianna.[17]

From Khersonesos we have a single dedication to Artemis of
c. first century B.C.[18]

At Knossos there is no portrayal of the goddess in the coinage
until a head is featured in the period *c.* 200–67 B.C.[19] But there is
an earlier epigraphic mention in the fifth-century treaty between
Knossos and Tylisos.[20]

The inclusion of Artemis in the oath of the Drerians has
already called for comment;[21] and so has her appearance beside

[9] Head 475; Guarducci IC 2 p. 241.
[10] IC 2.XXV.4–25 and Guarducci *ad loc.*
[11] IC 3.II.1.7; cf. p. 211 above. [12] *Ib.* III.5.13 f.
[13] IC 1.V.5; Willetts ASAC 141. [14] *Ib.* 6.
[15] *Ib.* 7–8. [16] *Ib.* 9.
[17] Head 459; Cook Z 1.623; Guarducci IC 1 p. 29; cf. St. Byz. s.v. Βίεννος.
[18] IC 1.VII.6. [19] Head 463.
[20] IC 1.VIII.4 b 7.
[21] *Ib.* IX.1 A 26; p. 179 above.

Lato at the city of Lato in the treaty with Olous.[22] At Lato a head of Artemis appears on coins of the period *c.* 200–67 B.C.[23]

Only a few fragmentary dedications remain from a temple of Artemis at Phaistos, of the first century B.C. or first century A.D.[24]

At Priansos, Artemis is featured on coins of the period 430–200 B.C.;[25] and a dedication to her survives from the first or second century A.D.[26]

A head of Artemis is portrayed on bronze coins of Gortyna of the period 200–67 B.C. After the Roman occupation, Ephesian Artemis appears on the tetradrachms struck at Gortyna *c.* 66 B.C.[27] The goddess is invoked in oaths appended to the treaty of the Gortynians and Hierapytnians with the Priansians at the beginning of the second century B.C.,[28] and also perhaps in the oath of the treaty with the Arcadians in the third century B.C.[29] It was in the temple of Artemis at Gortyna that Hannibal, according to Cornelius Nepos, made the pretence of depositing his wealth.[30]

1. APTERA

The cult of Artemis Aptera raises a problem of special interest, probably associated, as we have seen,[31] with the Minoan origin of Artemis as Mistress of Animals.

2. RHOKKAIA

There is some indication that Artemis was worshipped as Rhokkaia at, or in the neighbourhood of, Rhithymna. But the evidence is too slight for us to make any conjecture about the nature of the cult.[32]

3. SOTEIRA

The frequent epithet of protecting goddesses, Soteira ('Saviour'), was applied to Artemis at Lyttos,[33] where she had a temple,

[22] *Ib.* XVI.5.75.
[24] *Ib.* XXIII.6.
[26] IC I.XXIV.3.
[28] IC 4.174.59, 75.
[29] *Ib.* 171, 15: Ἄρ[τεμιν Halbherr, Blass, Guarducci; Ἄρ[εα Aly.
[30] *Hann.* 9.1 ff.
[31] Pp. 188–91.
[32] Ael. *NA* 14.20; Guarducci IC 2 p. 269.
[33] IC I.XVIII.12.4 f.

[23] Guarducci *ib.* p. 108; cf. Head 470.
[25] Head 476.
[27] Head 467.

and at Itanos, where Zeus was honoured under the same epithet.[34]

4. TOXIA

Artemis is referred to as Toxia ('the archer-goddess') in that passage of the Law Code of Gortyna where, in certain circumstances, a woman is obliged to take an oath of denial to the goddess.[35] It may be that Artemis is represented too under this aspect on coins of the period *c.* 200–67 B.C.[36]

5. ARTEMIS AS BEAR-GODDESS

We have seen that the autochthonous Kydonians who spread over western Crete in Achaean times and gave their name to Kydonia (modern Khania) on the north-west coast may have descended from Bronze Age emigrants into Crete from Asia Minor; and other likely Bronze Age emigrants were Pelasgians, perhaps from the far side of the Black Sea.[37] The Diktynnaion was under the jurisdiction of these Kydonians for long periods in historical times.[38] Not far eastward from Kydonia was the city of Aptera. The evidence for the cult of Artemis Aptera led to the conclusion that in Aptera Artemis was *kourotrophos*, close to her Minoan prototype of the Mistress of Animals, Diktynna in all but name; and that her cult was originally associated with a rite of initiation and purification performed by female *agelai*.[39]

Further confirmation for these conclusions is now provided by Faure's account of his recent survey of the district and, in particular, of the peninsula of Akrotiri, north-east of Khania.[40] The many Minoan remains discovered in caves and at other sites have persuaded Faure to infer with confidence that the whole peninsula was very densely populated at least by the end of the Bronze Age. At Kydonia itself these remains go at least as far back as the middle of the second millennium.

What the name of the peninsula was in antiquity is doubtful. Faure is sceptical about the identification of Akrotiri with the Κίσαμον ἄκρον (or Κίσμον or Κίαμον or Κύαμον) mentioned by

[34] *Ib.* 3.IV.13 (fourth/third century B.C.); cf. p. 248 above.
[35] *Ib.* 4.72.III.7 ff.; Willetts ASAC 91.
[36] Guarducci IC 4, pp. 34, 38. Cf. also Toxitis as epithet of Artemis in Kos: Maiuri *Nuova Silloge* 452; and Toxias of Apollo at Sikyon: Hsch., cf. Theognost. *Can.* 42.
[37] Pp. 135–6.   [38] P. 192.
[39] Pp. 189–90.   [40] BCH 84.209–15.

Ptolemy and perhaps of Asiatic origin, associated with the ancient Kydonians.[41] He argues instead, on the basis of ancient literary evidence and his knowledge of the terrain, in favour of the name Kynosoura ('Dog's-tail', i.e. the same as that of the constellation of the Lesser Bear).[42] This name, he decides, was given to the whole Kydonian peninsula and to the eponym of the region, who, before becoming the constellation of the Lesser Bear, had been the nurse and bride of Zeus, and companion of the Telkhines and Kouretes of Ida. The literary tradition implies a myth familiar to students of the coins of Kydonia. Zeus was here suckled by a bitch, who was metamorphosed into a bear. He adds that it is not surprising that the Kydonians, who claimed, like the Eteocretans, to be autochthonous, should also have claimed that Zeus was born on their territory; and he reminds us that coins of the Imperial period have Diktynna holding the young god. In fact, Kydonia is one of several places in western Crete which supply us with evidence for the cult of Zeus Kretagenes and his association with Diktynna.[43]

The local myth further implies, Faure's argument continues, a ritual involving a sacred bear, a cult of a divine *kourotrophos* in a cave similar to the Idaian Cave, whose worshippers were pre-Dorian. He associates all this myth and ritual with the cave on Akrotiri called Arkoudia ('Cave of the She-bear'), described under that name by other travellers for several centuries. This cave is consecrated to the Purification of the Virgin, whose local name is Panagia Arkoudiotissa, and the festival falls on the 2nd of February. Finds in the cave, which included several heads of Artemis, Classical and Hellenistic, point to a specific cult of Artemis in Classical times, among other divinities—one of them apparently Apollo. Thus a cult of a divine Mother has continued here from the Minoan Age at least, and the great central stalagmite in the shape of a bear (or a bitch) has to be linked with the myths of the birth and childhood of Zeus which ancient authorities associate with Kynosoura. Faure is confident that further investigation will confirm his interpretation of the evidence.[44]

[41] Ptol. 3.15.5; Guarducci IC 2 pp. 10, 94, 105; Fick VO 17.
[42] Hsch. s.v. Κυνόσουρα; Eratosth. *Cat.* 56 C. Robert; Hyg. *Astr.* 2.2; sch. *ad* Arat. Maass p. 185.
[43] Pp. 191, 207.
[44] 'Nous avons ici τὰ δεικνύμενα et, en partie, τὰ λεγόμενα: nous saurons un jour, après la fouille d'une masse énorme de terre dans la grotte, τὰ δρώμενα.' BCH 84.212.

Artemis as Bear-goddess is known elsewhere. In Arcadia the mother of that district's ancestor, Arkas, was changed into a bear shortly before he was born.[45] The mother's name was Kallisto, Megisto or Themisto, properly epithets of Artemis.[46] In Attica, at Brauron, Artemis Brauronia had her temple where girls, dressed in saffron, performed a bear-dance before they were married.[47] Kyzikos, on the Propontis, was built on a hill called the Bear Mountain; and here the nurses of Zeus were bears.[48]

It has been argued that the Bear-goddess belonged to the Pelasgians, who brought her to Arcadia from Attica, to Attica from Lemnos, and ultimately from the far shores of the Black Sea, reaching the Aegean by way of the Propontis; and that she was identified with Artemis, perhaps first in the Troad, because of the influence of the Ephesian goddess.[49] It seems now that the Cretans perpetuated a similar association on the peninsula of Akrotiri. It is to be hoped that further investigation in the bear-cave may help us to decide how this came about and so throw more light upon the reasons for the provenance of Diktynna within the limits of the old Carian domain.

---

[45] Apollod. 3.8.2, Paus. 1.25.1, 8.3.6–7, Eratosth. *Cat.* I, Hyg. *F.* 155, 176–7.
[46] Müller PWM 73–6, Farnell CGS 2.435; cf. Paus. 1.29.2, 8.35.8.
[47] Ar. *Lys.* 645 sch., Harp. ἀρκτεῦσαι; cf. Lys. *fr.* 82, E. *Hyps. fr.* 57.
[48] Str. 12.575, Nic. *Alex.* 6–8, A.R. 1.936 sch.
[49] Thomson SAGS 1.276–80.

CHAPTER 13

Athene

THE evidence relating to the Cretan cults of Athene in the historical period is of special interest because of the views which have been advanced concerning the ultimate origin of the goddess. Her name appears to be of pre-Greek origin, and the name of several towns, Athenai, have been adopted from that of the goddess, Athene. Her familiar association with the snake, the olive and the owl is a feature common to the Minoan goddess, to the domestic snake-cult, the tree-cult and the bird-epiphanies of Minoan religion. As the patron of skill and craftsmanship, she is no less directly connected with the Minoan household-goddess. Her association with war must be regarded as a later development of the Mycenaean period—and later still, intensified. For the Minoan household-goddess became the protector of the Mycenaean dynasts. When the kingship became superseded, Athene's function became more general. She was now protector of the *polis* and patron of the republican state, in all its forms, including the special link with the democracy at Athens. Therefore, her varied functions can be traced to different points along a line of evolution from the most primitive social forms, through the Minoan-Mycenaean palace organizations, to the historical *polis*.[1]

Athene is portrayed on the coins of several cities of western Crete. Allaria issued drachms of the third or second century B.C., with obverse head of Athene.[2] A head of the goddess is also found on coins of Aptera (*c.* 250–67 B.C.),[3] Kydonia (*c.* 400–67 B.C.),[4] Lappa (*c.* 200–67 B.C.),[5] Polyrhenia (*c.* 330–67 B.C.)[6] and Rhi-

---

[1] Kretschmer EGGS 418; Levi AJA 49.294; Nilsson HGR 26, MMR 489–501; Thomson SAGS 1.257–68; Persson RGPT 138; Guthrie GG 106–9; pp. 67–71, 118–19, 128–9 above. Cf. for Gortyna, p. 59 n. 21 above.

[2] Head 457.

[3] Guarducci IC 2 p. 13.

[4] Head 463; Guarducci *ib.* p. 114.

[5] Guarducci *ib.* p. 195.

[6] Head 475.

thymna (400–300 B.C.).[7] There is also some possibility of a cult of the goddess at Axos.[8]

In central Crete, epigraphic and literary evidence plays a more conspicuous part. The Athene standing, armed, on coins of Arcadia of the period *c.* 300–200 B.C., probably had a statue there in the same style in the fifth century B.C.[9] Coins of Khersonesos between *c.* 300 and 220 B.C. have a head of Athene.[10] As we might expect, Knossos had special early associations with Athene,[11] associations that are confirmed by the portrayal of a head of the goddess on coins from *c.* 350 to 67 B.C.[12] Athene was especially revered among the Rhittenians and had a temple in the city.[13]

At Gortyna, Athene is mentioned in the regulation of the early fifth century B.C. which specifies the deities to whom an oath is to be sworn;[14] an armed Athene appears on coins of the period 200–67 B.C.;[15] and in a temple at Gortyna her image replaces a naked goddess, in Classical and Hellenistic times.[16]

In eastern Crete, we know that there was a statue of Athene in the temple of Diktaian Zeus in the second century B.C.[17] There was also a statue of the goddess in Parian marble at Hierapytna, where she was invoked in oaths and where she appears, armed, on coins from *c.* 200 to 67 B.C.[18] Athene is mentioned too in the oath of the important decree from Praisos, defining the duties imposed on the Stalitai.[19]

1. DERAMIS

An inscription from Lato of the second century B.C. refers to the building of the temples and precinct of Athene Deramis and Eileithyia.[20] Apparently the title derived from the site of the

[7] Head 477.
[8] Guarducci IC 2 p. 47.
[9] IC 1.V.4 and Guarducci *ad loc.*; Head 459.
[10] Head 460.
[11] Paus. 9.40.3; Solin. 11.10; sch. P. O. 7.66. Cf. D.S. 5.72.3; Hsch. s.v. Τρίτα; and p. 282 below.
[12] Head 461–2.
[13] IC 1.XXVIII.19, 20 and p. 294; *ib.* 4.181.10 ff. and 182.20 f., and Guarducci *ad loc.*
[14] IC 4.51.2 f.
[15] Head 467
[16] JHS 75 (Sup.) 17; Levi GSAG 288.
[17] IC 3.II.7; cf. pp. 210–11 above.
[18] Guarducci *ib.* pp. 23–4.
[19] *Ib.* 3.VI.7 A.16; cf. Willetts ASAC 129.
[20] IC 1.XVI.26.8 and Guarducci *ad loc.*; cf. also perhaps *ib.* 5.70.

temple, since it is associated with words signifying 'ridge' or 'glen'.[21]

2. LINDIA

Among the documents which testify to the diplomatic means by which Rhodes was able to secure the neutrality or friendship of previously hostile Cretan cities at the beginning of the second century B.C. is a dedication from Lato by some Rhodian officials to Athene Lindia ('of Lindos').[22]

3. OLERIA

Athene Oleria was the special deity of the city of Oleros. It is possible that Oleros became subject to Hierapytna long before the Hellenistic period.[23] That such was the case by Hellenistic times the available evidence clearly demonstrates. For the Hierapytnians published treaties in the temple of Athene Oleria, invoked her in their oaths and apparently celebrated a festival in her honour.[24] An inscription from Oleros at the end of the second or early first century B.C. indicates that Hierapytnian officials were responsible for repairs to the temple of Athene Oleria.[25] A dedication in her honour of *c.* first century A.D. has also survived.[26]

4. POLIAS

Polias was a traditional epithet of Athene as the guardian deity of the *polis*. Though it has special associations with her oldest temple on the Acropolis at Athens,[27] the acropolis was similarly consecrated to Athene in many cities all over Greece,[28] confirm-

---

[21] Hsch. s.v.v. δέρα, δέραι, δειράδας, δειράδες. Guarducci (*ad loc.*) compares ἱαρὸν τῶ Ἄρεος τὸ Δέρᾳ (*ib.* XVI.3.17 f.; cf. 4 A 13), Apollo Δειραδιώτης at Argos, Artemis Δερεᾶτις on Mount Taygetos.

[22] IC 1.XVI.35.9 and Guarducci *ad loc.*; cf. Willetts ASAC 237. See also Nilsson MMR 495 n. 42.

[23] Willetts ASAC 144.

[24] IC 3.III. 3 B 11, 13, 19, *ib.* 4.174, 58 f., 74 (early second century B.C.); *ib.* 3.III.58., 12 (later second century B.C.); Xenion *ap.* St. Byz. s.v. Ὤλερος, cf. Eust. *ad Il.* 2.639.

[25] IC 3.V.1; cf. Willetts ASAC 144. [26] *Ib.* 2.

[27] Hdt. 5.82; S. *Ph.* 134; Ar. *Av.* 828; IG 1.²304.6; etc.

[28] Paus. 10.38.5 (Amphissa), 2.24.3 (Argos), 2.29.1 (Epidauros), 2.23.10 (Epidauros Limera), 4.34.6 (Korone), 3.26.5 (Leuktra), 7.20.3 (Patrai), 8.14.4 (Pheneos), 6.21.6 (Phrixa), 3.17.1 (Sparta), 2.32.5 (Troizen); Plb. 9.27.7 (Akragas, Rhodes); SIG 1007.40 (Pergamos); *Il.* 6.88 (Troy); Str. 14. 634 (Smyrna); X. *HG.* 3.1.21 (Skepsis); SGDI 345 (Thessalian Larisa).

ing the statement of Aristides that 'Athene reigns supreme over the summits of all cities'.[29] Naturally, then, we find evidence of the cult of Athene Polias in a number of Cretan cities.

The temple of Athene Polias was the principal one at Istron and here the decree of 201 B.C. relating to Teos had to be published.[30] Athene Polias and Pythian Apollo were the principal deities of Lyttos, where they had temples;[31] and the goddess was especially worshipped at Priansos.[32] She had a temple at Hierapytna, where decrees were published and she was invoked in oaths, and where high honour must therefore have been paid to her.[33] Similarly, decrees of Itanos had to be published in a temple of Athene Polias,[34] and the Itanian oath of loyalty begins with an invocation to the city's deities, including Athene Polias and other gods honoured in her temple.[35]

5. POLIOKHOS

Poliokhos ('protecting the *polis*') is an epithet similar to Polias and it occurs in Crete, as elsewhere,[36] applied to Athene. Athene Poliokhos is listed in the Drerian oath;[37] and also in oaths appended to treaties at Gortyna, in the first of which (a treaty with the Arcadians) she may be listed as an Arcadian goddess.[38]

6. SAMONIA

There was a temple and cult of Athene Samonia (Salmonia) on the promontory of the same name (now called Sidero) at the northwest tip of the eastern part of Crete. The forms *Salmone* and *Salmonion* are early, *Salmonion* becomes *Sammonion* and then *Samonion*. The name has been variously attributed to Phoenicians and Leleges;[39] but perhaps not enough attention has been paid to the

---

[29] Aristid. 1.15.   [30] IC 1.XIV.1.41 f., and Guarducci *ad loc.*

[31] IC 1 p. 182; *ib.* XVI 5.49 f.; *ib.* 3.III 3 B 12, and Guarducci *ad loc.*

[32] IC 1 pp. 279–80; *ib.* 3.III.4.80.

[33] IC 3.III.3 B 14, 20, C 10, 4.79, 80, 5.5 f.,12, 9.2 f., cf. 11.1.

[34] *Ib.* IV.3.25, 4.16.   [35] *Ib.* 8.4 ff.; cf. Willetts ASAC 128.

[36] Hdt. 1.160 (Chios); BCH 50.529 (Marathon); Ar. *Eq.* 581, *Nu.* 602, cf. *Av.* 827, Pi. *O* 5.10 (Athens).

[37] IC 1.IX A. 22 f. *(Πολιοῦχον)*.

[38] IC 4.171.14 (third century B.C.); cf. *ib.* 1.V.4 (*c.* fifth century B.C.); *ib.* 4.183.21 (*c.* second century B.C.).

[39] Assmann *Philol.* 67.164 f.; Bürchner in R.E. s.v. Σαλμώνη; Fick VO 76,116, 136; cf. Haley AJA 32.144.

suggestion that we have here a possible connexion with the king Salmoneus, who came from Pelasgian Thessaly, impersonated Zeus and imitated his thunders.[40]

The antiquity of the cult is confirmed by the story of Apollonios that a temple was consecrated on the promontory by the Argonauts in honour of 'Minoan' Athene.[41] Actual remains of a temple have been found perhaps dating to the sixth century B.C.[42] Inscriptions and drawings on the rocks in the locality from a very early period until Imperial times can be observed.[43]

In the oath attached to the treaty with Hierapytna of c. second century B.C., Athene Samonia is included among the list of deities invoked by the Hierapytnian colonists.[44]

Unless it was somehow brought from the eastern part of the island, the dedication at Soulia to Athene Samonia indicates that there was a cult of Samonia also in this city of western Crete.[45]

7. TRITOGENEIA

The epithet Tritogeneia applied to Athene was variously explained in antiquity. One explanation was that the epithet meant 'born beside the river Triton', a river which was located in Libya, Arcadia, Boiotia and Thessaly,[46] as well as Crete.[47] That the Cretan legend may perhaps have been localized near Knossos can be inferred from a gloss of Hesychios, explaining Trita as an alternative name of the city.[48] The possibility has been strengthened by Faure's examination of the topography in the light of the ancient evidence.[49]

8. WADIA

According to Pausanias,[50] when Herakles had taken and sacked Elis, the women, seeing that their land had been deprived of men in the prime of life, prayed to Athene that they might conceive at their first union with their husbands. This prayer was

[40] Harrison T 81 n. 2.
[41] A.R. 4.1688 ff.
[42] Guarducci IC 3 p. 156.
[43] IC 3 VII passim.
[44] Ib. III.5.13.
[45] Ib. 2.XXV.2.
[46] Phot., Suid., Hsch., EM., Et. Gud. s.v.; sch. Ar. Eq. 1189; Eust. D.P. 267, in Il. 696.38 f., 1265.7 ff.; in Od. 1473.11 f.; Paus. 8.26.6, 9.33.7, cf. Apollod. 1.3.6; sch. Paris. A.R. 1.109, cf. 4.1311; E. Ion 872, cf. Hdt. 4.180.
[47] D.S. 5.72.
[48] Hsch. s.v. Τρίτα.
[49] BCH 82.501-7.
[50] 5.3.2.

answered, and they established a shrine called after 'Athene the Mother'. Husbands and wives were so pleased at the outcome, moreover, that they named the place of this first union 'Bady' and the river that ran there was called 'Bady Water', this being a word of their native dialect. *Bādýs* then (i.e. *Wadýs*) was the Elean word for *hēdýs* = 'sweet', and is known in this form to be earlier than the fifth century B.C.[51]

An image dedicated to Athene Wadia (= *hadeîa*),[52] found at Kastri on the western slopes of Mount Ida, is therefore of unusual interest, being the only evidence of a cult of 'Sweet Athene' in Crete, evidence which can be related to the place in Elis called 'Sweet', where there was a cult of 'Athene the Mother'. Both in Elis and Crete, therefore, it seems that Athene continued to be worshipped as a fertility-goddess in a way that vividly recalls the Minoan goddess, who was both Mother and Maid. Nor was the epithet 'sweet' itself so unique, when we recall that Britomartis was also the 'Sweet Maid'.[53]

[51] Pherecyd. *fr.* 79 J; cf. Hsch. s.v. βαδύ.
[52] IC 2.XXX.2 (*c.* second century B.C.) and Guarducci's argument *ad loc.*; Bechtel 2.674, 830.
[53] P. 179 and n. 256.

CHAPTER 14

(a) Aphrodite

I T is generally agreed that, although her cults are relatively few
and her history therefore not plain to see, Aphrodite probably originated as an Oriental fertility-goddess. One indication
is that, like Hera and Artemis, Aphrodite was worshipped as a
goddess of childbirth.[1] Another is that the dove is an attribute
common to the Minoan goddess and to Aphrodite.

There is firm evidence for a cult of Aphrodite in no city of
western Crete;[2] and in eastern Crete only at Hierapytna, where,
along with Ares, she was invoked in oaths appended to treaties
with Lyttos (200–197 B.C.) and with the Hierapytnian colonists
(c. second century B.C.).[3]

More evidence is forthcoming from the cities of central Crete.
At Knossos we may infer that there was a cult of Ares and
Aphrodite in the mid-fifth century B.C., which possibly developed
under Argive influence.[4] In the Drerian oath, Aphrodite is coupled
with Ares in the list of deities invoked.[5] Like Knossos, Istron
also had a cult of Ares and Aphrodite, if an inscription of the
second century B.C., concerned with the building of a temple to
these deities, really belongs to Istron and not to Lato.[6]

Lato, in fact, supplies us with more epigraphic evidence than
any other city; and here Aphrodite had an old temple on the
borders of Lato and Olous.[7] Here also a new temple to the goddess
is mentioned as part of the general temple-building activity of
the Hellenistic period.[8]

---

[1] Nilsson HGR 132, MMR 336; Guthrie GG 101 n. 2; Farnell CGS 1.196, 2.444,
655–6.
[2] Cf. Guarducci IC 2 pp. 47, 114, 220.   [3] *Ib.* 3.III.3 B 14, 20 f.; 5.14.
[4] *Ib.* 1.VIII.4 b 14, and Guarducci *ad loc.*
[5] *Ib.* IX.1 A 27, viz. Ἀφορ(δ)ίταν; for the metathesis see Bechtel GD 2.711.
[6] *Ib.* XIV.2.3, and Guarducci *ad loc.*
[7] *Ib.* XVI. 5.70, cf. 75 (second century B.C.); 18.7 (second century B.C.).
[8] *Ib.* 24, 25 (second century B.C.); perhaps also *ib.* 27, though this may equally well
refer to the old temple.

At Gortyna the discovery of several statues of Aphrodite must be mentioned; and an invocation (perhaps along with Ares) in the oaths attached to the treaty of the Gortynians and Hierapytnians with the Priansians, of the second century B.C.[9]

I. ANTHEIA

The epithet Antheia ('flower-goddess') was associated with Hera at Argos and Miletos.[10] It is also used of the Horai.[11] But in Crete it was an epithet of Aphrodite at Knossos.[12]

That the title reveals an old link with herbal magic is confirmed by such attributes of Aphrodite as the apple, myrtle, poppy, rose and water-mint, and by her function as maker of the morning dew.[13]

2. SKOTIA

In our discussion of the festival of the Ekdysia at Phaistos, we saw that the festival and the associated myth combine elements of fertility, initiation and marriage-ritual. For the youth of Phaistos were apparently initiated into manhood, citizenship and marriage at the same period of life. The festival was connected with the local cult of Lato Phytia, a fertility-goddess, who promoted the growth of the young. When growth was achieved, the boy died as a boy and was born again as a man, cast aside his boyhood costume and wore man's clothes.[14]

Aphrodite was known in Phaistos as Skotia,[15] presumably because she was regarded as the special patron of those who were about to undergo initiation into manhood and marriage. Skotia took over when Phytia had done her work. The young men became *skotioi*, initiates who were about to undergo the crucial transition from boyhood to manhood, involving a period of seclusion outside the city for two months. The *skotioi* can thus be compared with the Spartan *krypteia*, whose members retired

[9] *Ib.* 4 174.59 f., 75. Cf. also perhaps *ib.* 189.2 (*c.* second century B.C.).
[10] Paus. 2.22.1; *EM* 108.47; *Milet.* 3 No. 31 (a). 5.   [11] Hsch. s.v.
[12] Hsch. s.v.
[13] Cook Z 2.491(6), 1043, 1165, 3.172.5; Paus. 2.10.5; Dsc. 2.154; *Pervig. Ven.* 15 ff.; Ael. *NA* 10.50; cf. pp. 78–9 above.
[14] P. 175.   [15] *EM* s.v. Κυθέρεια.

from the city into the countryside, in the process of their initiation into manhood.[16]

(b) Ares

The cults of Thracian Ares ('the Destroyer')[17] are generally even more rare than those of Aphrodite.

In Crete, there is no evidence from the west, and in the east Ares is mentioned only at Hierapytna, in oaths appended to two treaties.[18] Like Aphrodite, he was more prominent in central Crete, and here, in fact, rather more evidence is available for Ares than for Aphrodite.

We have already seen that he was associated with Aphrodite at Knossos, Dreros, Istron(?) and Gortyna(?).[19]

At Biannos there was a tradition of a festival to Ares called the Hekatomphonia ('sacrifice for a hundred slain enemies') celebrated there because Biannos derived its name (Bia = 'force') from the Cretan captivity of Ares by Otis and Ephialtes.[20] The prominence of the cult at Biannos is confirmed by inscriptions, from which it can be inferred that the temple of Ares was the principal one. For the decrees concerning Teos have to be published there.[21]

There was a cult and a temple of Ares at Knossos, the temple apparently being built on a ridge.[22]

There was certainly a cult of Ares at Gortyna, independent of any association with Aphrodite; and this evidence ranges from the fifth century to the second century B.C.[23] There is also evidence of a cult at Lato, and perhaps at Olous.[24]

---

[16] Willetts ASAC 14, 121–2; cf. pp. 116–17 above.
[17] Kretschmer *Gl.* 9.195.   [18] P. 284.
[19] Pp. 284–5.
[20] St. Byz. s.v. Βίεννος; cf. Serv. *ad* Verg. *A.* 3.578; Sall. *Hist. Fr.* 3.62; Stengel in RE s.v.
[21] IC 1.VI.1.11 (201 B.C.); *ib.* 2.24 (after *c.* 170 B.C.).
[22] *Ib.* VIII. 4 a 10 (fifth century B.C.); *ib.* XVI.3.17 f. and 4 A 13 (*c.* 120–116/15 B.C.); see p. 280 n. 21.
[23] *Ib.* 4 p. 4; 145.1; 174.75 cf. 59.
[24] *Ib.* 1.XVI.6 IV A 4 cf. 5.75 (second century B.C.); *ib.* XXII. 2.3 (second century B.C.), and Guarducci *ad loc.*

(c) Hermes

There seems to be little doubt that Hermes signifies 'the god of the stone-heap', the spirit immanent in stones set up as cairns or pillars to serve as boundaries, landmarks for the wayfarer and so on. He was a god of the countryside, having links with the Minoan pillar-cult and also with the Minoan Master of Animals.[25]

The cult of Hermes is attested in the western and central districts of Crete.

In the west a nude Hermes with wand and travelling-cap is featured on the coins of Aptera of the period *c.* 250–67 B.C.[26] Coins of Kydonia of the same period have a head of Hermes.[27] Here at Kydonia Hermes may have had very special associations with the old Minoan population. According to Ephoros,[28] certain festivals were regularly celebrated for the serfs of the district of Kydonia, during which no free persons entered the city; the serfs were masters of everything and even had power to flog the freemen. It is tempting to connect this account with the statement of Karystios[29] that festivals of Hermes were celebrated in Crete, and, while the serfs were feasting, their masters assisted in menial duties. On such carnival occasions the serfs were no doubt temporarily assuming the free status which their ancestors had once enjoyed.[30]

At Hyrtakina there is evidence from the third century B.C. of a statue to the god.[31] The name of Hermes may be written (*c.* first century B.C. to first century A.D.) on a stone at Phalasarna,[32] but there is no other evidence of a cult here. A promontory near Phoinix was called after Hermes and it is therefore possible that there was once a cult of the god in the vicinity.[33] Coins of Sybrita from *c.* fifth century B.C. include a number of interesting types portraying Hermes, one with the god stooping forward and placing his foot on a rock while he ties his sandal.[34]

---

[25] Nilsson HGR 109, MMR 515, GF 388; Guthrie GG 87–94; Chittenden *Hesperia* 16.89 ff.; Harrison T 365.
[26] Head 458; Guarducci IC 2 p. 13.   [27] Guarducci *ib.* p. 114.
[28] *Ap.* Ath. 6.263f.
[29] *Ap.* Ath. 14.639b; cf. Pl. *Ly.* 206d; Nilsson GF 393.
[30] Cf. Willetts H 86.3.
[31] IC 2.XV.3.   [32] *Ib.* XIX.3.
[33] Ptol. *Geog.* 3.15.3; Guarducci *ib.* p.227.
[34] Head 477; Seltman 173; Guarducci *ib.* p. 290.

There was a cult of Hermes in the stalactite cave of Melidhori in the Tallaia range between Axos and the sea. The earliest epigraphic evidence on the spot is possibly dated to the second century B.C. But the cult of Hermes here could have been older, or he may have taken the place of an older deity. Despite the reference to Hermes 'established on the Tallaian heights' in one inscription, it is most unlikely that Hermes was ever worshipped here at any time under the title of Tallaios.[35]

In central Crete, there is one piece of evidence for a cult of Hermes at Khersonesos, a dedication of the third century B.C.[36] At Dreros, there is numismatic evidence, confirmed to some extent by a reference in the oath.[37] Hermes is featured in the coinage of Lato in the period *c*. 200–67 B.C.;[38] and he is invoked in a treaty.[39] A seated Hermes, holding a wand, appears on coins of Phaistos, of the period 430–300 B.C.[40]

The god appears on coins of Gortyna in the period *c*. 480–430 B.C. and *c*. 200–67 B.C.;[41] he is included among the deities to whom oaths are to be taken;[42] and a region of the city was called the Hermaion as late as the first centuries of the Christian era.[43] The dedication by the clerks or supervisors of the market (*agoranomoi*), in the first century B.C., was probably made to Hermes.[44]

In the east, the only mention of Hermes is made in a Hellenistic epigram from Itanos.[45]

1. DAKYTIOS

In the treaty of the Gortynians and Hierapytnians with the Priansians, of the early second century B.C., Hermes is twice invoked as Dakytios (or Dakytinos).[46] The meaning of the epithet is unknown; and Maiuri's suggestion that it derives from the island Akytos near Kydonia appears to have no firm basis.[47]

---

[35] Pp. 146, 249; Guarducci IC 2 XXVIII *passim*.
[36] IC 1.VII.2.   [37] *Ib.* IX 1 A 28 and p. 82.
[38] Head 470.   [39] IC 1.XVI.5.55, 76 (second century B.C.).
[40] Head 473.   [41] IC 4, pp. 37–8; Head 467.
[42] IC 4.51.3 (early fifth century B.C.); cf. p. 258 above.
[43] *Ib.* p. 30.   [44] *Ib.* 254.
[45] *Ib.* 3.IV.37.9.   [46] *Ib.* 4.174.60, 75.
[47] Guarducci *ad loc.*

2. DROMIOS

A dedication to Hermes Dromios was offered by a Polyrhenian on his retirement from the office of *kosmos*, *c.* second century B.C.[48] This is the only reference to Hermes as 'god of the race-course'. But it gives grounds for supposing that the calendar month Dromeios at Priansos, and perhaps an associated festival, analogous to the Ekdysia, should be referred to Hermes as patron of the *epheboi* who exercised in the gymnasium, which the Cretans called *dromos*.[49]

A cult of Hermes at Polyrhenia is confirmed by the numismatic evidence.[50]

3. HEDAS

There was a tradition that Hedas was an epithet of Hermes at Gortyna.[51] It has been suggested that the word amounts to the same as *hedanos* (= 'sweet'), and therefore the title does not differ much from the known epithet of Hermes at Metapontion, Eukolos (= 'easy', 'agile').[52]

4. KRANAIOS

As we have seen,[53] the sacred cave near the village of Patso, although a centre of the worship of Hermes Kranaios in historical times, was once the centre of a Minoan cult. The epithet no doubt derives from the nature of the locality, i.e. 'rocky', 'rugged'.

(d) Poseidon

By origin Poseidon was a Thessalian Lapith, whose traditional sphere was the sea, but he was also 'Earth-shaker', god of horses and lord of springs as well as salt-water.[54] The evidence relating to his cult in Crete is not extensive.

[48] IC 2.XXIII.10.
[49] Willetts ASAC 12–13, 123; cf. p. 265: Guarducci *ad loc.*
[50] Guarducci *ib.* p. 241.　　　　　　　　　　　　　[51] *EM* s.v.
[52] Schwenck *Philol. Sup.* 2 (1863) 377; cf., of Asklepios at Epidauros, IG 4.1260.
[53] P. 146.
[54] Hom. *Il.* 15.190 f.; Nilsson HGR 120–1; Thomson SAGS 1.264; Guthrie GG 94–9.

In the west, a cult of Poseidon is attested at Axos by a reference to the god in the surviving fragment of a treaty of the sixth to fifth century B.C.[55] At Lappa, there is a head of Poseidon on coins of the period *c.* 200–67 B.C.[56] The trident on coins of Phalasarna and Rhithymna (*c.* 400–300 B.C.) is presumably to be associated with Poseidon.[57]

In the east, there is a single mention of Poseidon, in the oath of the decree of Praisos concerning the Stalitai, in the early third century B.C.[58]

In central Crete, there is evidence of a cult of Poseidon at Mount Juktas, near Knossos, in the fifth century B.C.;[59] he is included in the Latian oath of the treaty with Olous, of the second century B.C.;[60] he features in the coinage of Priansos (*c.* 430–200 B.C.) and Rhaukos (*c.* 300–165 B.C.);[61] and there is a possible indication of a cult at Gortyna in the early fifth century B.C.[62]

1. ASPHALEIOS

The epithet Asphaleios ('the Securer') is associated with Poseidon elsewhere in Greece,[63] and is mentioned once as a quite specifically Cretan epithet in an inscription from Kisamos of the second century A.D.[64]

2. HIPPIOS

The epithet Hippios, alluding to Poseidon as a god of horses, and to his erstwhile equine form, emphasizes that he was by no means exclusively a sea-deity. The Cretan evidence, which indicates that his cult was relatively common in central districts, away from the coast, reinforces the point.

Among the coins of Rhaukos there are several types portraying Poseidon, including, from the earliest period (*c.* 430–300 B.C.), Poseidon Hippios, naked, holding a trident and standing beside his horse, the horse's foot sometimes on a prow.[65]

---

[55] IC 2.V 6.1; cf. *ib.* 11 b for a possible further mention.
[56] Head 470.
[57] IC 2 pp. 220, 269.
[58] *Ib.* 3.VI 7 A 16.
[59] *Ib.* 2.VIII 4 a 15.
[60] *Ib.* XVI 5.74.
[61] Head 476–7.
[62] IC 4.66.
[63] Ar. *Ach.* 682; Paus. 3.11.9, 7.21.7; Plu. *Thes.* 36.
[64] IC 2.VIII 1.4 f.
[65] Head 477; cf. Guarducci IC 1 p. 291.

(e) The Twelve Gods

'The Twelve Gods' were united under Ionian influence at an early date to form a kind of official Olympian organization.[66] The canon usually consisted of Zeus, Hera, Poseidon, Demeter, Apollo, Artemis, Ares, Aphrodite, Hermes, Athene, Hephaistos, Hestia. There are sometimes minor modifications in this list. For example, Dionysos replaces Hestia in the representation of the Twelve on the east frieze of the Parthenon.

In Crete, there is evidence of a cult of the Twelve Gods only at Hierapytna, which flourished in the Hellenistic period.[67] Its origin is not known, but presumably it developed under overseas influence.

[66] Weinreich in Roscher LGRM s.v. Zwölfgötter; Cook Z 3.1055; Guthrie GG 110–12.

[67] IC I.VIII B.25, cf. IC 3 p. 17; IC 3 III 9.2, cf. 10.

CHAPTER 15

Strangers to Olympos

IT is the intention of the present chapter to mention a few non-Olympian cults which, either as survivals from the past or stimulated by foreign influence in the historical period, and although not of major importance, yet deserve some special notice because of their intrinsic interest.

In the first place, it is surely appropriate to refer to the evidence indicating a cult of the hero Minos at Itanos as late as the first century B.C.[1] The coupling together of Gaia and Ouranos in the Drerian oath must be taken as another proof of the archaic nature of that document.[2] Of more importance is the inscription dated to the second century B.C., found in a village near the site of Phaistos, which refers to a temple of the Great Mother.[3]

A dedication was made, some time in the latter half of the third century B.C., by the Phalasarnians on behalf of Ptolemy III Euergetes and his wife Berenike to gods who were clearly dear to the royal couple. They are described as *Theoi Megaloi* ('Great Gods').[4] These must be the Kabeiroi, divinities worshipped especially in Lemnos, Samothraike and Boiotia, who are likened by Strabo to the Korybantes.[5] This inscription is therefore of interest not only for the general light it throws upon relations between Phalasarna and Ptolemy, but, in particular, as an indication that one outcome of these relations was the establishment on Cretan soil of a cult which can have been foreign only in name.

Elsewhere, and with other deities, the influence of Egypt is more conspicuous. Osiris-Apis, under his name of Sarapis, was worshipped throughout the countries of the Mediterranean world during the Hellenistic Age.[6] Sarapis and Isis were the

---

[1] IC 3.IV 38.15, cf. *ib.* 37.19.
[2] IC 1.IX 1 A 31–2; cf. Willetts ASAC 119–23 and further in H 85.281.
[3] *Ib.* XXIII 3.2, 9; Nilsson MMR 463–4.　　　　[4] *Ib.* 2.XIX.2.
[5] P. 98.　　　　[6] Cf. Rundle Clark 98.

principal deities worshipped in a temple at Gortyna devoted to Egyptian cults. Epigraphic evidence from the site, as well as the temple remains, indicate that the cult of Sarapis and Isis was already in vogue there by the second century B.C.[7]

A dedication to Sarapis and Isis of the second century B.C. survives from Olous.[8] A dedication to Sarapis by a Parian was made in the same century at Khersonesos.[9] A man from Lyttos and another from Gortyna dedicated arms to Sarapis.[10] A dedication to Isis of the first to second century A.D. survives from Lasaia.[11] At Phoinix, a dedication was made to Iuppiter Sol Maximus Sarapis in the time of Trajan,[12] and a temple was consecrated (or restored) to Sarapis at Poikilasion as late as the third century A.D.[13] The sculptures found there show that the district near Hierapytna was also penetrated by Egyptian cults.[14]

The nature of Minoan-Mycenaean religion is such as to make us suppose that a Cretan cult of Helios can have very ancient associations. Although a dedication to Helios at Polikhna is dated to the second century B.C., he was honoured at Gortyna and at Dreros at an early date.[15]

The cult of Enyalios (the 'Warlike'), ultimately of Carian origin, survived among the Arcadians in historical times. The deity is mentioned only once (if we except a reference in an epigram) in the Cretan epigraphic record, namely in the treaty between the Gortynians and the Arcadians, of the third century B.C. It is possible then that the Gortynians had a cult of this deity as well as the Arcadians.[16]

Thermolaios was the name of a month at Lato; and a festival Thermoloia was celebrated at Gortyna.[17] Although the forms are slightly different, we may assume that, just as a festival derived from the month-name was celebrated at Lato, so this month also existed in the Gortynian calendar. Unfortunately, we do not know with what deity the festival and month-name could have been associated.

---

[7] IC 4.243–9; also *ib.* p. 10; cf. Cook Z 1.188 ff., 435.
[8] IC 1.XXII.11. [9] *Ib.* VII.3.
[10] Call. *Epigr.* 38; IC 4.243. [11] IC 1.XV.2.
[12] *Ib.* 2.XX.7 and Guarducci *ad loc.* [13] *Ib.* XXI.1 and Guarducci *ad loc.*
[14] *Ib.* 3 p. 23.
[15] *Ib.* 2.XXII.1; *ib.* 4.65, 7 f.; *ib.* 1.IX 1 A 28.
[16] *Ib.* 4.171.15, and Guarducci *ad loc.* Cf. *ib.* 244.17.
[17] *Ib.* 1.XVI 5.86 (second century B.C.); *ib.* 4.144.3 (late fifth–early fourth century B.C.).

We can, however, suggest a plausible hypothesis concerning the character of a festival at Lyttos, called the Periblemaia or Periblemata.[18] The name occurs in the text of a treaty between Malla and Lyttos, and it shows the responsibility of the *kosmoi* for the annual ritual graduation of the youth. It is therefore reasonable to infer that the festival was also concerned with this ceremony. Etymologically the name suggests a rite involving the 'putting on of garments', the opposite of Ekdysia.

But the contradiction with the Ekdysia may be only apparent.[19] For it may be suggested that, while the Ekdysia emphasizes one aspect of the ritual ceremony of graduation into citizenship, namely, the putting off of boy's garments, the Periblemaia or Periblemata emphasizes another aspect, the assumption of men's garments. Both names may thus have originated as terms for complementary aspects of what was essentially a single ceremony.[20]

---

[18] IC i.XIX.i (*c.* third century B.C.).   [19] Cf. Nilsson GF 469.

[20] Cf. p. 176. The ritual for the taking off of the old and putting on of new vestments appropriate to the new office in the ordination of a sub-deacon and a deacon, in the Greek Orthodox Church, provides a suggestive parallel.

Part Four

CRETAN KOSMOS

But the dreams their children dreamed
  Fleeting, unsubstantial, vain,
Shadowy as the shadows seemed,
Airy nothing, as they deemed,
  These remain.

MARY COLERIDGE

Part Four

CRETAN KOSMOS

CHAPTER 16

Religion and Law

I T was suggested, at the beginning of this inquiry, that the history of Cretan religion would be better understood if it were to be seen in close relation with the economic and social history of Crete, dominated as that history was by the overriding influence of tradition. We are now in a better position to examine the ways in which the religious practices of Crete helped to shape the characteristic features of the Cretan *polis*.

The Cretan *polis* was, from the onset of the historical period, abidingly aristocratic. Although close oligarchy was modified in various ways in the course of the historical period, and so long as Greece remained independent, the aristocracies resisted fundamental change, primarily because the Cretan *polis* continued to be based upon serf labour. For the survival of a large serf-class which never effected a transition to small-scale, independent production meant that narrowly based groups of aristocrats perpetuated their political dominance.

The native system of land tenure, with its roots in the Minoan-Mycenaean past, had been skilfully adapted to the tribal institutions of the Dorians. When Aristotle observed that the older population of Crete continued to practise the laws of Minos,[1] he implicitly confirmed that there had been a more cautious treatment of the subject population of Crete than was the case in Sparta. Hence, just as the economy remained backward and old-fashioned, so Minoan-Mycenaean religious traditions exerted a powerful and enduring influence. Here too there is evidence of widespread and skilful adaptation.

Although it is not possible to argue an exclusively Cretan origin for more than a few of the institutions which are described in Plato's *Laws*, the general impression created by that work was

---

[1] *Pol.* 1271b.

probably consistent with actual contemporary social and political practices which were alike familiar and congenial to Plato's temperament.[2] Now the concentration of political power in the hands of old men is one of the marked features of the *Laws*. And these old men invoke the sanctions of dogmatic religion in support of law and order. Their state is a theocratic state, stubbornly resisting innovation. We must suppose therefore that Plato's admiration for the achievement of Cretan law was matched by a corresponding recognition of the complementary role of Cretan religion.

The scene of the *Laws* is set in Crete, and its argument unfolds during a walk from Knossos to the cave of Zeus on Mount Ida. Of its three old men, one is Athenian, one Spartan and one, Kleinias, a Cretan. The Athenian opens the argument by asking whether the others attribute the origin of their laws to god or man. The Cretan promptly replies that a god is certainly responsible. His fellow-Cretans call Zeus their lawgiver; Minos held converse with Zeus and was guided by his advice; Rhadamanthys won his reputation as a wise judge because of his righteous administration of justice.[3]

It is supposed, for the sake of promoting the argument of the work, that most of Crete is engaged in the undertaking of founding a colony. The Knossians are in charge, Kleinias is their representative, and he has nine colleagues. Their terms of reference are to frame a set of laws, following the model of Crete or other countries, without prejudice, guided only by respect for superior quality.[4]

Bearing in mind that, wherever a *polis* has a mortal and not a god for its ruler, there the people have no respite from toils and troubles, the correct procedure, it is suggested, is to imitate the life of the age of Kronos, as tradition pictures it; to manage homes and states in conformity with the element of immortality within us, giving to the ordering of reason the name of 'law'.[5]

The founder must place the model *polis* as near as possible in the centre of the territory. It is then to be divided into twelve parts, but not until temples have been founded to Hestia, Zeus and Athene, in a place which will be called the Acropolis. The citizens are also to be divided into twelve parts. Twelve allot-

[2] Willetts ASAC 153–4. Cf. Morrow 17–39.
[4] *Ib.* 702b–d.
[3] *Lg.* 624a–625a.
[5] *Ib.* 713e–714a.

ments are to be assigned to twelve gods, each named after the god to whom it has been allotted and consecrated.[6] At least as much care is to be taken about the appointment of religious as of other state officials.[7]

The starting-point of legislation for this *polis* is religion. The subdivisions of the community are to be regarded as sacred, corresponding to the months and to the revolution of the universe. When each section has been endowed with the name of a god, or of the child of a god, altars and sacred rites are to be bestowed. At these altars sacrificial assemblies are to be convened twice a month—twelve assemblies for the tribes and twelve for the city—the first purpose of which is to ensure the blessing of the gods and to promote religion, and secondly to encourage social intercourse, with a view to the arrangement of suitable marriages.[8]

When it is considered how best to prevent the youth of the city from wanting to imitate new fashions in dance and song, no better way of bringing this about than that adopted by the Egyptians can be recommended; namely, by consecrating traditional types.[9] (It is interesting that Plato should recall, in the Cretan setting of the *Laws*, the conservative traditions of Egypt, just as Aristotle, in discussing the Cretan 'caste-system', found its parallel in Egypt, both having been inherited from the Bronze Age.)[10] When the festivals have been fixed by compiling an annual calendar to show what feasts are to be celebrated, on what dates, and in honour of what gods, children of gods and spirits; when the hymns to be sung at each of the divine festivals and the dances with which each one is to be graced have been determined; then the whole citizen body is to make public sacrifice to the Fates and all the other gods, consecrating by solemn libation each hymn to its respective divinity. If anyone tries to introduce hymns and dances to any of the gods other than those prescribed, the priests and priestesses, acting together with the guardians of the law, and in obedience to the principles of both religion and law, shall expel him from the festival. If he does not submit to this excommunication, he shall be liable for life to be indicted for impiety by anyone who so desires.[11]

[6] *Ib.* 745b–d.　　　　　　　　　　　　　[7] *Ib.* 759a–760a.

[8] *Ib.* 771a–772e.　　　　　　　　　　　　[9] *Ib.* 799a.

[10] *Pol.* 1329b; Willetts ASAC 161; p. 19 above. Cf. Morrow 5–6, 18 n. 8, 344–5, 355.

[11] *Lg.* 799a–b; cf. *ib.* 656d–657b.

When the punishment of offences and related modes of procedure are considered, the punishment for robbing temples is first discussed. If the intending robber is not cured of his fatal impulse by supplication and by association with the virtuous, but goes on to commit the crime, he shall be branded in the face and hands, should he be a slave or foreigner, and cast out naked beyond the borders. If he be a citizen, he shall be regarded as incurable and subject to the death penalty. After some discussion of further details, it is significantly stated that, after religion, it is the preservation of the constitution which is the first object of the law.[12]

Since religion is then the foundation of this social order, atheism, impiety and erroneous beliefs are to be treated as crimes. This proposal, made, so far as we know, for the first time, together with the further proposal for an inquisition to suppress heresy, gives to Book X of the *Laws* its great historical interest as one of the few Platonic theories which have been vigorously applied in practice. Plato holds dogmatically that there are gods, that they care for men, and that they cannot be bribed to do injustice. Therefore it is proposed that the impious man shall be subjected to fines and imprisonment, or the death penalty, depending on the degree of his error.

In order to discourage impiety further, it is to be enacted that no man shall possess a shrine in his house. He must go with others to pray and sacrifice in the temples.

Thus theocracy and oligarchy go hand in hand; religion and law consolidate the state, sanctify and support the status quo.

[12] *Ib.* 854a–856a.

CHAPTER 17

The Role of the *Polis*

'THE *Laws*, today the least generally known of Plato's major compositions, is in some respects his most characteristic work,' wrote A. E. Taylor[1] nearly thirty years ago. The same remark could be made with equal truth today. Part of the reason for the neglect is that the *Laws* is a sombre and depressing work, especially when it is set beside the more vital, energetic and expansive achievements of earlier Greek thought or of Aristotle's more buoyant realism.

But the *Laws* will repay study; and not only because it contains prophetic recommendations about the bond which might be forged by the state between religion and law in pursuit of conservative orthodoxy. We must also be alive to the possibility, in studying this characteristic work of Plato, of gaining some insight into the characteristics of the Greek *polis* as typified in its aristocratic phase without the perspective of advance to higher forms. Such was the Cretan *polis* in Plato's time. Long after his time it remained a centre of antiquarian practices, where old men were powerful and young men constrained.

As we continue to examine concrete aspects of the service of religion in the everyday life of the Cretan *polis*, we may see more of the reality behind the major work of Plato's old age.

I. THE POLIS AS CULT-CENTRE

The 'Heroic Age' of the Greek world signifies the collapse of Bronze Age culture. It also marks the transition to the rule of the landed aristocracy. To this transitional period we can trace the beginnings of the process whereby a city of a new type—the *polis*—was created, organized on the basis of new relations of production brought into being by the introduction of iron.

[1] Taylor xi.

Generally speaking, transition from village or tribal settlement to *polis* must have been gradual. The process by which it came about (*synoikismos*) caused outlying villages to be abandoned and a central village to develop as a market-town, with its *agora*; the sacred images of the clans were transferred from the dwellings of clan-chiefs to temples built in the towns; and the clan-cults eventually became state-cults. At Athens the *synoikismos* was associated with the name of Theseus and was therefore traditionally dated to the Mycenaean period. But this early date was exceptional.

In Crete, this whole schematic development must have been modified by the legacy of Minoan urbanization. The *agora*, for instance, had had an old and flourishing past. Yet a relatively isolated community like the Arcadians seem not to have been subject to such modification. For their name applies not so much to a settled township as to a group of villages in Cretan Arcadia inhabited by a people who had affinities with the ancient Arcadians of the Peloponnese. It is significant that the Arcadian inscriptions are from different places in the whole Arcadian area. Thus the constitutional forms of government, normally associated with the central role of the typical *polis*, are there characteristic of a kind of federation in process of evolution from tribal forms.[2]

On the whole, however, if the basic features of the *polis* are understood to be on the one hand the *agora*, on the other the temple, we must, in the case of Crete, place most emphasis on the temple. The temple points the contrast between the organization of Minoan religion and the organization of state religion in the historical *polis*. Its existence is just as characteristic of the Cretan *polis*, centre of the political life of the state, as the houses, *syssitia* and gymnasia of the ruling classes of landowners.

The epigraphic evidence indicates that the building and restoration of temples were among the chief duties of state officials. Indeed, we know that one of the *kosmoi* was especially charged with religious matters and given the title of *hiarorgos*. Thus, an inscription from Gortyna, from the early second century B.C., preserves a list of eleven *kosmoi*, who were apparently charged with the responsibility of constructing a hero's shrine.[3] The fifth *kosmos* is specifically designated as *hiarorgos*. Two rather later

[2] Willetts ASAC 147 and n. 1.   [3] IC 4.259.

inscriptions from Gortyna[4] also mention a *hiarorgos*. In the first of these he is placed second in the list; and in the other the *kosmoi* are made responsible for the sacrifice of a bull and a she-goat, and here too the *hiarorgos* is named next after the president. A secretary of the *hiarorgos* is also mentioned here. With one possible exception, however—again from Gortyna[5]—there is no other reference to this latter official.

The above evidence illustrates the degree to which the state bureaucracy of a larger city like Gortyna could be developed in relation to religious affairs. It also incidentally illustrates a point made by Aristotle, who writes of a kind of superintendence concerned with divine worship, in this category being priests and superintendents of matters connected with the temples, the preservation of existing buildings and the restoration of those that are ruined and other duties relating to the gods. Sometimes these functions belong to a number of officials who are not members of the priesthood, for example Sacrificial Officers and Temple-Guardians and Stewards of Sacred Funds. (Plato, we recall, was anxious to ensure that regulations for the appointment of similar state officials should be properly fashioned.) In other places, however, the management of such matters constituted a single office, for example in the small cities.[6] Arcadia, even in the second (?) century B.C., must have belonged to this second category described by Aristotle, if we can judge from the inscription which records the responsibility of the *kosmoi* for work on the temple of Artemis.[7] For the state is responsible for defraying expenses and no special officers are named. Hence the two men who are cited as *ergepistatai* may have been priests, fulfilling the single office of a small state.

There is hardly need to emphasize further the role of the temple as the official repository of state documents, including treaties, which have been referred to repeatedly in this work.

But there is some point in referring again to Aristotle's statement that, out of all the crops and cattle produced from the public lands of Crete, and the tributes paid by the serfs, one part was assigned for the worship of the gods. For we have seen that the

---

[4] *Ib.* 195 b, 260. Cf. also *ib.* 1.XVII (Lebena) 2 a 5, b 4, where Guarducci suggests that it is the Gortynian *hiarorgos* who is referred to.

[5] *Ib.* 409, *c.* first century B.C.   [6] *Pol.* 1322b 18–26.

[7] IC 1.V.5.

epigraphic evidence throws an interesting light on this statement, as also on the general historical development of the tribute system.[8] In particular, the evidence concerning the revenues of the temple of Diktynna shows how these revenues had become part of the state treasury, used not only for religious purposes but for public works.[9]

Yet the old cult traditions of the serfs permeated the whole official religious structure and sometimes, as we have seen, they observed their own sanctioned religious festivals. There were other compensations. Although, by the fifth century B.C., a serf could lose his serf-status and be sold as a slave, a runaway serf could not be sold within a year if he had taken refuge in a temple. And though the cities were now administered by aristocratic land-owners, the naming of these cities, or parts of them, like Lato or Aptera, Latosion or Hermaion or Artemitai, reflected the presence of older inhabitants within the framework of the *polis* than its citizen class. If we compare such nomenclature with Plato's recommendations in the *Laws*, and with the context of these recommendations, we are justified in supposing that it supplies further evidence about the preservation of the old tribal divisions of land until a late date in Crete.[10]

The *prytaneion* ('town-hall') was regarded in antiquity as another universal feature of the *polis*.[11] We have some dozen inscriptions from various cities of Crete which show that the *prytaneion* was used as a centre for official hospitality, where magistrates and other officials dined and where official documents were sometimes published.[12]

The *Koina Hestia*, or Public Hearth, is also mentioned in inscriptions, as a place which served a similar function.

The *prytaneion* had originally been the house of the king, chief or headman (*prytanis*) of an independent village or town. It contained a fire which was kept constantly burning, and from which live faggots were transferred when a colony was sent out; and it developed into the familiar building of the historical *polis*, housing the sacred public hearth, with its perpetual fire, and associated with the cult of Hestia. Hence, in the oath of the Drerians, Hestia takes precedence even over Zeus, invoked as Hestia in the *Prytaneion*, as sacred personification of the Public

---

[8] Cf. Willetts ASAC 139–40, *Philol*. 105. 1/2.
[9] P. 192.
[10] Cf. Willetts ASAC 28 and n. 1.
[11] Aristid. *Pan*. 103. 16 sch.; Liv. 41.20.
[12] Willetts ASAC 198–9.

Hearth.[13] Although her anthropomorphic shape is scarcely realized, the cult of Hestia has a special relation to the *polis*. For the sanctity of the hearth, of which she is the patent abstract conception, is Greek and not Minoan.[14]

2. THE RELIGIOUS ASPECT OF CITIZENSHIP

The temple and the hearth, the market-place, gymnasium and town-hall, with all that they connoted, were institutions which helped to shape the *polis*, the city-state, as a specifically Greek form of social organization. The idea of the *polis* is a basic assumption in Greek thought until the Hellenistic period, until Alexander had demonstrated that it was out of date. But, for Alexander's tutor, Aristotle, the *polis* was still the most sovereign and inclusive form of political association, and man was an animal intended by nature to live in a *polis*.[15] Aristotle also defined the *polis* as an association of clans and villages.[16] In the process of association the clans and the villages underwent radical changes, becoming both a city and a state. The clansman in time became a *polites*, a citizen.

The Cretan evidence throws interesting sidelights on this development. For example, the word *agora* is used at Gortyna in the earlier fifth century B.C. to mean an assembly of the citizens, and was probably thus used in earlier times.[17] In the Gortyn Code we find the same blending of two meanings, 'place of assembly' (i.e. 'market-place') and 'muster', common in the frequent Homeric use of the word. The Assembly is still associated with its tribal origin. But by the third, if not the fourth, century B.C., the word *polis* replaces *agora*, to mean, at Gortyna as elsewhere, 'assembly' or 'community of citizens'. Citizen and *polis* have become synonymous.

For, in the Cretan aristocratic *polis*, the state does not emerge as an impersonal and abstract power, but is closely associated with a particular section of the community. The personal responsibility of state officials for state actions, which is an accepted practice, illustrates the point.[18]

---

[13] IC 1.IX.1.16; cf. Pl. *Lg.* 745b, 848d; Paus. 5.14.4.

[14] Nilsson HGR 124. For other references to Hestia in Crete see IC 1.XVIII (Lyttos) 9, c.4; *ib.* 3.III (Hierapytna) 3, B 13, 19; 5.11; *ib.* 4 (Gortyna) 171.12, 174.57, 72.

[15] *Pol.* 1252a, 1253a; cf. *EN* 1.7.6, 8.12.7, 9.9.3.   [16] *Pol.* 1281a.

[17] IC 4.72 (Cols. X and XI); 80; cf. *ib.* 13 g–i; Willetts ASAC 116.

[18] Willetts ASAC 105.

This lack of even apparent impartiality is due to the close and abiding relationship between the Cretan state and its tribal origins, the distant Minoan and the nearer Dorian. Nowhere is this relationship more apparent than in the religious aspect of citizenship, and particularly in the cults specially devoted to the initiation of the citizen-novices, as is demonstrated by the evidence which has been brought forward in the earlier argument and elsewhere.[19] It is only necessary here perhaps to dwell upon a few points emerging from this evidence.

Firstly, at such annual ceremonies as the Ekdysia, when the novices laid aside their boyhood garments, before assuming the warriors' costumes which they had received after their period of seclusion, they were reborn as citizens; and so the city itself was also reborn. Moreover, this aspect of rebirth was extended to the oaths taken at these annual ceremonies, whether of personal loyalty or attached to state treaties and agreements. Legal sanction is not therefore absolute, but has a cycle of birth and death, must also be renewed. The citizen is thus a descendant of the 'priest-king', whose sacral functions have been distributed among the whole citizen-body of the *polis*, modified to the new framework of a city-state.

Secondly, these cults of the novices, with all their traditional lore, were deliberately fostered by the Cretan aristocrats as a means of perpetuating their rule, of controlling the youth, and as a further means of preventing innovation leading to the kind of conflict between old and young citizens which was envisaged by both Plato and Aristotle as a possibility, and which actually did occur in Crete.[20]

In a more general sense, the annual oath of the new citizens is a major demonstration of several ways in which the binding obligation of oaths was practised by the authorities to bring about a close and formal relationship between the state and official religion.[21]

It can be inferred from the evidence of the Drerian oath that the very terms *dromeus* and *apodromos* ('adult' and 'minor', one who could and one who could not take part in the public athletic exercises) are to be referred ultimately to the cult practices of an agricultural community which had linked the death and the

---

[19] *Ib.* 7–9, 12–14, 16–19, 24–6, 81, 120–3, 126, 141, 155, 173, 243.
[20] *Ib.* 191.
[21] See the evidence relating to oaths *ib. passim.*

rebirth of initiation with the fertility of the crops, with marriage, and later with citizenship and the calendar; moreover, that these archaic practices were encouraged and controlled by the leading magistrates so as to ensure the legality of the new citizens. For not only does an ordeal that took the form of a race appear to be closely associated with a formal injunction to all new citizens, at the annual ceremony, to plant olive-trees, but a heavy penalty was incurred by those who were negligent in assuming the responsibility. It is quite possible that the cult of the sacred tree had, in Dreros, been harnessed to the necessity of confirming tenure of a plantation-holding by the state control of the old-established ritual of the *agela*.[22]

Basic components of this ritual which still flourished were the Ekdysia, the Periblemaia or Periblemata, and the *agon* of the Dromeia, the ritual race by which the victor, the chief *kouros*, became known.

[22] Willetts H 85.381-4. Cf. pp. 201-2 above.

CHAPTER 18

Poetry and Music

THE dominant conclusion which emerges from a study of the Cretan cults is that so many of the pre-Olympian, indeed quite primitive, strata were perpetuated officially within the general social framework. This characteristic is fully consistent with the nature of the social framework itself—an aristocratic *polis* organization subject to relatively little, and certainly to no radical, change in the historical period. Because of the obvious ritual origins of Greek poetry and music, no survey of Cretan cults would be complete without a chapter on Cretan poetry and music. But, in the nature of things, such a chapter has to be brief. An explanation of this necessity may serve as an apt conclusion to the work as a whole.

It has been said that the three main forms of Greek poetry were, in the order of their maturing to the level of conscious art: epic, lyric and drama. Regarded from the standpoint of their origins, however, this chronological order is reversed. For, since it combines song, dance and impersonation, drama preserves the original unity of mimetic magic; choral lyric combines song and dance; and epic is merely recitation. The least differentiated of the three, and hence the most primitive, was the last to mature; the first to mature was the least primitive. Drama, however, marks the consummation of all three, because it includes recitation, and, though its structure is the most primitive in the sense of being the oldest, its technique is not, nor is its content. The three art forms correspond to three successive phases in the growth of Greek society—the early monarchy, the landed aristocracy, democracy.[1]

Little has survived of Greek lyric poetry. Almost all of those examples which have survived are self-conscious masterpieces. The choral odes used in normal temple worship must have been

[1] Thomson SAGS 1.463–4.

much less sophisticated, based on the solo-and-chorus convention exemplified in the luckily surviving Hymn of the Kouretes.[2] These closely related facts are the major cause of the brevity of this chapter. For there is a direct relation between the backwardness of Cretan society and the poverty of its literary art, a poverty which is, by and large, faithfully reflected in the range and content of the surviving epigrams and ritual verses.[3]

The aged Plato was at least consistent in his sociology, his theology and his aesthetics. For the *Laws* is a testament not only to his repudiation of the democratic institutions of his native city, but also of its traditions of bold and restless innovation in the arts.

'In God's name, stranger,' says the Cretan Kleinias,[4] 'do you suppose that is how poets set to work in other cities at the present time? So far as my own observations go, I am not aware of any practices such as you now describe, except among the Spartans or among ourselves. Rather, innovation prevails in dancing as all other forms of art, introduced, not in response to law, but to some sort of arbitrary taste, which, so far from displaying the consistency and stability which you ascribe to the Egyptians, is absolutely inconsistent.'

'Very true, Kleinias,' replies the Athenian. 'However, the obscurity of my formulation may well have been responsible for giving you the impression that the practices to which you refer are actually prevalent. You thought that this was what I have in mind probably because of the way in which I stated what I would like to see done about the arts. For it is sometimes unpleasantly necessary to censure matters which are advanced in error and beyond the scope of remedy. Come, do you agree that such practices as I have described are more congenial to the Spartans and to you Cretans than to any other Greeks? For we see eye to eye in these things.'

'What you say is true,' says Kleinias.

'Might we say,' asks the Athenian, 'that these practices would be an improvement upon the present state of affairs, if they were generally adopted elsewhere?'

---

[2] Cf. Thomson *ib.* 467.

[3] IC *passim*. Some have a curious interest, e.g. those for guiding the dead in the other world; IC 2.XII.31, cf. *ib.* XV.3, XXX.4; Murray, appx. *ad* Harrison PSGR; Guthrie OGR 173; Burn 388.

[4] *Lg.* 660b–d.

'If matters were arranged as they are among us Cretans,' agrees Kleinias, 'and among the Spartans, and in fact just as you were now saying they ought to be arranged, then a considerable improvement would be likely.'

What are these practices which Plato has described as desirable theoretical propositions, which only Sparta and Crete among Greek states actually emulate?

It has been earlier stated that the gods, out of compassion for the wearisome lot of mankind, ordained the cycle of their festivals to provide respite from troubles, giving the Muses and Apollo, the leader of the Muses, and Dionysos, to share the festivals with mankind with due observance, and also the spiritual nourishment derived from the presence of gods. A human child, like other young animals, is restless, leaps, skips, dances, plays and cries out. But, in the case of the human child, originally spontaneous cries and movements are purposefully co-ordinated by means of songs and dances. Education thus owes its origin to Apollo and the Muses. But the link between the arts, education and morality is now to be forged in such a way as to prevent any spontaneous growth. Standards of artistic composition are to be canonized as they have been in Egypt, to the exclusion of all innovation and without regard to the wishes of an audience.[5]

The inference from all this is that the artistic side of Cretan life in the time of Plato (and probably for a long time afterwards), to a considerable extent corresponded with his petrified ideal. The old oligarchs of the Cretan cities were presumably powerful enough to ensure that new generations skipped and danced and sang according to the right traditional precepts. We are tempted to conclude that it is perhaps only when we are most devotedly antiquarian that we can afford to regret that so little remains of those Cretan arts of later antiquity which were presided over by Apollo and the Muses.

But such a conclusion would not be wholly satisfactory. We may not treasure the Hymn of the Kouretes for the delight of its form or the profundity of its content. But such a fragment reveals the extent to which poetry and music were a part of normal life; it serves as a model by which other, more sophisticated, examples may be more accurately judged; and, most important, its very archaism serves to remind us that there was a time, even in Crete, when this kind of composition was fresh, vital and new. Similarly,

[5] *Ib.* 653c–659e.

the nature of some of the festivals which we have examined is such as to throw light on the ritual basis of Greek drama. We can infer, from *The Cretans*, that Euripides took this view and respected Cretan legend and paid attention to Cretan cult. In different social conditions legend and cult might well have combined in the advance to higher forms, just as in Athens.

For tradition indeed confirms that Greek poetry and music did once owe a debt to Cretan innovation, in the days before innovation was arrested.

We have seen how the Cretan reputation for dancing is reflected in the Homeric poems; in what we know of the ritual of the Kouretes; and also in the worship of the Cretan Zeus.[6] Although our knowledge of the work of the Cretan Thaletas is slight, it can be said that he and his school must have played a part of distinct importance in combining the dance with the song and metre of aristocratic choral lyric. Thaletas flourished in the seventh century B.C. and was born either at Elyros, or Knossos or Gortyna. The advice of the Delphic oracle was said to have been responsible for his journey to Sparta, to cure a plague by means of his music. Whilst at Sparta he introduced musical reforms of such a drastic kind that they amounted to an artistic revolution. These innovations included the elaboration of the Cretan *hyporkhema*, a mimetic dance originally closely connected with the cult of Kronos and the Titans, of Leto and the Cretan Zeus; and also probably the Cretic and Paeonic metres. The Paean itself was not so very different from the *hyporkhema*, was traditionally Cretan in origin and likewise connected with the name of Thaletas.[7]

Thaletas came to Sparta to purify from pestilence and to help in the fashioning of new forms of art in the consolidation of the Dorian aristocratic social order as Sparta emerged to the leadership of the Peloponnese. The role of the semi-legendary but also undoubtedly historical Cretan poet and prophet Epimenides was in some ways similar. He too played his part as a Cretan missionary in adapting the ritual arts of earlier Cretan religion to newer forms and purposes. For he seems to have visited Athens with the express intention of introducing purificatory rites developed out of Cretan cathartic practices. His legendary association with Solon was directed to a series of religious reforms whose

---

[6] Pp. 98 f., 123 f., 199 ff.
[7] Plu. *De Mus.* 9, 10, 42; Arist. *Pol.* 1274a 28; Suid. s.v. Θαλήτας; Paus. 1.14.4; Croiset 2.284–7; Farnell GLP 5–6, 28–9, 38; Swindler 56–7.

consequence was, so far as we can judge, to diminish the importance of the religious rites of women; and of a kind paralleled in
the early legislation of historical Crete itself.[8]

The direct evidence relating to Cretan poetry and music is
therefore certainly not extensive. But if we turn to the earliest of
Greek poetical forms, the epic, we do find indirect evidence of the
influence of the early Cretan aesthetic imagination, and of a kind
which indicates its origin in a major characteristic of Minoan
religion. The testimony of the Minoan monuments leaves no room
for doubt that the bird is a form of the divine epiphany.[9] Now in
Homer the gods sometimes change themselves into birds, but
never into other animals.[10] This recurrent type of metamorphosis
has affected a common category of image which describes the
speed of descent of deities from Ida or Olympos.

A simple formula occurs in the form 'as swift as a wing or a
thought'.[11] This is elaborated in a passage of the *Iliad* as follows:

'Thus he spoke and white-armed Hera obeyed. From the hills
of Ida she darted to Olympos, and, as a man who has travelled far
turns over many thoughts, musing rapidly, "If only I were there or
there!" so rapidly did Hera fly.'[12]

A similar formula of introduction and conclusion is introduced
in this description of Iris:

'Thus she spoke and wind-footed Iris obeyed. She descended
the peaks of Ida down to Troy, as when a chill storm of snow or
hail sweeps from the clouds under a northerly blast. So swiftly
did Iris fly.'[13]

In other contexts the comparison with the flight of birds is
pointedly emphasized.

'Thus he spoke and Apollo did not turn a deaf ear to his father,
but went down from the mountains of Ida like a swift dove-
killing hawk, the swiftest creature on wings.'[14]

---

[8] Pl. *Lg.* 642d; Arist. *Ath.* 1; Plu. *Sol.* 12; Harrison PSGR 401; Guthrie GG
196–7; Dodds 141–2; Willetts ASAC 216 and n. 6. Cf., on the plastic arts, Boardman 159: 'In the sixth century there is a falling-off in the artistic activity in the
island . . . but now too we begin to hear the names of Cretan artists working far
from home. Dipoinos and Skyllis of Gortyn were said to be pupils of Daidalos and
the first sculptors in marble. They worked mainly in the Peloponnese, apparently in
the early sixth century. Khersiphron of Knossos and his son Metagenes were the
architects of the great Artemision at Ephesos in the mid-sixth century. But the island
is empty of sculpture and architecture which might match the achievements of her
artists overseas.'

[9] Nilsson MMR 330–40. Cf. pp. 51, 73 above.   [10] *Ib.* 491.
[11] *Od.* 7.36.   [12] *Il.* 15.78–83.
[13] *Il.* 15.168–72.   [14] *Il.* 5.236–8. Cf. *ib.* 13.62, 18.616, 19.350.

'Wand in hand mighty Hermes made his flight. He arrived at Pieria from the upper skies and thence alighted on the sea. He darted over the waves like a gull, which drenches its wing-feathers with spray as it goes in pursuit of the fishes through the dread gulfs of the unharvested sea.'[15]

Such passages can be assessed as similes referring only to speed and not to an assumption of the form of birds. But elsewhere there can be no doubt that real bird-epiphanies are described. The species of bird vary, but any of them may be the form of a divinity. That pre-Greek Athene so often appears as a bird is a further indication of the Minoan source of the imagery.

A passage from the Fifth Book of the *Iliad* is particularly convincing. For Athene and Hera set out for the battle to help the Greeks 'with steps like shy doves'.[16] If it is intended to remind us of the strides of heroic warriors, this simile is most unsuitable. Nor can it be intended as mockery.[17] We must assume that the goddesses here appear in the shape of birds.[18]

Later, Athene and Apollo combine with a sacred tree to present a scene strikingly Minoan in its detail. The deities have come to watch the battle.

'Athene and Apollo of the Silver Bow also sat down, in the form of vultures on a lofty oak-tree sacred to aegis-bearing Zeus.'[19]

Hera sets out with Sleep and they travel with speed to Ida.

'Here Sleep halted, and to avoid the sight of Zeus, went up into a tall pine-tree, the tallest on Ida, which had pierced its mists and reached through to the clear sky. There he sat, covered up by the branches of the pine-tree, in the form of a sweet-toned mountain bird.'[20]

Reproached by Athene, Zeus has agreed that Odysseus should be allowed to return home. Athene then suggests that Hermes be sent to Kalypso to inform her of this decision, while she herself goes to Ithaca to encourage Telemachos. Her departure is described.

'Thus she spoke and bound a pair of lovely sandals under her feet, divine sandals of gold, which carried her swift as the blasts

[15] *Od.* 5.49–53.
[17] Cf. Myres *ad loc.*
[19] *Il.* 7.57–60.
[16] *Il.* 5.778.
[18] Nilsson MMR 492.
[20] *Il.* 14.286–90.

of wind over sea or boundless land. Down she went, darting from the crests of Olympos.'[21]

Arrived in Ithaca, she assumes the appearance of a Taphian chieftain called Mentes, is welcomed as a guest by Telemachos, gives him advice and then takes her leave.

'Thus she spoke and Athene of the flashing eyes disappeared, flying up into the air like a bird. As for Telemachos, his heart was imbued with courage and confidence and he was even more mindful of his father than he had been before. He understood, he was astonished, he knew he had been with a god.'[22]

After the debate in the Assembly at Ithaca, on the following day, the people disperse to their homes, the suitors return to the palace and Telemachos seeks the solitude of the seashore. He washes his hands in the surf and prays for further help to her who had already revealed her divinity to him. Athene promptly answers his prayer by appearing in the guise of Mentor. As Mentor she accompanies him on his voyage to Pylos. They find Nestor and his sons at a feast with the assembled people of Pylos. The goddess commends Nestor for inviting Telemachos to visit his palace.

'Thus she spoke and Athene of the flashing eyes disappeared in the form of a sea-eagle. They were seized with wonder at the sight. The old man was amazed at what he had seen. He took Telemachos by the hand and addressed him. "My friend, no fear that you will be a rogue and a weakling. Because, of all those who live on Olympos, that was no other than the daughter of Zeus."'[23]

Odysseus takes leave of Kalypso and sails away. Poseidon sees him and raises a storm. Odysseus is in dire straits. But the goddess Leukothea, formerly Ino, daughter of Kadmos, takes pity on him and settles on his boat. She offers him a veil to wind round his waist, which will save him from destruction.

'Thus she spoke and the goddess gave him the veil and promptly sank into the rolling sea in the form of a sea-gull; and the dark water covered her over.'[24]

During the battle with the suitors, Athene again puts on the form of Mentor to visit the scene. For the time being she allows the fighting to continue without interfering.

'And she herself darted up and perched on the smoky roof-beam of the hall, in the actual form of a swallow.'[25]

---

[21] *Od.* 1.96–102.
[22] *Od.* 1.319–23.
[23] *Od.* 3.371–8.
[24] *Od.* 5.351–3.
[25] *Od.* 22.239–40.

After this survey of old traditional deposits in the Homeric poems, it will be fitting to conclude by mentioning what could be an element in the founding of a new tradition under Cretan influence.

We have seen that the Hymn of the Kouretes may have been sung by initiates as part of a festival celebrating the epiphany of Zeus Kretagenes.[26] It has been claimed[27] that the earliest representation of Zeus occurs on the Geometric lid from a tomb at Fortetsa near Knossos. That this divine epiphany is traditionally Cretan is indicated by the presence of birds, one of them carried on the left hand of the figure supposed to be Zeus, who strides towards a tripod. There is another bird on top of the tripod; between the figure and the tripod is yet another, larger, bird with its head lifted towards the handle of the tripod. The principal figure carries in his right hand an object which consists of three wavy verticals—the thunderbolt, or at least fire.[28] Underneath the tripod is a human protome—perhaps the Minoan goddess herself, associated with, not yet displaced by, Zeus.[29]

If we do have represented here a double epiphany of Cretan Zeus and the old Cretan goddess, heralded by the birds of Minoan tradition, further details of interpretation may be suggested of a scene which, despite its crudity, has been put at the head of a long and glorious series of monumental works of Hellenic art.[30]

The thunderbolt of Zeus was traditionally looked upon as a means of bringing death so that immortality might be conferred.[31] The tripod—a three-legged cauldron to be put over a fire—goes back in its origins to the fourteenth century B.C.[32] Real or simulated boiling in a cauldron is a familiar prelude to rejuvenation, immortality and apotheosis. The infant Dionysos-Zagreus, so closely akin to the Cretan Zeus, was slain, his limbs cooked in a cauldron, and restored to life again.[33] In the boiling cauldron

---

[26] P. 214.

[27] With varying conviction: Payne JHS 53.292; Cook Z 3.1150; Demargne CD 297; M. Robertson ABSA 43.114; Levi, *Hesperia* 14.29, GC 311 ff.; Guarducci RIA 6 (1937) 11; Brock 123; cf. p. 199.

[28] Payne pointed out a close resemblance to the bolts depicted on Syro-Hittite reliefs. Cf. Brock *ib.* and n. 4.

[29] Brock, who adds *ib.* n. 6: 'The legend that Gaia rescued the infant Zeus may be an attempt to reconcile the two cults.'

[30] Levi, *ibid.*   [31] See Cook Z 2.9, cf. *ib.* 23–9.

[32] Levi *ib.* 305.

[33] Harrison PSGR 491. On the cauldron of apotheosis see Cook Z 1.676, 2.210.

mortality and old age are shed, perennial youth is gained. Rebirth follows upon death. The initiate is born again.

Thunderbolt and tripod can be accompaniments of initiation; and Cretan Zeus is an initiation god. It is tempting to suppose that the Mystery of the greatest Kouros, of Cretan Zeus himself, celebrated by the Hymn of the Kouretes, is celebrated in another form in the scene on the Knossos lid, in the form of a double epiphany, reflecting the combination of the Dorian with the traditional social background, newly Hellenic yet abidingly Minoan.

The Song of Hybrias the Cretan

THE Song of Hybrias the Cretan is quoted by Athenaios to conclude his collection of Attic σκόλια, with the qualification that the poem is called a σκόλιον by some.[1] Others presumably disputed the description and it seems to have been regarded by Hesychios as a marching-song.[2] The poem adds nothing to our knowledge of Cretan religion, but it does add to our knowledge of the nomenclature of Cretan serfdom[3] and it was, until the discovery of the Hymn of the Kouretes, the only possible example of Cretan lyric. There is still no certainty about its author, its text, its date or its specific lyrical genre—it is sometimes presented as a single stanza, sometimes as two. But if we may assume, with Athenaios, that there was a Cretan Hybrias, his song must have some bearing on what has been said about the relation between Cretan poetry and Cretan social life. I give the text as now generally presented:

> ἔστι μοι πλοῦτος μέγας δόρυ καὶ ξίφος
> καὶ τὸ καλὸν λαισήϊον, πρόβλημα χρωτός·
> τούτῳ γὰρ ἀρῶ, τούτῳ θερίζω,
> τούτῳ πατέω τὸν ἁδὺν οἶνον ἀπ' ἀμπέλω,
> 5 τούτῳ δεσπότας μνοΐας κέκλημαι.
> τοὶ δὲ μὴ τολμῶντ' ἔχειν δόρυ καὶ ξίφος
> καὶ τὸ καλὸν λαισήϊον, πρόβλημα χρωτός,
> πάντες γόνυ πεπτηῶτες ἐμὸν κυνέοντι, δεσπόταν
> καὶ μέγαν βασιλῆα φωνέοντες.

4 ἀμπέλων ACE; ἀμπέλου Eust. 6 τολμῶντες ACE, Eust. corr. Hermann. 7 πρόβλημά τε χρωτός AE corr. ς. 8 πεπτηότες ACE, corr. Eust.; προσκυνεῦντί με δεσπόταν Bergk; πεπτηῶτες ἁμὸν αἰεὶ σέβοντι προσκυνέοντί τε Hiller 'exempli causa'; πάντες σέβοντι Stadtmüller; πάντες γόνυ πεπτηῶτες ⟨ἀμφὶ⟩/⟨ἁμὸν⟩ κυνέοντι δεσπόταν ⟨ἐμὲ δέσποτᾶν⟩ Crusius. 9 βασιλεα ACE, Eust.

The poem has been analysed in some detail by Sir Maurice

---

[1] 15.695 f. Cf. Eust. 1574.7.   [2] S.v. Ἰβικτήρ.
[3] Willetts ASAC 46, 48.

Bowra.[4] He disagrees with the conclusion arrived at by Wilamowitz that the poem derives at least from the fourth century but
in its present state dates to the third or second centuries B.C. He
argues that the main metrical combinations of the poem can be
found in quite early lyric poetry, with parallels from monody or
folk-song. His own conclusion is that, so far as sentiment, style
and metre are concerned, the song could be placed in the sixth
century—which is the traditional view—but of course it might
still be later.

Bowra agrees that the text of what he regards as the first stanza
looks sound as presented in its usual form (ll. 1–5) and he trans-
lates: 'My great wealth is my spear and sword, and the fine targe,
which guards my skin; with this I plough, with this I reap, with
this I tread the sweet wine from the vine, with this I am called
master of the serfs.' Rightly he points out that we have here an
indisputable piece of evidence that the song is connected with
Crete in the reference to μνοῖα, serfs.

In my view the text of the following verses (6 ff.) makes sense as
it stands: 'But those who dare not hold the spear and sword, and
the fine targe, to guard their skin, all fall and kiss my knee, calling
me master and great lord.'

But in Bowra's view there is clearly something wrong here with
the text. It can be made grammatical, however, with some small
additions. Γόνυ needs a preposition such as ἀμφί to bring it into
the sentence and a word for 'me' seems to be missing as the object
of κυνέοντι. A second difficulty, he thinks, is that there is not complete responsion between second and first strophes. After the first
two verses the correspondence is very vague. Therefore we must
either assume that much more has fallen out than the sense seems
to require or we must accept the difference between the two
strophes and regard it as quite appropriate for a poem of this kind.
Bowra chooses the second of these alternatives: 'It seems that at a
certain popular level of composition exact correspondence was
not demanded, and we can understand that in a song like that of
Hybrias the difference of metre might reflect some difference in
the actual movement of the dance and the weapon-play.' He consequently makes the following minimum alterations in his second
stanza:

> πάντες γόνυ πεπτηῶτες ἀμφ'ἐμὸν
> κυνέοντί με δεσπόταν
> καὶ μέγαν βασιλῆα φωνέοντες.

[4] GLP 398–403.

and maintains that the meaning is then quite clear: 'Hybrias announces his contempt for those who have not won a place like his own through their weapons and must therefore do obeisance to him as if he were a great king. There is no specific reference to Crete or to serfs. Hybrias' claim is more exorbitant than when he started, and his contempt embraces all who are not so successful as he is.' There is no explanation of the place which Hybrias is supposed to have won through his weapons.

Bowra imagines, however, that Hybrias had soldiered abroad. His first piece of evidence for this hypothesis is not convincing. He says that the presence of Greek mercenaries in foreign lands in the seventh and sixth centuries is well known and in later centuries Crete was a great source of supply of them. If by later centuries is meant the Hellenistic period, then it is quite true that Crete was at that time a major source of supply.[5] But what is required is evidence that Cretan mercenaries were commonly abroad earlier, if Hybrias is to be regarded as 'a successful soldier of fortune' who could have flourished before Hellenistic times. However, from this initial statement Bowra proceeds to argue that additional confirmation for his view of Hybrias as a soldier of fortune can be derived from the second stanza of the poem, where Hybrias is supposed to announce his contempt for those who have not won a place like his own, and so on.

For the chief interest, Bowra continues, lies in the last line with its mention of μέγαν βασιλῆα, which can only refer to some Oriental monarch whose ways are known to Hybrias and whose titles and ceremonies he appropriates to himself. This monarch must be the Persian king. The word κυνέοντι describes a practice familiar at the Persian court, known to Herodotos,[6] deplored by Aristotle and Demosthenes[7] as barbarian and unworthy of Greeks. Δεσπότας is commonly used for the Persian king, by Herodotos of Kambyses,[8] by Thucydides of Asiatic rulers in general,[9] in the form δέσποτα δεσποτᾶν by Persian elders of the Ghost of Dareios.[10] The appellation βασιλεὺς μέγας is thoroughly appropriate to the Persian king, for Herodotos calls him by this title and Aeschylus refers to satraps as βασιλῆς βασιλέως ὕποχοι μεγάλου.[11]

[5] Evidence in Willetts ASAC 246.
[7] Arist. Rh. 1361a 36; D. 21.106.
[9] 6.77.1.
[11] Hdt. 1.188.1; A. Pers. 24.

[6] 1.119.1, 3.86.2, 8.118.4.
[8] 3.89.3.
[10] A. Pers. 666.

Hence Bowra's conclusion is that these three claims made by Hybrias are expressed in language normally applied to the Persian monarchy, and, though it is conceivable that they might have been applied to the kings of Babylon or Assyria or Lydia, there is no evidence that they were. They suggest that the song was written after the accession of Cyrus. How long after we cannot say, but it need not have been very long. The song seems to have been written by a Cretan soldier of fortune who had seen service under the Persian king and returned home to glory in his success and declared his intention of applying his Asiatic methods in Crete.

In the nature of the case it is difficult to refute the possibility that Hybrias could have seen service under the Persian king. It is even more difficult to prove. Nor is our knowledge of contemporary Cretan conditions extensive. But we do know enough to be sceptical about the idea of a returned mercenary declaring his intention, in a lyrical manifesto, of applying Asiatic methods in Crete, which was fashioning a set of social traditions far removed from those of Oriental despotism. The fact is that Bowra's interpretation bears no relation to what we know of the realities of life in ancient Crete.

For our scepticism is not lessened by an examination of the points of proof offered to demonstrate that μέγαν βασιλῆα can be none other than the Persian king. First, the word κυνέοντι does not describe a practice familiar at the Persian court. The appropriate word, in the passages cited by Bowra from Herodotos, Aristotle and Demosthenes, as elsewhere,[12] is προσκυνέω (προσκύνησις). If Bowra is right to suspect that the word λαισήϊον, found twice in Homer and once in Herodotos,[13] is used by Hybrias with a sense of its antique, heroic air, not to describe a modern weapon, then we are justified in supposing that κυνέοντι is used, not to describe a modern Asiatic practice, but in its old-fashioned, and indeed unchanging,[14] sense of 'kiss': as when Priam goes up to Achilles, grasps his knees and kisses his hands;[15] or when Amphithee throws her arms round the neck of Odysseus, kisses him on the forehead and on both his eyes;[16] or when Penelope, bursting into tears, throws her arms round his neck and kisses his head.[17]

Even more to the point are several passages of the *Odyssey*

---

[12] See LSJ s.v.
[14] See LSJ s.v.
[16] *Od.* 19.417.

[13] *Il.* 5.453, 12.426; Hdt. 7.91.
[15] *Il.* 24.478.
[17] *Od.* 23.208.

involving the serf, the swineherd Eumaios, and his master Odysseus or his master's son Telemachos. When Eumaios runs forward to meet his young master Telemachos, kisses his forehead, his eyes, his right hand and his left,[18] the tears stream down his cheeks, says Homer; and Eumaios is like a fond father welcoming back his only son after nine years abroad, the son who has been the centre of his anxious thoughts, as he throws his arms round Telemachos and showers kisses upon him as if he had escaped from death.[19] In the same way, when Odysseus reveals his identity to the swineherd and the cowherd, who have prayed for his return, they burst into tears, fling their arms round his neck and kiss him lovingly on forehead and shoulders. Odysseus responds in the same way.[20]

Hybrias might have liked to think that the same idyllic relationship existed between him and his serfs; that, though arms were the emblems of mastery over serfs, they did not prevent these serfs from embracing their master and acknowledging him as their lord.[21] For the common meaning of δεσπότας, as in the first stanza of the poem, is 'master', 'lord'; and βασιλεύς is used by Homer and Pindar in the same sense.[22] Nor have we any reason to suppose that βασιλεύς was alien to a Cretan context;[23] and the title (μέγας) βασιλεύς is used by Greek writers of the Persian king *after* the Persian War.[24]

To return to Eumaios. He was the son of a king of Syros. Kidnapped in early childhood by Phoenician pirates, he was bought by Odysseus' father, Laertes, and then brought up with the family.[25] Because of the prominent part he plays in the plot of the *Odyssey* we know and respect Eumaios, and we learn to understand the patriarchal relationship, the mutual ties of obligation and loyalty that could exist between a master and the servile members of his household in an early aristocratic society before chattel slavery became widespread in the city-states. Eumaios and others like him look after their master's cattle. Before he went to the Trojan War, Odysseus had intended to give him a house, land and a wife.[26] He would then presumably have abandoned his servile status. Now the serfs of Cretan Gortyna were allowed by law to

---

[18] *Od.* 16.15.   [19] *Ib.* 21.

[20] *Od.* 21.224–5.

[21] Cf. Arist. *Pol.* 1264a 12–23 and my remarks in ASAC 170.

[22] *Il.* 18.556; Pi. *O.* 6.47.   [23] Hdt. 4.154. Cf. IC 2.XVI.1.

[24] LSJ s.v.   [25] *Od.* 15.403–84, 363–70.

[26] *Od.* 14.62–4.

assume the tenure of their master's estate in the absence of normal heirs.[27] They too could abandon their servile status by working a piece of land in their own right. They had other rights and privileges; and there is no evidence that they, or other Cretan serfs, ever revolted. Their status, broadly speaking, cannot have been so very different from that of Eumaios in the *Odyssey*. The old patriarchal way of life persisted in Crete long after it had broken up elsewhere.

In this old order, wealth was landed wealth and nobility was equated with its possession. But by the sixth century the power of the landed aristocracy was being attacked and broken in other parts of the Greek world, where it had been successfully challenged by tyranny and the onset of democracy. In Lesbian Mytilene, Sappho and Alkaios saw the overthrow of the ruling Penthelidai and the appointment of Pittakos (590–580 B.C.) to hold the balance, as Solon did in contemporary Athens, between the rival factions. At Megara, the tyranny of Theagenes (c. 640 B.C.) was followed by conflict between oligarchs and democrats, by revolution and counter-revolution, in the lifetime of Theognis.

The complacent, self-assured voice of Hybrias speaks out of a settled tradition with a secure future. It is in marked contrast with the tone of the poets who may have been his near-contemporaries and who were faced with violent change. Alkaios seems to be speaking of this situation and its consequences when he writes of a ship in a storm:

'I do not understand the winds' strife; for one wave rolls from this side, another wave from that side and we, in the midst, are carried along in our black ship, sorely pressed by the mighty storm.'[28]

Theognis had seen democracy in power. He speaks of the people with contempt, with arrogance, with fear; and sometimes his only consolation is a grim despair:

'The noble marries the base, the base the noble. Wealth has confounded birth.'[29]

'Shame has perished. Shamelessness and insolence have got the better of justice and possess the earth.'[30]

'This city is still a city, but its people are changed now; there was a time when they knew nothing of justice, nothing of laws,

---

[27] *Leg. Gort.* V 25–8. Cf. Arist. *Pol.* 1271b; Willetts ASAC 10 n. 2.
[28] Alc. 18; cf. Bowra GLP 153.   [29] 189–90.
[30] 291–2.

but wore out goatskins on their flanks and pastured like the deer outside this city. They are nobles now and the former nobles base. Who can bear the sight of this?'[31]

'Trample on the empty-headed people, goad them hard and let their yoke be heavy. That is the way to make them love their masters.'[32]

'Rejoice, my heart. Soon there will be other men and I be dead, black earth.'[33]

'Not to be born is best, not to see the sunshine; or, once born, to pass as soon as may be through the gates of death and lie beneath a heap of earth.'[34]

To sum up: the text of the Song of Hybrias, as presented above, can be translated as it stands and yields good historical sense. Why then should we suppose that Hybrias was anything but a Cretan aristocrat who spent his life at home in Crete and without experience of Persia, Babylon, Assyria or Lydia? His poem, imperfect though it may be, seems to be a true reflexion of Cretan life in the long heyday of the Cretan aristocracies. It may well date to the sixth century B.C., even earlier, in some form. But the scanty traces of Cretan dialect in the text are sufficient reminder that the poem probably suffered change in its transmission from its Cretan home to the common stock of Greek lyric; and the older the poem the greater the change is likely to have been. However, it is more than usually difficult to assess the extent of such change simply because the poem has no close parallel. Our knowledge of Greek lyric poetry as a whole is strictly limited. Of Cretan lyric we know next to nothing. Therefore emendation and interpretation based on metrical combinations, strophic arrangement, strophic responsion or the lack of it carry little weight.

[31] 53–8.
[32] 847–9.
[33] 1070–1.
[34] 425–8.

Bibliography

Where an English translation of a foreign work is specified, the references are to its pages. Lists of epigraphical publications and of periodicals, with the abbreviations used for them, are given at the end of the bibliography.

ALEXIOU, S. ʽΗ μινωϊκὴ θεὰ μεθ᾽ ὑψωμένων χειρῶν, KK (1958).
ALLEN, T. W., HALLIDAY, W. R., and SIKES, E. E. *Homeric Hymns.* 2 ed. Oxford, 1936.
ALY, W. *Der kretische Apollonkult.* Leipzig, 1908.
AUTRAN, C. *La prehistoire du Christianisme.* Paris, 1941.
BACHOFEN, J. J. *Das Mütterrecht.* Stuttgart, 1861.
BANTI, L. *Myth in Pre-Classical Art.* AJA 58.
BARNETT, R. D. *The Epic of Kumarbi and the Theogony of Hesiod.* JHS 65.
BAUDISSIN, W. W. *Kyrios als Gottesname im Judentum und seine Stelle in der Religionsgeschichte.* Giessen, 1929.
BAUNACK, J. and T. *Die Inschrift von Gortyn.* Leipzig, 1885.
BAUR, P. V. C. *Eileithyia: The University of Missouri Studies* I:4. 1902.
BEATTIE, A. J. *A Plain Guide to the Ventris Decipherment of the Mycenaean Linear B Script.* Mitteilungen des Instituts für Orientforschung. 6.1 (1958).
—Mr. *Ventris' Decipherment of the Minoan Linear B Script.* JHS 76.
—The *'Spice' Tablets of Cnossos, Pylos and Mycenae* in *Minoica.* 6–34.
BECHTEL, F. *Die griechischen Dialekte.* Berlin, 1921–4.
BELOCH, K. J. *Griechische Geschichte.* 2 ed. Strasbourg, 1912–27.
BELON, P. *Observations sur plusieurs singularitez.* Paris, 1553.
BÉRARD, J. *Les Hyksos et la légende d'Io.* S 29.
BERNHÖFT, F. *Die Inschrift von Gortyn.* Stuttgart, 1886.
BISCHOFF, H. RE s.v. *Kalender.*
BITTEL, K. *Die Ruinen von Bogazköy der Haupstadt des Hethiterreichs.* Berlin/Leipzig, 1937.
BLASS, F. *Die kretischen Inschriften,* in SGDI III.2.3, 227–423. Göttingen, 1905.
BLEGEN, C. W. *The Coming of the Greeks.* AJA 32.
BLINKENBERG, C. *The Thunder-weapon in Religion and Folklore.* Cambridge, 1911.
BOARDMAN, J. *The Cretan Collection in Oxford.* Oxford, 1961.
BOISACQ, E. *Dictionnaire étymologique de la langue grecque.* 4 ed. Heidelberg, 1950.
BONNER, R. J., and SMITH, G. *The Administration of Justice from Homer to Aristotle.* Chicago, 1930–8.
BOSANQUET, R. C. *The Palaikastro Hymn of the Kouretes.* ABSA 15.
BOSSERT, H. T. *Die Beschwörung einer Krankheit in der Sprache von Kreta.* OL 34.
—The *Art of Ancient Crete.* London, 1937.
BOWRA, C. M. *Greek Lyric Poetry.* 2 ed. Oxford, 1961.
—Heroic Poetry. London, 1952.
—Homer and his Forerunners. Edinburgh, 1955.

BRANDENSTEIN, W. *Bermerkungen zur Völkertafel in der Genesis, Festschrift Debrunner.* Bern, 1954, 66–70.

BRAUSE, J. *Lautlehre der kretischen Dialekte.* Halle, 1909.

BRIFFAULT, R. *The Mothers.* London, 1927.

BROCK, J. K. *Fortetsa.* Cambridge, 1957.

BÜCHER, K. *Arbeit und Rhythmus.* 5 ed. Leipzig, 1919.

BUCK, C. D. *Comparative Grammar of Greek and Latin.* Chicago, 1933.

—*The Greek Dialects.* Chicago, 1955.

BUDGE, E. A. W. *The Gods of the Egyptians.* London, 1904.

BURKITT, M. C. *Prehistory.* 2 ed. Cambridge, 1925.

BURN, A. R. *The Lyric Age of Greece.* London, 1960.

BURY, J. B. *History of Greece.* 3 ed. by R. Meiggs, London, 1951.

BUSOLT, G. *Griechische Staatskunde,* in I. von Müller's *Handbuch der klassischen Altertums-Wissenschaft,* IV. 1.1. 3 ed. Munich, 1920–6.

Cambridge Ancient History. Cambridge, 1925–39.

CARNOY, A. *Dictionnaire étymologique du proto-indo-européen.* Louvain, 1955.

CARY, M. *Geographic Background of Greek and Roman History.* Oxford, 1949.

CAUDWELL, C. *Illusion and Reality.* 2 ed. London, 1957.

CHADWICK, H. M. *The Growth of Literature.* Cambridge, 1925–39.

—*The Heroic Age.* Cambridge, 1912.

CHADWICK, J. *The Greek Dialects and Greek Pre-History,* GR 3.1.

CHAMOUX, F. *Cyrène sous la monarchie des Battiades.* Paris, 1953.

CHANTRAINE, P. *Grammaire homérique.* Paris, 1942.

—*Études sur le vocabulaire grec.* Paris, 1956.

—*Morphologie historique du grec.* Paris, 1945.

CHAPOUTHIER, F. (and others). *Fouilles exécutées à Mallia (Rapports 1, 2, 3).* Paris, 1928–42.

CHILDE, V. G. *The Aryans.* London, 1926.

—*The Bronze Age.* Cambridge, 1930.

—*The Bronze Age.* PP 12.

—*The Date and Origin of Minyan Ware.* JHS 35.

—*The Dawn of European Civilization.* 6 ed. London, 1957.

—*History.* London, 1947.

—*Piecing Together the Past.* London, 1956.

—*The Prehistory of European Society.* London, 1958.

—*Progress and Archaeology.* London, 1944.

CHISHULL, E. *Antiquitates Asiaticae.* London, 1728.

CHRIMES, K. M. T. *Ancient Sparta.* Manchester, 1949.

CLARK, G. *From Savagery to Civilisation.* London, 1946.

CLARK, R. T. RUNDLE. *Myth and Symbol in Ancient Egypt.* London, 1959.

COHEN, R. *La Grèce et l'hellénisation du monde antique.* 2 ed. Paris, 1939.

COLLINGWOOD, R. G. *The Idea of History.* Oxford, 1946.

COMPARETTI, D. *Le leggi di Gortyna e le altre iscrizioni arcaiche cretesi edite ed illustrate.* MA 3.

COOK, A. B. *Zeus.* Cambridge, 1914–40.

—*Who Was the Wife of Zeus?* CR 20.

—*Zeus, Jupiter and the Oak.* CR 17.

COOK, S. A. *The Religion of Ancient Palestine in the Light of Archaeology.* London, 1930.

BIBLIOGRAPHY

CORNFORD, F. M. *The* Ἀπαρχαί *and the Eleusinian Mysteries* in Quiggin 153.
—*The Origin of the Olympic Games* in Harrison, T. 212.
—*Principium Sapientiae.* Cambridge, 1952.
CORTSEN, S. P. *Die Lemnische Inschrift, Gl.* 18.
CROISET, A. and M. *Histoire de la littérature grecque.* 3 ed. Paris, 1901-21.
DAREMBERG, C., and SAGLIO, E. *Dictionnaire des antiquités grecques et romaines.*
Paris, 1877-1919.
DAWKINS, R. M. *The Sanctuary of Artemis Orthia at Sparta.* London, 1929.
DE SANCTIS, G. *Storia dei Greci dalle origini alla fine del secolo V.* Florence, 1939.
DEITERS, P. *De Cretensium titulis publicis quaestiones epigraphicae.* Diss. Jena,
1904.
DEMARGNE, P. *La Crète dédalique.* Paris, 1947.
DEMETRAKOS, D. *Μέγα λεξικὸν τῆς ἑλληνικῆς γλώσσης.* Athens, 1936-.
DESBOROUGH, V. R. D'A. *Protogeometric Pottery.* Oxford, 1952.
DEUBNER, L. *Attische Feste.* Berlin, 1932.
DIAMOND, A. S. *Primitive Law.* 2 ed. London, 1950.
—*The Evolution of Law and Order.* London, 1951.
DIETERICH, A. *Mutter Erde.* Leipzig/Berlin, 1905.
DIKAIOS, P. *The Excavations at Vounous-Bellapais in Cyprus, 1931-2. Arc.* 88.
DODDS, E. R. *The Greeks and the Irrational.* Oxford, 1951.
DUNBABIN, T. J. *The Greeks and their Eastern Neighbours.* London, 1957.
DURKHEIM, E. *Les formes élémentaires de la vie religieuse.* 2 ed. Paris, 1912.
EARTHY, E. D. *Valenge Women.* Oxford, 1933.
EDELSTEIN, E. J. and L. *Asclepius: A Collection and Interpretation of the Testi-
monies.* Baltimore, 1945.
EGGER, A. E. *Études historiques sur les traités publics.* 2 ed. Paris, 1866.
EHRENBERG, V. *The Greek State.* Oxford, 1960.
ELDERKIN, G. W. *The Marriage of Zeus and Hera.* AJA 41.
ELDERKIN, K. M. *Jointed Dolls in Antiquity.* AJA 34.
ENGNELL, I. *Studies in Divine Kingship in the Ancient Near East.* Uppsala, 1943.
EVANS, A. J. *Knossos Excavations, 1903.* ABSA 9.
—*The Mycenaean Tree and Pillar Cult.* JHS 21.
—*The Palace of Minos.* London, 1921-35.
—*Shaft Graves and Beehive Tombs of Mycenae.* London, 1929.
—*The Ring of Nestor.* JHS 45.
FARNELL, G. S. *Greek Lyric Poetry.* London, 1891.
FARNELL, L. R. *Cults of the Greek States.* Oxford, 1896-1909.
—*Greek Hero Cults.* Oxford, 1921.
FAURE, P. *Grottes crétoises.* BCH 80.
—*Nouvelles recherches de spéléologie et de topographie crétoises.* BCH 84.
—*Spéléologie et topographie crétoises.* BCH 82.
FICK, A. *Hattiden und Danubier in Griechenland.* Göttingen, 1909.
—*Vorgriechische Ortsnamen als Quelle für die Vorgeschichte Griechenlands.* Göt-
tingen, 1905.
FINLEY, M. I. *The World of Odysseus.* London, 1956.
FONTENROSE, J. *Python.* Berkeley/Los Angeles, 1959.
FORMAN, W. and B., and POULÍK, J. *Prehistoric Art.* London, 1955.
FORREST, G. *The First Sacred War,* BCH 80.
FORSDYKE, J. *Greece before Homer.* London, 1956.

—*Minos of Crete.* JWCI 15.
—*The Pottery called Minyan Ware.* JHS 34.
FOTHERINGHAM, J. K. *Cleostratus.* JHS 39.
FRANKFORT, H. *Cylinder Seals.* London, 1939.
—*Kingship and the Gods.* Chicago, 1948.
FRAZER, J. G. *Apollodorus.* London 1921.
—*Folklore and the Old Testament.* London, 1919.
—*Lectures on the Early History of the Kingship.* London, 1905.
—*Pausanias's Description of Greece.* London, 1898.
—*The Golden Bough.* London, 1923–7.
—*The Prytaneum, The Temple of Vesta, The Vestals, Perpetual Fires.* JP 14.
—*Totemica.* London, 1937.
—*Totemism and Exogamy.* London, 1910.
FRÖDIN, O., and PERSSON, A. W. *Asine.* Stockholm, 1938.
FROST, K. T. *The Critias and Minoan Crete.* JHS 33.
FURTWÄNGLER, A. *Aegina. Das Heiligtum der Aphaia.* Munich, 1906.
GARDNER, P. *The Types of Greek Coins.* Cambridge, 1883.
GEMOLL, A. *Das Recht von Gortyn.* Striegau, 1889.
GLOTZ, G. *La civilisation égéenne.* Paris, 1923. *Aegean Civilisation.* London, 1926.
—*La cité grecque.* Paris, 1928
GORDON, C. H. *Ugaritic Handbook.* Rome, 1947.
—*Ugaritic Literature.* Rome, 1949.
—*Ugaritic Manual.* Rome, 1955.
GROENEWEGEN-FRANKFORT, H. A. *Arrest and Movement.* Chicago, 1951.
GRUMACH, E. *Bemerkungen zu M. Ventris-J. Chadwick, Evidence for Greek Dialect in the Mycenaean Archives.* OL 52.7/8.
—(ed.) *Minoica.* Berlin, 1958.
GRUPPE, O. *Griechische Mythologie und Religionsgeschichte.* Munich, 1906.
GUARDUCCI, M. *Note sul calendario cretese, Epigraphica* 7.72.
GUIRAUD, P. *La propriété foncière en Grèce jusqu'à la conquête romaine.* Paris, 1893.
GURNEY, O. R. *The Hittites.* London, 1952.
GUTHRIE, W. K. C. *Early Greek Religion in the Light of the Decipherment of Linear B.* BICS 6.
—*Orpheus and Greek Religion.* 2 ed. London, 1952.
—*The Greeks and their Gods.* London, 1950.
HALBHERR, F. *Cretan Expedition.* AJA 9 (1894), 11 (1896), 1 (1897), 2 (1898), 5 (1901).
—*Iscrizioni cretesi, Mus. It.* 3.
—and COMPARETTI, D. *Epigrafi arcaiche di varie città cretesi, Mus. It.* 2.
—and FABRICIUS, E. *Leggi antiche della città di Gortyna.* Florence, 1885.
HALEY, J. B. *The Coming of the Greeks.* AJA 32.
HALL, H. R. *The Civilisation of Greece in the Bronze Age.* London, 1928.
HALLIDAY, W. R. *The Hybristika.* ABSA 16.
HAMMOND, N. G. L. *A History of Greece.* Oxford, 1959.
HANSEN, H. D. *Early Civilisation in Thessaly.* Baltimore, 1933.
HARRIS, J. R. *Boanerges.* Cambridge, 1913.
—*The Origin of the Cult of Hermes.* Manchester, 1929.
HARRISON, J. E. *Myths of the Odyssey.* London, 1882.

BIBLIOGRAPHY

—*Prolegomena to the Study of Greek Religion*. 3 ed. Cambridge, 1922.
—*Primitive Hero Worship*. CR 6.474, 7.74.
—*Sophocles' Ichneutae and the Dromena of Kyllene and the Satyrs*. Quiggin 136.
—*The Kouretes and Zeus Kouros*. ABSA 15.
—*Themis*. 2 ed. Cambridge, 1927.
HARTLAND, E. S. *Primitive Paternity*. London, 1909–10.
HASEBROEK, J. *Staat und Handel in alten Griechenland*. Tübingen, 1928. *Trade and Politics in Ancient Greece*. London, 1933.
HASLUCK, F. W. *Cyzicus*. Cambridge, 1910.
HASTINGS, J. *Encyclopaedia of Ethics and Religion*. Edinburgh, 1908–18.
HAWES, MRS. H. A. (BOYD). *Excavations at Gournia, Crete* (By Harriet A. Boyd). Washington, 1908.
HAWKES, C. F. C. *The Prehistoric Foundations of Europe*. London, 1940.
HAZZIDAKIS, J. *Tylissos à l'époque minoenne*. Paris, 1921.
HEAD, B. V. *Historia Numorum*. 2 ed. Oxford, 1911.
HEICHELHEIM, F. *Wirtschaftsgeschichte des Altertums*. Leiden, 1939. *An Ancient Economic History I*. Leiden, 1958.
HEURTLEY, W. A. *Prehistoric Macedonia*. Cambridge, 1939.
HOBHOUSE, L. T. *The Simplest Peoples*. BJS 7.2.
—WHEELER, G. C., and GINSBERG, T. *Material Culture and Social Institutions of the Simpler Peoples*. London, 1930.
HOCART, A. M. *Kingship*. Oxford, 1927.
HOECK, A. *Kreta*. Göttingen, 1823–9.
HOLLIS, A. C. *The Masai, their Language and Folklore*. Oxford, 1905.
—*The Nandi, their Language and Folklore*. Oxford, 1909.
HOMOLLE, T. *Comptes des hiéropes du temple d'Apollon délien*. BCH 6.
HOOKE, S. H. (editor). *The Labyrinth*. London, 1935.
—*Myth and Ritual*. Oxford, 1933.
—*Myth, Ritual and Kingship*. Oxford, 1958.
HOW, W. W., and WELLS, J. *A Commentary on Herodotus*. 2 ed. Oxford, 1928.
JARDÉ, A. *Les céréales dans l'antiquité grecque I*. Paris, 1925.
JEANMAIRE, H. *Couroi et Courètes*. Lille, 1939.
—*Dionysos*. Paris, 1951.
—*La cryptie lacédémonienne*. REG. 26.
JEFFERY, L. H. *The Local Scripts of Archaic Greece*. Oxford, 1961.
JUNOD, H. A. *The Bantu Heritage*. Johannesburg, 1938.
—*Life of a South African Tribe*. 2 ed. London, 1927.
KAHRSTEDT, U. *Griechisches Staatsrecht I*. Göttingen, 1922.
KANTOR, H. J. *The Aegean and the Orient in the Second Millennium B.C.* Bloomington, 1947.
KARSTEN, R. *The Civilisation of the South American Indians*. London, 1926.
KAZAMANOVA, L. N. *Rabovladenie na Krite v VI–IV vv. do n.e.* VDI 3 (40).
KENNA, V. E. G. *Cretan Seals*. Oxford, 1960.
KIRCHHOFF, A. *Studien zur Geschichte des griechischen Alphabets*. 4 ed. Gütersloh, 1887.
KIRSTEN, E. *Die Insel Kreta im fünften und vierten Jahrundert*. Diss. Leipzig, 1936.
KLINGENDER, F. D. *Palaeolithic Religion and the Principle of Social Evolution*. BJS 5.2.
KOHLER, J., and ZIEBARTH, E. *Das Stadtrecht von Gortyn*. Göttingen, 1912.

KOVALEVSKY, M. M. *Tableau des origines de l'évolution de la famille et de la propriété.* Stockholm, 1890.

KRETSCHMER, P. *Einleitung zur Geschichte der griechischen Sprache.* Göttingen, 1896.

—*Die Stellung der lykischen Sprache Gl.* 27.256, 28.101.

—*Mythische Namen Gl.* 8.

KRIGE, E. J. *Social System of the Zulus.* London, 1936.

—and KRIGE, J. D. *The Realm of a Rain-Queen.* London, 1943.

KUBITSCHEK, W. *Grundriss der Antiken Zeitrechnung: Handb. der Altertumswissenschaft.* I, t. VII. München, 1927.

—*Die Kalenderbücher von Florenz, Rom und Leyden, Wiener Denkschr.* Bd. 57. Abh. 2.

KUNZE, E. *Kretische Bronzereliefs.* Stuttgart, 1931.

LANDTMAN, G. *Origin of the Inequality of the Social Classes.* London, 1938.

LANGDON, S. *The Babylonian Epic of Creation.* Oxford, 1923.

—*Babylonian Menologies and Semitic Calendars.* London, 1935.

LARSEN, J. A. O. *Perioeci in Crete.* CP 31.

LAYARD, J. *Stone Men of Malekula.* London, 1942.

LEAF, W. *Homer and History.* London, 1915.

LEGRAND, E. *Descriptions des îles de l'Archipel par Christophe Buondelmonti.* Paris, 1897.

LEJEUNE, M. *Traité de phonétique grecque.* Paris, 1947.

LEKATSAS, P. Ἡ Ψυχή. Athens, 1957.

LETHABY, W. R. *The Earlier Temple of Artemis at Ephesus.* JHS 37.

LEVI, D. *Gli scavi del 1954 sull'acropoli di Gortina, Annuario. 1955–6.*

—*Gleanings from Crete.* AJA 49.

LILLEY, S. *Men, Machines and History.* London, 1948.

LLOYD, S. *Early Anatolia.* London, 1956.

LORIMER, H. L. *Homer and the Monuments.* London, 1950.

LOWIE, R. H. *Primitive Society.* New York, 1929.

MAINE, H. J. S. *Dissertations on Early Law and Custom.* London, 1883.

MAIURI, A. *Il calendario cretese.* RL 19.

—*Studi sull'onomastica cretese.* RL 19–20.

MARINATOS, S. *The Cult of the Cretan Caves.* RR 5.

MASON, O. T. *Woman's Share in Primitive Culture.* London, 1895.

MATZ, F. (ed.) *Forschungen auf Kreta 1942.* Berlin, 1951.

—*Frühkretische Siegel.* Berlin, 1928.

—*Kreta, Mykene, Troja.* Stuttgart, 1956.

MEILLET, A. *Aperçu d'une histoire de la langue grecque.* 4 ed. Paris, 1935.

—*Introduction à l'étude comparative des langues indo-européennes.* 8 ed. Paris, 1937.

—and VENDRYES, J. *Grammaire comparée des langues classiques.* 2 ed. Paris, 1927.

MEISTER, K. *Der syntaktische Gebrauch des Genetivs in den Kretischen Dialektinschriften. Indogerman. Forsch.* 18.

MENDELSOHN, I. *Slavery in the Ancient Near East.* New York, 1949.

MENSIGNAC, DE C. *Recherches ethnographiques sur la salive et le crachat.* Bordeaux, 1892.

MERRIAM, A. C. *Law Code of the Kretan Gortyna.* AJA 1 (1885) and 2 (1886).

MEYER, E. *Geschichte des Altertums.* 2 ed. Stuttgart, 1937.

MICHELL, H. *Economics of Ancient Greece.* 2 ed. Cambridge, 1957.

BIBLIOGRAPHY

MICHELL, H. *Sparta*. Cambridge, 1952.
MOMMSEN, A. *Feste der Stadt Athen*. Leipzig, 1898.
MORGAN, L. H. *Ancient Society*. 2 ed. Chicago, 1910.
MORROW, G. R. *Plato's Cretan City*. Princeton, 1960.
MÜLLER, K. *Frühmykenische Reliefs* in *Jahrb*. 30 (1915).
MÜLLER, K. O. *Die Dorier*. 2 ed. Breslau, 1844. *The History and Antiquities of the Doric Race*. Oxford, 1830.
—*Orchomenos und die Minyer*. 2 ed. Breslau, 1844.
—*Prolegomena zu einer wissenschaftlichen Mythologie*. Göttingen, 1825.
MURRAY, G. *The Hymn of the Kouretes*. ABSA 15.
—*The Rise of the Greek Epic*. 3 ed. Oxford, 1924.
MUTTELSEE, M. *Zur Verfassungsgeschichte Kretas im Zeitalter des Hellenismus*. Diss. Hamburg, 1925.
MYLONAS, G. E. *Ancient Mycenae*. London, 1957.
MYRES, J. L. *Homer and his Critics*. London, 1958.
—*Who were the Greeks?* Berkeley, 1930.
NEUGEBAUER, O. *The Exact Sciences in Antiquity*. Princeton, 1952.
NILSSON, M. P. *Das frühe Griechenland von innen gesehen*. Hist. 3.3.
—*Die Entstehung und Religiöse Bedeutung des griechischen Kalenders*. Lunds Universitets Årsskrift. N.F. Aud. 1, 14.21. Lund, 1918.
—*Die Grundlagen des spartanischen Lebens*. K 12.
—*Geschichte der griechischen Religion*. Munich, 1941–50.
—*Greek Piety*. Oxford, 1948.
—*Greek Popular Religion*. New York, 1940.
—*Griechische Feste von religiöser Bedeutung mit Ausschluss der attischen*. Darmstadt, 1957.
—*History of Greek Religion*. 2 ed. Oxford, 1949.
—*Homer and Mycenae*. London, 1933.
—*Minoan-Mycenaean Religion*. 2 ed. Lund, 1950.
—*Mycenaean Origin of Greek Mythology*. London, 1932.
—*Opuscula Selecta* 1–2. Lund, 1951–2.
—*Primitive Time Reckoning*. Lund/Oxford, 1920.
—*Sonnenkalendar und Sonnenreligion*, Arch. f. Religionswiss. 30.
—*Studia de Dionysiis Atticis*. Lund, 1900.
—*The New Inscriptions of the Salaminioi*. AJP 59.
OVERBECK, J. *Die antiken Schriftquellen z. Geschichte d. bildunden Künste bei d. Griechen*. Leipzig, 1868.
PAGE, D. L. *History and the Homeric Iliad*. Berkeley/Los Angeles, 1959.
PALMER, L. R. *Achaeans and Indo-Europeans*. Oxford, 1955.
PARKE, H. W., and WORMELL, D. E. W. *The Delphic Oracle*. Oxford, 1956.
PARKER, R. A. *The Calendars of Ancient Egypt*. Chicago, 1953.
PASHLEY, R. *Travels in Crete*. Cambridge/London, 1837.
PAULY, A., WISSOWA, G., and KROLL, W. *Realencyclopädie der classischen Altertumswissenschaft*. Stuttgart. 1894–.
PENDLEBURY, J. D. S. *Archaeology of Crete*. London, 1939.
PERNIER, L., and BANTI, L. *Il palazzo minoico di Festos*. Rome, 1935–51.
PERSSON, A. W. *Der Ursprung der eleusinischen Mysterien*. Arch. f. Religionswiss. 21.
—*The Religion of Greece in Prehistoric Times*. Berkeley/Los Angeles, 1942.
PFUHL, E. *Malerei und Zeichnung der Griechen*. Munich, 1923.

BIBLIOGRAPHY

PICARD, C. *Ephèse et Claros*. Paris, 1922.
—*Les Origines du Polythéisme Hellénique*. Paris, 1930.
—*Les Religions Préhelléniques*. Paris, 1948.
—*Sur la patrie et les pérégrinations de Déméter*. REG 40.
PICKARD-CAMBRIDGE, A. *Dithyramb, Tragedy and Comedy*. Oxford, 1927.
—*The Dramatic Festivals of Athens*. Oxford, 1953.
POLITES, N. G. Παραδώσεις τοῦ ἑλληνικοῦ λαοῦ. Athens, 1904.
—Παροιμίαι. Athens, 1899–1902.
PRELLER, L. VON. *Griechische Mythologie*. 4 ed. by C. Robert. Berlin, 1887–1926.
PRITCHARD, J. B. (ed.). *Ancient Near Eastern Texts*. Princeton, 1950.
Proceedings of the Second International Congress of Classical Studies. Copenhagen, 1958.
QUIGGIN, E. C. *Essays and Studies Presented to William Ridgeway*. Cambridge, 1913.
RANSOME, H. M. *The Sacred Bee*. London, 1937.
REICHEL, A. *Die Stierspiele in der kretisch-mykenischen Cultur*. AM 34.
RIDGEWAY, W. *The Early Age of Greece*. Cambridge, 1901–31.
RIVERS, W. H. R. *Kinship and Social Organisation*. London, 1932.
ROBERT, C. *Sosipolis in Olympia*. AM 18.
ROBERT, L. *Les Asklepieis de l'Archipel*. REG 46.
ROBERTSON SMITH, W. *Religion of the Semites*. 3 ed. London, 1927.
RODENWALDT, G. *Tiryns*. Athens, 1912.
ROHDE, E. *Psyche: Seelencult und Unsterblichkeitsglaube der Griechen*. Freiburg, 1898.
ROSCHER, W. H. *Ausführliches Lexicon der griechischen und römischen Mythologie*. Leipzig, 1884–1937.
—*Selene und Verwandtes*. Leipzig, 1890.
ROSCOE, J. *The Baganda*. London, 1911.
—*The Bagesu and Other Tribes of the Uganda Protectorate*. Cambridge, 1924.
—*The Bakitara or Banyoro*. Cambridge, 1923.
ROSE, H. J. *Primitive Culture in Greece*. London, 1925.
—*Handbook of Greek Mythology*. 5 ed. London, 1953.
ROSTOVTZEFF, M. *A History of the Ancient World I*. 2 ed. Oxford, 1930.
—*The Social and Economic History of the Hellenistic World*. 2 ed. Oxford, 1957.
ROUSE, W. H. D. *Greek Votive Offerings*. Cambridge, 1902.
SCHAEFFER, C. F. A. *Cuneiform Texts of Ras Shamra*. London, 1939.
SEAGER, R. B. *Excavations on the Island of Pseira, Crete*. Boston/New York, 1912.
—*Explorations in the Island of Mochlos*. Philadelphia, 1910.
SEEBOHM, H. E. *The Structure of Greek Tribal Society*. London, 1895.
SELTMAN, C. *Greek Coins*. 2 ed. London, 1955.
—*Masterpieces of Greek Coinage*. Oxford, 1949.
SEMENOFF, A. *Antiquitates iuris publici Cretensium*. Petrograd, 1893.
SHREWSBURY, J. F. D. *The Plague of the Philistines*. JH 47.
SINCLAIR, T. A. *Hesiod, Works and Days*. London, 1932.
SINGER, C., HOLMYARD, E. J., HALL, A. R., and WILLIAMS, T. I. (editors). *A History of Technology*. 1–2. Oxford, 1954–6.
SPRATT, T. A. B. *Travels and Researches in Crete*. London, 1865.
STUBBINGS, F. H. *Mycenaean Pottery from the Levant*. Cambridge, 1951.

BIBLIOGRAPHY

SVORONOS, J. N. *Numismatique de la Crète ancienne*. Macon, 1890.
SWINDLER, M. H. *Cretan elements in the Cults and Ritual of Apollo*. Bryn Mawr, 1913.
SWOBODA, H. *Lehrbuch der griechischen Staatsaltertümer*. 6 ed. Tübingen, 1913.
TARN, W. W., and GRIFFITH, G. T. *Hellenistic Civilisation*. 3 ed. London, 1952.
TAYLOR, A. E. *The Laws of Plato*. London, 1934.
THIEL, J. H. *De Feminarum apud Dores condicione*. M 57.
THOMPSON, J. E. S. *The Rise and Fall of Maya Civilization*. London, 1956.
THOMSON, G. *Aeschylus and Athens*. 2 ed. London, 1946.
—*Aeschylus, Oresteia*. Cambridge, 1938.
—*Aeschylus, Prometheus Bound*. Cambridge, 1932.
—*From Religion to Philosophy*. JHS 73.
—*Studies in Ancient Greek Society*. 1: *The Prehistoric Aegean*. 2 ed. London, 1954.
2: *The First Philosophers*. London, 1955.
—*The Greek Calendar*. JHS 63.
—*The Greek Language*. Cambridge, 1960.
—*The Wheel and the Crown*. CR 59.
THOMSON, J. A. K. *Studies in the Odyssey*. Oxford, 1914.
THUMB, A. *Handbuch der griechischen Dialekte*. 2te Auflage von E. Kieckers. Heidelberg, 1932.
THURNWALD, R. *Economics in Primitive Communities*. London, 1932.
TOD, M. N. *Teams of Ball-Players at Sparta*. ABSA 10.
TOMBE, F., and DUBUC, G. *Le Centre Préhistorique de Ganties-Montespan: Archives de l'Institut de Paléontologie Humaine, Mémore 22*. Paris, 1947.
TREVOR-BATTYE, A. *Camping in Crete*. London, 1913.
TRISP, A. *Die Fragmente der griechischen Kultschriftsteller*. Geisen, 1914.
TRITSCH, F. J. *Die Agora von Elis und die altgriechische Agora. Jahresh. 27*.
—*Die Stadtbildungen des Altertums und die griechische Polis*. K 22.
—*Lycian, Luwian and Hittite. Symbolae Hrozny, Pt. 3. Archiv Orientální. 18.1–2*.
TYLOR, E. B. *Primitive Culture*. 3 ed. London, 1891.
VAN DER MIJNSBRUGGE, M. *The Cretan Koinon*. New York, 1931.
VAN DER POST, L. *The Lost World of the Kalahari*. London, 1958.
VAN EFFENTERRE, H. *À propos du serment des Drériens*. BCH 61.
—*Inscriptions archaïques crétoises*. BCH 70.
—*La Crète et le monde grec de Platon à Polybe*. Paris, 1948.
VAN GENNEP, A. *L'état actuel du problème totémique*. Paris, 1920.
—*Les rites de passage*. Paris. 1909.
VENTRIS, M., and CHADWICK, J. *Documents in Mycenaean Greek*. Cambridge, 1956.
—*Evidence for Greek Dialect in the Mycenaean Archives*. JHS 73.
VOLLGRAFF, W. *Inscription d'Argos (Traité entre Knossos et Tylissos)*. BCH 37.
VON HAGEN, V. W. *The Incas of Pedro de Cieza de León*. Oklahoma, 1959.
WACE, A. J. B. *A Cretan Statuette in the Fitzwilliam Museum*. Cambridge, 1927.
—*Chamber Tombs of Mycenae*. Arc. 82.
—*Excavations at Mycenae*. ABSA 25.
—*Mycenae*. Princeton, 1949.
—*Mycenae, Ant. 10.*
—*Mycenae 1939*. JHS 59.
—*The Treasury of Atreus, Ant. 14.*

BIBLIOGRAPHY

WACKERNAGEL, J. *Sprachliche Untersuchungen zu Homer, Gl.* 7
WADE-GERY, H. T. *The Poet of the Iliad.* Cambridge, 1952.
WEBSTER, H. *Primitive Secret Societies.* 2 ed. New York, 1932.
WELCKER, F. G. *Kleine schriften.* Bonn, 1844–67.
—*Griechische Götterlehre.* Göttingen, 1857–63.
WESTERMARCK, E. A. *Origin and Development of Moral Ideas.* London, 1906–8.
—*The History of Human Marriage.* 5 ed. London, 1921.
WIDE, S. *Lakonische Kulte.* Leipzig, 1893.
WIDENGREN, G. *The King and the Tree of Life in Ancient Near Eastern Religion.* Uppsala Universitets Årsskrift, 1951–4.
WILAMOWITZ–MOELLENDORFF, U VON. *Der Glaube der Hellenen.* Berlin, 1931–2.
WILLETTS, R. F. *Aristocratic Society in Ancient Crete.* London, 1955.
—*A Neotas at Dreros?* H 85.3.
—*Cretan Eileithyia.* CQ 8.3–4.
—*Europa.* E 1.
—*Καρποδαῖσται. Philol.* 105. 1/2.
—*Some Elements of Continuity in the Social Life of Ancient Crete.* IRSH 2.3.
—*The Myth of Glaukos and the Cycle of Birth and Death.* K 37.
—*The Neodamodeis.* CP 49.
—*The Servile Interregnum at Argos.* H 87.4.
WOOLLEY, L. *A Forgotten Kingdom.* London, 1953.
WU TA-K'UN. *An Interpretation of Chinese Economic History.* PP 1.1.
XANTHOUDIDES, S. A. *The Vaulted Tombs of Mesara.* London, 1924.
ZANOTTI-BIANCO, U. *Archaeological Discoveries in Sicily and Magna Graecia.* JHS 57.
ZERVOS, C. *L'Art de la Crète.* Paris, 1956.

EPIGRAPHICAL PUBLICATIONS

CIG   A. Böckh, *Corpus Inscriptionum Graecarum.* Berlin, 1827–77.
Delphinion   A Rehm, *Das Delphinion in Milet,* in *Milet: Ergebnisse der Ausgrabungen und Untersuchungen seit dem Jahre 1899,* III, 362–406. Berlin, 1914.
DHR   R. Dareste, B. Haussoullier, T. Reinach, *Recueil des inscriptions juridiques grecques.* 1 série, Paris, 1891–5; 2 série, Paris, 1898–1904.
Die Inschriften von Magnesia am Maeander, ed. O. Kern. Berlin, 1900.
F. Durrbach, *Choix d'Inscriptions de Délos.* Paris, 1921.
Heikel   I. A. Heikel, *Griechische Inschriften sprachlich erklärt.* Helsingfors, 1924.
Hicks-Hill   E. L. Hicks and G. F. Hill, *A Manual of Greek Historical Inscriptions.* Oxford, 1901.
IC   *Inscriptiones Creticae opera et consilio Friderici Halbherr collectae.* 1. *Tituli Cretae mediae praeter Gortynios.* Rome, 1935. 2. *Tituli Cretae Occidentalis.* Rome, 1939. 3. *Tituli Cretae Orientalis.* Rome, 1942. 4. *Tituli Gortynii.* Rome, 1950. *Curavit Margarita Guarducci.*

BIBLIOGRAPHY

IG   *Inscriptiones Graecae.* Berlin, 1873–.

IGA   H. Roehl, *Inscriptiones Graecae antiquissimae praeter Atticas in Attica repertas.* Berlin, 1882.

IGR   *Inscriptiones Graecae ad res Romanas pertinentes.* Paris, 1911–27.

IIGA   H. Roehl, *Imagines inscriptionum Graecarum antiquissimarum.* 3 ed. Berlin, 1907.

IPE   *Inscriptiones orae septentrionalis Ponti Euxini,* ed. B. Latyshev. Petersburg, 1885–1901: I² = vol. i, 2 ed., 1916.

Inscr. Cos.   *The Inscriptions of Cos,* ed. W. R. Paton and E. L. Hicks. Oxford, 1891.

Inscr. Perg.   *Die Inschriften von Pergamon,* in *Altertümer von Pergamon* viii, ed. M. Fraenkel. Berlin, 1890–5.

MAMA   *Monumenta Asiae Minoris Antiqua.* Manchester/London, 1928–.

Michel   C. Michel, *Recueil d'inscriptions grecques.* Paris/Brussels, 1900–27.

OGI   *Orientis Graeci Inscriptiones Selectae,* ed. W. Dittenberger. Leipzig, 1903–5.

Roberts   E. S. Roberts, *An Introduction to Greek Epigraphy,* I. Cambridge, 1887.

Schwyzer   E. Schwyzer, *Dialectorum Graecarum exempla epigraphica potiora* (3 ed. of P. Cauer's *Delectus inscriptionum Graecarum propter dialectum memorabilium*). Leipzig, 1923.

SGDI   *Sammlung der griechischen Dialekt-Inschriften,* ed. H. Collitz, F. Bechtel, O. Hoffmann. Göttingen, 1884–1915.

SIG   *Sylloge Inscriptionum Graecarum,* ed. W. Dittenberger. 3 ed. Leipzig, 1915–24.

Solmsen   F. Solmsen, *Inscriptiones Graecae ad inlustrandas dialectos selectae* (4 ed. by E. Fraenkel). Leipzig, 1930.

Tod   M. N. Tod, *Greek Historical Inscriptions.* I., to the end of the fifth century B.C. 2 ed. Oxford, 1946. II, from 403 to 323 B.C. Oxford, 1948.

PERIODICALS

ABSA   *Annual of the British School at Athens.* London, 1894–.

AJA   *American Journal of Archaeology.* v.p. 1885–.

AM   *Mitteilungen des deutschen archäologischen Instituts, Athenishe Abteilung.* 1876–.

Ann. Ép.   *L'Année épigraphique,* published in *Revue Archéologique.*

Annuario   *Annuario della regia Scuola Archeologica di Atene.* 1914–.

Ant.   *Antiquity.* London, 1926–.

Arc.   *Archaeologia.* London, 1770–.

Arch. Anz.   *Archäologischer Anzeiger,* in *Jahrbuch des (kaiserlich) deutschen archäologischen Instituts.* 1886–.

Ἀρχ. Δελτ.   Ἀρχαιολογικὸν Δελτίον. Athens, 1915–.

Ἀρχ. Ἐφ.   Ἀρχαιολογικὴ Ἐφημερίς. Athens, 1910–.

Arch. f.
Religionswiss. *Archiv für Religionswissenschaft.* Freiburg im Breisgau,
          1898–.
Archiv Orientální. Prague, 1929–.
Ausonia   *Ausonia, Rivista della Società italiana di archeologia e storia
          dell'arte.* 1906–.
BCH   *Bulletin de correspondance hellénique.* Paris, 1877–.
Berl. Sitzb. = *Sitzungersberichte der Preussischen Akademie der Wissenschaften.*
          Berlin, 1882–.
BICS   *Bulletin of the Institute of Classical Studies.* London, 1954–.
BJS   *British Journal of Sociology.* London, 1950–.
BSLP   *Bulletin de la société de linguistique de Paris.* Paris, 1869–.
CP   *Classical Philology.* Chicago, 1906–.
CQ   *Classical Quarterly.* London, 1907–.
CR   *Classical Review.* London, 1887–.
CRA   *Comptes rendus de l'Académie des Inscriptions et Belles-Lettres.*
          1857–.
E   *Eirene. Studia Graeca et Latina.* Prague, 1960–.
Epigraphica *Epigraphica. Rivista italiana di epigrafia.* Milan, 1938–.
ʾΈφ. ʾΑρΧ. ʾΕφημερὶς Ἀρχαιολογική, περίοδος τρίτη. Athens, 1893–1909.
Gl.   *Glotta.* Göttingen, 1907–.
GR   *Greece and Rome.* Oxford, 1931–.
H   *Hermes.* Berlin–Wiesbaden, 1866–.
Hesperia *Hesperia: Journal of the American School of Classical Studies at
          Athens.* Cambridge, Mass., 1932–.
Hist.   *Historia, studi storici per l'antichità classica.* Milan/Rome,
          1927–.
Indogerman. Forsch. *Indogermanische Forschungen.* Strassburg/Berlin, 1891–.
Iraq   London, 1934–.
IRSH   *International Review of Social History.* Assen/Netherlands,
          1956–.
Jahrb. *Jahrbuch des (kaiserlich) deutschen archäologischen Instituts.*
          1886–.
Jahresh. *Jahreshefte des österreichischen archäologischen Institutes.* Vienna,
          1898–.
JAOS   *Journal of the American Oriental Society.* New Haven, 1843–.
JCP   *Jahrbücher für classische Philologie.* Leipzig, 1855–.
JH   *The Journal of Hygiene.* Cambridge, 1901–.
JHS   *Journal of Hellenic Studies.* London, 1880–.
JP   *Journal of Philology.* London, 1868–1920.
JRAS   *Journal of the Royal Asiatic Society.* London, 1834–.
JWCI   *Journal of the Warburg and Courtauld Institutes.* London,
          1937–.
K   *Klio, Beiträge zur alten Geschichte.* Leipzig, 1901–.
Kerameikos *Kerameikos: ergebnisse der ausgrabungen.* Berlin, 1939–.
KK   *KPHTIKA XPONIKA.* Herakleion, 1946–.
M   *Mnemosyne.* Leiden, 1852–.
MA   *Monumenti antichi pubblicati per cura della Reale Accademia dei
          Lincei.* Rome–Milan, 1890–.

BIBLIOGRAPHY

Mus. It.	*Museo italiano di antichità classica.* Florence, 1885–90.
OL	*Orientalistische Literaturzeitung.* Leipzig, 1897–.
Philol.	*Philologus.* 1846.
PP	*Past and Present.* London, 1951–.
Praktika	Πρακτικα τῆς ἐν ᾿Αθήναις ἀρχαιολογικῆς ἑταιριάς.
RA	*Revue Archéologique.* Paris, 1844–.
REA	*Revue des études anciennes.* Bordeaux, 1930–.
REG	*Revue des études grecques.* Paris, 1888–.
Rev. Phil.	*Revue de Philologie.* Paris, 1877–.
RF	*Rivista di filologia e di istruzione classica.* Turin, 1873–.
RHR	*Revue de l'histoire des religions.* Paris, 1880–.
RIA	*Rivista del R. Instituto d'Archeologia e Storia dell'Arte.* Rome, 1929–.
Rivista di storia antica. Padua/Messina, 1895–1910.	
RL	*Rendiconti della Reale Accademia nazionale dei Lincei.* Rome, 1873–.
RM	*Rheinisches Museum für Philologie.* Frankfürt, 1842–.
RR	*Review of Religion.* New York, 1936–.
S	*Syria.* Paris, 1919–.
SK	*The Sacral Kingship.* (*Studies in the History of Religions IV*). Contributions to the Central Theme of the 8th International Congress for the History of Religions. Leiden, 1959.
VDI	Вестник Древней Истории. Moscow–Leningrad, 1947–.
Wiener Denkschr.	*Denkschriften der Akademie der Wissenschaften in Wien, Phil.-hist. Klasse.*
Wien. Sitz.	*Sitzungsberichte der (Kaiserlichen) Akademie der Wissenschaften in Wien, Phil.-hist. Klasse.* 1849–.
WS	*Wiener Studien.* 1879–.

I. Subject Index

Accounts 9, 35, 192
Administration 11, 30, 32–3, 40
Adoption 7
Aetiology 161, 197
Age-grades 44–7, 49, 65, 112, 175
Agela 41, 45, 65–6, 109, 112, 116–17, 125, 175, 179, 190–1, 201, 204–6, 214, 275, 307
Agon 109, 195, 205–6, 213, 307
Agora (*see also* Market-place) 234, 302, 305
Agoraios (*Agoraia*) 234
Agoranomoi 288
Agrianios 105–7
Agriculture 7–11, 14, 18–20, 24–5, 30, 33, 38, 42, 56–7, 63, 75, 78, 80, 92–3, 100, 102, 113, 148, 160, 166–7, 202, 306
Agyios 105–7, 259
Aigolioi 217
Aisymnetai 97–8
Alienation 41–2
Alliances 32, 107, 121, 153, 204, 263
Alphabet 12–13, 25, 41, 133, 153
Alphesiboiai 124
Altars 46, 50, 82, 113–14, 124, 144–5, 164, 186, 205, 210, 212, 222, 226, 234, 237, 249, 259, 263, 268, 299
Amber 9, 29, 270
Amyklaios 104–7, 261
Ancestors 6, 44, 56, 59, 63, 66, 78, 97, 116, 166, 197–8, 238, 277, 287
Anebos 47
Animals xi, 5–6, 19, 43–5, 55–7, 59–60, 70–5, 77–8, 84, 86–7, 100, 110–11, 142, 144–6, 151, 161–2, 164–6, 186, 205, 218, 222, 240, 257, 260, 266, 310, 312
Anoros 47
Anthropomorphism 68, 70, 74–5, 77, 79, 100, 163, 166, 218, 224, 238, 305

Apageloi 47
Apellaios 105–7, 258
Apetairoi 41
Aphanes 182
Apodromos 47, 202, 306
Apotheosis 90, 315
Aqueducts 26
Arabic 13
Archaeology 6, 9, 13, 15, 20, 23, 25, 27, 54, 67, 82, 88, 90, 94, 126, 141, 157, 210, 241, 268
Archaic period 144, 186, 190, 210, 249, 254, 258, 263–4
Architecture 17, 21–3, 29, 37, 45, 128, 210
Archon 49, 83, 97
Aristocracy ix, 39–42, 116, 297, 301, 304–6, 308, 311, 321–3
Arourai 31
Art xi, 16–17, 20, 24, 38, 55, 64, 76, 82, 85, 87, 89–90, 112, 128, 148, 167, 190, 209, 217, 224, 262, 309–11, 315
Artemision 49, 115
Artisans 9–11, 16, 26, 28, 32, 174
Asklapieia 225
Assembly 39, 46, 225, 234, 299, 305, 314
Atheism 300
Athletics 45, 47–8, 112, 186, 206, 306
Axes xi, 4–5, 8, 11, 43, 69–70, 73, 75, 82, 84, 114, 142–3, 145, 236, 240

Babylonian 13
Badys (*Wadys*) 283
Bakinthios (Hyakinthios) 105–6, 222
Barbarians 5, 7, 29, 35, 156, 319
Bards 119, 128
Barley 5, 113, 226
Basilai 49, 52
Basileus 49, 83

Batromios 50
Beads 9
Bee 44, 61, 66, 216–18, 257
Bee-keepers, 217
Bellows 10
Betarmones 98
Birds 43, 51, 57, 66, 71–5, 78, 101,
    144, 146, 152, 163, 177, 217, 236,
    245, 251, 278, 284, 312–15
Bison 55
Boedromion 49, 107, 170
Bondage 41
Bouagoi 45
Bouai 45, 112
Bouphonia 113–15
Boutypoi 114–15
Bow 80, 187, 191, 258, 261, 269–70,
    272–3, 313
Bracelets 85, 145
Brick 8, 17
Bridges 25–6
Bronze 9–11, 13, 18, 30, 32, 37–8,
    58, 84, 100–1, 113, 124, 127–8,
    142–6, 153, 177, 187, 210, 217, 222,
    248, 257–8, 263, 271, 274
— Age 3–4, 9–10, 13, 17–18, 25–6,
    30, 32, 36–8, 40–1, 54, 62, 69–70,
    75, 77, 81, 91–2, 101–2, 119, 133–5,
    146–7, 184, 190, 252, 275, 299, 301
Builders 11
Building 6, 17, 22, 25–6, 37, 110,
    147, 173, 209, 227, 249, 279, 284,
    302–4
Bull xi, 43–4, 49–50, 65, 71, 85–7,
    97, 99–103, 108–13, 115, 117–18,
    124, 144–5, 152–3, 156–7, 159–60,
    162–8, 177, 182, 205–6, 213,
    219–21, 238, 240–1, 248, 250, 253,
    303
Bull-games 112
Bureaucracy 30, 35–6, 303
Burials 8, 20–1, 56, 62, 126, 141–2,
    163

Calendar 44, 49–50, 78, 92–111,
    201–2, 221, 238, 254, 258–9, 261,
    264, 293, 299, 307
Capital 12, 26
Carnival 287

Carpenters 14, 16
Carts 10, 145
Carving 16, 114
Caste 16, 18–19, 31–2, 40, 299
Casting 10, 101, 144
Cats 78
Cattle 5, 7, 19, 40, 45, 56, 102,
    112–13, 115, 122, 125, 131, 163,
    167, 192, 212, 303, 321
Caves xi, 3, 20, 52, 55, 58–9, 73, 87,
    90, 115, 141–7, 149–50, 152, 169,
    172, 186, 209, 215–17, 235, 237,
    242–3, 252, 275–7, 288–9, 298
Cement 17
Centralization 23–4, 30, 32–3, 38, 40,
    75, 91–2, 118
Cereals 5, 7
Chariots 15, 30, 34–5, 90, 144
Childbirth 52, 58, 79, 160, 168–9,
    171, 175, 177, 284
Cire-perdue process 10–11, 101
Cities (*see* Towns)
Citizens 39–41, 46–9, 107–8, 115,
    174, 191, 200–2, 204, 206, 210,
    213–14, 233–4, 254, 261, 269, 298–
    300, 304–7
Citizenship 173, 176, 202, 285, 294,
    305–7
City-states 10, 13, 39, 41–2, 44–5, 54,
    60, 81, 83, 93, 104, 214, 234, 278,
    280–1, 297–308, 321
Civilization 3, 9, 13, 26, 35, 41, 75,
    82, 119, 128, 163
Clan 6–7, 12, 18–19, 21, 30, 40–4, 59,
    77–8, 111, 114, 117, 196–8, 270,
    272, 302, 305
Classes 10, 25–6, 31–3, 40–2, 174,
    297, 302, 304
Classical period x, 15, 48, 68, 71,
    205, 210, 234, 242, 260, 276,
    279
Classificatory system 6
Clay 4–5, 13, 15, 21–2, 55–7, 145,
    182
Climate 5, 22
Cloaks 45, 48, 65, 85–6, 221
Cloth 128
Clothes (*see* Dress)
Cock 177–8, 250–1

Coinage 41, 43, 71, 103, 115, 149–50, 152–3, 167–8, 171, 177, 180, 187, 190–1, 193, 195, 207, 220–1, 231–3, 235, 238, 243, 246, 249, 251, 253–60, 262, 270–6, 278–9, 287–8, 290
Colonization 35, 88, 207, 244, 247, 250, 254, 273, 282, 284, 298, 304
Columns 17, 22–3, 27, 68–9, 73, 142, 145
Combs 16
Commerce (see Trade)
Commodities 10, 24–6, 29, 192
Communications 28, 35
Comparative methods x, 30, 117
Compasses 101
Confederacy 39
Conquest 31–2, 40, 136, 154
Copper 4, 6, 8, 10–11, 14, 25, 243
Coppersmiths 8
Corn 19–20, 70, 102, 128, 131, 149–51, 163, 212
Corn-Spirit 150
Cornucopia 52
Coronation 117, 176
Cosmetics 11
Council 39, 83
Cow 60, 62, 64–6, 100, 102, 110–12, 115, 117, 144, 156, 163–5, 177, 209, 239, 253, 273
Cowherds 31, 166, 239, 321
Crafts 9, 15–16, 18, 32, 37, 124, 278
Craftsmen 8, 11, 15–18, 21, 25, 28, 32–3, 36
Crane Dance 50, 96, 124, 263
Crocus sativus 15
Crops 5, 58–9, 67, 70, 80–1, 102, 112–13, 148, 152, 160, 163, 165, 202, 214, 269, 303, 307
Crown 49, 90, 160, 188–90, 201, 220, 253, 255, 266
Cuckoo 51
Cultivation 5–8, 19, 41, 59, 69–70, 102, 197, 201, 211
Cultivators 7, 26, 31–3, 40–1, 56, 74
Cuneiform 12
Curse 197–8, 234, 245
Cymbals 144

Daemons xi, 98, 245
Daitroi 114
Dances xi, 45–6, 50, 55–6, 58, 75, 79, 96–8, 102–3, 111–13, 116, 123–6, 186, 189, 193, 196–7, 213, 216–17, 263, 277, 299, 308–11, 318
Daphnaphoria 96
Decentralization 30, 37
Decrees 171, 188, 208–9, 225, 243, 246, 248–9, 258, 261, 263, 269, 279, 281, 286, 290
Deification 91
Delphinios 105–7, 264
Delphis 262
Democracy 42, 196, 278, 308–9, 322
Descent 6, 59
— matrilineal 7, 20, 56, 77, 79–80, 166
— patrilineal 7, 20, 166
Desert 5, 162
Despotism 83, 91, 118, 320
Dew 178, 285
Dialects 12, 154, 260, 323
Diasia 245
Didymeia 264
Diktynnaois 104, 106, 188
Diktyon 181–2
Dionysia 104, 109, 202–5
Dionysios 104, 106, 221
Dipolieia 113
Dirge 189
Diseases 198, 227
Disks 13–14, 23, 102, 270
Dithyramb 113, 213
Divination 60–1, 64
Divorce 40
Dogs 72, 144–5, 191–2, 248–9, 270, 272, 276
Dolphin 84, 262
Doric 39, 106, 171, 173, 258
Dove 43, 71–2, 78, 144, 146, 216, 284, 312–13
Dowry 125
Dramas 110, 124, 241, 308, 311
Dreams 69, 216, 227
Dress 6, 29, 51, 76–7, 81–2, 84, 86, 89, 116, 123, 145–6, 150, 169, 175–6, 191, 197, 201, 205, 215, 217, 240, 285, 294, 306

Dromeia 106, 201, 265, 307
Dromeios 106, 201, 264
Dromeus 47, 201-2, 206, 306
Drums 216-17
Dues 11, 261
Dyeing 11, 15
Dyeworks 11
Dynasties 28, 31-2, 34, 36-7, 82, 89, 121, 278

Eagle 144, 152, 167, 177, 232-3, 243, 246, 249, 251, 253, 314
Earth 27, 56, 75-6, 80, 142, 150, 162-3, 165, 237, 264, 322-3
— goddess 158-9, 164, 189, 196, 215, 268
Earthquakes 27, 289
Ebion 47
Ebionsa 47
Economy 5-10, 13-14, 16-20, 24-6, 28, 30-3, 35-42, 55, 70, 75-6, 80, 83, 91-3, 102, 118-19, 125, 165-6, 231, 297
Education 41, 45-9, 310
Egdramein 201
Egyptian 13, 25
Eiren 45-6
Ekdysia 108, 175-8, 201, 265, 285, 294, 306-7
Elaphebolion 49, 109
Elders 44-5, 298, 301, 306, 310, 319
Elephants 16, 85
Eleusinia 105, 170
Eleusinion 52, 170
Eleusinios 105-7, 109, 170
Enatai 97
Endogamy 128-9
Eniautos Daimon 127
Ennaeteris 93, 95
Enneoros 94-5
Enuma elish 220
Epheboi 48-9, 65, 115, 125, 185, 195-6, 205, 213-15, 233, 266
Ephors 87, 96
Epic 67, 94, 308, 312
Epigrams 242, 244, 288, 293, 309
Epigraphy 39, 49, 107, 115, 133, 146, 153, 167, 170-5, 179-80, 182, 188, 191-2, 197-8, 200-1, 204,

206-15, 219, 221, 223-7, 232-4, 237-50, 253-6, 258-9, 261-9, 272-5, 279-94, 302-7
Epiouros 120
Epiphanies 51, 146, 202, 213, 251, 278, 312-16
Epitaphs 219
Epithets 67, 125, 146, 170-1, 177-9, 182, 185, 188, 200, 207, 210, 231, 233-4, 236-7, 239, 244, 246-7, 249, 256, 260, 262, 264-7, 270, 274-5, 277, 280-2, 285, 288-90
Epopsios 238
Epoptai 98
Equinox 49-50, 94, 107-9
Ergepistatai 303
Estates 40-1, 129, 131, 322
Ethnography 5-7, 29, 43, 82, 126, 131-2, 134-5, 203
Ethnos 32
Exchange 10, 17, 24-6, 33
Exogamy 6
Exports 14, 25-6

Faction 30
Factories 24
Faience 9, 76, 249
Family 7, 14, 41, 46, 121, 129, 142, 209, 273, 321
Farmers 5-6, 15, 31, 75
Farms 8, 130
Feasts 51, 114, 116-17, 195-6, 202-3, 205, 240, 266, 287, 299, 314
Fertility-cults xi, 44, 52, 55-7, 78-9, 92-3, 100-1, 111, 113, 149, 152, 160-1, 165-7, 176, 186, 193-4, 197, 202, 214, 251, 259, 283-5, 307
Festivals ix, xii, 46, 48-50, 62, 87, 94, 96, 104, 106-9, 113-15, 117, 151-2, 170, 175-6, 178-80, 186, 194-7, 201-6, 213-14, 219, 222, 225, 238-41, 243, 245, 250, 254, 264-6, 268-9, 276, 280, 285-7, 293-4, 299, 304, 310-11, 315
Field tillage 7, 19, 56, 113, 166
Figurines 9, 55-9, 72, 74-6, 78, 145-6, 260
Fire 27, 262, 304, 315
Fish 63, 313

Fishermen 6, 181–2
Flocks 35, 211–12, 214, 261, 266
Florentine Hemerologion 104, 106
Flowers 15, 63, 75, 79, 151, 160, 167,
    178, 222, 253, 255, 273, 285
Folklore 44, 70, 74, 88, 100, 127,
    215, 257
Food 5–6, 10, 19, 21, 40, 56, 66, 71,
    145
Food-gatherers 3, 5
Food production 5, 26, 56, 102
Fortetsa lid 315–16
Fortification 9, 22–3, 29, 33–4, 48
Foundries 11
Fowlers 11
Freedmen 174, 192
Frescoes 15–17, 22, 34, 77, 84–5,
    90–1, 152
Fruits 7, 60, 63, 69, 108, 115, 145,
    162, 242, 266, 270, 285
Furniture 16

Games 103, 115, 188–9, 197
Garden tillage 7–8, 19–20, 56, 70
Gatekeepers 11
Genos 19, 31, 114
Geography 10, 20, 23, 26, 30, 75,
    127, 146, 215, 282
Geometric 37, 59, 142, 145, 315
Geraphoros basileon 50
Ghosts 66, 69, 73, 198, 319
Goats 5, 7, 43–4, 52, 72, 78, 144–5,
    163, 215–16, 218, 221, 226, 242,
    257–8, 263, 267–8, 271, 303, 323
Gold 9, 11, 62, 128, 143–4, 150, 242,
    313
Goldsmiths 14
Gorgoneion 263
Gortyn Code 47, 112, 198, 261, 275,
    305
Grain 5–6, 71, 115, 143–4
Granaries 21
Grapes 220
Grass 5
Graves 21, 28, 58, 64, 66, 68, 142
Greek xii, 87, 94, 133, 135, 158, 179,
    188, 203, 205, 269
Grooms 11
Guilds 11–12, 16–18, 63

Gymnasium 40, 45, 47, 289, 302, 305
Gypsum 23

Haliaios 105–6, 108, 110
Halieia 105
Halios 110
Hamlets 8, 14, 29–30
Handicrafts 33
Harbours 6, 10, 17, 24–6, 33, 51,
    143, 253, 261–2
Hares 78
Harness 10
Harvest 49, 80, 109, 149–50, 152,
    162–3, 197, 206, 266
Hawk 144, 312
Hearth 4, 142, 264, 304–5
Hebrew 12–13
Hecatombs 163, 239
Hedanos 289
Hedgehogs 72
Hedrai 97
Hegemony 28, 30, 33, 35, 92, 118,
    136, 154
Heirs 40, 322
Hekatomboia 239
Hekatomphonia 286
Hellanodikai 97–8
Hellenistic period 41–2, 49, 63, 71,
    142, 192, 200, 207, 220, 225, 269,
    276, 279–80, 284, 288, 291–2, 305,
    319
Hellotia 158–62
Heraia 105, 254
Heraion 51, 253–4
Heraios 105–6, 254
Herbs 61, 63, 79, 160–1, 167–8, 178,
    241, 255, 285
Herds 35, 45–7, 49, 60, 65, 100,
    110–12, 164, 167, 212
Herdsmen 32, 240
Heresy 300
Hero 30, 66, 84, 121, 131, 133, 153,
    196, 224, 256, 292, 302, 313, 320
Heroic Age 29, 94, 119, 121, 301
Hetaireia 40–1
Hiarorgos 302–3
Hides (*see* Skins)
Hierarchies 31–2, 84, 118, 224
Himalios 105–6, 109, 264

Historical period 7, 21, 38, 44, 54, 60, 65, 74, 77, 81, 97, 104–10, 112, 117, 125, 132–5, 141, 146–8, 150, 154–5, 166–7, 172, 175, 179, 184, 210, 221, 224, 231, 234–5, 238, 244, 253, 256, 265, 268, 272, 275, 278, 289, 292–3, 297, 302, 304, 308, 312
Hittite 13, 25
Hoe 7, 19, 56
Honey 52, 60–3, 66, 217, 226, 242
Hormos 125
Horns 43, 52, 112, 144, 162, 165, 167, 220, 263, 265
— of consecration 80, 145–6
Horse 52, 144, 289–90
Household (see also Oikos) 14, 21, 24, 26, 41, 75, 77–8, 125, 128, 131, 212, 321
Household-goddess 75, 278
Houses 4, 8, 14, 21–2, 27, 29, 40, 74, 83, 141, 144, 149, 187, 209, 245, 250, 265, 270, 300, 302, 304, 321
Hunting 5–6, 55–6, 63, 72, 74–6, 78, 80–1, 85, 90, 98, 116, 141, 162, 183, 186–7, 191, 205, 257, 272
Hyakinthia 105, 201, 222, 266
Hyakinthios 105–6
Hydrophoroi 114
Hymns 205, 213, 220, 299
— Homeric 137, 151, 181, 262
— of the Kouretes 209–14, 239–40, 244, 309–10, 315–17
Hyperboia 108–9, 239
Hyporkhema 311

Ice Age 5
Idaei dactyli 242
Idols 58–9, 73, 142, 146, 182, 260, 264
Immigration 3, 5–6, 8, 18–20, 63, 94, 135–6, 154–6, 166, 184, 275
Immortality 63, 66, 74, 117, 212, 298, 315
Imperial times 104, 149, 153, 192, 247, 257, 259, 272–3, 276, 282
Impiety 83, 299–300
Incantation 256
Incarnation 60, 206, 245

Incubation 226–7
Indo-European xi, 169, 199
Industry 6, 11, 15, 24, 28, 38
Ingots 25
Inheritance 41, 79, 125, 322
Initiation x, 7, 43–53, 55–8, 60, 63–5, 81–3, 98–9, 112–13, 116–17, 125, 144, 173, 175–7, 179, 181–2, 185, 187–91, 193–7, 200–2, 204–6, 213–15, 217, 240–2, 266, 275, 285–6, 306–7, 315–16
Inquisition 300
Intercalation 93
Intermarriage 6
Ionios 105–7
Iron 11, 38, 144–5, 242, 301
Iron Age 37–42, 54, 57, 119, 132, 190
Irrigation 10–11, 18, 30, 92
Ivory 15–17, 76
Ivy 220

Jars 21, 60–3, 66
Jewellers 8, 14
Jewellery 9, 11, 29, 85, 87, 91

Kanneios (Karneios) 105–7, 265–6
Kantharos 220
Karneia 97, 105, 110, 195, 201, 265–6
Karnos 265
Karonios 105–7
Katharmata 161
Katharsia 161–2
Keleoi 217
Kentriadai 114
Keras 265
Kerberoi 217
Keryx 195
Khartiobiarios 105–7
Kilt 34, 81, 89
Kings 12, 23, 28, 30–2, 39, 49–50, 83, 86–92, 103, 108, 110, 119, 124–5, 127, 130–1, 155, 166, 180, 191, 207, 241, 245, 282, 292, 304, 319–21
Kingship 44, 49–50, 82–3, 87–8, 91–2, 94–8, 108, 118, 156, 215, 278, 308

Kinship 6–7, 16, 18–19, 21, 39, 41–2, 67, 150, 197–8
Klaros 40–1
Kleinoi 116–17, 214
Koina Hestia 304
Kokkos 161
Komnokarios 105–6, 108
Komos 195, 205–6
Kosmoi 39, 200, 204, 206, 209, 294, 302–3
Kosmos xii
Kouroi xi, 98–9, 124, 195, 206, 212–14, 307, 316
Kourotrophos 182–3, 186, 188, 190, 193, 275–6
Kronion 49, 115
Krypteia 46–7, 285

Labour 6–7, 30, 32–3, 42, 57, 70, 113, 297
Labour service 11, 26
Labrys 82, 236
Labyrinth 22, 50, 102–3, 110, 123–4, 187, 232, 253
Lada 173
Laioi 217
Land 6, 19, 24, 29, 31–2, 39–42, 102, 115, 131–2, 136, 211, 225, 301, 303–4, 308, 314, 321–2
Land tenure 7, 26, 30–1, 297
Landlords 40, 302, 304
Language 12–13, 27, 39, 71, 83, 131, 133, 135, 157
Lapidaries 8
Launderers 11
Laurel 68, 231–2, 246, 249, 256–7, 268
Law 83, 101, 205, 214, 216, 233, 239, 252, 258, 297–301, 306–7, 309, 312, 321–2
Lead 9, 234
Legislation 19, 31–2
Leskhanasios 267
Leskhanorios 104–7, 267
Leukippos 178
Levy 131, 262
Libations 145, 299
Libraries 12
Lightning 81, 118–19, 162, 245

Limestone 4, 23
Linear A 25
Linear B ix–xii, 25, 36
Lions 84, 144
Liquidambar orientalis 270
Literacy 12
Luxuries 10–11, 25, 29, 33
Lyre 256–8
Lyric 308, 311, 317–18, 320, 323

Maeander pattern 115, 195, 232
Magic 55–9, 63, 66, 70, 78–80, 86, 102–3, 111, 114, 123, 127, 160–1, 165, 167–8, 178, 187, 206, 214, 224, 234, 241, 244, 255, 285, 308, 311
Magistrates 39, 83, 97, 107–8, 202, 273, 304, 307
Maimakterion 107
Maize 70–1
Mannos (Monnos) 246
Manufactures 6, 9–11, 32, 86
Marble 9, 225
Market 14, 25, 29, 35, 38, 302
Market-place 24, 26, 97, 205, 234, 288, 305
Marneion 187
Marriage 6, 40–1, 46–7, 57–8, 112, 116–17, 121, 124–5, 128–9, 152, 166–7, 176–7, 181, 188, 193, 202, 206, 218, 252, 277, 285, 299, 307
— matrilocal 125, 156
— sacred 51–2, 110–18, 148, 150, 158, 167–8, 176–9, 181, 188, 219, 251–3
Masks 55, 110, 145, 162
Masonry 22
Matriarchy 57, 129, 150, 165, 181, 189, 196
Meat 5, 31, 205, 240
Medicine 224–7
Megaron 29, 149
Melleiren 46
Men's House 116, 266
Mercenaries 42, 319–20
Merchandise 17
Merchants 6, 9, 12, 25–6, 33, 91
Metageitnion 107
Metals 8–11, 13, 38, 75
Metamorphosis 63, 179, 189, 312

Metics 174
Metre 211, 311, 318, 323
Mice 60, 66–7, 72, 269
Militarism 12, 22–3, 29–30, 32–4, 36,
    40, 81, 84, 86–7, 102, 118
Military training 46, 48–9
Milk 5, 52, 144, 215, 226, 242
Minoan god 79–81, 90–2, 98, 119,
    160, 165–6, 199, 251
Mogostokos 168–9
Money 25, 40–1, 243
Monopoly 32, 35–6
Monotheism 75–6
Month 92–4, 100, 186, 200, 202, 225,
    239, 250, 254, 258–9, 261, 264–7,
    285, 293, 299
Moon 49, 65, 71, 78–9, 92–3, 96,
    100, 102, 108, 110–11, 115, 117,
    128, 145, 158, 164, 177–8, 180–1,
    193, 200, 262, 266
— goddess 78, 92, 111, 158, 160,
    177, 253
— worship 78, 100, 178, 181
Mother-goddess xi, 20, 44, 50–2, 54,
    74–80, 82–5, 90–2, 98–100, 119,
    144–5, 149–52, 156–7, 159–60, 165,
    168, 181, 193, 251–2, 255, 268, 276,
    278, 283–4, 315
Mourning xi, 48, 65, 67, 149–50,
    167, 194, 219
Mulberry 61, 64–6, 100
Mummification 92
Murex 14
Music 45–6, 189, 217, 271, 308–16
Myrton 161
Mysteries 51, 53, 98, 150–1, 198, 221,
    237, 240, 242, 316
— Eleusinian 53, 83, 150–1, 161,
    170, 198
Mythology x, 18, 20, 43–4, 50–1,
    53–4, 60, 62–7, 71, 74, 78, 80, 94,
    96, 99–102, 110–11, 113, 117,
    119–20, 149–50, 152, 156–7, 162,
    164, 174–83, 189, 195–6, 199–200,
    209, 215–18, 220, 222, 231, 241,
    253, 276, 285

Nature x, 5, 43, 46, 56, 70, 74, 77,
    80, 99, 102, 108, 186, 195, 305

Necklaces 90, 246
Nekysia 105, 109
Nekysios 105–7, 109
Neoi 115
Neolithic Age 3–8, 10, 14, 54, 56–9,
    70, 72–9, 81, 141–3, 146, 155, 160,
    167–9
Nickel 11
Nine 87, 93–5, 97–9, 115, 129, 131,
    179, 181–2, 242, 298, 321
Nisan 108
Nomads 5, 22

Oaristes 121
Oases 5
Oaths 48, 107–8, 110, 171, 173–4,
    191–2, 198, 200, 202, 204, 206–9,
    211, 233, 243, 246–7, 253–4, 258,
    261, 269, 274–5, 279–82, 284–6,
    288, 290, 306
— Drerian 173, 179, 191, 200–1,
    206, 233, 248, 263, 273, 281, 284,
    288, 292, 304, 306
Obsidian 4, 9, 142
Ochre 56, 145
Octennium 50, 88, 92–9, 111, 118
Officials 40, 83, 87, 97, 107, 111, 115,
    192, 205, 280, 299, 302–5
Oikos 21, 41–2
Oktaeteris 93
Oligarchy 42, 297, 300, 310, 322
Olives 7, 14, 35, 65, 96, 191, 201,
    266, 278, 307
Olive-oil 26, 29, 128, 192, 226
Olympic Games 52, 97–8, 201, 206,
    219, 266
Omphalos 68, 258–9
Oracles 61, 102, 110, 156, 164, 177,
    268, 311
Orchards 6, 14, 70, 75, 197
Orchestra 102, 123, 205
Ordeal 44, 63, 112, 118, 124, 176,
    185, 189, 196, 198, 201, 205–6, 307
Orgia x, 193
Orientalizing 142
Orima 47
Ornithogonia 217
Orphism 198, 221, 237
Oskhophoria 195–7, 266

Othrys 121
Owl 61, 66, 217, 278
Ownership 6, 30, 41
Oxen 45, 72, 85–6, 102, 111–17, 124, 144–5, 163, 166, 205, 213, 258

Paean 311
Painters 17, 152
Palaces xii, 17–19, 21–7, 29, 36–7, 51, 75–8, 82–6, 89, 96–7, 103, 111–12, 117–18, 125, 127–8, 131, 142, 149, 156, 159, 250, 252, 278, 314
Palaeolithic Age 3, 5–7, 55–9, 72, 141
Panamia 105
Panamos 105–6
Pangenei 198
Panoptes 111
Pantheons 118–19, 148, 157, 162, 165, 231, 235
Panther 220
Pantomime 62, 124
Parastathentes 116, 205, 213
Parian Marble 58, 89, 120, 279
Partridge 101
Pasture 41
Peace 24, 33–4, 49, 80, 115, 157, 212
Peasantry 8, 26, 33, 35, 67
Periblemaia (Periblemata) 108, 294, 307
Perioecic communities 243, 261, 269, 272
Persian War 321
Philosophy 31, 45
Phoenician 12–13
Phonemes 12
Phratry 40, 97
Phthinoporios 105–7, 109–10
Physicians 225, 248–9
Pictographs 25
Pigs 5, 7, 43–4, 72, 78, 145, 152, 161, 216, 218
Pillars xi, 23, 43, 68–9, 75, 238, 259–60, 263, 287
Piracy 42, 88, 131, 321
Plague 198, 249, 311
Plants xi, 5–6, 60, 62–3, 65, 77, 79, 100, 162, 178

Plough 7, 10, 19–20, 56, 102, 113–14, 318
Poetry 149, 308–23
Police 33–4, 46
Polis (*see* City-state)
Polites 305
Polytheism xi, 54, 76
Pompe 205–6
Population 8, 10, 12, 14, 19–20, 37–8, 40, 48, 122–3, 133, 136–7, 141, 165, 261, 275, 287, 297
Ports 9, 12, 51, 132, 134, 171–2, 195, 209, 224, 261
Pottery 4–6, 8, 10–11, 13–15, 29, 37, 82, 101, 123, 142–3, 145–6, 217
Prayers 49, 68, 110, 115, 198, 266, 282, 300
Prehistory 44, 60, 82, 85, 88, 94, 108, 148, 222, 244
Priestesses 52, 78, 111, 115, 150, 185, 268, 299
Priests 11–12, 25, 31–3, 49, 83, 85–7, 91, 94, 97, 108, 111, 115, 150, 161–2, 187, 226, 247, 262, 299, 303
Priest-king 25, 35, 52, 82–92, 111, 117–18, 121, 167, 236, 246, 306
Processions 86, 96, 99, 115, 159, 185, 195, 197, 205, 213
Produce 6, 8
Production 7, 9–11, 14, 19, 22, 24–6, 33, 39, 75, 297, 301
Property 30, 35, 86,
Prophecy 66, 269, 311
Prophylactic offerings 72
Protogeometric 37, 59
Proto-Phoenician 157
Prytaneion (*see* Town-hall)
Prytanis 304
Puberty 7, 44, 47, 56, 67, 81, 195
Public service 12
Puppets 58, 161
Purple 15, 49
Pyanopsion 107
Pyramids 92
Pythia 269

Queens 28, 110, 180
Quince 134, 226

Racing 46–7, 103, 109, 112, 116, 185, 195, 201, 206, 265–6, 307
Rain 6, 71, 92, 118–19, 162–3, 186
Ram (*see* Sheep)
Rations 31
Rats 66
Raw materials 10, 21
Relationship 6, 41, 131, 252, 321
Rent 32, 40–1
Resources 10, 13–14, 18, 20, 29–30, 34, 37, 121, 131, 166
Revenue 32, 88, 192, 304
Riddles 64, 66
Rings xi, 62, 85, 90, 125, 186
Ritual 7, 54–7, 60, 63, 65–8, 75, 79–82, 84, 86, 98, 103, 109–14, 117–18, 125, 148, 150–2, 162–3, 166, 174–7, 189, 193, 196–7, 199–200, 204–6, 214, 222–3, 241–2, 253, 276, 285, 294, 307–9, 311
Rivers 5, 14, 135, 143, 163, 189, 242, 282–3
Roads 25–6, 33, 134, 192, 205, 242
Roman period 42, 46, 49, 142–4, 146, 153, 169–70, 181, 191–2, 197, 207, 241, 243, 274
Rosetta Stone 87

Sacred stone 67–71, 78, 259
Sacred tree 43, 66–71, 75, 78, 145, 152, 185–7, 190, 197, 217, 255, 268, 270, 278, 307, 313
Sacrifices 31, 43, 49–50, 52, 72, 78–9, 86–7, 90, 97, 108–10, 113, 115–17, 124, 145, 151–2, 161–6, 186, 196, 203–6, 208, 213, 218, 222, 226–7, 233, 239, 242, 253, 258, 264, 273, 286, 299–300, 303
Saffron 15, 35, 277
Sails 10
Sanctuaries 55, 58–9, 73–4, 82, 141, 144, 150, 174, 177, 190–1, 209, 217, 225–6, 253, 258
Satraps 319
Scribes 11, 28
Sculptors 11, 273
Sculpture 16, 54

Sea 3, 6, 55, 63–4, 75, 114, 119–20, 125–6, 128, 130–1, 134, 146, 179, 181, 189, 197, 213–14, 225, 236, 238, 242, 261–2, 288–90, 313–14, 322
Sea-power 22–3, 82, 84, 88–9
Seals xi, 9, 15, 25, 34, 82, 86, 90, 112
Seal-cutters 14
Seasons 62, 80, 93, 100, 102, 162–3, 212, 266
Seeds 5, 20, 79–80, 115, 149–52, 199, 206
Semitic 11–12, 78, 101, 135, 157
Serfs 40–2, 156, 287, 297, 303–4, 317–19, 321–2
Serpent (*see* Snake)
Services 31–3, 46, 225, 320
Shaft Graves 28
Sheep 5, 7, 72, 145, 163, 166, 242, 244–5, 253, 265, 267
Shekels 11
Shepherds 11
Shields 34, 48, 80, 85–7, 123, 144, 210, 212, 216–17, 318
Ships 10–11, 17, 88–9, 121–2, 126, 128–30, 132, 134–5, 144, 154, 173, 213–14, 262, 290, 314, 322
Shipyards 11
Shrines 24, 52, 58, 67–8, 73–4, 76, 82, 141–2, 171–2, 184, 186–7, 193, 205, 207, 209, 225, 233–4, 240, 243, 265, 268, 283, 300, 302
Silver 9, 11–12, 123, 128, 143–4, 313
Sisyropoioi 221
Skins 34, 72, 85–7, 102, 110–11, 114, 240, 248, 266, 323
Skotioi 47, 285
Sky 75, 103, 159, 166, 199, 245, 313
Skyla 248
Skylax 248
Skyllos 248
Skylos 248
Slavery 26, 41, 130–1, 134, 156, 192, 300, 304, 321
Smelting 10, 38
Sminthoi 269
Smiths 11, 14

Snake 43–4, 50, 52, 60–2, 64, 66, 71,
73–5, 78, 144, 150–3, 164, 224, 227,
245–6, 268, 278
Soil 5, 10, 32–3, 40, 186
Solar cycle 167
Soldiers (*see* Warriors)
Solstice 108, 238
Soul 60–1
Specialists 16, 18–22, 25–6, 29–30,
33, 36, 63, 70
Spell 198
Spermios 105–7, 109
Spinning 5–6, 10
Spitting 61, 63
Springs 3, 51, 68, 162–4, 177, 203,
268, 289
Stars 87, 96, 103, 110, 238, 262
State 9–12, 30–2, 34, 39–42, 45, 47–8,
52, 86, 104, 174, 179, 196, 205, 210,
268–9, 278, 298–307, 310
Staters 201, 243
Statues 52, 56, 81, 112, 142, 145,
169, 174, 177, 180, 186, 205, 210–
11, 225, 227, 233, 235, 254–5,
263–4, 272–3, 279, 283, 285, 287,
293
Steel 38
Stephanephoros 49
Stepterion 96, 268
Stoa basileios 97
Stoats 72
Stock-breeders 5, 7–8, 19–20, 102,
166
Stone 4, 10, 13, 17, 20, 23, 29, 55–6,
61, 71, 82, 126, 142, 145, 211, 215,
218, 238, 242, 264, 270, 273, 287
Storax 270
Streams 3, 55, 135, 167–8, 171–2,
177
Stucco 16, 82
Sun 22, 44, 52, 71, 93, 96, 98–9,
100–3, 110–11, 117, 128, 143, 145,
165, 167, 177–8, 180–1, 236, 238,
248, 253, 262, 270, 323
Surgery 227
Surplus 10–11, 14, 16, 21, 26, 30,
32–3, 42
Swastika 232
Swineherds 31, 131, 321

Synoikismos 302
Syntagmata 32
Syssitia 40, 42, 302

Tablets x, 12, 15, 25, 101, 145, 234,
243
Taboo 114–15, 218
Taxes 11, 31
Techniques 3–6, 10–11, 13–20, 25,
28–30, 33, 36–8, 63, 101–2, 227,
308
Temenos 145, 174
Temples 12, 16, 24, 48, 82–3, 97,
103–4, 150, 156, 159, 170–4, 180,
182, 184, 186–8, 190–3, 204, 208–
11, 225–7, 233, 243, 246–50, 254,
256–7, 261–4, 268–9, 272–4, 277,
279–82, 284, 286, 292–3, 298, 300,
302–5, 308
Terracotta 58, 72–3, 142, 144, 146,
210, 243, 260, 263
Teshrit 108
Tetradrachms 232, 257, 274
Thalamos 149
Thalassocracy 35–6
Thargelia 50, 96
Thargelion 50, 96
Theatres 48, 103, 123, 205
Theocracy 24, 298, 300
Thermolaia (Thermoloia) 104–5,
293
Thermolaios (Thermoloios) 104–6,
293
Thesmoi 152
Thesmophoria 105, 109, 151–2,
160–1
Thesmophorios 105–7, 109
Thiodaisia (Theodaisia) 105, 107,
109, 202–6, 213
Thiodaisios (Theodaisios) 105–7,
202, 221
Tholoi 9, 21–2
Tholos Tomb Dynasty 28
Thunderbolt 71, 118, 162, 217, 232,
237, 242, 246, 315–16
Thunder-stone 215, 241–2
Thyrsos 220
Tillers 5, 10, 39–40
Tin 10

Tithes 261, 269
Tombs 21–2, 37, 57–8, 61–2, 65–6, 68–9, 86, 89, 91, 197–8, 203, 219, 222, 233, 242, 315
Tongs 10
Tools 4–6, 9–11, 43, 69, 142
Tortoises 72
Totemism 6, 43–5, 51, 55–6, 59–60, 63, 66–7, 70, 72–4, 78, 81, 99–100, 115, 218
Towns 6, 8–13, 16, 18–19, 24–5, 27, 29–30, 33–4, 36–8, 40–2, 47, 49, 63, 75, 77, 83, 92, 94, 102, 107, 115–16, 118, 122, 127, 130–2, 134, 164, 170, 172, 188, 200, 203–4, 206, 210, 213–14, 220, 225, 231–3, 240, 256–8, 261, 264, 266, 273, 278, 280–1, 284–6, 299, 301–6, 309–10, 322–3
Town-hall 264, 304–5
Trade 8–10, 12, 17–18, 20, 24–6, 29, 31, 33, 35, 37, 41, 51, 75, 92, 134, 157, 166, 253
Tradesmen 31
Transport 6, 11, 14–15, 121
Treaties 107, 171, 173–4, 179–80, 191, 200–1, 204, 206–9, 211, 223, 233, 243–4, 246–8, 253–5, 257–8, 263–5, 269, 273–4, 280–2, 284–6, 288, 290, 293–4, 303, 306
Tree-cults xi, 66, 68, 70–1, 236
Tribe 6, 12, 18, 29–30, 35, 39–41, 43, 45–8, 77, 97, 114–15, 118, 131–2, 178, 195–6, 205, 213, 245, 266–7, 297, 299, 302, 304–6
Tributary relations 9–10, 26, 35, 40, 42, 92
Tribute 26, 30, 32–3, 35–6, 40, 50, 88, 96, 173, 197, 261–2, 303–4
Trident 290
Triopis (Triottis) 246
Tripods 232, 315–16
Trojan War 121–2, 130–1, 321
Tyranny 35, 82, 322

Unwritten Laws 198

Vases 9, 14, 34–5, 66, 84–7, 89–91, 141–5, 260, 263

Vassalage 40
Vegetation-cults x–xi, 62, 75, 79, 158, 163, 193–4, 222, 231
Vegetation cycle 44, 62, 66, 70, 74, 78, 80–1, 92, 99, 110, 148, 199, 251, 266
Vehicles 15
Villages 3, 6, 8, 14, 21, 24, 38, 40, 101, 170, 195, 235–6, 289, 292, 302, 304–5
Vines 14, 195–7, 248, 266, 318
Visions (see Dreams)
Votive offerings 143–6, 210, 242, 260, 263

Wainwrights 11
Wanax 120
War 15, 24, 28, 30, 32, 34–6, 42, 80–1, 85, 88, 98, 125, 129–30, 278, 293
Warehouses 24
Warriors 11, 31–4, 46, 65, 80, 85–7, 121, 144, 175, 187, 190–1, 205, 306, 313, 319–20
Water 65, 68, 86, 114, 126, 162–4, 177, 203, 226, 283, 285, 289, 314
Weapons 6, 28, 30, 33–5, 43, 48, 75, 80–1, 84–6, 90, 98, 103, 123, 125, 129, 142–5, 190–1, 193, 205, 216–17, 248, 257–8, 261, 269–70, 272–3, 279, 293, 313, 318–21
Weasels 72
Weather-god 118–19
Weaving 5–6, 10, 128
Weights 11, 25
Welkhania 104–6, 250
Welkhanios 104–7
Wheat 5, 113, 143
Wheel 10, 13–15, 101–2, 110, 123, 145
Willow 152, 168, 177, 242, 250
Winds 3, 6, 118, 126, 236, 312, 314, 322
Wine 26, 61, 66, 131, 144, 192, 203, 226, 318
Wolf 267
Wood 6, 8, 10, 14, 17, 22–3, 27, 51, 69–70, 143, 177, 180, 185, 209, 211, 215, 240–1, 253–5

Woodpecker 71, 217
Wool 11, 128, 192, 242
Workshops 11, 24
Wreaths 96, 123, 159–62, 191, 232, 249, 256–7, 268
Writing 9, 12–13, 25, 41, 145

Youth 41, 44–9, 60, 65, 81, 84, 87–8, 91, 98–9, 103, 109, 112, 115–18, 123–5, 128, 175–6, 182, 185, 193, 195–7, 200–1, 204, 206, 213–14, 220, 245, 266, 285, 294, 299, 301, 306, 310, 316

II. Index of Deities, Persons, Places

Achaeans xii, 15, 27, 29–30, 32, 37, 67, 88, 90, 121–3, 129, 131–6, 154–5, 158, 199, 260, 275
Acheloos 189
Achilles 123, 320
Acropolis 280, 298
Adonis 80, 148, 163, 199, 219, 222, 238
Adrasteia 242
Aegean xi, 4, 13, 15, 28–9, 35, 94, 119, 131, 136, 190, 277
Aerope 121
Aeschylus 62, 244, 319
Africa 5, 10, 42, 56, 235
Agamemnon 30, 122, 125
Agathokles 218
Agenor 156
Agra 160, 185
Ahmosis 157
Aigaion 215
Aigina 106, 179, 181–2, 263
Aigolios 217
Aiolians 137
Aiolis 135, 155
Aiolos 245
Aithon 130
Aitolia 259
Akakallis 257, 270–1
Akarnanians 265
Akharnai 260
Akrotiri 275–7
Akytos 288
Alalakh 12, 17
Alea 185, 203
Aleppo 16
Alexander 153, 305

Alexandretta 12
Aliyan 162–3
Alkaios 322
Alkathoos 121
Alkinoos 127–8
Alkman 178
Allaria 256, 278
Alpheus 154
Alps 14
Amaltheia 52, 215, 242
Amen-Ra 235
Ametoridai 257, 270, 272
Amnatos 209
Amnisiades 172
Amnisos 51, 130, 143, 169, 172, 249, 252
Ampelos 33
Amphithee 320
Amphritite 207
Amyklai 154, 222, 260
Amyklaioi 261
Amyklaion 261
Anat 157, 163
Anatolia 3, 6, 8, 10, 58, 82, 136, 185, 259
Androgeos 50, 96, 124
Andron 133, 147
Ankhiale 216
Anthedon 63–4, 189
Antimachos 210
Antioch 82, 170
Anu 108
Aphaia 179, 181–2, 188
Aphrodite 47, 101, 119, 124–5, 148, 160, 194, 207–8, 284–6, 291

— Antheia 285
— Skotia 47, 285–6
Apollo 39, 50, 61, 66, 68, 96, 98, 100,
    169, 171–2, 174–6, 186–8, 190–1,
    222, 231–2, 239, 250–1, 256–72,
    276, 291, 310, 312–13
— Agyieus 259–60
— Amyklaios 260–1
— Dekataphoros 257, 261–2, 269
— Delphinios 173, 258, 262–4
— Didymeus 264
— Dromaios (?) 264–5
— Enauros 265
Apollo Karneios 265–6
— Leskhanorios 266–7
— Lykeios 267
— Pythios 173–5, 179, 207–8, 233,
    261–2, 267–9, 281
— Smintheus 67, 269–70
— Styrakites 257, 270
— Tarrhaios 270–1
Apollodoros 60, 63, 65, 158
Apollonia 257, 262
Apollonios 282
Apollonios Tyanensis 192, 225
Aptera 104–6, 171, 184, 188–91, 225,
    231, 235, 255–6, 264, 275, 278, 287,
    304
Aradena 195
Arbios 235
Arcadia 52, 154, 166, 185, 218, 232,
    235, 239, 260, 273, 277, 279, 282,
    302–3
Arcadians 154, 204, 225, 233, 274,
    281, 293, 302
Ares 164, 207–8, 252, 284–6, 291
Arete 128
Argolis 35, 135, 155, 224
Argonauts 282
Argos 48, 51, 61, 65, 106, 110–11,
    119, 159, 244, 253–4, 259–60, 267,
    284–5
Ariadne 62, 103, 120, 123–5, 193–7,
    232
Aristides 281
Aristonymos 227
Aristophanes 62, 113–15, 183
Aristotle 18–19, 31, 262, 297, 299,
    301, 303, 305–6, 319–20

Arkalokhori 143, 215
Arkas 277
Arkoudia 276
Armenians 16
Artemis 50, 96, 115, 119–20, 158,
    160, 170, 173–5, 179–84, 187–8,
    190–1, 207–8, 211, 222, 234, 264,
    270, 272–7, 284, 291, 303
— Agrotera 185
— Aptera 188–91, 274–5
— as Bear-goddess 275–7
— Brauronia 277
— Ephesian 185–7, 274, 277
— Limnatis 185
— Lygodesma 185
— Orthia 46, 176, 185, 188, 190
— 'Persian' 190
— Rhokkaia 274
— Soteira 160, 274–5
— Toxia 275
Artemitai 272, 304
Arvad 195
Arvi 236
Asherat 156, 162, 165
Asia 4–5, 8–10, 13, 16–17, 20, 23–4,
    42, 75, 83, 113, 121, 134, 155–6,
    166, 194, 225, 276, 319–20
Asia Minor 4–5, 29, 118, 133, 135,
    153, 172–3, 184, 190, 256, 264, 275
Asine 9
Asios 121
Asklepios 62, 74, 209, 224–7
Assyria 13, 15, 128, 144, 203, 320,
    323
Astarte 167, 186, 236
Asterion 166–7
Asterios 110, 166–7
Asteros 166
Astypalaia 184
Atchana 17
Athenai 278
Athenaios 218, 317
Athene 83, 98, 101, 119, 128–9, 159,
    164, 208, 211, 233–4, 258, 278–83,
    291, 298, 313–14
— Deramis 279–80
— Hellotis 161
— Lindia 280
— Oleria 208, 246, 280

Athene Polias 207–8, 233, 280–1
— Poliokhos 207, 281
— Samonia 208, 281–2
— Tritogeneia 282
— Wadia 282–3
Athens 18, 47–51, 65, 82–3, 96–8, 101, 108–9, 113, 115, 120, 151, 183–5, 195, 204–5, 224, 226, 232, 239, 257, 260, 263, 266, 278, 280, 298, 302, 309, 311, 322
Atkinson 177, 250
Atlantic 55
Atlas 211
Atreidai 121
Atreus 121
Attica 18, 35, 94, 126, 135, 151, 155, 159–60, 178, 205, 277, 317
Attis 148, 222
Atymnos 167
Augeias 65
Augustus 153, 207, 225
Auxesia 52
Axos 146, 148, 231, 239, 243, 256, 272, 279, 288, 290

Baal 157, 162–3, 186
Babylon 320, 323
Babylonia 10, 50, 93–4, 108, 118, 220
Bacchus 163
Bacis (Bacchis) 100
Bady 283
Baikal 55
Bakchylides 166
Bakkhos 240
Barnett 16
Beattie ix
Bellerophon 158
Beloch 132
Belos 156
Berenike 292
Bianna 273
Biannos 105–6, 170–1, 273, 286
Black Sea 136, 190, 275, 277
Boiai 160
Boios 217
Boiotia 108, 159, 164, 203–5, 218, 282, 292
Boros 121

Bowra 318–20
Brauron 277
Britomarpeia (Britomartia) 180
Britomartis 179–94, 207, 249, 271–2, 283
Brittany 15
Bushmen 55
Busiris 32
Byzantium 166, 222

Canaanites 157, 162, 165
Cappadocia 15
Caracalla 187
Caria 39, 156, 173–4, 184–5, 293
Carians 88–9, 173, 185, 277
Caucasia 38
Chaironeia 218
Chalcedon 244
Chalkis 263
Childe 8
China 14–15, 30–2
Chios 108, 263
Christians 67, 70, 85, 143, 187, 219, 240, 288
Cilicia 15, 153, 156
Constans 240
Constantius 240
Cook, A. B. 100, 110, 144, 158, 161, 164, 167–8, 177, 180–1, 237, 241, 245, 250, 270
Corcyra 244
Corinth 159, 161, 164
Corinthian Isthmus 28
Cretans 13–14, 23, 36
Cuzco 71
Cyclades 8–9, 35, 39, 58, 88
Cyprus 12, 29, 38, 250
Cyrene 191, 227
Cyrus 320

Daidalidai 18
Daidalos 18, 101, 103, 110, 122–4, 180
Daktyloi 98–9, 216, 242
Damascus 17
Damoia 52
Damokhares 258
Danaos 157
Danube 57

Daphne 176–7
Dareios 319
De León, Pedro de Cieza 71
Deipnophoroi 196
Delos 50, 96, 108, 124, 169, 174–5, 180, 188, 263
Delphi 94, 96, 102, 108, 122, 156, 164, 174, 190, 195, 254, 257, 262–3, 267–8, 271, 311
Delta 3, 5
Demandros 227
Demargne 145
Demeter 20, 39, 52, 97, 113, 148–52, 159–60, 170, 180–1, 194, 197–8, 215, 232, 291
— Achaia 159
— Eleusinia 160, 170
— Europa 156, 159
— Thesmophoros 151, 156, 159
Demetrios 98
Demosthenes 319–20
Deukalion 117, 120–1, 130
Dia 120, 195
Didyma 264
Didymaion 264
Dieukhidas 260
Diktaian Cave 145, 186, 200, 215–17
Diktaion 182–3, 233
Dikte 182–3, 186, 193, 207–12, 216, 218–19, 233, 237
Diktynna 104, 158, 179–94, 200, 207, 210, 272–3, 275–7, 304
— Sebaste 191
Diktynnaion 146, 182–4, 191–3, 275
Diktynnaios 193
Diodoros 31–2, 137, 151, 209, 227
Dione 252
Dionysos x–xi, 49–50, 120, 125, 163, 178, 193–4, 196, 202–3, 205, 213, 220–1, 232, 235, 240–1, 260, 291, 310, 315
— Eleuthereus 205
— Skyllatis 248
— Theodaisios 202
Dipylon 62
Domitian 191, 243
Dorians 37–42, 46, 60, 94, 97, 115, 131–3, 136–7, 154–5, 158, 174, 222,

231, 246, 260, 265, 297, 306, 311, 316
Doris 133, 137
Doros 137
Doulikhion 130
Drepanum 203
Drerians 263
Dreros 105–8, 110, 190, 201–2, 233–4, 263, 269, 286, 288, 293, 307
Drios 218
Dymanes 39

Egypt 4, 6, 8–10, 12–16, 19, 24, 29, 31–2, 35–6, 58, 81–2, 87, 89, 91–3, 100, 103, 110–11, 118, 126, 128, 130–1, 134, 151, 156–7, 162, 235, 249, 292–3, 299, 309–10
Eileithyia 51–2, 143, 168–72, 207, 252, 279
— Binatia (Inatia) 171–2
El 101, 156–7, 162
Elam 15
Eleuseiniai 170
Eleusis 150–1, 170
Eleutherai 205
Eleutherna 149, 169–71, 221, 232, 257, 270, 272
Elis 52, 129, 135, 155, 213, 282–3
Elyrians 257, 271
Elyros 257, 271, 311
Ennius 219
Enyalios 293
Ephesos 175, 185–8
Ephialtes 286
Ephoros 287
Epidauros 224, 226–7
Epimedes 52
Epimenides 216, 242, 263, 311
Eratosthenes 89
Erech 14, 24
Erekhtheus 119
Erinyes 197–8
Ertaios 209
Eteocretans 122, 131–3, 135–7, 155, 158, 199, 209, 245, 276
Etruscans 135, 154
Euboia 51, 127, 159, 203
Euboulos 271

Eumaios 129–31, 321–2
Euphrates 15
Euripides 47, 62, 159, 164, 183, 189,
　221, 240–1, 311
— The Cretans 239–41, 311
Europa 94, 101, 120, 124, 152–68,
　216, 238, 240, 251, 265
Europe 3, 14, 42, 56, 103, 141, 155,
　168
Eurotas 46, 185
Eurytione 161
Eurytos 175, 178
Eustathius 98–9
Euthykhion 227
Eutykhides 115
Evans 25, 28, 34, 54, 57, 67–8, 70,
　74, 80, 82–5, 89–91, 117, 132, 142,
　145, 157

Fates 299
Faure 146, 275–6, 282
Faustina Iunior 187
Finley x
Firmicus 221, 240–1
Forsdyke 85–6, 88–90
Fortetsa 315
Frazer 70, 80, 103, 110, 117, 158, 180

Gaia 215, 292
Galatea 175, 178
Ganymede 117
Gardner 150
Gaza 187
Geta 187
Glaukos 60–7, 74, 100, 124, 189
Gortyna 7, 20, 40, 47, 104–7, 110,
　122, 126, 134–5, 148, 152–5, 158–9,
　161, 166–8, 174, 177, 200, 209, 221,
　224–5, 227, 232–4, 236, 238–9,
　242–3, 247, 250–1, 253–5, 258,
　260–1, 266–9, 274, 279, 281, 285–6,
　288–90, 293, 302–3, 305, 311, 321
Gortynians 156, 166, 171, 174, 207,
　209, 227, 233, 242–3, 246–7, 255,
　261, 269, 274, 285, 288, 293
Gortynios 154
Gortys 153–5
Gournia 8, 27, 34, 73, 142, 150
Gravettian 55–6

Great Mother 199, 292
Greece x–xi, 3–4, 8, 20, 29, 39, 44–5,
　48–51, 65, 81, 83, 93–4, 96, 108,
　118, 133, 136, 141, 148, 151, 157,
　159–61, 172, 189–90, 221, 225, 235,
　245, 253, 259, 280, 290, 297
Grumach ix
Gumelnita 57
Guthrie x–xi, 202–3
Gytheion 222

Hadad 162
Hades 120, 149–50, 215
Hadrian 187, 192
Hadrianopolis 153
Haghia Triada 19, 25, 27, 34, 37,
　72–3, 84–6, 89–91, 250
Halbherr 145, 250
Haliartians 203
Halikarnassos 260
Hannibal 274
Harmonia 153, 164
Harrison, Jane 63, 66, 151, 195–6,
　213, 245
Hatshepsut 89
Hattusas xi
Haussoullier 171
Hazzidakis 145
Hebe 252
Hekate 181
Helen 189
Helios 98, 177, 207, 293
Hellenospelio 146
Hellespont 136
Hellotia 157, 159–60
Hellotis 153, 155, 158–9, 161–2,
　164–5, 168
Hephaistos 101, 118, 123, 128, 291
Hera 50–1, 83, 111, 118–19, 160,
　168, 177, 207–8, 211, 215, 233,
　244, 246–7, 252–5, 264, 284, 291,
　312–13
— Antheia 285
— Melikhia 245, 254
— Parthenos 51, 253
Herais 255
Herakleidai 265
Herakleion 143, 195
Herakles 39, 51–2, 96, 252, 282

Hermaion 288, 304
Hermes 146, 207, 232, 234, 249, 258,
  265, 287–9, 291, 313
— Dakytios (Dakytinos) 288
— Dromios 289
— Eukolos 289
— Hedas 289
— Kranaios 146, 289
Hermione 51, 253
Hermonthis 100
Herodotos 31, 88–9, 122, 126, 133,
  135, 137, 151, 155–6, 158, 184, 192,
  319–20
Hesiod 67, 98, 166, 215, 252
Hestia 207–8, 215, 243, 246–8, 254,
  291, 298, 304–5
Hesychios 47, 109, 172, 181–2,
  201–2, 236, 239, 248, 250, 259,
  265, 282, 317
Hieraptyna 98, 105–7, 135, 142,
  148–9, 174, 202, 204, 207–11, 216,
  220–1, 233, 235, 237, 239, 245–7,
  254, 257–8, 261, 264–5, 269, 273,
  279–82, 284, 286, 291, 293
Hierapytnians 171, 174, 204, 209, 243,
  246–7, 255, 257, 274, 280, 285, 288
Hittites 12, 22–3, 30, 32, 150, 162,
  185
Hoeck 180
Hogarth 145
Homer 27, 29–30, 36, 67, 88, 91, 94,
  96–8, 118–37, 148–9, 151, 164,
  168–9, 172, 181, 244, 262, 269, 305,
  311–15, 320–2
Horai 285
Horus 87
Hyakinthos 222–3, 251, 260
Hybrias 317–23
Hygieia 150, 224–5
Hyginus 60–1, 65–6
Hyksos 157–8
Hylax 129
Hylleis 39
Hyllos 39, 96
Hyria 122
Hyrtakina 148, 254, 264, 271, 287

Iapygia 122
Iardanos 126, 135

Iasion 52, 113, 148
Iasios 52
Ida 52, 132, 143–4, 146, 193, 216,
  218–19, 239, 241–3, 249, 276, 283,
  298, 312–13
Idaian Cave 52, 144, 241–3, 276
Idas 52
Idomeneus 88–9, 120–3, 125, 129–
  32, 177–8
Ikaros 124
Imbros 136
Inatos 171–2, 235
Incas 71
India 15–16
Ino 314
Io 65, 100, 111, 155, 157
Ionians 49, 83, 94, 170, 190, 291
Iran 5, 14, 38
Iris 312
Ishtar 80, 148, 199
Isis 80, 199, 292–3
Isokrates 32
Istron 281, 284, 286
Italy 29, 226
Itanos 207–8, 210–11, 216, 225, 233,
  238, 248, 254, 268–9, 275, 281,
  288, 292
Ithaca 129–30, 313–14
Ithome 218
Iuppiter Sol Maximus Sarapis 293

Jacob 69
Jeanmaire 63
Juktas 73, 142, 290
Jupiter Laprios (Labrios) 236

Kabeiroi 98, 292
Kadmeioi 155–7, 159, 164–6, 204
Kadmos 96, 102, 153, 156–9, 164,
  314
Kairatos 3
Kalabis 227
Kallimachos 181–2, 203, 219
Kallisto 277
Kalymna 222
Kalypso 313–14
Kamares 143–4
Kambyses 319
Kamikos 122

Kantanos 233
Karmanor 270–1
Karme 271
Karneatai 266
Karnos 265
Kartemnides 155
Karteros 143
Karystios 287
Kasos 249
Kastor 129
Kastri 283
Katakhthonioi theoi 197–8
Kaudians 209
Kaudos 243, 261, 269
Kaÿstros 185
Keleos 217
Kerberos 217
Khersonesos 180, 225, 232–3, 258, 273, 279, 288, 293
Khryse 161, 269
Khyan 157
Kikones 151
Kilix 156
Killa 269
Kisamos 207, 257, 290
Kissousa 203
Kithairon 51, 177
Klaros 186, 188
Kleinias 298, 309–10
Klingender 55
Knidos 222
Knossos 3–4, 8, 12, 15, 17, 19, 22, 24–5, 27, 33–5, 37, 51, 57, 59, 82–5, 88–9, 91, 102–3, 105–7, 109–11, 120–3, 125, 130–2, 134, 142–3, 148–51, 153, 157, 165, 167, 171–2, 183, 193, 195–6, 203–4, 208–9, 211, 219, 223, 225, 232–3, 235, 242, 244, 248, 250, 252–3, 258, 262–3, 266–7, 273, 279, 282, 284–6, 290, 298, 311, 315–16
Koiranos 60–1
Kokkygion 51
Kolophon 186
Komo 33, 134–5
Konon 154
Kore 52, 170
Korybantes 98–9, 113, 193, 208, 216–17, 292

Korybas 113
Kos 50, 97, 115, 222, 224–5, 244, 248
Kouretes 60, 63, 65–6, 98–100, 113, 144, 191, 193, 201, 206–9, 211–17, 240, 242, 266, 276, 311
Kremnia 153, 155
Krios 265
Krisa 262
Kronos 49, 52, 101, 215–16, 218, 244, 298, 311
Kteatos 178
Kybele 113, 208, 217
Kydon 133, 256
Kydonia 80, 133–5, 148–9, 182, 184, 191–3, 207, 220, 232, 244, 255–7, 275–6, 278, 287–8
Kydonians 126, 131–7, 182, 184, 275–6
Kynosoura 276
Kyrbas 98
Kyzikos 153, 237, 277

La Ferrassie 55
Laconia 52, 126, 160, 170, 177, 184
Lactantius 236
Ladon 176
Laertes 131, 321
Lagash 24
Laïos 217
Lakrateides 115
Lampros 175, 178
Lapith 289
Lappa 149, 197, 257, 272, 278, 290
Larisa 135, 153, 155
Las 184
Lasaia 225, 293
Lasithi 142
Latians 173, 207, 245, 253, 258, 263
Lato 97, 105–7, 109, 170–1, 173, 179–80, 188, 200–2, 204, 209, 221–2, 233, 248, 269, 274, 279–80, 284, 286, 288, 290, 293, 304
Latosioi 174
Latosion 174, 304
Lebadeia 156, 159
Lebena 153, 209, 224–7
Leda 152
Leleges 88, 185, 281
Lemnos 136, 277, 292

Lenormant 150
Les Combarelles 55
Lesbos 322
Leskhe 266
Lesky 158
Leto (Lato) 168–9, 171–9, 181–8, 190, 207–8, 264–5, 272, 274, 311
— Mykhia (Nykhia) 177
— Phytia 175–7, 201, 285
Leukai 189
Leukippos 175–6
Leukothea 314
Leviathan 162
Libya 8, 85, 130, 155–6, 235, 245, 282
Libyans 225
Lindos 280
Lisos 184, 191–2, 200, 207, 271
Lloyd, Seton 22
Lokris 259
Lorimer 132
Lotan 162
Lucian 62, 124–5
Lucilla 187
Lycia 156, 158, 267
Lycians 156, 158, 267
Lydia 121, 135, 155, 218, 236, 320, 323
Lykaion 218
Lykastos 122
Lykosoura 97
Lyktos 122
Lyttians 174, 206–7, 243, 246–7, 257
Lyttos 105–8, 143, 145, 173–4, 180, 198, 200, 204, 206, 209, 215, 225, 232, 243, 246, 250, 254, 268–9, 274, 281, 284, 293–4

Macedonia 67, 136, 154
Magas 191, 207
Magasa 4, 142
Magna Mater 148
Magnesia 49–50, 99, 115, 250
Maiuri 288
Malia 126
Malla 105–8, 222, 239, 246, 269, 294
Mallia 19, 27, 37, 84
Mannhardt 70
Marathon 159, 164

Marduk 108
Marinatos 143, 249
Marna (Marnas) 187, 192
Marseille 184
Massilia 263
Master of Animals xi, 287
Mattia 149
Maurospelaion 143
Maya 70
Media 203
Mediterranean 5, 10, 12, 17, 36, 56, 292
Megalopolis 260
Megara 260–1, 322
Megisto 277
Melidhori 288
Melidoni 146
Melissai 217
Melos 4, 154
Mên Askaënos 82
Menelaos 90, 122, 125, 134
Mentes 314
Mentor 314
Meriones 117, 122
Mesopotamia 10, 12, 15, 50, 92–4, 108
Messara 21–2
Messenia 218
Messogis 218
Metapontion 289
Miamu 141
Middle East 5, 13
Milesians 258
Miletos 49, 108, 122, 263–4, 285
Minoans 3, 7–38, 41, 43–5, 50–119, 123, 127, 129, 132–4, 141–6, 148, 152, 154–60, 165, 167, 169, 173, 175, 179, 186, 189–90, 193–5, 197–9, 206, 210, 222–4, 231–2, 236, 238, 245–6, 248–53, 255, 259, 262–4, 266, 268, 274–6, 278, 282–4, 287, 289, 293, 297, 302, 305–6, 312–13, 315–16
Minos 17, 19, 22, 31, 35, 50, 60–2, 65, 82–4, 87–90, 94–6, 100–1, 110–11, 117, 120–3, 130–2, 134, 156, 158, 166, 172–3, 179–82, 187, 189, 197, 203, 216, 219, 232, 238, 292, 297–8

Minotaur 50, 96, 101, 103, 110, 167, 232
Mistress of Animals 190, 222, 274–5
Moirai 217
Mokhlos 8, 21, 25, 27
Molione 178
Molos 117, 176, 178
Montespan 55
Morges 242
Mot 162–3
Mountain-mother 183, 193, 240
Müller 85
Murray 214
Muses 189, 203, 310
Mycenae x, 12, 15, 22, 27–37, 51, 83, 90–1, 136
Mycenaeans xi, 83, 85, 111, 118–19, 134, 141, 157, 166–7, 182, 184, 188, 231, 235, 238, 248, 260, 268, 278, 293, 297, 302
Myres 137, 145
Mytilene 322

Nagas 14
Nauplia 51, 253
Naxos 194, 218, 256
Neanthes 218
Near East x–xi, 3, 9–10, 13–14, 16, 56
Neda 218
Nemea 178
Nepos 274
Nero 225
Nestor 97, 122, 125, 314
Nile 92
Nilsson x–xi, 59, 70, 72, 83, 90–1, 94, 136, 161–2, 172, 183, 190, 194, 202, 214, 245, 249
Nirou Khani 27
Nonnos 219
Nymphs 52, 153, 172, 207–8, 217–18, 222, 242, 270

Oaxos (Oaxes) 256
Odysseus 67, 120, 122, 126–7, 129–31, 313–14, 320–1
Oidipous 90
Oiketas 265

Oinomaos 121, 176
Okhe 51
Olbia 263
Oleros 280
Olountians 249, 253, 258, 263
Olous 105–7, 109, 170–1, 173, 179–80, 200–1, 204, 206, 209, 225, 232, 243, 245, 248–9, 254, 258, 264, 269, 274, 284, 286, 290, 293
Olympia 49, 52, 176, 195, 201, 206, 219, 234, 266
Olympos xii, 118–19, 148, 215, 222–4, 231, 235, 244, 252, 254, 269, 291–4, 312, 314
Omphalian plain 249, 263
Onga 164
Orchomenos 28
Oreioi 191, 207
Orestes 185
Oropos 263
Orpheus 151
Orsilokhos 129
Ortygia 175
Osiris 80, 91, 163, 199, 222, 292
Othryoneus 121
Otis 286
Ouranos 215, 292

Paionios 52
Palaikastro 4, 8, 27, 72–3, 142, 150, 210–11, 240, 244
Palaiokhora 249
Palestine 10, 13, 16, 29, 38
Pamphyloi 39
Panagia Arkoudiotissa 276
Pandia 178–9
Pandion 178–9
Pandionis 178
Paphlagonia 237
Paphos 119
Paribeni 72, 85–6
Parthenon 291
Pasiphae 60–1, 110, 124, 177–8, 193
Patso 146, 289
Pausanias 110, 154, 164, 170, 172, 177–8, 190, 257, 282
Pelagon 164
Pelasgians 131–2, 135–7, 155, 275, 277, 282

Peloponnese 3, 28, 35, 52, 121, 133, 135, 154, 159–60, 185, 188, 265, 267, 302, 311
Pelops 121
Pendlebury 27–8, 33
Penelope 67, 130–1, 320
Penthelidai 322
Pergamon 97, 218, 225
Persephone 149–50, 180–2, 189, 194, 197–8, 232
Persia 14, 122, 319–21, 323
Persson x, 60, 62, 64
Petsofa 72
Phaiacia 97–8, 126–30
Phaidra 120, 124
Phaistians 176
Phaistos 19, 22, 24, 27, 37, 47, 121–2, 126, 134, 143, 152, 175–7, 179, 188, 201, 249–51, 265, 274, 285, 288, 292
Phalaris 227
Phalasarna 184, 191–2, 234, 256, 287, 290, 292
Phalasarnians 292
Phaneromeni 142
Pharaoh 32, 82, 157
Pherekydes 98
Philistines 82, 187
Phoenicia 16–17, 101, 129–30, 153, 155–9, 162, 164–5, 167, 195, 203, 236, 240, 281, 321
Phoinix 120, 156, 287, 293
Phokis 184
Phrontis 126
Phrygia 102, 150, 193, 199, 218, 237, 245
Phylakis, 257, 271
Phylandros 257, 271
Physkoa 176
Phytalidai 197
Phytalos 197
Picard x, 186
Pieria 313
Pindar 52, 244, 321
Pisa 176
Pittakos 322
Plataiai 51
Plate 27
Plato 87, 90, 95, 101, 117, 154, 178, 297–301, 303, 306, 309–10

— Laws 297–301, 304, 309–10
Plautilla 187
Pliny 79, 242
Plutarch 46, 87, 117, 124, 176–7, 195–7, 203, 234
Pluto 197
Poikilasion 191, 207, 293
Polikhna 293
Polikhnites 122
Pollux 246
Polyidos 60–4, 66–7, 124
Polyrhenia 184, 191–2, 207, 220, 255, 257, 272, 278
Polyrhenians 192
Porphyrios 219, 239
Porti 9
Poseidon 97, 119, 156, 207–8, 215, 289–91, 314
— Asphaleios 290
— Hippios 290
Praisians 122, 133, 209, 218
Praisos 104, 106, 133, 142, 207–8, 210, 221, 258, 269, 279, 290
Priam 97, 320
Priansians 171, 174, 209, 243, 246–7, 255, 274, 285, 288
Priansos 106, 150, 171, 201, 239, 243, 247, 254, 264–5, 274, 281, 290
Prokris 120
Propontis 136, 277
Pseira 8, 27
Psychro 73, 145, 215, 235
Pteras 190
Ptolemy 276
Ptolemy III Euergetes 292
Ptolemy V 87
Pyloros 225
Pylos 97, 129, 314
Pyrgos 142
Pythagoras 242
Pythieis 174
Pythion 174, 268
Pytho 164, 262, 268
Python 268, 271
Pythoness 122

Ras Shamra (see Ugarit)
Reichel 112
Rekhmara 89

Resheph 81
Rhadamanthys 90, 120, 127, 166, 198, 203, 298
Rhaukos 148–9, 290
Rhea 52, 98, 144, 199, 201, 208–9, 211–12, 215, 217, 242
Rhetia 98
Rhithymna 257, 274, 278–9, 290
Rhittenians 243, 279
Rhodes 39, 98, 105, 108, 156, 222, 270, 280
Rhytion 122, 247
Romans 226
Roscher 178, 180
Rufus, Poplius Granius 226
Russia 15

Sabazios 150
St. Paul 219
Salmoneus 282
Samians 133–4, 184, 192–3
Samonia 258, 281
Samos 51
Samothraike 136, 151, 292
Saphon 163
Sappho 322
Sarapis 292–3
Sarpedon 156, 158, 166
Satyr 193
Schaeffer 12, 163
Selene 177–9
Seleukeia 153
Seleukos 159
Senmut 89
Septimius Severus 187
Sesostris 19, 31–2
Seth 162
Shor-El 162, 165
Sicily 29, 35, 122, 151, 170
Sidero 238, 281
Sidon 153, 167
Simonides 101
Sipylos 218
Sirens 189
Skheria 127
Skoteino 142
Skylla 248
Soarkhos 227
Solon 311, 322

Sophocles 62, 182
Sosipolis 49–50, 52
Sosos 227
Sotades 64
Soulia 247, 254, 273, 282
Sounion 126
Sparta 40, 45–8, 65–6, 81, 87, 96–7, 108, 110, 122, 125–6, 154, 160, 170, 176, 184–5, 201, 222, 234, 261, 263, 265–6, 285, 297–8, 309–11
Sphinx 90, 144, 211
Stalitai 208, 279, 290
Standia 195
Staphylodromoi 195, 201, 266
Staphylos 133
Stephanos 153, 155
Strabo 47, 95, 98–9, 112, 133–5, 137, 172, 182, 192–3, 206, 209, 292
Styrakion 270
Sumer 14–15, 21
Sutekh 162
Svoronos 150
Sybrita 200, 220, 232–3, 257, 287
Syria 3, 10–16, 29, 35, 38, 75, 81, 89, 157–8, 162
Syros 321

Taleton 52
Tallaia 146, 249, 288
Talos 52, 100–1, 124, 248–9
Tammuz 80, 148, 163, 199, 219, 238
Tanagra 244
Taramelli 143–4
Tarne 121
Tarrha 270–1
Tauris 185
Taygeton 52, 170
Taylor 301
Tegea 154, 260, 267
Tegeans 154
Tektamos 137
Telekiöi 67
Telemachos 97, 125, 130, 313–14, 321
Telkhines 98, 276
Tenedos 269
Teos 171, 220, 246, 262–4, 281, 286
Termilai 156